Assertion Training:
A Facilitator's Guide

Assertion Training:
A Facilitator's Guide

Colleen Kelley

University Associates, Inc.
8517 Production Avenue
P.O. Box 26240
San Diego, California 92126

Copyright © 1979 by International Authors, B.V.

ISBN: 0-88390-146-3

Library of Congress Catalog Card Number 78-69787

The materials that appear in this book (except those for which reprint permission must be obtained from the primary sources) may be freely reproduced for educational/training activities. There is no requirement to obtain special permission for such uses. We do, however, ask that the following statement appear on all reproductions:

Reproduced from
Assertion Training: A Facilitator's Guide
Colleen Kelley
San Diego, CA: University Associates, 1979

This permission statement is limited to the reproduction of materials for educational/training events. *Systematic or large-scale reproduction or distribution — or inclusion of items in publications for sale — may be done only with prior written permission.*

Printed in the United States of America

Preface

I have written this book with the hope that it will serve as a practical, comprehensive, and easy-to-use guide for assertion trainers. I have used the assertion components presented here in training events in the United States and in various foreign countries over a period of almost six years. During this time a great deal of the assertion literature has been developed, and innovation and research continue to increase our knowledge and change our perspective. It is my hope that this book will contribute to these efforts and, most of all, that it will be used by trainers for the benefit of many people who would like to develop their assertion skills.

Thanks for technical assistance on the book go to my editor, Rebecca Taff; my readers, Mary Ann Tucker and Sharon Young; graphic artist, Merilyn Britt; and typists, Barbara Dodson and Mary Lou Jensen. My appreciation goes also to my mentors (especially Frank Feigert, John Feldhusen, Jay Minn, Jorge and Edda Pratts, Anne Ancelin-Schutzenberger, Simone Clamens, and Robert Crang), who continue to help and inspire me, and to my friends, who patiently waited while I finished the book. I would like to thank Bill Pfeiffer for his invitation to write the book. My special thanks go to John Jones for his constant caring, encouragement, and support and to my family, who from the beginning taught me to be assertive, for their love, understanding, and confidence in me.

La Jolla, California   *Colleen Kelley*
May 1979

Table of Contents

Introduction to the Book

Many people react to the word "assertion" as though it were spelled with four letters and were synonymous with aggression or manipulation. Such reactions are understandable because assertion, aggression, and a variety of other response styles have been taught as "assertive." But assertion in its original sense, and as it is used here, is based on humanistic values.

This book was written for group facilitators or trainers who want to teach their clients to express themselves appropriately without violating their own basic human rights *or* the basic human rights of the others involved. Although therapists may find the book useful, it is written for the professional whose clients have *situational* rather than *general* assertion needs. Such clients "respond in a nonassertive or aggressive manner in a specific situation or with specific individuals" (Cotler & Guerra, 1976, p. 11; Alberti & Emmons, 1974, pp. 60-62) but are generally assertive in their lives; they have a command of basic interpersonal skills and do not require in-depth emotional or psychological support from the trainer; i.e., they cope adequately but wish to enhance their assertive abilities. In a therapy setting, on the other hand, intense support and work are possible over a broader range of skills and needs. The therapy setting is more suited to the client who responds in a nonassertive or aggressive manner in many situations, does not have a command of basic interpersonal skills, and/or requires in-depth emotional or psychological support from the trainer.

AN OVERVIEW OF THE BOOK

This book is neither an encyclopedia of all possible assertion information nor a manual on a favored technique. An attempt has been made to integrate what is available in the field into a functional guide. The book is based on a logical skill-component system. In the first ten chapters (Part I), ten assertion skill components, arranged in a logical design sequence, are presented. Each chapter contains (a) an introduction, in which the skill component is defined and explored and implementation guidelines are listed, (b) one or more lecturettes[1] for the facilitator to use when teaching the skills involved, and (c) two or more structured experiences[2] useful for teaching the skill component. Some implementation guidelines may not be understood by a facilitator until he or she has read the entire chapter, as the guidelines occasionally refer to specific lecturettes or structured experiences.

Part II presents three assessment forms that are designed to be used at various points in the skill-component sequence: "Assertive Vignettes Matrix Form," "Sixty Assertive Situations," and "Assertion Skills Check List."

Part III, "Professional Considerations," contains two chapters. Chapter Eleven, "Workshop Design Considerations," explores considerations in the design of an assertion training event and presents five sample designs. Brief implementation guidelines are also listed. Chapter Twelve, "Readings on Professional Issues," contains four articles: "Issues in Assertive Behavior Training," "Ethical Considerations," "Screening Procedures," and "Assessment Procedures for Assertive Behavior." Part IV contains "Resources for Training: The State of the Art," devoted to a brief history of assertion and an in-depth discussion of available resources in the field (literature, films, tapes, and other aids). Reference citations from the book and further readings are listed at the end of the book in "Bibliographical Sources."

AN OVERVIEW OF ASSERTION

Assertion trainers are in general agreement on the definition and thus the overall goal of assertion: self-expression through which one stands up for his or her basic human rights without violating the basic human rights of others. Implicit in the concept of assertion training is the assumption that assertion can be learned[3] — that there are no assertive people, only people who have learned assertive skills and applied them in specific situations. However, the question of which skills and which procedures constitute assertion training has been answered only partially. As Rich and Schroeder (1976, p. 1085) have said: "The term assertiveness defines the target of the training procedure rather than the nature. The lack of a standard treatment package of assertiveness training has limited the generalizations that might be drawn from research [and] different therapists use 'brand names' to refer to roughly the same procedures

---

[1]Lecturettes are generally brief, simply worded statements of theoretical positions intended for the use of a trainer or facilitator who wishes to introduce theory or background information to a group.

[2]Structured experiences are specific, practical group experiences to be used by a trainer or facilitator to focus on individual behavior, constructive feedback, processing, and psychological integration.

[3]Learning is described by psychologists as "any relatively permanent change in behavior that results from an individual's interaction with the environment" (Adler, 1977, p. 21).

(e.g., modeling, behavioral rehearsal, role-playing therapy, etc.) leading to further confusion and chaos." In the absence of any predominant school of thought, each therapist claims to be teaching *the* assertion skills using *the* best procedures. Some use only verbal techniques; others concentrate on nonverbal techniques; and still others focus on active practice or thought patterns. Although there are indications that many different approaches are helpful, not enough empirical evidence exists in support of any one view.

RATIONALE FOR THE DESIGN SEQUENCE OF THIS BOOK

The assertion area has been organized in this book into a logical design sequence for training purposes. The rationale for the sequence is as follows. A stated *goal* for participants already exists: self-expression through which they stand up for their own basic human rights without violating the basic human rights of others. It is then necessary to decide what *techniques* or procedures to use to teach the *skills* to reach that goal. Logically, it should first be decided which skills are to be taught and then appropriate techniques should be selected to develop those skills. (See Figure 1.)

Choice of Skills

The skills chosen will depend to some extent on (a) the skills and needs participants bring to the training session and (b) the target interaction/ setting/person(s) participants want to learn assertion for. I have called skills that clients bring to the training session (or need to develop prior to practicing the actual assertive response) *preparatory skills;* skills that clients need for an assertive response *core skills;* and skills of a more specific and accessory nature that clients may find useful in special situations or to fill special needs *accessory skills.* Preparatory skills vary according to the skills and needs that clients enter training with, and accessory skills vary according to the target interaction/ setting/person(s). Thus, assertion skills can be presented as a three-stage model consisting of *preparatory* skills, *core* skills, and *accessory* skills, as shown in Figure 2. Preparatory skills are necessary but not sufficient for assertive behavior; core skills are vital to an assertive response; and accessory skills are useful supplements to the core skills but, in general, not necessary for assertive behavior. I have determined specific skill components within each of these skill stages by considering three criteria:

1. What skills have *trainers* reported to be useful or functional in helping people to become more assertive? Which have produced desired results?
2. What skills does assertion *research* show make a difference?
3. What skills does *logic* dictate should be included? Which skills does it

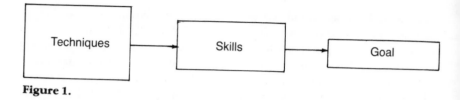

Figure 1.

make sense, because of their very nature, to include? What skills build on the preceding skills?

Core skills are relatively easy to identify because there is almost universal agreement from research and training reports, as well as from logic. The core skills are to speak, act, and think assertively in a given situation: (a) to use words appropriate to the situation (*verbal* skills), (b) to express physical and paralinguistic cues appropriate to the situation (*nonverbal* skills), (c) to think rational and realistic thoughts appropriate to the situation (*cognitive* skills), and (d) to combine all three of these skills into a congruent assertive response (*integration* skills).

Assuming, according to our earlier definition of training (versus therapy) clients, that the client responds in a nonassertive or aggressive manner in only some situations, has a command of basic interpersonal skills (including primary communication skills), has a functional self-confidence, has confidence in most of his or her basic human rights, and does not require in-depth emotional or psychological support from the trainer, the major preparatory skills that seem to contribute to building more assertive behavior are (a) an understanding of and ability to apply assertion *theory;* (b) the ability to identify one's own positive traits and abilities and to talk about and act on these in a positive way (*self-confidence*, self-acceptance, self-esteem); (c) an ability to *identify the basic human rights* involved in an assertive situation; and (d) *confidence in one's basic human rights* and those of others.

Accessory skills include (a) the ability to use assertion skills specifically designed for *special application areas* and (b) the ability to use assertion skills that are necessary only under special circumstances (*special needs*).

The criteria of usefulness, comprehension, and logic are very helpful in determining skills that could be used in any assertion program; to narrow the focus to a particular training program requires that the trainer make some assumptions about the types of skills that are appropriate for a particular clientele. If the client's skills are not proficient enough for a training program, he or she may require a therapy setting and therapy techniques.

Preparatory Skills

Preparatory skills are considered prerequisites for the core skills, and so are developed prior to practicing specific assertive responses. The very act of asserting oneself (core skill) presupposes that one believes in oneself and has an assertive belief system. Because preparatory skills involve developing confidence levels and belief systems, they take longer to learn than do other skills. Although a person can formulate an assertive verbal, nonverbal, and cognitive response on the spot, confidence must be built up over time. Most training participants have already developed preparatory skills to a functional level in most areas.

Without belief and confidence in oneself and one's worth as a person, it is very difficult to believe in one's rights and very difficult to act in an appropriate manner. A person who lacks self-confidence tends to respond nonassertively or aggressively. So, sequentially, the first preparatory skill (after a founding in theory) is the possession of a positive self-concept or self-confidence.

The ability to identify the basic human rights involved in an assertive situation is the next preparatory skill because it is difficult to stand up for one's rights if one does not know what they are.

The final preparatory skill is confidence in one's basic human rights and those of others; it is very difficult to stand up for basic human rights if one does not believe in those rights. As can be seen, each preparatory skill builds on the previous one, and all serve as a foundation for learning core skills.

Core Skills

Core assertion skills involve actually saying what one wants to say in an assertive situation, with appropriate physical and mental behaviors.

Assertion usually necessitates some kind of verbal exchange of information. Thus, besides being able to develop an assertive message, verbal assertion involves appropriate complementary communication skills.

Nonverbal assertion may involve voice qualities, such as tempo, pitch, or loudness, and physical characteristics, such as dress, touch, or proximity (how close people stand, seating arrangements, etc.). Nonverbal language that is not assertive can cancel an assertive verbal message or send a confusing double or mixed message.

Cognitive assertion involves what one is thinking in an assertive situation; basically it involves blocking any counterproductive thoughts and replacing them with more realistic ones. Even though one may know how to speak assertively and how to behave assertively, one may diffuse the motivation to be assertive by telling oneself that assertion is not possible or will bring terrible consequences.

Integrating and practicing verbal, nonverbal, and cognitive assertion skills concurrently in a simulated situation is important because it is the closest approximation of a real-life situation.

The core skills could be sequenced in several ways, but training participants are most often eager to know what to *say* in a given situation. Once they know what to say, they are less inhibited about practicing an accompanying nonverbal message, after which they can deal (through cognitive assertion) with counterproductive thoughts about using power or the negative consequences of being assertive that arise during verbal and nonverbal skill practice, as participants mentally ask, "What if I really do this?" Therefore, typically, verbal skills are taught before nonverbal skills and nonverbal skills before cognitive skills — the sequence used in this book. However, some trainers have found it more useful to vary the sequence, e.g., to deal with counterproductive beliefs or fear of consequences first, especially if participants seem pessimistic about being assertive. Other trainers prefer to switch back and forth between integration and the three other core skills. This latter approach requires more direction and closer supervision on the part of the trainer. In the majority of training events the most functional and logical sequence seems to be verbal assertion, nonverbal assertion, and cognitive assertion, followed by integration of all three in a practice situation.

Accessory Skills

Accessory skills are less broadly based than are the preparatory or core skills, which are used in all situations. Accessory skills are used in unique situations in which special guidelines are helpful or needed. These skills can be subclassified as those helpful in applying assertion to *special application areas* and those necessary only under special circumstances — *special needs*.

Special application areas are categories of situations for which additional guidelines are helpful. These include types of interchange (requests, compliments, criticisms) and types of people or situations (consumer, job, family). Because special-application-area skills require refinements of basic skills and provide a narrower and more in-depth focus, they are taught after the core-skill sequence.

Special needs skills are those necessary under special circumstances. For example, participants occasionally encounter a particularly difficult situation in which they are overly anxious or feel the need to develop assertion at a more gradual pace. Because assertion is taught in a hierarchical sequence, i.e., those situations that are not highly difficult are practiced first, special needs — if they exist at all — do not become apparent until the core skills have been established.

Theory

Common sense dictates that preparatory skills be taught before core skills, that accessory skills be taught once the basics are learned, and that participants develop a competency in each skill in turn and continue to practice that skill along with each successive skill. Of course, an understanding of theory (a preparatory skill) is important at all levels of the three-stage model. Participants must understand assertion theory, be able to recognize an assertive response and distinguish it from other types of responses, understand how and why each skill component relates to assertion, find meaning for what they are doing, and learn some broad concepts and principles to apply to new situations.

An understanding of the differences between assertive, nonassertive, and aggressive responses is vital to *all* phases of assertion training. Without a cognitive understanding of what skill to use and why, how, when, and where each is used, a person sometimes learns how to be assertive only in specific situations, which leaves him or her dependent on the trainer and unable to apply these skills intelligently to new situations. Through an understanding of theory, one learns to apply skills selectively in response to various nuances and variables. Sufficient theory cannot be given or absorbed in a three-hour lecture at the beginning of an assertion-training session, so theory must be interspersed throughout. The basic assertion concepts are particularly important at the beginning of the training session, but theory is also crucial to the teaching of each new assertion skill in succession, since each skill is embedded in theory. (See Figure 3.)

A Sequence of Skills

The sequence of skills in assertion training should be logical, and each skill should be built on the previous one, although the sequence is somewhat flexible. Galassi has suggested that skills can be combined in sequence in a variety of ways based on the preliminary assessment of assertive behavior (Galassi & Galassi, 1977), and Jakubowski states that skill steps in a training program she proposes can occur in "virtually any order" (Jakubowski-Spector, 1973a, p. 79). Some clients may have a high competency and understanding of some of the skills; if this is true, there is obviously no need to spend time on these skills. The needs of certain clients may be met best by a different sequence. The skills that are selected for the program, however, should follow a logical, functional order. In the sequence used here, as I have said, preparatory skills precede core skills, which precede accessory skills, and assertion theory is a component of them all (Figure 3). Within the preparatory skills, self-confidence precedes identification of one's rights, which precedes confidence in one's rights; within the core skills a logical sequence is verbal assertion, nonverbal assertion, cognitive assertion, and integration. Figure 4 depicts the major assertion skills in the proposed sequence.

Selection of Techniques

A great diversity of techniques in the field exists for several reasons:

1. *There is usually more than one way to develop a skill; thus, more than one technique may be legitimate and even appropriate* (Flowers & Booraem, 1975), especially if the techniques focus on different aspects or competency levels of the skill.

2. *Because different trainers emphasize different assertion skills, the techniques they teach vary.*

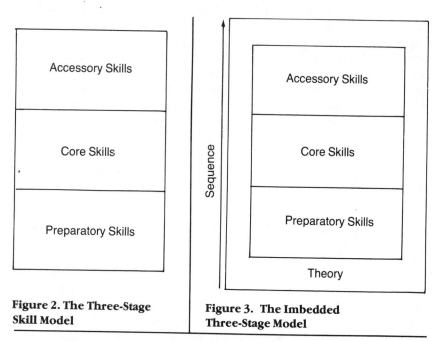

**Figure 2. The Three-Stage
Skill Model**

**Figure 3.   The Imbedded
Three-Stage Model**

3. *Different clients have needs for different skills* (Lange & Jakubowski, 1976); because the trainer must serve a clientele with particular problems, needs, and skill levels, he or she may use different assertion techniques from those used by the therapist.

4. *Techniques may vary with the target interaction, setting, or person(s).* Some techniques or procedures may be specific to such interactions as making a request, such settings as the job, or such target person(s) as friends.

When choosing techniques "the point is not to choose which way is best . . . the point is to choose which intervention and which manner of application is best for which . . . client population . . . try it, evaluate it, modify it, and try it again" (Flowers & Booraem, 1975, p. 29). Widely used techniques can be divided into experiential techniques, behavior-modification techniques, rational-emotive techniques, written instruments, instruction, and group discussion. The skills most often being taught can be grouped into five functional areas: (1) behavior (nonverbal assertion and integration), (2) thought (self-confidence, identification of rights, confidence in rights, cognitive assertion), (3) the spoken word (verbal assertion, special applications), (4) anxiety reduction (special needs), and (5) theory.

Combining functional skill areas with widely used techniques provides some useful guidelines for choosing appropriate techniques to develop specific skills. Behavioral skills are usually taught through such behavior-modification techniques as behavior rehearsal, role reversal, modeling, and escalation.

Thought skills are usually taught through experiential (structured experience), rational-emotive (thought identification), and behavior-modification techniques (thought stopping and thought substitution). Word skills are usually taught through such experiential techniques as structured activities and scripting. Anxiety-reduction skills are usually taught through such behavior-modification techniques as relaxation, covert rehearsal, covert modeling, and covert reinforcement; systematic desensitization is occasionally used. Theory is usually taught through structured activities, instruction, theoretical models, guidelines, examples, and written instruments. All-purpose techniques include demonstration, guided practice, shaping, reinforcement, homework and self-management, coaching, films, readings, and small-group discussion. All techniques are discussed in more detail in their respective chapters.

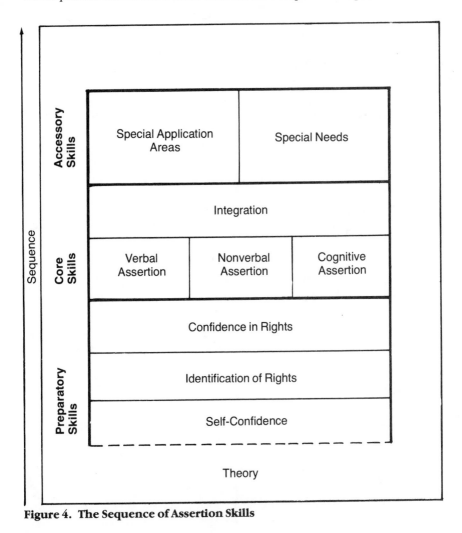

Figure 4. The Sequence of Assertion Skills

PART I

COMPONENTS OF ASSERTION

PREPARATORY SKILLS

Chapter One

Assertion Theory

Assertion theory provides the underlying framework and rationale for training. An introduction to theory early in a workshop or course gives participants an overview of what they will be doing, answers many of the questions they may have, and provides a basic understanding of assertion concepts and terms.

A knowledge of theory is vital to *all* phases of assertion training. Without it a person sometimes learns only how to be assertive in the specific situation practiced, which leaves the learner dependent on the trainer and unable to apply assertion skills intelligently to new situations. A foundation in theory enables a person to articulate the reasoning behind assertion and to apply skills selectively in response to nuances and variables of each situation. "Give a person a fish and he eats for a day; teach him to fish and he eats for a lifetime." Without theory, the participant has only a set of tools and no understanding of how or why to use them.

It is important that participants be able to recognize an assertive response and distinguish it from other types of responses, understand how and why each skill component relates to assertion, and make sense of their own behavior in assertive terms.

Theory is taught at every stage of the training sequence, even though it is a preparatory skill. It is more practical to present a general overview of theory and basic assertion concepts at the beginning of training and to be more specific about the theory underlying each skill immediately preceding practice of that skill or at the time the applicable situation arises; there is only so much theory a person can absorb at one time. Each chapter of this book begins with a discussion of the theory appropriate to each skill component and contains lecturettes on the same topic.

Besides a concise and useful definition of assertion, some important aspects of theory that it makes sense to present early are the philosophy underlying assertion, the three possible response styles in an assertive situation (Table 1) as well as ways to recognize these response styles and functional distinctions among them, an overview of assertion skills, and a rationale for the sequence in which they are to be practiced.

DEFINITION OF ASSERTION

Assertion is defined for the purposes of this book (Jakubowski-Spector, 1973a, p. 76) as self-expression through which one stands up for one's own basic human rights without violating the basic human rights of others. Assertion theory assumes that *all* people have certain basic human rights, that these rights should be respected, and that assertion skills can be developed.

Most definitions of assertion agree on the fact that assertion involves self-expression and respecting the rights of others and oneself in any situation. It follows that an assertive response is also honest and appropriate to the culture, the situation, and the other people involved.

THREE POSSIBLE RESPONSE STYLES

"Response" refers to one's way of approaching a situation, whether it is initiating a conversation or responding to others. The response is specific to the *situation*, not necessarily to a particular remark. Bower and Potter (1976, p. 27) offer some ways of discriminating among the three response styles (see Table 1) and identifying assertive, nonassertive, and aggressive response patterns. It is important to realize that response styles exist on a continuum and that sometimes a response may be between two styles. Jakubowski-Spector (1973b) describes the assertion continuum in terms of the quality of assertive responses. For example, when a person's verbal message clearly indicates that he or she wishes to be assertive, but his or her nonverbal language is somewhat incongruent, the assertion is of a lower quality or gives a less clear message than when the verbal and nonverbal messages are congruent.

Origins of Response Styles

People develop the responses they use (a) by watching other people (modeling); (b) by being positively reinforced or punished for a certain response; (c) by inventing a response; (d) by not thinking of a better way to respond; (e) by not developing the proper skills for a better response; or (f) by consciously choosing a response style. Through teaching assertion skills, the trainer increases the options available to participants and gives them a choice; of course they have no obligation to be assertive in each and every situation.

Some of the reasons why a person may choose not to be assertive are that

(a) the risks involved are too great; (b) it is not worth the time or energy to be assertive; (c) the costs to the other person outweigh the benefits of assertion; and (d) the other person has already changed his or her behavior or the situation appropriately.

Motivation

People decide to be assertive for a variety of reasons: (a) it is respectful of both oneself and others; (b) it usually leads to better feelings on both sides; (c) it gives a person more control over his or her behavior; (d) it usually "works" better than nonassertion or aggression, and people are more apt to come out with a win-win result; (e) it provides more independence, responsibility, and power to choose; (f) it means increased calm; (g) it helps one to communicate what one is, feels, thinks, and wants; and (h) it helps to let others know "the real you" and you to know "the real them."

It is important to recognize whether a participant is truly motivated to change his or her behavior in a situation or whether he or she simply wishes to

---

Table 1. The Three Response Patterns

NONASSERTIVE	ASSERTIVE	AGGRESSIVE
Too little too late	Enough of the appropriate behaviors at the right time	Too much too soon
Too little never		Too much too late
Effects	*Effects*	*Effects*
Interpersonal conflicts	Solves problems	Interpersonal conflicts
Depression	Feels good about others	Guilt
Helplessness	Feels satisfied	Frustration
Poor self-image	Feels good about self	Poor self-image
Hurts self	Is good to self & others	Hurts others
Loses opportunities	Creates & makes the most of opportunities	Loses opportunities
Stress	Relaxed	Stress
Feels out of control	Feels in control of self	Feels out of control
Dislikes self & others	Likes self & others	Dislikes others
Addiction		Addiction
Loneliness		Loneliness
Feels angry		Feels angry

Reprinted from p. 27 of the Instructor's Manual for ASSERTING YOURSELF: A PRACTICAL GUIDE FOR POSITIVE CHANGE, by Sharon A. Bower and Beverly A. Potter, copyright © 1976, by permission of Addison-Wesley Publishing Company, Inc., Reading, Mass.

complain or do any of a number of things other than learn to deal with the situation assertively. Such a person can be referred to an appropriate professional or program.

Effect on Others

Assertion will not turn a pushy person into a "mushy" person or vice versa. However, this kind of flip-flop (sometimes called the pendulum swing) between behaviors may occur for a period of time, usually of short duration, before an assertive style can be established (Jakubowski-Spector, 1973b; Wolpe & Lazarus, 1966). Gaw (1978, p. 143) terms this phenomenon "a necessary evil in the growth cycle." Two possible explanations are *overcompensation* — a person suddenly trying to stand up for his or her own rights to the exclusion of some of the other person's rights or learning to stand up for the rights of others while neglecting his or her own; and *past behavior patterns* — nonassertion and aggression. These are more alike in terms of their dynamics than they are different, so many times both patterns are more familiar and easier to practice than is assertion itself.

It is important to inform participants of the pendulum phenomenon, assure them that it is not a permanent change but a natural occurrence whenever one is trying to learn a new skill, and encourage them to inform people with whom they interact of their new skills and the possible temporary effects of the training and to solicit their patience and cooperation. Those with whom a person interacts generally are used to having him or her act in certain ways and have expectations with regard to his or her behavior. Any change can be uncomfortable or threatening to the other people involved in the relationship. Many couples prefer to enroll in different, but simultaneous, assertion courses so that they can change their relationship as a joint effort or understand the change in their partners. One common situation is that the other person in a relationship may label the participant's behavior aggressive, even though the participant is acting assertively. This usually occurs when the participant has been nonassertive in the past. The contrast can seem great to a person who is used to "running the show." Or, if the participant has routinely been "nice" to a person to avoid hurting his or her feelings, when the participant decides to act assertively, the other person may be hurt by both the "new" assertive message and by the fact that the message was not shared earlier.

Situational Versus Generalized Assertion

There are no assertive, nonassertive, or aggressive people — only assertive, nonassertive, or aggressive responses to situations. It is useful to look at these behaviors not as "good" or "bad," but as more or less helpful or desirable. *Situational* nonassertion or aggression means that the response is not part of an overriding pattern (*generalized* nonassertion or aggression) but occurs only in certain types of situations. It is not the result of a deep emotional problem, and basic interpersonal skills are not lacking. "In the case of situational non-assertiveness we may assume we are dealing with a relatively healthy person who wishes to develop new ways of handling situations which are now uncomfortable, self-denying and non-adaptive for him. If he did nothing about these situations, he would still be able to function in a realtively healthy manner" (Alberti & Emmons, 1974, p. 21).

Aggression and Nonassertion

Aggression and nonassertion are response styles that tend to hide the real message a person wishes to send. At times the message may simply be understated or exaggerated; at other times the real message may not be stated at all. A person who habitually uses a nonassertive response in a given situation may build up resentment until he or she bursts out in a flash of aggression; or he or she might act aggressively toward a person over whom he or she feels more power.

People may respond aggressively in situations because of an accumulation of bad feelings, frustration, a transfer of reactions to past emotional experiences into the present, a belief that aggression is the only thing that will work, a feeling of power derived from the aggressive act, a reaction to feeling vulnerable or threatened, a wish to avoid backing down and being nonassertive, a belief that one's self-image and self-respect are built on this aggressive image, or because aggression has been a means to get one's way without direct negative feedback from others.

In the long run, both nonassertion and aggression result in a loss. Nonassertion rarely helps people get what they want or lets others know how they feel, and "it also shows . . . a subtle lack of respect for the other person's ability to take disappointments, to shoulder some responsibility, to handle his own problems" (Lange & Jakubowski, 1976, p. 9). The nonassertor often discounts himself or herself by thinking that what he or she has to say is not important enough. The nonassertive respondent must realize that small points are not necessarily unimportant ones. An aggressive response often results in long-term loss of friendship and even of the original goal because others find a way to get back at the person who has acted aggressively.

An assertive person can express anger, but in doing so he or she directs anger at the behavior or issue, not at the person, and lets it be known exactly what is desired without trying to dominate, humiliate, or insult the other person. Sometimes people skirt the border between aggression and nonassertion with an indirect, mixed response that seems nonassertive but the effect on others is the same as an aggressive response. This is sometimes known in the literature as "indirect aggression" (Phelps & Austin, 1975; Adler, 1977). A person appears to go along with what another says, but in reality he or she has the definite goal of being aggressive. The methods used may range from guilt induction to sabotage.

There are also times when the person to whom an assertive response is directed does not know how to stand up for his or her own rights and to make a response in kind. In such a situation, the assertor has the responsibility to ascertain as clearly as possible what the other person's position is, rather than simply taking advantage by making assumptions about the feelings of the unskilled person. The underlying philosophy of assertion is humanistic and aimed at a win-win solution.

OVERVIEW OF THE CHAPTER

Chapter One contains a lecturette, "Assertion Theory," in which assertion is defined and the three response styles are explored, and two structured experiences, "Yes-No" and "Assertion Response Discrimination Index (ARDI)." The former is designed to lead to a discussion of assertion theory, to raise energy and involvement levels, and to help participants identify some of the nonverbal cues and feelings associated with assertion, nonassertion, and aggression. The "ARDI" contains a paper-and-pencil instrument to help participants discriminate among assertive, nonassertive, or aggressive verbal responses.

PROFESSIONAL CONSIDERATIONS

The facilitator should believe in and practice whatever is taught, since modeling can be a powerful force in assertion training. On the other hand, participants must be reminded that trainers are people too, and that although they may have the skills necessary for assertion, they may not always decide to use those skills or may not always use them properly.

Ideally, any theory of assertion presented in training should make sense in terms of current knowledge in the field; should be consistent with the definition of assertion; should "work" in the sense that it is useful and practical; and should be easy to grasp. Alberti et al. (1977) describe several dimensions of assertive behavior that should be taken into account. Among these are:

Intent. Whether the assertor intends to express himself or herself appropriately and stand up for his or her own rights as well as the rights of the other people involved in the situation.

Behavior. From an objective observer's viewpoint, whether the assertor's words and actions were assertive in the cultural context in which they were expressed, and whether in the context of the situation and person to whom they were addressed all rights were respected.

Sometimes participants have the idea that assertion is "just for friends," but assertion skills provide an effective way to respond to strangers as well; assertion is a useful and humanistic way to live with all people. Although sometimes pushy people do get their way, they can usually be challenged at least as effectively with assertion as with counteraggression.

Sometimes people associate assertion only with conflict situations, but assertion can be positive as well as negative. It can be used in social conversation, expressing affection, giving and receiving compliments, and other positive situations.

Some possible negative reactions that others may have to assertion include backbiting, aggression, temper tantrums, psychosomatic reactions, over-apologizing, and revenge (Alberti & Emmons, 1974, p. 189). Less extreme negative reactions can include impatience and sarcasm. Participants should be made aware of these and of ways to deal with them.

Audio- and videotapes or films can be used to discriminate among the three response styles.

When using "Yes-No," people sometimes have trouble understanding that the total conversation consists of the words "yes" and "no." This must be clearly stated. It also helps to state that this activity may sound strange, but that it is generally found to be fun and useful by other participants. Also, people sometimes become involved in which word was easiest for them to use. It is important to point out that this varies from person to person, and that the emphasis is on the nonverbals. Assertion involves the ability to say yes or to say no with confidence, and one cannot say yes assertively if one cannot also say no assertively.

Assertion Theory

A friend asks to borrow your new, expensive camera . . . Someone cuts in front of you in a line . . . A salesperson is annoyingly persistent . . . Someone criticizes you angrily in front of your colleagues . . .

For many people these examples represent anxious, stressful situations to which there is no satisfying response. One basic response theory being taught more and more frequently in training programs is a theory called Assertiveness or Assertion.

Some important aspects of Assertion theory include (1) the philosophy underlying assertion, (2) the three possible response styles in an assertive situation, (3) some means of outwardly recognizing these response styles, (4) some functional distinctions between the three styles, and (5) six components of an assertive situation.

THE PHILOSOPHY OF ASSERTION

Assertion theory is based on the premise that every individual possesses certain basic human rights. These rights include such fundamentals as "the right to refuse requests without having to feel guilty or selfish," "the right to have one's own needs be as important as the needs of other people," "the right to make mistakes," and "the right to express ourselves as long as we don't violate the rights of others" (Jakubowski, 1977, pp. 175-176).

THREE RESPONSE STYLES

People relate to these basic human rights along a continuum of response styles: nonassertion, assertion, and aggression.

Adapted from Colleen Kelley, "Assertion Theory," pp. 115-118 of the *1976 Annual Handbook for Group Facilitators*. J. William Pfeiffer and John E. Jones (Eds.). La Jolla, CA: University Associates, 1976.

Assertion

Self-expression through which one stands up for one's own basic human rights without violating the basic human rights of others is termed assertion (Jakubowski-Spector, 1973, p. 76). It is a response style that recognizes boundaries between one's individual rights and those of others and operates to keep those boundaries stabilized.

When one of her friends asked to borrow Jan's new sports car for a trip, she was able to respond assertively by saying, "I appreciate your need for some transportation, but the car is too valuable to me to loan out." Jan was able to respect both her friend's right to make the request and her own right to refuse it.

Nonassertion

The two alternative response styles represent an inability to maintain adequately the boundaries between one person's rights and those of another. Nonassertion occurs when one allows one's boundaries to be restricted. In Jan's case, a nonassertive response would have been to loan the car, fearing that her friend might perceive her as petty or distrustful, and to spend the rest of the afternoon wishing she had not. Thus, Jan would not have been acting on her right to say no.

Aggression

The third response style, aggression, takes place when one person invades the other's boundaries of individual rights. Aggression, in Jan's case, might sound like this: "Certainly not!" or "You've *got* to be kidding!" Here, Jan would be violating the other person's right to courtesy and respect.

RECOGNIZING RESPONSE STYLES

Some helpful keys to recognizing these nonassertive, assertive, and aggressive response styles in any given situation are (1) the type of emotion experienced, (2) the nonverbal behavior displayed, and (3) the verbal language used.

Emotion

The person responding nonassertively tends to internalize feelings and tensions and to experience such emotions as fear, anxiety, guilt, depression, fatigue, or nervousness. Outwardly, emotional "temperature" is below normal, and feelings are not verbally expressed.

With an aggressive response, the tension is turned outward. Although the aggressor may have experienced fear, guilt, or hurt at one time in the interchange, this feeling has either been masked by a "secondary" emotion such as anger, or it has built up over time to a boiling point. In an aggressive response, the person's emotional temperature is above normal and is typically expressed by inappropriate anger, rage, hate, or misplaced hostility — all loudly and sometimes explosively expressed.

In contrast to the other two response styles, an individual responding assertively is aware of and deals with feelings as they occur, neither denying himself the right to the emotion nor using it to deny another's rights. Tension is kept within a normal, constructive range.

Nonverbal Behavior

Each response style is also characterized by certain nonverbal or body-language cues. A nonassertive response is self-effacing and dependent; it "moves away" from a situation. This response may be accompanied by such mannerisms as downcast eyes, the shifting of weight, a slumped body, the wringing of hands, or a whining, hesitant, or giggly tone of voice.

Aggression represents a nonverbal "moving against" a situation; it is other-effacing and counterdependent. This response may be expressed through glaring eyes, by leaning forward or pointing a finger, or by a raised, snickering, or haughty tone of voice.

Assertion, instead, faces up to a situation and demonstrates an approach by which one can stand up for oneself in an independent or interdependent manner. When being assertive, a person generally establishes good eye contact, stands comfortably but firmly on two feet with his hands loosely at his sides, and talks in a strong, steady tone of voice.

Verbal Language

A third way of differentiating between assertion, nonassertion, and aggression is to pay attention to the type of verbal language being used. Certain words tend to be associated with each style.

Nonassertive words can include qualifiers ("maybe," "I guess," "I wonder if you could," "would you mind very much," "only," "just," "I can't," "don't you think"), fillers ("uh," "well," "you know," "and") and negaters ("it's not really important," "don't bother").

Aggressive words include threats ("you'd better," "if you don't watch out"), put downs ("come *on*," "you must be kidding"), evaluative comments ("should," "bad"), and sexist or racist terms.

Assertive words may include "I" statements ("I think," "I feel," "I want"), cooperative words ("let's," "how can we resolve this"), and emphatic statements of interest ("what do you think," "what do you see").

Emotional, nonverbal, and verbal cues are helpful keys in recognizing response styles, but they should be seen as general indicators and not as a means of labelling behavior.

FUNCTIONAL DISTINCTIONS

Outwardly, the three response styles seem to form a linear continuum running from the nonassertive style, which permits a violation of one's own rights; through the assertive style; to the aggressive position, which perpetrates a violation of another's rights.

Functionally, however, as indicated in Figure 5, nonassertion and aggression look both very much alike and very different from assertion. Nonassertion and aggression are dysfunctional not only because they use indirect methods of expressing wants and feelings and fail to respect the rights of *all* people, but also because they create an imbalance of power in which the two positions may mix or even change positions with each other. In refusing to stand up for his rights, the nonassertive responder creates a power imbalance by according everyone else more rights than himself, while the aggressive responder creates a power imbalance by according himself more than his share of rights.

This power imbalance is unstable; the restricted nonassertive responder can accumulate guilt, resentment, or fear until he becomes the aggressive responder in a burst of rage, or he may mix a nonassertive "front" with a subversive "behind the scenes" attempt to "get back" at the person.[1]

The assertive responder seeks a solution that equalizes the balance of power and permits all concerned to maintain their basic human rights. Thus an imbalance of power, caused by a failure to respect the rights of *all* people and perpetuated by the use of indirect methods, creates a very vulnerable position for both the nonassertive and the aggressive responders, while the more functional assertive responder respects all human rights, uses direct methods, and seeks a balance of power.

COMPONENTS OF AN ASSERTIVE SITUATION

Assertion theory can be helpful in situations in which a person is anxious about

---

[1]The mixed, or indirect, response can range from guilt induction to subversion in style and is represented in Figure 5 by the broken-line area.

standing up for his basic human rights. These situations include saying yes and no with conviction, giving and receiving criticism, initiating conversations, resisting interruptions, receiving compliments, demanding a fair deal as a consumer, dealing with sexist remarks, and handling various other specific situations encountered in one's personal, social, and professional life.

It is important to remember that assertion does not always "work," i.e., assertion involves letting another person know what one's response, opinion, thoughts, or wants are in a particular situation. Sometimes these needs are met, opinions or responses agreed with or acknowledged, and sometimes not. The main goal of assertion is not to get one's way, although that is a pleasant bonus, but to know that one has communicated honestly, appropriately, and directly with another person while respecting the rights of all parties involved.

A person may feel capable of being assertive in a situation but make a conscious decision not to be so, because of such things as power issues or the time or effort involved. Before making a decision to be assertive, it is helpful to examine the six components of an assertive situation.

1. The potential asserter's basic human rights and his level of confidence that he has these rights;
2. The specific behavior to which the potential asserter is responding;
3. The potential asserter's feeling reactions to this specific behavior;
4. The specific behavior the potential asserter would prefer;
5. The possible positive and negative consequences for the other person if he behaves as the potential asserter wishes him to behave;
6. The potential consequences of the assertive response for the potential asserter.

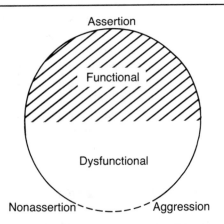

Figure 5. Functional and Dysfunctional Assertive Response Styles[2]

[2]Adapted from J. William Pfeiffer and John E. Jones, "Openness, Collusion and Feedback," in J. William Pfeiffer and John E. Jones (Eds.), *The 1972 Annual Handbook for Group Facilitators*. La Jolla, Calif.: University Associates, 1972, p. 199.

Once the situational assertive components have been determined, assertion training techniques provide a means of formulating and enacting an assertive response.

CONCLUSION

Assertion theory offers a model for those who wish to stand up for their own rights without violating the human rights of others. It is a model that can be used in all types of situations — personal, professional, and social — to facilitate honest, direct, functional communication.

REFERENCES

Jakubowski-Spector, P. Facilitating the growth of women through assertive training. *The Counseling Psychologist*, 1973, *4*(1), 75-86.

Jakubowski-Spector, P. Self-assertive training procedures for women. In E. Rawlings & D. Carter (Eds.), *Psychotherapy for women: Treatment toward equality*. Springfield, Ill.: Charles C Thomas, 1977.

Pfeiffer, J. W., & Jones, J. E. Openness, collusion and feedback. In J. W. Pfeiffer & J. E. Jones (Eds.), *The 1972 annual handbook for group facilitators*. La Jolla, Calif.: University Associates, 1972.

Yes-No: Energizer and Introduction to Assertion

Goals

I. To raise energy and involvement levels.
II. To increase awareness of the nonverbal and affective aspects of assertion.
III. To develop an understanding of assertion theory.

Group Size

An unlimited number of groups of three.

Time Required

Forty-five minutes to one hour.

Materials

Newsprint, felt-tipped markers, and masking tape for the facilitator.

Process

I. The facilitator announces the goals of the experience and asks participants to form groups of three.

The yes-no dialogue appears frequently in the literature; however, the structure and goals of the activity vary widely.

II. The facilitator tells two participants in each group to stand, facing one another, and designates the third person as an observer. One of the two facing people is told to choose the word "yes" and the other is to choose the word "no."

III. The facilitator explains that the exchange will be very simple. One person will say "yes," and the other will reply "no," the first person will repeat "yes," the second person will repeat "no," and so on. The following guidelines are given:

A. Continue the conversation until directed to stop.

B. During the conversation, be aware of what specific nonverbal cues (posture, tone of voice, etc.) are demonstrated when you feel most confident or least confident.

C. Do NOT focus on which word (yes or no) you feel most or least confident with. The words have nothing to do with the goals of the activity.

D. The observer is to note what nonverbal cues the participants demonstrate and decide when they seem most and least confident.

IV. The facilitator tells participants to begin the conversation. After two or three minutes, he or she announces that the yes-no conversation will continue without words.

V. After one to two minutes of silent dialogue, the facilitator asks each triad to compare and try to find some basic principles from its observations.

VI. Steps IV and V are repeated, with each of the three members of the triads taking a role he or she has not played.

VII. The facilitator asks for specific examples of nonverbal cues observed and posts these cues on newsprint under the headings "most confident" and "least confident."

VIII. The facilitator indicates that usually those cues experienced as "most confident" correspond to the assertive posture and those as "least confident" to the nonassertive and aggressive postures.

IX. The facilitator indicates which of the posted cues are usually seen by others as assertive, nonassertive, and aggressive stances and gives a brief lecturette on assertion theory, using the posted lists as a point of departure.

Variations

I. Three rounds may be run to give all members of each triad the opportunity to play all three roles.

II. Other words may be substituted for yes-no, such as: I want it — I won't give it to you.

Assertion Response Discrimination Index: Practice in Recognizing Assertive Responses

Goals

    I. To practice discriminating among assertive, nonassertive, and aggressive responses to various situations.

    II. To test recognition of the differences among assertive, nonassertive, and aggressive response styles.

Group Size

    An unlimited number of participants.

Time Required

    One hour.

Materials

    A pencil and copies of the Assertion Response Discrimination Index (ARDI) and Assertion Response Discrimination Answer Key for each participant.

Process

    I. The facilitator gives a brief lecturette on assertion theory, focusing on the differences among assertive, nonassertive, and aggressive response styles.

II. The facilitator distributes the ARDI and pencils and gives participants ten minutes to complete the index.

III. The facilitator asks participants to form groups of four to six and to discuss their responses and reasons for the responses. (Ten minutes.)

IV. The facilitator distributes the ARDI Answer Key to participants and asks the small groups to compare their responses and reasons for the responses with those indicated on the scoring sheet. (Fifteen minutes.)

V. Participants present a summary of their findings, as well as any unanswered questions, to the facilitator in a final large-group discussion.

Variations

I. The ARDI Answer Key may be distributed immediately following Step II and answers may be discussed in the large group.

II. The facilitator can post the ten situations and have participants try to write assertive, nonassertive, and aggressive responses to each situation.

Assertion Response Discrimination Index (ARDI)

The ARDI is designed to gauge your ability to recognize assertive, nonassertive, and aggressive responses in a variety of situations. For each situation, three different responses are given. Imagine yourself in each of the situations, and mark each response as assertive, nonassertive, or aggressive. You may mark two responses to a situation the same way if indicated, or a response may be *both* assertive and nonassertive. Tone of voice, inflections, and nonverbal behaviors have not been included in this activity. However, keep in mind that nonverbal behavior and tone of voice play an important role in self-expression.

Situation 1

Your friend has just arrived an hour late for dinner. He/she did not call to let you know that he/she would be detained. You are annoyed about his/her lateness. You say:

1a.	Come on in. Dinner's on the table.	☐ assertive ☐ nonassertive ☐ aggressive
1b.	I've been waiting for an hour. I would have appreciated your calling to let me know you would be late.	☐ assertive ☐ nonassertive ☐ aggressive
1c.	You've got a lot of nerve coming late. That's the last time I'll invite you.	☐ assertive ☐ nonassertive ☐ aggressive

Situation 2

A co-worker has just criticized your spouse/boyfriend/girlfriend. You feel the criticism is unjustified. You say:

Reprinted from "Exercise Module 2: Discriminating Nonassertive, Aggressive, and Assertive Behavior," pp. 19-29 of *Assert Yourself! How To Be Your Own Person* by Merna Dee Galassi and John P. Galassi. Copyright © 1977 by Human Sciences Press, 72 Fifth Avenue, New York, NY 10011. Used with permission.

2a. Shut up. You're so stupid and prejudiced.

☐ assertive
☐ nonassertive
☐ aggressive

2b. Well, I see what you mean.

☐ assertive
☐ nonassertive
☐ aggressive

2c. I feel your criticism is unfair. He/she is not like that at all.

☐ assertive
☐ nonassertive
☐ aggressive

Situation 3

A friend has just complimented you on your new suit. It's the first time you've worn it and you really like it. You say:

3a. Thank you.

☐ assertive
☐ nonassertive
☐ aggressive

3b. This? It's nothing special.

☐ assertive
☐ nonassertive
☐ aggressive

3c. Well . . . I picked it up at a sale . . . well. . . .

☐ assertive
☐ nonassertive
☐ aggressive

Situation 4

You're out with a group of friends. You're all deciding which movie to see. One person has just mentioned a movie you don't want to see. You say:

4a. You always pick movies I don't like. You only think about yourself. You're very selfish.

☐ assertive
☐ nonassertive
☐ aggressive

4b. I don't want to see that one. How about a movie over at the Plaza Theatre?

☐ assertive
☐ nonassertive
☐ aggressive

4c. Well, I don't know much about that movie. But, I guess, if you want to, we can see it.

☐ assertive
☐ nonassertive
☐ aggressive

Situation 5

You are returning a faulty item to the department store. You bought a shirt/blouse. When you took it home, you found a misweave in it. You do not want the item as it is. The clerk has just said no one will ever notice it. You say:

5a. Well, I'd still like to return it or exchange it. I do not want this one.
☐ assertive
☐ nonassertive
☐ aggressive

5b. Look, give me my money. I don't have all day for you to waste my time.
☐ assertive
☐ nonassertive
☐ aggressive

5c. Well, are you sure no one will notice it?
☐ assertive
☐ nonassertive
☐ aggressive

Situation 6

You love your spouse/boyfriend/girlfriend very much and want to express this feeling to him/her. You've just finished a quiet dinner in your home and are sitting alone. You say:

6a. I enjoyed the dinner. Oh ... well ... how do you feel?
☐ assertive
☐ nonassertive
☐ aggressive

6b. I really love you. You're great.
☐ assertive
☐ nonassertive
☐ aggressive

6c. Well, what's new?
☐ assertive
☐ nonassertive
☐ aggressive

Situation 7

Your parents have just called and said they are coming to visit tonight. You already have plans for the evening that you do not want to break. You say:

7a. Mom, I've seen you twice this week. Enough is enough. You are always bugging me. You're a pain.
☐ assertive
☐ nonassertive
☐ aggressive

7b. Sure, I'd be glad to see you tonight, but couldn't you come tomorrow?

☐ assertive
☐ nonassertive
☐ aggressive

7c. Mom, not tonight. I already have plans for the evening.

☐ assertive
☐ nonassertive
☐ aggressive

Situation 8

You'd like your child to go down the block and pick up a package at your friend's house. You say:

8a. Billy, I'd like it if you would go over to Mrs. Smith's and pick up a package for me. I'd appreciate it if you could do it by 3 o'clock.

☐ assertive
☐ nonassertive
☐ aggressive

8b. If you aren't too busy, well … will you be going to Mrs. Smith's today?

☐ assertive
☐ nonassertive
☐ aggressive

8c. Hey, it's about time you did something worthwhile. Go down to Mrs. Smith's and pick up a package for me. No back talk. Stop being such a lazy thing. Go on.

☐ assertive
☐ nonassertive
☐ aggressive

Situation 9

A co-worker keeps giving you all of his/her work to do. You've decided to put an end to this. Your co-worker has just asked you to do some more of his/her work. You say:

9a. I'm kind of busy. But if you can't get it done, I guess I can help you.

☐ assertive
☐ nonassertive
☐ aggressive

9b. Forget it. It's about time you do it. You treat me like your slave. You're an inconsiderate S.O.B.

☐ assertive
☐ nonassertive
☐ aggressive

9c. No, Sue/Tom, I'm not going to do any more of your work. I'm tired of doing both my work and your work.

☐ assertive
☐ nonassertive
☐ aggressive

Situation 10

A new person/family has just moved in next door. You really want to meet him/her/them.

10a. You smile as your neighbor(s) walk by, but say nothing.

☐ assertive
☐ nonassertive
☐ aggressive

10b. You go next door and say, "Hi. I'm Sue/Tom. I live next door. Welcome to the neighborhood. I'm glad to meet you."

☐ assertive
☐ nonassertive
☐ aggressive

10c. You watch your neighbor through your window.

☐ assertive
☐ nonassertive
☐ aggressive

ASSERTION RESPONSE DISCRIMINATION INDEX
ANSWER KEY

Responses to Situation 1

1a. Nonassertive, because you pretend that nothing has happened. You neither mention that your friend is late nor that you are displeased by his/her behavior.

1b. Assertive, because you tell your friend that he/she is late, that you have been waiting, and that you feel he/she should have called.

1c. Aggressive, because you put your friend down (you've got a lot of nerve) and threaten him/her (won't invite you again).

Responses to Situation 2

2a. Aggressive, because you behave hostilely toward your co-worker and call him/her a name (stupid).

2b. Nonassertive, because you don't agree with what your co-worker said, but you imply that you do (I see what you mean).

2c. Assertive, because you express how you feel (I feel your criticism is unfair).

Responses to Situation 3

3a. Assertive, because you accept and acknowledge the compliment.

3b. Nonassertive, because you do not accept the compliment. You say it's nothing special, although you know it's the first time you've worn it, and you really do like it.

3c. Nonassertive, because you do not accept the compliment.

Responses to Situation 4

4a. Aggressive, because you attack your friend (you're very selfish) rather than saying, "I don't want to see that one" and then suggesting another one.

4b. Assertive, because you express your opinion (I don't want to see that one) and make another suggestion.

4c.   Nonassertive, because you don't express your opinion. You say, "If you want to, we can see it," but you don't really want to see it.

Responses to Situation 5

5a.   Assertive, because you tell the clerk exactly what you want. While acknowledging his point of view, you still want to return or exchange the shirt.

5b.   Aggressive, because you accuse the clerk of wasting your time.

5c.   Nonassertive, because you do not want this faulty merchandise.

Responses to Situation 6

6a.   Nonassertive, because you do not express how you feel. You talk about dinner rather than your feelings of affection.

6b.   Assertive, because you state how you feel.

6c.   Nonassertive, because you do not express what you want to say. You engage in small talk when you really want to express your affection.

Responses to Situation 7

7a.   Aggressive, because you put your mother down. You tell her she's a pain and she bugs you. You never tell her that you already have plans for this evening so she can't come.

7b.   Nonassertive, because you only imply that perhaps tomorrow would be better while at the same time saying you'd be glad to see her tonight. The point is you already have plans tonight. You have given her a double message.

7c.   Assertive, because you tell your mom you have a previous engagement and therefore can't see her tonight.

Responses to Situation 8

8a.   Assertive, because you ask your child directly to do a favor for you. You neither demand nor threaten him/her. Your request is stated in such a manner that he/she is free to respond to it.

8b.   Nonassertive, because you never ask your child to pick up the package. You never come to the point.

8c. Aggressive, because you demand rather than ask your child to do a favor for you. You also insult him/her.

Responses to Situation 9

9a. Nonassertive, because you do not tell your co-worker you're tired of doing his/her work. You agree to help even though you do not want to.

9b. Aggressive, because you make accusations and engage in name calling.

9c. Assertive, because you express how you feel (I'm tired of doing your work) and what you plan to do (I'm not going to do your work any more).

Responses to Situation 10

10a. Assertive/nonassertive. This response gets two ratings because the nonverbal behavior is assertive. You smile to your neighbor to show your interest, but your verbal behavior is nonassertive; you don't say anything. You need to introduce yourself to your neighbor if you want to meet him/her/them.

10b. Assertive, because you go and introduce yourself.

10c. Nonassertive, because you will not meet your neighbor(s) by just watching.

Chapter Two

Self-Confidence

Self-confidence, identification of basic human rights, and confidence in basic human rights are the three preparatory skills that must precede any assertive act. Of these skills, self-confidence is the most basic. Without belief and confidence in oneself and one's worth as a person, it is very difficult to stand up for oneself and one's rights in an appropriate manner. Simpson and Hastings (cited in Egan, 1976, p. 16) define self-esteem as "the evaluation that an individual makes and customarily maintains in regard to himself. It is a personal judgment of one's worthiness as a person, indicating the extent to which he believes himself to be capable, significant and successful." Generally, the path to self-confidence is built on self-knowledge, self-acceptance, and self-esteem. Egan (1976, p. 16) believes that "self-esteem is one of the most important dimensions of your self-concept. Your ability both to develop interpersonal skills and to use those you do develop depends to a great extent on the quality of your self-esteem." Those with a lack of self-confidence tend to raise doubts about their own worth and their ability to develop assertion skills.

Percell (1977, p. 61) credits Alberti and Emmons as "two of the first to explicate the relationship between assertiveness and self-acceptance." According to Alberti and Emmons (1974, p. 20), "the generally nonassertive person is one who finds his own self-esteem very low and for whom very uncomfortable anxiety is generated in nearly all social situations. His feelings of inadequacy, his lack of acknowledgement of his own self-worth and his physical discomfort brought on by generalized anxiety may call for in-depth treatment." The situationly nonassertive person — the training client — does not bring needs of such magnitude to the training event, but it is important to be sure that the client does have a degree of self-confidence that will allow him or her to participate in the training group and progress through the skills sequence at about the same rate as other participants. It is equally important to raise the consciousness of participants about their strengths and confidence levels in preparation for an identification of their rights. If a person does not believe in himself or herself to some extent, it will be very difficult for him or her to stand up for his or her rights; and if a person has a very difficult time with the self-confidence activities, it is doubtful that that person will be able to continue in an assertiveness training program without some intensive practice in building self-confidence.

A person who lacks self-confidence tends to respond nonassertively or aggressively in a situation. Self-confidence is often associated with a person's liking himself or herself and being aware of his or her personal assets. Self-confidence is paradoxical in a sense, because one needs some confidence before attending an assertion workshop, and yet an enhanced self-esteem and self-acceptance are some of the results many clients take away from assertion training (Percell, 1977, pp. 62-64). Self-confidence feeds on itself through assertive action, making assertion inherently rewarding; even if one does not receive what one wants in an assertion situation, one has the satisfaction of knowing that one has said what one wanted to say. The following diagrams illustrate the circular dynamics of assertion (Bloom, Coburn, & Pearlman, 1975, p. 138; Fensterheim & Baer, 1975, p. 31):

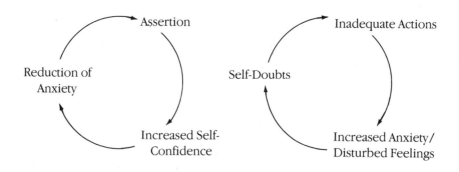

There is such a strong connection between self-confidence and assertion that Fensterheim and Baer (1975) suggest that if one has doubts about whether a specific act was assertive, one need only ask oneself whether it increased his or her self-respect even slightly. If it did, it was assertive. If not, it was unassertive. If one has self-esteem, it is expressed in assertive action, because the person neither shies away from a situation nor hides behind an aggressive front. "Assertiveness is simply the behavior based on valuing yourself enough to insist on getting what you want and need by using reasonable and fair means" (Porat & Quackenbush, 1977, p. 110).

Assertion techniques foster self-confidence because:

1. People take small, successful steps rather than trying more than they can handle.

2. Assertion provides positive reinforcement, rewarding people for what they have done right and gradually increasing "correct" behaviors, as opposed to putting emphasis on dysfunctional behaviors.

3. Assertion provides active practice and feedback, in which the participant has actual experience with assertion skills, hears about his or her ability to be assertive through feedback from the group, and develops his or her own self-evaluation skills.

4. The group supports each person's attempts to be assertive.

5. Assertion training covers theory and encourages understanding of the dynamics behind each assertion skill so that participants know how to apply their skills on a long-term basis.

6. Anxiety is reduced.

7. Assertion is self-reinforcing.

Percell (1977, p. 63) puts forth a three-step process "which may explain why assertive people usually feel good about themselves": (a) the client expects to feel better about himself or herself as a result of assertion; (b) the client's self-esteem is enhanced through reinforcement; and (c) the person's perception of himself or herself changes to a more positive one.

OVERVIEW OF THE CHAPTER

This chapter contains a lecturette, "Improving Your Self-Esteem," that describes how one acquires self-esteem, its characteristics, and some useful ways to build self-confidence. Two structured experiences are included, both of which can be used to help people break the ice and get acquainted. "Boasting" focuses on awareness and confident sharing of one's own strengths. It raises energy levels quickly and involves everyone in the experience. "Introductions" focuses on the identification of strengths in others and a sharing of those observations with them. It is better suited to small groups, because people must take turns, and it may be used as a follow-up to "Boasting" to help individuals learn one another's names and begin practicing feedback on a relatively nonthreatening level. It is somewhat more anxiety provoking than the boasting experience because participants must wait and then speak in front of the entire group.

PROFESSIONAL CONSIDERATIONS

Assertion training assumes that participants have functional levels of self-confidence, i.e., although participants can benefit from confidence-building techniques, the main function of the activities is to remind people of their strengths, to point out the importance of self-confidence to assertion, and to begin the process of asserting oneself that will bring new confidence levels.

A person with low self-confidence is not always nonassertive. People who seem very aggressive may also be very insecure and sensitive. This is the "bully-baby" syndrome in which a person pushes others around but is terribly hurt if anyone reacts assertively in response to his or her behavior.

People sometimes defeat themselves by setting unrealistic goals. One important focus when building confidence during training is to have participants set goals that are relatively easy to achieve and then to move gradually to more challenging activities.

A good way to approach self-confidence during a training session is to have participants examine their own levels of self-confidence through awareness of their strengths, skills, and accomplishments, and to share these strengths with the other participants.

Self-esteem is enhanced when one *chooses* to do something good for oneself, rather than when one does what he or she has been told should be done. One way to help participants think about the choice dimension is to have them explore how much of their time is spent doing things they *should* do, but do not really enjoy, as opposed to the amount of time they spend doing things they enjoy. (If you feel good about what you are doing, your self-esteem is generally increased.)

Much confidence is gained through experiences with others, but once it has been gained, the assertor must take control of the process. This can be encouraged through emphasizing the need to begin reinforcing oneself for assertive acts and the intrinsic satisfaction of assertion. As Virginia Satir (1972, p. 24) says, "No genes carry the feeling of worth. It is learned" from the experiences one has with the people around one and the messages these people give one. A support system is important to building and maintaining that self-confidence, but it is also important to transfer the locus of control to oneself, to like oneself in spite of what others may think.

Improving Your Self-Esteem

Whether or not you are assertive is determined by your self-concept — by a blueprint or mental picture that you maintain of your strengths, your weaknesses, your personality. You call your self-concept to mind when you predict whether your performance will succeed. It influences your hopes, aspirations, moods, and actions.

We all acquire our self-concept in much the same way — from what other people tell us about ourselves and from our observations of our behavior and its consequences. As we grow up, our parents, teachers, and other adults gradually impart by instruction and example the values, norms, and rules of conduct of their culture. The norms tell us what behaviors are considered appropriate. For example, eating moderately at mealtimes is acceptable; stuffing oneself all day long is unacceptable. Resting at the end of a workday is a reward that is deserved; sleeping all day is laziness. The media also teach us an enormous set of norms about behaviors expected from girls versus boys, from children versus adults, from pupils versus teachers, from husbands versus wives, and from parents versus children.

We tend to be judged in society largely according to how we measure up to the relevant norms. Thus, with respect to her peers, Joyce may be exceptional in athletics, average in reading, and poor in mathematics. Adults constantly make comparisons about all aspects of the behavior of children — their intelligence, beauty, manners, work habits, ability to play with other children, and so on. In addition, adults label children as loving or spiteful, friendly or mean, reasonable or selfish, cooperative or uncooperative, outgoing or shy. As we mature, these comparisons and labels are applied to all of us — first by adults, increasingly by our peers, and eventually by ourselves.

Excerpted and adapted from pp. 26-29, 34-35 of ASSERTING YOURSELF: A PRACTICAL GUIDE FOR POSITIVE CHANGE by Sharon A. Bower and Gordon Bower, copyright © 1976, by permission of Addison-Wesley Publishing Company, Inc., Reading, Mass.

Having internalized the standards and beliefs of those who judge us, we gradually come to describe ourselves in terms of how we deviate from the norm. For instance, we may say to ourselves, "I'm a good bridge player, but I'm pretty stupid at balancing the checkbook." We make such self-judgments not only about our athletic, artistic, and scholastic talents, but also about our social and personal adjustments.

These social comparisons are important because they are hooked directly into the pay-off system of the culture. People who equal or exceed a positive norm are rewarded by gifts, promotions, money, praise, and admiration. Presumably, they are then "successful." Those who fall short of what is expected receive disapproval, loss of privileges, demotions, penalties, and other punishments. Consequently, people become anxious when their performance is being closely evaluated because they fear punishment for possible failure.

THE TOLL OF A NEGATIVE SELF-CONCEPT

Your self-concept is wrapped up in a set of descriptions and images — of good success scenes or bad failure scenes that you've experienced. It is also carried in a set of personality trait labels you use to tell yourself and others what you are really like. Your self-evaluations are important because they influence most areas of your behavior, defining the limits of what you will attempt. You avoid an activity if your self-concept predicts you will perform so badly as to humiliate yourself. For instance, if your self-concept includes the belief that you would be a poor ice skater, you might never try it, and will indeed remain a poor ice skater. Often people excuse themselves with "That's just the way I am." By using this excuse, they deny themselves opportunities for personal growth.

If you could listen in, you would hear nonassertive people saying all kinds of negative sentences to themselves. They selectively remember some criticism of themselves, exaggerate it to monstrous proportions, and repeat it over and over like a chant. The man battling his bulging waistline might be saying, "I am ugly, fat, and disgusting. No one can stand to look at me. I am a fat worm. I've got no will power." The shy, retiring boy at a dance might be saying, "Those girls are whispering about me. My pimples are horrible. If I talk to that girl, she'll insult and ridicule me. I never know what to say to girls. I'll die if she cuts me down."

The fact is that people are often their own worst Downers. They say to themselves, "I am irrational, emotional, stupid, dull, ugly, shy, cold, submissive, fat, ineffectual, overbearing, bitchy, childish, a bully, a miserable father (mother), a lousy speaker, a failure, and over-the-hill." We all have our own lists. People can be terribly brutal with themselves. Out of the whole animal kingdom, only humans are endowed with this capacity to make themselves miserable. Can you imagine your pet cat or dog moping around, saying such brutal things to himself?

Worse yet, in many cases our negative view of ourselves may be communicated to new acquaintances before they have time to form an independent impression of us. If we tell people we are inadequate, they may do us the disservice of believing us. A woman in an assertiveness class repeatedly advertised herself poorly by prefacing each remark with, "I doubt if my idea is worth anything, but . . ." Without realizing it, the class did indeed pay less and less attention to her ideas — at least until they stopped to examine the subtle message her remark conveyed.

The toll of a negative self-concept is that it limits what we are willing to try, forestalling opportunities for growth and enjoyment. Doomsday prophesies about our social failures tend to be self-fulfilling. The shy woman who retreats from friendly overtures is indeed judged to be cold, aloof, disdainful, and the man who was turned down for approaching her is even less likely to make another overture to her (or vice versa!). The student with anxiety about taking a test "goes blank" to such an extent that he does indeed fail just as miserably as he had feared.

Many people are plagued by images of failures they have experienced during social encounters. For example, one man experienced difficulty in public speaking because each occasion for a speech reactivated a memory-image of a time when he had lost his voice, blocked and stammered in front of a large audience, and was forced to retreat from the stage in utter humiliation.

Sometimes people imagine bizarre metaphors to symbolize their passivity, inadequacy, or weakness. One timid individual reported that when she thought about the sarcastic replies her Downer might make to her assertion, she visualized herself "melting into a little puddle on the floor!" Images that prevent people from asserting themselves are based on memories of their weaknesses and their prior failures and embarrassment in specific situations. People may also imagine punishments for assertion, such as their spouses hitting them or leaving them, or their friends snubbing or ridiculing them.

To sum up, negative sentences and images continually inhibit nonassertive people. By concentrating on negative evaluations of themselves, these people miss valuable opportunities for growth and enjoyment. . . .

CHANGING YOUR SELF-CONCEPT

To become assertive, you must have a positive self-concept and believe that you can act effectively. . . . Think for a moment, then list three to five good personal attributes of yourself or of your life — positive beliefs about your appearance, intelligence, range of interests, life's achievements, or whatever. These should be truthful and concrete, for example, "I have a nice smile," "I am well informed about current affairs," "I have raised four happy children," or "I am a good billiards player." . . .

Now, your goal is to increase how often you recall these self-enhancing thoughts. You can do this by following each positive statement with an immediate reward. Many everyday activities will qualify as rewards: eating, drinking, arranging flowers, playing a game, phoning a friend, taking a bath, resting, reading the newspaper, watching TV, having sexual relations, and so on. Now, to increase how often you think good things about yourself, whenever you are about to carry out one of these rewarding actions, say a few of your positive, self-enhancing sentences to yourself just before the rewarding activity. That way you reward yourself for thinking positive thoughts and so the positive thoughts are strengthened by the pleasurable act that follows!

Simply saying the self-congratulatory sentences whenever you have an idle moment (say, while driving a car or waiting in a line) can increase their frequency even when a reward does not follow. If you find that you are forgetting to practice your positive sentences, you can remind yourself by a periodic "message" which cues you to rehearse. One woman carried her list of positive statements in her change purse, so that she was reminded to rehearse them whenever she opened her purse. An executive wrote "Now" at several specific times on his daily time schedule to cue himself to rehearse his good points for a few minutes.

A middle-aged woman doubted her drafting ability even though she was appointed head of the entire drafting department of her firm. She wrote a positive statement for herself, "I am good at drafting." After reading and rehearsing the statement for several days, she took the next step and posted it on the bulletin board of the department. Her colleagues were astonished and asked, "Of course, you're terrific at drafting. That's why you're head of the department. But why put up that message?" She replied, "Because I need to see it right up front in order to convince myself." Posting her positive statement brought her many compliments and confidence that the statement was true.

Publicly posting a statement about yourself is neither conceited bragging nor "fishing for compliments." You are simply telling others what you like about yourself. It is up to them to agree or not. . . .

Developing a positive self-concept and maintaining it is an important skill, since self-esteem is the cornerstone of assertion. By remembering and amplifying what is good about you, you can develop your self-confidence into a solid foundation on which to build other assertion skills.

Boasting: Building Self-Confidence Levels

Goals

 I. To help participants identify, own, and share their personal strengths.
 II. To explore feelings and reactions to sharing "boasts" with other participants.
 III. To experience an enhanced sense of personal power and self-confidence by announcing one's strengths to others.

Group Size

No more than thirty participants.

Time Required

Forty-five minutes to one hour.

Materials

 I. Newsprint, a felt-tipped marker, and masking tape for the facilitator.
 II. A copy of Six Questions to Encourage Boasting for the facilitator to post.
 III. Blank paper and a pencil for each participant.

Adapted from pp. 49-50 of *The 1976 Annual Handbook for Group Facilitators*. J. William Pfeiffer and John E. Jones (Eds.). La Jolla, CA: University Associates, 1976.

Process

I. The facilitator gives paper and a pencil to each participant, posts the Six Questions to Encourage Boasting, and asks participants to respond to each privately, in writing, in preparation for a group get-acquainted and confidence-building activity. The facilitator may wish to mention that self-confidence is the foundation on which all other assertion skills rest.

II. The facilitator tells the participants:

> "Move around the group and share your name and one item from your list with each person you encounter. When two people have shared an item, they should move to new partners. The idea is to share with as many people as possible in the time allowed and to practice sharing in as confident a way as possible. Do not discount yourself, give negative comments, or share your weaknesses. Brag and boast even more than you may feel is permissible in your day-to-day life. Be aware of your feelings, reactions, and reservations during this experience." (Fifteen to twenty-five minutes.)

III. The facilitator leads a discussion of the experience, using the following guidelines:

A. Did you write down or boast about everything you could have? Why or why not?

B. How did it feel to share your boasts with other group members?

C. How did you share your boasts: were your body language and words congruent?

D. How did you feel about yourself during the experience? How are you feeling about yourself now?

E. Did it become easier to boast with practice?

F. How much do you boast in your day-to-day living?

G. What are some appropriate and useful times to practice boasting?

IV. The facilitator gives a short lecturette on self-confidence/self-image building, the importance of self-confidence in assertion, and the use of boasting.

Variations

I. Following Step IV, participants can share their boasts "on stage," doing a short "commercial" to sell themselves to the other participants.

II. Step II can be done in triads or quartets rather than in dyads.

III. Step III can be done in dyads, triads, or quartets before discussing general themes within the large group.

IV. Instead of answering the Six Questions to Encourage Boasting, participants can be instructed to create a "strengths collage" by cutting pictures or parts of pictures and phrases from magazines. These clippings should be chosen to portray one's strengths, skills, and strong points and pasted on a piece of newsprint or cardboard. Participants share their names and one aspect of their collages with each person they encounter.[1]

---

[1] This variation is based on pp. 116-117, "Strengths Building" in *Help Yourself: A Guide to Self Change*, by Jerry A. Schmidt. Champaign, IL: Research Press, 1976.

SIX QUESTIONS TO ENCOURAGE BOASTING

1. What natural abilities do you have?

2. What things do you do better than most people?

3. How have you grown in the last year?

4. What are the most difficult things you have accomplished?

5. What are you proudest of?

6. What about yourself would you most like to receive compliments on?

Introductions: Identifying and Recognizing Group Member Strengths

Goals

   I. To build self-confidence.
  II. To help participants learn about each other.
 III. To identify and give recognition to group member strengths.

Group Size

From ten to thirty participants.

Time Required

Forty-five minutes to one and one-half hours.

Process

   I. The facilitator states the goals of the experience and explains that self-confidence is the foundation underlying all other assertion skills.
  II. The facilitator explains that participants are to practice assertive, positive introductions and demonstrates the technique by making eye contact with a participant in the group and introducing him/herself to that person by name. That person is to respond by giving his/her name. ("Hi, I'm Chris"; "Hi, Chris, I'm Dale.")

Adapted from pp. 70-72 of *Responsible Assertive Behavior*, by Arthur J. Lange and Patricia Jakubowski. Champaign, IL: Research Press, 1976. Used with permission.

III. The person who receives the introduction (the respondent) then introduces himself or herself to someone else in the group who has not been introduced. This exchange continues until each member has responded to an introduction and has introduced himself or herself to one other person. Participants should respond by stating their names for each introduction so that two people have actually interacted before the respondent moves to the next introduction. (Five to fifteen minutes, depending on number of participants.)

IV. The facilitator asks each person, beginning with the first respondent, to tell the introducer something specific and positive about the way the other person introduced him/herself ("Chris, I really liked the way you smiled, and I found your voice easy and smooth"). The focus is on the nonverbal qualities, since very little is actually being said. This feedback must be positive and as behaviorally specific as possible. (The facilitator may wish to give some examples of the types of behaviors that participants might focus on: eye contact, facial expression, body and hand positions, voice qualities.) (Ten to thirty minutes.)

The facilitator states that it is normal to have forgotten someone's name. If participants cannot remember the names of the people they were introduced by, the facilitator encourages those people to continue to ask for names until they can remember them. If a participant cannot remember something good about his/her introducer's self-presentation, the facilitator directs the participant to ask the introducer to repeat the self-introduction. The facilitator may also ask for help from other members of the group when focusing on positive feedback.

V. The facilitator directs participants to simultaneously ask the names of those participants whose names they do not remember.

VI. The facilitator leads a discussion of the experience, focusing on changes in self-confidence levels, awareness of personal strengths, and ways of raising self-confidence levels and increasing awareness of personal strengths in day-to-day living.

Variations

I. Participants can mill around, introducing themselves to each other and telling others something they like about the others' introductions.

II. Step IV can be expanded to include any favorable impression or positive strength observed in the introducer.

Chapter Three

Identification of Rights

Identification of rights involves the ability to identify the basic human rights in assertion situations. Identification of rights differs from confidence in rights, which deals with one's commitment and willingness to stand up for one's rights. Identification of rights is important because it is difficult to develop confidence in one's rights (and those of others) or to stand up for them if one does not know what they are, i.e., cannot identify them in an assertive situation.

Both identification of rights and confidence in rights are important skills for building a psychological and emotional framework that can support assertive behavior. The concept of rights itself is useful in assertion because (Lange & Jakubowski, 1976, p. 57) "(1) Talking about human rights often helps individuals feel more comfortable about [the right to be assertive]; (2) The concept of rights also helps individuals feel that they can justify their assertive acts; (3) [Learning to] identify and accept . . . rights often helps reduce those internal injunctions which prohibit individuals from acting assertively . . . The net effect of . . . rights is to give individuals permission to be 'themselves,' in other words, to act in ways that are different from other people and to express their real thoughts, feelings, and needs" in a responsible way.

The idea of basic human rights was first introduced to assertion by Alberti and Emmons (Alberti, 1977, p. 355): "No procedure shall be utilized in the name of assertive behavior training which would violate those freedoms or rights [of a person to be treated as a person of value]." Bower and Bower (1976) add:

> Our human rights flow from the idea we are all created equal in a moral sense and we are to treat one another as equals. In social relations between two equals, neither person has exclusive privileges, because the needs and goals of each person are to be equally valued. As equals, two people (say a husband and wife) may work out — "fall into" — a diverse set of agreements, compromises and rules to "govern" themselves. Such agreements, often inexplicit, allow the day-to-day

business of the relationship to proceed without daily arguments and negotiations about who is to do what and when. There is no universally correct form for these social accommodations; any arrangement or division of labor is O.K. provided both parties are satisfied with it and the arrangement does not infringe upon the rights of others. But whatever the agreement, it rests on the premise that we are equals with the same rights. This means that each party has a moral right to renegotiate what he thinks is an unfair or inequitable arrangement ... [and to try to negotiate a behavior-change contract agreeable to both parties]. (p. 6)[1]

A basic human right, in the context of assertion, is anything one considers all people are entitled to be, have, or do by virtue of their existence as human beings. One wants permission and freedom for oneself and for all people to assert these rights. Rights are anything one feels no human being should be deprived of. The overriding value is for a humanistic existence. When there is a difference of opinion on rights, this value takes priority. When rights are in conflict, negotiation of differences may be necessary.

Some questions that can be used to identify basic human rights in any particular situation are the following:

1. What are some of the basic things I believe people in this situation are entitled to be, have, or do because they are human beings?

2. Is this something that can be given to all people; do I accord this right to others?

3. What rights are necessary in this situation for all involved to be treated fairly, with dignity, and as people of worth? (Galassi & Galassi, 1977).

4. What rights do people in this situation need in order to make their own decisions and to live their own lives without violating the rights of others?

5. What permission am I taking away in this situation; what rights am I denying myself?

6. Which rights are most relevant for the message I want to give in this situation?

OVERVIEW OF THE CHAPTER

Chapter Three offers a lecturette, "What Are My Rights?," that contains a definition of basic human rights, some sample rights and corresponding responsibilities, and some of the limitations of rights. Two structured experiences, "Human Rights/Role Rights" and "Basic Human Rights," are included.

---

[1]Reprinted from ASSERTING YOURSELF: A PRACTICAL GUIDE FOR POSITIVE CHANGE, by Sharon A. Bower and Gordon Bower, copyright © 1976, by permission of Addison-Wesley Publishing Company, Inc., Reading, Mass.

The first is designed to help participants distinguish between the two types of rights, which are often confused. The second, designed to accompany "What Are My Rights?," is designed to help participants understand the origin, definition, and importance of rights in assertion and identify their own rights in particular situations. Participants practice identifying the basic human rights in sample situations and then in their own personal situations.

PROFESSIONAL CONSIDERATIONS

Participants should practice identification of basic human rights until they can identify them readily and articulate them, if required, in a real-life situation.

It is helpful for participants to keep lists of those rights that they identify as basic human rights. The lists can be useful in developing confidence in rights and in defining personal belief systems.

One right that people have trouble agreeing on is the right to maintain one's dignity by being properly assertive — even if it hurts someone else. This right sometimes raises all the ogres participants bring to a session regarding assertion as aggression. Usually it helps to discuss what causes other people to be hurt when one is being properly assertive. Typical responses are: "The other person would be disappointed because he assumed I would do what he wanted" or "The other person would be hurt because she is used to violating my rights and would be losing something she had." In both cases, the person wants something he or she was never "entitled" to but has become accustomed to and now can no longer have. Usually, looking at these causes will convince participants that in those situations in which they are being properly assertive, the other person will be hurt because he or she is legitimately disappointed — and that it is O.K. to feel this legitimate feeling — or because he or she has a history of aggressive or nonassertive behavior and does not want or does not know how to give that up. The assertor should make it clear to the person that the change is not a reflection on him or her, but reflects the new willingness of the assertor to say what he or she wishes to say.

When identifying basic human rights, participants can begin practicing by identifying all the possible rights in a situation; they eventually will learn to identify only those rights that are most important or relevant to the people involved.

In "Human Rights/Role Rights" sometimes participants become confused regarding one or two rights. For example, when generalizing from boss's rights to employee's rights, participants may not be able to determine whether a right results from a role or is a basic human right. The trainer can restate the question: "Do both boss and employee have this right?" or "Do all people have this right?" If people still do not agree, the trainer can simply point out that all people do not recognize or agree on all categorizations of human and role rights, usually due to borderline cases or different background situations.

What Are My Rights?

A Universal Declaration of Human Rights has been issued by the United Nations listing certain rights deemed necessary to all human beings in order to live a decent life. Assertion is based on the similar premise that all human beings require certain basic human rights in order to live well together and that these should not be violated. Webster's (1975, p. 741) defines a right as: "something to which one has just claim" or "something that one may properly claim as due." A basic human right, in the context of assertion, is anything one considers all people are entitled to be, have, or do by virtue of their existence as human beings. Assertive rights are anything one feels no human being should be deprived of. The underlying premise of assertiveness training is humanistic: not to produce undue stress in others and to support self-fulfillment of each person — to "care about one another."

Because there is no "declaration of basic assertive rights," each person must develop his or her own declaration. However, people do seem able to agree on many of these rights. For example, the right to have and express one's own opinion is legally protected in the United States. Many rights are so much a part of people's daily lives that they simply take them for granted or naturally bestow them without writing them down or legalizing them. When someone violates one of these rights, a person may have a sense of discomfort but be unaware that the discomfort is due to the violation of a particular basic right. One of the first skills needed to prepare for assertion is to understand what basic human rights are and to become aware of and able to identify these rights in particular situations.

IDENTIFYING RIGHTS

Obviously, due to the variety of human activities, there are many possible rights, although they can be grouped into categories. In general, the *right to be* is the right to exist and to express one's human abilities; the *right to have* is the right to own certain things; and the *right to do* is the right to engage in certain activities. Some examples of possible rights in each of these categories are (a) to be — the right to be left alone, the right to be independent, the right to be successful, (b) to have — the right to have your own feelings and opinions, the right to have rights, the right to get what you pay for, and (c) to do — the right to refuse requests without feeling guilty or selfish, the right to ask for what you want, and the right to make mistakes — and then to be responsible for them. There are so many basic human rights and so many ways to express them that it would be impossible to list them all or to agree on them all, but it is important to be familiar with those that are discussed most often in assertion situations and to practice identifying some of them. Some of the rights most often mentioned in assertion groups are:

1. *The right to be left alone.* This is the right to spend some time by oneself, even when one feels pressure from others to socialize or do things with others.

2. *The right to be independent.* This is the right to maintain a separateness and individuality in leading one's own life.

3. *The right to be successful.* This right does not guarantee success, but gives the person who has excelled or done well the right to be good at what he or she does and to succeed even though others may not have the capacity to do as well.

4. *The right to be listened to and taken seriously.* This is the right to be heard when one has something to say, or to have one's point of view respected. This right can be abused when a person speaks without thinking or speaks for an inordinate length of time or repeats himself or herself or tries to force his or her views on the other person.

5. *The right to get what one pays for.* This is the right to receive the product or service one purchased. Damages incurred when a service is performed or product defects that exist when the merchandise is sold should be corrected free of charge. This right (and similar rights) is now being regulated or backed by law.

6. *The right to have rights*, i.e., *to act in an assertive manner.*

7. *The right to refuse requests without feeling guilty or selfish.* This is the right to say no even though others believe that to say no is selfish or wrong. (One possible consequence of exercising this right is that people who refuse others' requests are sometimes refused in turn.)

8. *The right to ask for what you want.* This right is directly related to the right to refuse requests. Anyone making a request should be prepared to hear yes or no and to respect the other's right to accept or refuse. It is important not to assume that simply because one has granted requests in the past others have tacitly agreed to return the favor.

9. *The right to make mistakes and to be responsible for them*. This is the right to do something without needing to be perfect. So many people accept this right that it is sometimes called "the right to be human," i.e. the right to err and to bear the consequences of those errors.

10. *The right to choose not to assert oneself*. One has a choice if he or she has mastered the skills involved in assertion. A person may know how to be assertive but choose not to be so. The most frequently cited reasons for making this choice are that it is not worth the cost in terms of time or energy expended or that the risks involved are too high.

RIGHTS AND RESPONSIBILITIES

It is important to remember that just because one has certain rights, they do not give one carte blanche to do as one pleases, nor do they guarantee that others will bestow these rights. All rights have attendant responsibilities: the right to be successful presumes that one is successful or simply gives one permission to strive for such an outcome; the right to be independent carries the responsibility to meet one's own needs, etc. Rights carry the responsibility to accord those rights to others as well.

Fulfilling responsibilities associated with one's basic human rights helps ensure that others will respect those rights, although some people may never recognize them. People who live very aggressively, for example, are sometimes not willing to accord others any rights at all, or people from other cultures may hold a different set of values. The point is that assertion is sometimes one sided, i.e., standing up for one's own rights without violating the rights of others, even if the other person does not acknowledge or believe in these rights. Sometimes the payoff is simply knowing that one's position has been communicated.

CONFLICTING RIGHTS

Sometimes there is a difference of opinion as to who has the rights in a given situation, or it is unclear, even to the assertor, where the limits of one's own rights end and those of the other person begin. Some examples of such situations are listed in Table 2. Unless personal integrity is involved, the best way to handle these situations is to discuss them with the other person involved and negotiate a solution that gives both parties the most freedom to lead a humanistic existence.

Role Rights Versus Human Rights

One type of right that is commonly confused with human rights is the role or contingency right. Human rights can be generalized to all people, but role

Table 2. Comparison of Rights, Limitations, and Responsibilities

INTERPERSONAL RIGHTS	LIMITATIONS	RESPONSIBILITIES
You have a right to use your own judgment to decide whether another person's request is reasonable. You have a right to deny the request *even if* the other person (a) badly wants you to grant this request, (b) is an authority figure, or (c) has "emotional problems."	It is unclear whether you have the right to change your mind midstream about fulfilling commitments you've made.	You may have the responsibility to fulfill the commitment if the other person will be seriously inconvenienced by your changing your mind.
You have a right to tell someone else what your needs are *even if* the other person (a) feels that your needs are illogical or unwarranted, (b) doesn't want to hear about your needs, (c) feels hurt or upset about your needs, or (d) if you feel that you "ought" not to have these needs.	It is unclear whether you have the right to always demand that the other person fulfill your needs once you've expressed them. It may depend on the nature of your relationship with that person (whether a friend, lover, acquaintance), how often you make the demands, etc.	You may have the responsibility not to take advantage of someone else's willingness to take care of your emotional needs. You may have the responsibility to be sensitive to another's needs without letting this sensitivity cow you into being a martyr.

Reprinted from p. 10 of *An Introduction to Assertive Training Procedures for Women*, by P. Jakubowski-Spector. Washington, DC: American Personnel and Guidance Association, 1973. Copyright ©1973 by American Personnel and Guidance Association. Reprinted with permission.

rights are those a person holds by virtue of a formal or informal contract to take on certain responsibilities or use certain skills. Such contracts include those between a boss or subordinate, parent or child, physician or patient, and owner or buyer. For example, a boss has the right to hire and fire, a subordinate does not. An easy way to distinguish a basic human right from a role right is to ask "Is it a right that can be accorded to *all* people?"

SUMMARY

To summarize, a basic human right is anything one considers all people to be entitled to by virtue of their existence as human beings. The underlying value system is humanistic — everyone should be accorded personal dignity. To identify one's basic human rights, it helps to be familiar with some of the rights most often identified by other people and to ask questions that help identify the rights involved in any situation. Every right carries with it a responsibility. Because not all people recognize the same basic human rights, there may be conflicts. Since assertion is based on the ability to stand up for one's own basic human rights without violating the rights of others, one preparatory skill in becoming more assertive is learning to define and identify basic human rights as distinct from role rights and to understand their origins and limitations.

Human Rights/Role Rights: Identifying and Understanding Rights

Goals

I. To identify basic human rights.

II. To understand the difference between basic human rights and role rights.

III. To increase awareness of one's own rights.

Group Size

No more than thirty participants.

Time Required

One hour.

Materials

I. Newsprint, felt-tipped markers, and masking tape for the facilitator.

II. Blank paper and a pencil for each participant.

Process

I. The facilitator gives each participant paper and a pencil and asks individuals to list rights they feel belong to each of two specified complementary

Adapted from pp. 91-92 of *Responsible Assertive Behavior*, by Arthur J. Lange and Patricia Jakubowski. Champaign, IL: Research Press, 1976. Used with permission.

pairs, such as parent/child, employer/employee, man/woman, etc. (Ten minutes.)

II. The facilitator posts items on separate sheets of newsprint with the appropriate headings as participants read items from their lists.

III. The facilitator asks participants which of the rights listed for only one group could be generalized to both and adds those that participants nominate and agree about to the appropriate list. (Fifteen minutes.)

IV. The facilitator points out that human rights can be generalized to all people; rights that cannot be generalized are "role" rights.

V. The facilitator gives a short lecturette on the identification of human rights and leads a discussion of the basic principles involved.

VI. The facilitator asks participants to make individual lists of their basic human rights and role rights and to continue to add to the lists as they become aware of other rights on their own.

Variation

The facilitator may also have participants distinguish between those rights that are guaranteed them by law (legal rights) and those that are not.

Basic Human Rights: Identifying Assertive Rights

Goals

  I. To develop an understanding of basic human rights.
 II. To learn to identify basic human rights in specific situations.

Group Size

No more than twenty-eight participants, preferably a number divisible by four.

Time Required

One hour.

Materials

  I. Newsprint, felt-tipped markers, and masking tape for the facilitator.
 II. The Sample List of Basic Human Rights for posting.
III. Blank paper and a pencil for each participant.

Process

  I. The facilitator discusses the definition and importance of basic human rights in assertion as well as the importance of the ability to identify the basic human rights involved in any situation.

II. The facilitator posts the Sample List of Basic Human Rights and asks for additions to the list.

III. The facilitator lists some sample assertion situations[1] on newsprint and leads a discussion of some of the rights involved in two or three of the situations.

IV. The facilitator gives each participant paper and a pencil. Participants are told to form dyads, choose an assertive situation from the sample list, and identify the basic human rights involved in the situation they have chosen. (Five minutes.)

V. Participants are told to share the situation they have chosen and the rights they have identified in the large group. The facilitator leads a discussion of any problem situations and helps identify rights in situations where a dyad has had difficulty doing so.

VI. The facilitator tells dyads to form groups of four. Each participant is to choose a situation from his or her personal experience, share it within the group, and identify the rights involved, with the help of the other group members. (Ten to fifteen minutes.)

VII. The facilitator leads a discussion in the large group, helps to clarify any problem situations, and helps identify rights in situations where a group has had difficulty doing so.

Variations

I. The facilitator may ask participants to generate a list of basic human rights and sample assertion situations through brainstorming.

II. The Sample List of Basic Human Rights may be used as a handout.

---

[1] The "Sixty Assertive Situations" form (p. 249) may be useful for generating such a list.

SAMPLE LIST OF BASIC HUMAN RIGHTS

The right to have and express your own feelings and opinions.

The right to refuse requests without having to feel guilty or selfish.

The right to consider your own needs.

The right to set your own priorities and make your own decisions.

The right to change.

The right to decide what to do with your own property, body, and time.

The right to make mistakes — and be responsible for them.

The right to ask for what you want (realizing that the other person has the right to say no).

The right to ask for information (including from professionals).

The right to choose not to assert yourself.

The right to do anything as long as it does not violate the rights of someone else.

The right to maintain your dignity by being properly assertive — even if the other person feels hurt — as long as you do not violate the other person's basic human rights.

The right to be independent.

The right to be successful.

The right to have rights and stand up for them.

The right to be left alone.

The right to be treated with respect and dignity.

The right to be listened to and taken seriously.

The right to get what you pay for.

The right to initiate a discussion of the problem with the person involved and so clarify it, in borderline interpersonal cases where the rights involved are not clear.

This list of rights was compiled from the following sources: "The Seven Basic Inalienable Rights of Women," pp. 62-64 of *How To Be an Assertive (Not Aggressive) Woman*, by Jean Baer. New York: Rawson Associates Publishers, Inc., 1976. Used with permission; "Basic Human Rights," pp. 175-176 of *Psychotherapy for Women*, Edna I. Rawlings and Dianne K. Carter (Eds.). Springfield, IL: Charles C Thomas, 1977. Used with permission; p. 49 of *Don't Say Yes When You Want To Say No*, by Herbert Fensterheim and Jean Baer. New York: David McKay Company, Inc., 1975. Used with permission; and "Everywoman's Bill of Rights," p. 24 of *The New Assertive Woman*, by Lynn Z. Bloom, Karen Coburn, and Joan Pearlman. Copyright © 1975 by Lynn Z. Bloom, Karen Levin Coburn, and Joan Crystal Pearlman. Reprinted by permission of DELACORTE PRESS.

Chapter Four

Confidence in Rights

Confidence in one's rights is believing that the rights identified in any particular situation are one's own (and also belong to the other person). Having confidence in rights gives one a commitment to and willingness to stand up for those rights once they have been identified.

Whereas identifying rights involves understanding what those rights are and being able to identify them in any situation, confidence in rights involves ownership of the rights and the willingness of participants to act on those rights appropriately. At the identification stage, however, many participants think in terms of what people "should" have, what they "want," or "this is how people should be." At the confidence stage, the question is not what, but *how much* you believe — whether your belief in a particular right is embedded in a personal philosophy and how confident you are in terms of taking action on or exercising these rights. Jakubowski-Spector (1973b, p. 9) lists four reasons why it is important to develop a belief system "which will help participants support and justify their acting assertively: . . . The participant (a) can continue to believe in her right to act assertively even when she is unjustly criticized for her assertion, (b) can counteract any irrational guilt that may later occur as a result of having asserted herself, (c) can be proud of her assertion even if no one else is pleased with this behavior, and (d) will be more likely to assert herself."

When developing confidence in rights it is sometimes helpful to ask: "Would you accord this right to others? If so, why not accord it to yourself?" Rights have been called "reasonable expectations," i.e., "the right to expect to be treated with dignity and respect," etc. Being assertive does not guarantee that one will get what one wants nor that the other person will respect one's rights, but it usually does allow a person to express himself or herself and let others know his or her beliefs and preferences.

Rights require varying degrees of cooperation from others, and there are some rights one has the power to grant only to others, not to oneself. Once a person is aware of some specific rights in which he or she wishes to build confidence, the person can rate them in terms of his or her control over them. People usually find it easier to begin developing confidence in rights over which they have some control and fewer ogres because there are fewer risks.

FREEDOM, PERMISSION, AND THE LAW

Once some rights have been identified, it is helpful to ask what power base one has with regard to exercising each right. The right may be based on a potential ability one has as a human being and need only be given the freedom to use, or it may be based solely on a humanistic assertion belief system, in which case others must cooperate to give this right. Or the right may be supported by law or other legitimate backing (in a family, parents; in an office, the boss). The power bases of rights are not always clear-cut, but generally can be placed on a continuum from high (belief in the right with attendant power to act on the belief) to low (belief in the right with the need for cooperation from others) (Figure 6).

As can be seen, when the right is largely based on an ability or power of the assertor, it is much more difficult to violate that right; physical or legal force must be used. When the exercise of the right depends on the cooperation of others, others have only to refuse to cooperate. No one has complete power over his or her own rights. Even the right to life is dependent on the cooperation of others. In almost all situations, one at least has the power to let the other person know one's feelings, i.e., to state one's belief in the right and to choose to relate to people who respect that right. When both people are being assertive, respect of rights is usually possible, unless compromise of personal integrity is involved.

The payoff in assertion comes from the knowledge that one has expressed oneself appropriately, standing up for one's own rights and the rights of others, and sometimes from "getting what one wants." The latter depends on one's skill or ability to act on rights *and* on the cooperation of others, so it is usually easier for participants to begin building confidence in rights that do not require a great deal of cooperation from others.

OVERVIEW OF THE CHAPTER

The chapter contains a lecturette, "Developing a Belief System," and two structured experiences: "Rights Circle" and "Rights Fantasy." The lecturette discusses the basic tenets of an assertion belief system and the importance of having these beliefs and focuses on methods of building confidence in one's rights and the role played by conflicting beliefs.

"Rights Circle" asks participants to state their beliefs in some of their rights

High   *Belief + Personal Ability or Power*

Some Rights	*Some Powers of Others*	*Others' Powers Checked By*
Right to have and express one's own feelings and opinions	To physically gag or restrain a person from speaking To make laws against freedom of speech	Existing laws Desire for equal treatment Belief in the right
Right to be left alone	To physically invade a person's privacy To hassle the person	Existing laws Assertor's ability to move elsewhere Assertor's refusal to join others Desire for equal treatment
Right to be listened to and taken seriously	To refuse to listen, laugh, or disregard one's comments To leave	Authority figures who enforce right Desire for equal treatment Assertor's direct power to deny same right

Low   *Belief + Cooperation from Others*

Figure 6. An Assertor's Power Continuum

(Left vertical axis label: **Assertor's Power Base**)

---

confidently. Other participants give encouragement and positive reinforcement in an intensive structure to help build confidence in rights. This structured experience can be a very powerful and uplifting experience.

"Rights Fantasy" is a guided fantasy in which participants explore the possibilities of possessing rights they cannot easily accept for themselves. Participants explore what having or not having the rights does to their self-images and how people deny these rights to themselves. "Rights Fantasy" is relatively nonthreatening and helps participants get in touch with their personal motivations and blockages.

PROFESSIONAL CONSIDERATIONS

Sometimes participants become so enchanted with the idea of basic human rights and their newly found confidence in them that they stand up for every right that someone else violates, whether it is important to them or not. Some clients tend to believe they *must* be assertive at every opportunity. The trainer should caution participants not to overdo, but to stand up for their rights only "when your rights are violated and it is objectionable to you that the violation occurred" (Galassi & Galassi, 1977, p. 124). Those who have assertion skills have the freedom to choose (in view of possible consequences, risks, and costs) whether they want to be assertive or not in any particular situation. Assertion is an *option*.

Some people are overly confident of their rights to the point at which they are aggressive and take advantage of the rights of others. These people may need to work more on building confidence in the rights of other people than on building confidence in their own.

Conflicting beliefs sometimes make it difficult for a person to develop confidence in a basic right. Cognitive assertion techniques can be helpful to participants who find that "socialization messages" block their confidence in rights. (See Chapter Seven.) Participants for most training events are assumed to have only minor problems in this area. If a socialization message or counter-belief has been held for a long time, is extremely well learned, very emotionally based, or originates in a traumatic or often-repeated event, it may be too deep-seated to deal with in the group, and the participant may be referred to a competent professional for work in a one-on-one situation.

Some participants may have difficulty fantasizing in the "Rights Fantasy." A technique in the Chapter Ten lecturette, "Covert Techniques," can be used to help develop this ability.

In the "Rights Circle," when participants are playing the part of the "encourager," it is important that they give the assertor some reasons to own this right that make sense to the assertor. If the encourager can think of nothing else to say, he or she can say, "You do have this right."

In the "Rights Circle" there is a tendency for participants to go quickly around the circle in order to avoid any feeling of discomfort. Participants should be encouraged to proceed at a moderate pace to give each encourager time to respond to them in a meaningful way.

Developing a Belief System

The philosophy underlying assertion is that everyone has certain basic human rights. Many people are able to identify these rights objectively and understand that they should have these rights. However, it is one thing to be able intellectually and hypothetically to identify those rights; it is another to have enough confidence in those rights to act on them. Once people have enough confidence in specific rights to want to stand up for them, they need only learn *how* to stand up for them.

OWNING A BELIEF SYSTEM

The first step toward confidence in one's own and others' basic human rights is to examine the philosophy underlying assertion. Most people have a fairly well defined set of beliefs (belief system) that encompasses attitudes, values, and ideas. To be assertive, it is important that a person have a belief system that supports the idea of basic human rights and gives him or her confidence in ownership of specific rights. Confidence in these rights comes partly from an understanding of and commitment to the basic tenets of an assertion philosophy, which can be expressed as follows: 1) "assertion rather than manipulation, submission, or hostility enriches lives and ultimately leads to more satisfying relationships with people, 2) everyone is entitled to act assertively" (Lange & Jakubowski, 1976, pp. 55-56) and to decide what is important to him or her. From these tenets comes a belief in specific human rights.

Belief in Specific Rights

Most people who come to assertion training sessions have already developed an assertive belief system but may still have difficulty with specific applications of that belief system. For example, a person may agree that assertion rather than manipulation, submission, or hostility enriches lives and ultimately leads to more satisfying relationships with people. Still, he or she may have difficulty with some of the specific applications of that belief such as:

> 1) When we do what we think is right for us we feel better about ourselves and have more authentic and satisfying relationships with others ... 2) Sacrificing our rights usually results in destroying relationships or preventing new ones from forming ... 3) Sacrificing our rights usually results in training other people to mistreat us ... 4) If we don't tell other people how their behavior negatively affects us we are denying them an opportunity to change their behavior ... 5) By trying to govern our lives in order never to hurt anyone we end up hurting ourselves and other people. (Jakubowski, 1977, p. 176)[1]

To many people it is helpful to make a list of some specific human rights (see the sample list on page 66) and to mark those on which they act most or in which they most believe, and those on which they act least or in which they least believe. In this way a person can focus on those rights in which he or she most needs to develop confidence.

Lack of Belief in Rights or Incompatible Beliefs

It is very difficult to stand up for rights one does not have confidence in. For example, a woman wanted to ask for a raise and identified her right to do so as "the right to ask for what you want"; however, she did not feel comfortable with accepting the right for herself in this situation because she believed that (a) the best way to get a raise was to work hard enough to deserve it and to wait until someone recognized her work; (b) the boss might not agree with her belief that she should have a raise, and it is better not to request something and then be turned down; and (c) one should not ask for money from an employer because this might imply a criticism of the employer's judgment. In this particular case, the woman had some personal beliefs that were incompatible with an assertive belief system. Some people, on the other hand, encounter situations for which they have no particular belief system, but in which they do not feel comfortable acting. Both incompatible personal beliefs and lack of beliefs can prevent people from having confidence in their basic human rights.

Building Confidence

A personal assertion belief system provides an underlying rationale for asser-

---

[1]Excerpted from Patricia Ann Jakubowski, "The Basic Tenets of an Assertive Philosophy," in Edna I. Rawlings and Diane K. Carter (Eds.), *Psychotherapy for Women*, 1977, pp. 176. Courtesy of Charles C Thomas, Publisher, Springfield, Illinois.

tive actions. Reminding oneself of one's beliefs is very often enough to help one feel confidence in specific rights in specific situations. Once one has identified the belief involved, confidence in that right comes almost automatically.

However, most people also have several rights that they find difficult to accept for themselves or to give to other people, even after they have identified the rights involved and see that the rights are consistent with their beliefs in the tenets of an assertive philosophy. In this case, the assertor may need to raise his or her consciousness about these rights by: (a) hearing from others who believe they have this right, (b) hearing others' beliefs that the assertor has this right and others' views about why the assertor owns this right, or (c) hearing the feelings of others in reaction to the assertor's intent not to exercise his or her basic rights. This positive approach to building confidence usually helps people to accept their rights.

Counterbeliefs

In a few cases it is not sufficient to raise confidence in a right. The assertor may be holding counterbeliefs. A counter- or conflicting belief may be of one's own invention, or it may have been learned through the past modeling of other people, through advice or messages from others, or through deductions made from interactions with others. For example, many people have difficulty believing in their right to maintain their dignity by being properly assertive when the other person may feel hurt. The assertor may have learned from a favorite teacher, from parental messages, or from watching the interactions of others that one should never do anything that will make the other person feel bad.

Regardless of the source, it is important to identify countermessages and examine their validity and usefulness in light of one's desire to be assertive. Recognizing the source of the difficulty is helpful so that it can be discussed in terms of more appropriate and useful beliefs.

Some questions that may help to focus on the source of difficulty are: (1) If you accord this right to others, why can't you give yourself the same right? (2) Does some experience you have had cause you to believe that you do not have this right? (3) What would happen if you gave yourself permission to accept these rights? (4) What makes you think you do not have these rights? (Lange & Jakubowski, 1976). Some general examples of conflicting beliefs and philosophy and resulting responses to assertive situations are shown in Table 3.

People who have taken advantage of someone in the past may not react favorably to that person's becoming assertive and standing up for himself or herself. Even when other people do not reward the behavior, confidence in rights helps people understand why they are being assertive and helps them feel good about themselves and their assertion.

Table 3. Conflicting Beliefs and Resulting Behavior

	NONASSERTION	ASSERTION	AGGRESSION
Conflicting Philosophy	Take care of other people's rights and hope others will worry about yours (or *then* worry about yours)	Take care of your rights and respect the other person's rights	Take care of your own rights . . . Others' rights don't count
Conflicting Belief	I have no basic human rights or I don't know how to stand up for my rights	I have basic human rights and so do you or I know how to stand up for my rights and to respect yours too	Some of us have basic human rights and some of us don't (or I have rights— you don't) or I don't know how to respect your rights
Some Potential Behaviors	Hidden bargains Manipulation (guilt, etc.) Retreating, giving up	Confrontation Honesty Negotiation	Tirades Put-downs Cutting remarks

SUMMARY

A personal belief system that supports the idea of basic human rights is necessary for assertion. Two major beliefs of this type are that assertion means more satisfying relationships with people and an enriched life in the long run and that all people are entitled to be assertive and to express their thoughts, feelings, and beliefs. Most people have a well-developed assertion belief system but need to become more aware and confident of specific assertive rights. Many people can identify basic human rights but do not believe these rights belong to them. A first step in such a case is for a client to realize that the right is consistent with his or her assertive belief system. It is also helpful to hear from others in a group who believe in the right for themselves and believe that this right also belongs to the assertor and why, and to hear how they would feel if the assertor did or did not stand up for this right when interacting with them. Sometimes people have difficulty accepting rights for themselves because they have never thought about owning the rights; at other times people may hold counterbeliefs derived from past experiences. In the latter case, their confidence levels must be raised by methods such as challenging these beliefs with more correct or useful ones, exploring the origin of the belief, using cognitive-assertion techniques, or doing more in-depth work with a qualified professional. On a scale from zero to ten, few people score a consistent ten on their beliefs in every one of their basic human rights, but it is important to have a functional level of confidence in the rights in any situation before one can sincerely stand up for those rights.

Rights Circle: Developing Confidence in Rights

Goals

   I. To increase confidence in one's basic human rights.

  II. To determine one's level of confidence in various rights.

Group Size

Nine to fifteen participants per group, each group with its own facilitator.

Time Required

One hour.

Materials

A copy of a Sample List of Basic Human Rights (p. 66) and a pencil for each participant.

Process

   I. The facilitator distributes a copy of the Sample List of Basic Human Rights and a pencil to each participant, answers any questions concerning the

Adapted from pp. 91-92 of *Responsible Assertive Behavior*, by Arthur J. Lange and Patricia Jakubowski. Champaign, IL: Research Press, 1976. Used with permission.

list, and asks participants to add to the list any additional rights that are important to them or that are identifiable in situations they are presently dealing with in their own lives.

II. Participants are asked to check off five rights from the list that they feel comfortable accepting for themselves.

III. The facilitator forms participants into circles of from nine to fifteen members. Each group should include a facilitator. Each participant, in turn, is told to read his or her list of five rights to the group in the following format: "I have the right to . . .," practicing good eye contact and confident tone of voice, body posture, and gestures. (Ten minutes.)

IV. Participants are asked to select one right from the Sample List of Basic Human Rights that they do not feel comfortable accepting for themselves.

V. Participants take turns standing in front of each participant in the circle, repeating: "I have the right to . . .," completing the phrase with the right they have difficulty accepting for themselves, practicing eye contact and confident tone of voice, body posture, and gestures. (Twenty minutes.)

VI. Each person being addressed in the cirlce is to respond with various "permission"messages such as: "Yes, you do have the right (permission) to say no. I would actually feel closer to you if you said no when that's what you really want to say."

Note: An easy and orderly method of taking turns within the circle[1] is as follows: One participant begins by standing in front of the first person on his or her left and continues around the circle in a clockwise direction. As soon as two persons have responded to the first participant, the first person who responded may start around the circle. As participants complete the circle, they take their original places.

V. The facilitator leads a discussion in the large group of reactions to the experience, changes in levels of confidence, and ways of incorporating the technique "back home" (using friends to give "permission," giving oneself "permission," etc.).

Variations

I. Instead of using a circle, participants may simply mill around until they have interacted with all other participants.

II. Participants may use a partner in Steps II and IV to help identify and

---

[1]This idea was taken from p. 95 of *A Handbook of Structured Experiences for Human Relations Training* (Vol. II, Rev.). J. William Pfeiffer and John E. Jones (Eds.). La Jolla, CA: University Associates, 1974.

choose rights they feel comfortable accepting and those they have difficulty accepting for themselves.

III. Participants may be instructed to apply a ten-point confidence scale to their rights lists in Steps II and IV to help gauge their level of confidence in the rights listed.

Rights Fantasy: Accepting Basic Human Rights

Goals

    I. To develop confidence in one's basic human rights.

    II. To increase awareness of how one denies one's rights.

Group Size

No more than thirty participants.

Time Required

One hour.

Materials

Newsprint, felt-tipped markers, and masking tape for the facilitator.

Process

    I. The facilitator announces the goals of the experience and asks the participants to brainstorm a list of basic human rights, which the facilitator posts.

    II. The facilitator directs the participants to clarify, modify, delete or add to

Adapted from pp. 88-91 of *Responsible Assertive Behavior*, by Arthur J. Lange and Patricia Jakubowski. Champaign, IL: Research Press, 1976. Used with permission.

the rights list. This may include a discussion of any limitations on the rights or the responsibilities that accompany the rights.

III. The facilitator directs participants to silently select one of the rights on the list that they feel most uncomfortable accepting.

IV. The facilitator gives the following instructions:

> "Move into a comfortable position . . . close your eyes . . . take a deep breath . . . hold it as long as you can . . . let is out slowly . . . Now imagine that you have the right you selected from this list . . . Imagine how life would change as you accept this right . . . How you would act . . . How you would feel about yourself . . . How you would feel about other people . . ."

This fantasy continues for two minutes, after which the trainer says:

> "Now imagine that you no longer have the right . . . Imagine how your life would change from what it was moments ago . . . How would you now act . . . and feel about yourself . . . How would you feel about other people . . ."

This fantasy continues for one minute. (Participants usually find it easier to imagine the right being taken away than to accept the right.)

V. The facilitator directs participants to form pairs and to discuss the following questions:

  A. What right did you select?

  B. Had you been denying it to yourself? In what way?

  C. How did you feel when you accepted the right?

  D. How did you act differently when you had the right? When you no longer had the right?

  E. What did you learn about yourself during this activity?

VI. The facilitator conducts a general group discussion of findings from Step V.

VII. The facilitator leads the group in a discussion of what methods participants may have used to deny themselves their rights, what methods they used to help accept these rights, and how they can continue to use these methods to increase the range of rights they readily accept for themselves.

COMPONENTS
OF ASSERTION
CORE SKILLS

Chapter Five

Verbal Assertion

Verbal assertion focuses on the words used to communicate in an assertive situation. Being able to put the correct words together to form an assertive statement is a core assertion skill. Of course, assertion situations generally also include some dialogue following or leading up to an assertive statement, so besides the ability to develop a verbal message in which a person stands up for his or her own rights without violating the rights of others, it is important to possess communication skills to respond to all parts of the conversation appropriately.

Our society communicates primarily by means of verbal messages. It makes sense to practice verbal assertion skills before nonverbal skills in a workshop design because nonverbals — tone of voice, inflection, gestures, and posture — are normally developed to accompany and enhance verbal statements. Verbal assertion has gradually evolved from very general types of guidelines (disagree, greet people, ask why, talk about yourself [Dawley & Wenrich, 1976]) and the simple modeling of an assertive response to a more systematic approach. Specific communication skills are now taught.

Scripting, or the use of a set of verbal components to form assertive statements or "scripts," is a technique that can be taught quickly and grasped easily and that builds on communication skills. It has evolved from Lange and Jakubowski's (1976) proposed system of six different types of assertion and the four-component "I-language" statements articulated by Gordon (1970). Scripting gives participants concrete and useful verbal assertion skills and makes them more willing to practice nonverbal and cognitive assertion, which are more foreign and, therefore, more difficult for most people to master. Bower and Bower (1976) have developed the scripting/components approach into a logical assertive technique known as "DESC scripting." A modified version of that technique is presented in this chapter.

In addition to communication skills and the scripting or components approach, a third verbal assertion method espoused by Manual Smith (1975) involves tactics for getting what one wants in a difficult situation or for defending oneself. Some of these techniques are considered protective skills (broken record, selective ignoring) and are included in the chapter on special applications; some are considered aggressive rather than assertive and so are not included.

OVERVIEW OF THE CHAPTER

The chapter contains a lecturette, "Communication Skills," that describes some of the communication skills most relevant to assertion: self-disclosure, active listening, open-ended questions, giving and responding to free information, and describing an experience. "Communication Triads," a structured experience designed to aid in the practice of these skills, is also included. A second lecturette, "Scripting," describes a systematic method of deciding what one wants to say in an assertive situation, and a structured experience, "Assertive Words" provides practice in using this method.

PROFESSIONAL CONSIDERATIONS

Participants should be encouraged to be as brief and concise as possible when being assertive so that they do not dilute their statements. A flood of words, including apologies, justifications, or explanations, lessens the impact on the listener.

Some participants object that "people don't talk this way" when practicing verbal assertion. It is important to point out that certain characteristics of verbal behavior are being practiced in an isolated form for intensive learning purposes, even if this makes conversation a bit stilted. It is helpful to discuss appropriate lead-ins to the verbal skills, as well as how to use these skills in the context of one's own personal style and of the situation. Scripting elements, for example, can be used in various positions within a statement.

Participants sometimes ask how active listening is assertive. It is assertive because the listener speaks up and lets the speaker know what is heard rather than just letting him or her ramble on. The biggest problem with teaching active listening is that people have been taught not to interrupt. Yet it is important that listeners speak up occasionally to check on what they are hearing rather than to tune out. It is also assertive to speak up when one is not listening or when one has not heard what one is supposed to be listening to or when one is not able to listen because of other things on the mind (Porat & Quakenbush, 1977).

Sometimes participants wonder how scripting can help them and what to do if their statements do not fit the other person's statements when they start talking. Some participants are able to spontaneously develop assertive statements they feel will express what they want to say. When they cannot, scripting is a point of departure for learning how to be spontaneous. Scripting is flexible and can be used to help people focus on what they want to talk about and how they can say it as a conversation progresses. Scripting also provides criteria for determining whether a statement is assertive and helps focus on what (which components) one needs more or less of in any assertive statement (Cooley & Hollandsworth, 1977).

Some additional points should be made about DESC. It is sometimes best to begin learning DESC by focusing on the words "describe," "express," "specify," and "choose." When using the unabridged version, there is a tendency for participants to over*explain*, to *empathize* to the point of feeling more for the other person than for themselves, to be over*considerate* of the possible consequences to others, and to exaggerate the possible *consequences* to themselves. Also, some clients may find it difficult to remember more than four components in the early assertion practice stages.

One of the most important abilities in verbal assertion is to be objective and descriptive and to speak in the first person rather than being evaluative, judgmental, or blaming. In this way, other people can listen and respond nondefensively. If one has decided to negotiate, it helps to look for a win-win solution.

Sometimes participants devise a script that they feel says what they want to say, but they still come away from the situation feeling that they have not expressed themselves adequately. This can be because the focus changed during an interaction but the assertive message remained the same. People often respond to one behavior and later must respond to a very different behavior as the interchange continues. For example, a cousin asks if she can borrow Fred's car. Fred explains that he does not wish to lend the car. The cousin tells her aunt and uncle, Fred's parents, about Fred's decision, and the parents and cousin combine to pressure Fred into lending the car. Fred continues to state that he does not want to lend the car, but he no longer feels good about his assertion. Although Fred's first reactions were to the request for the car and he stated his own wishes, his second reactions were to the tactics of his cousin and the hassle with his parents following his refusal. Yet Fred's verbal response continued to be to his cousin's original request. A person must at all times ask: "What am I reacting to *now* in this situation? What behavior or feeling should I be describing now?" In the example, Fred might have shared his feelings about the behavior of his parents and cousin and told them how he would prefer to be treated.

Sometimes communication skills and scripting are so rewarding for participants in the workshop setting that they overuse them. One woman, after learning the active-listening technique, went home and used it to reflect back every sentence her husband said. Participants should be cautioned to introduce assertive language into their lives gradually — choosing receptive people and nonstressful times when people are more willing to listen. An additional overkill occurs in scripting with participants who feel obligated to use all the DESC elements in one assertive statement.

Some participants raise the question of whether it may be "too late" to assert themselves about a situation because some time has passed. Usually, if the risks have been examined and accepted and the participant wishes to be assertive in the situation, it is not too late. However, unless the behavior or situation is ongoing, the passage of time makes it more difficult for others to recall the behavior or situation being described. Also, letting situations go for long periods of time without confronting them can build emotions to the point at which it is hard to avoid an overreaction. The time it takes to realize that one should have been assertive can be shortened through practice. It is also possible to ask for time to think about a reply in an assertive situation.

Sometimes mistakes occur in assertion. A person may incorrectly interpret a situation or assert himself or herself incorrectly. In this case, a good approach is to simply acknowledge the mistake and continue practicing assertion with that person and other persons when it seems appropriate. "It is more important that the nonassertive client learn to accept her 'aggressive mistakes' than it is for that client to learn a 'perfect' assertive response or learn a 'perfect' distinction between assertion and aggression" (Jakubowski-Spector, 1973a, p. 85).

If a person reacts negatively to another's assertion, and the assertor has examined his or her own behavior and the comments of the other person in the situation, has asked the other person for clarification of aspects of the assertor's behavior that caused the negative reaction, and still feels that the behavior was appropriate, Galassi and Galassi (1977) suggest that the assertor restate to clarify his or her position and to be sure it was heard correctly, and then, if necessary, ignore the unfavorable reaction.

In "Communication Triads," it can be pointed out that open-ended questions typically begin with "what" or "how." "Why" generally should not be used, as it frequently causes defensiveness by seeming to ask for justification.

Communication Skills

Assertion is a communication skill — it involves getting the message across to other people. Many times this message is delivered in the context of a dialogue or conversation. Whether the message is confrontive ("I need to talk with you about a problem") or social ("I would like to get to know you") or somewhere between, three communication skills — the use of free information, open-ended questions, and active listening — are helpful to know about. One way to look at [communication] is as a search for common interests. This doesn't mean that you only want to meet people who agree with you, for this would become boring. But in order for a conversation to work, the participants have to be interested in at least discussing the same topics. . . .

UTILIZING FREE INFORMATION

Sometimes an initial exchange of facts or a few clichés leads naturally into a satisfying conversation. In other cases, however, things don't progress so smoothly. Here's a familiar scene: You've just met another person. You've introduced yourselves to each other and told where you live, what you do for a living, and where you're from. You've commented on the weather. Then comes an awkward silence. After a few moments of averted glances and shifting about, either you or your partner can't stand the tension any more. One of you blurts out "Nice talking to you" or "I've got to get going," and the conversation is over before it really ever started.

It usually isn't necessary to feel at a loss for words in these situations. Most people will give you plenty of opportunities to develop a conversation by

Adapted and excerpted from "Establishing Relationships Through Conversation Skills," from *CONFIDENCE IN COMMUNICATION: A GUIDE TO ASSERTIVE AND SOCIAL SKILLS*, by Ronald B. Adler. Copyright © 1977 by Holt, Rinehart and Winston. Reprinted by permission of Holt, Rinehart and Winston.

offering free *information* — data that goes beyond what you've requested or commented on. Your skill in using free information is an important part of the conversational process. Whether consciously or not, people share whatever part of themselves they are willing to discuss. In this sense free information is often a sort of invitation to talk about whatever the person who offers it feels is appropriate.

Most conversations contain more free information than you could possibly use. . . .

The free information you choose to pursue will depend on your own interests. If you're genuinely interested in getting to know the other person, there's likely to be some data offered that you'd like to know more about.

Free information includes nonverbal clues as well as the words another person speaks. Articles of clothing, physical features, smiles, frowns, and so on often can form the basis for a conversation. . . .

ASKING OPEN-ENDED QUESTIONS

Sometimes the person you're talking to will offer plenty of free information, making your conversation flow along effortlessly. But what about the partner who, out of nervousness or lack of skill, doesn't share anything to which you can respond? . . .

The answer lies in questions. . . . *Closed-ended questions* — ones that can be answered in one or at most a few words . . . [evoke replies that contain] no free information and thus leave [one] no closer to knowing his partner than before he had asked them. In contrast . . . *open-ended [questions]* are worded in such a way that they call for a more detailed response.

Instead of "Is there a lot to do in Fargo, North Dakota?" try "What kinds of things are there to do in Fargo, North Dakota?"

Instead of "Are you happy with your job as a nurse?" try "What are some good (or bad) things about being a nurse?"

Instead of "Are you still practicing Transcendental Meditation?" try "I'd like to hear what your experiences have been with Transcendental Meditation."

One big advantage of open-ended questions is that they allow you to direct a conversation toward whatever communication level seems appropriate at the time.

SELF-DISCLOSURE

In any conversation it's important that both participants practice at least some *self-disclosure*, for a relationship can grow only when the people involved share something about themselves.

Suppose that you've met someone whom you think has the qualities of a potential good friend. Using your newfound skills of asking open-ended questions and following up on the resulting free information, you become even more certain that you'd like to get to know your partner better. Now look at this exchange from the other person's perspective: What might his feelings be toward you? The answer to this question depends to a great extent on how much of yourself you've shared. It's unrealistic to expect that others will become interested in you unless you give them some data on which to form a personal opinion. Many of the people who wonder why their relationships never seem to get off the ground don't realize the importance of being willing to let others know who they are — their likes and dislikes, their talents, opinions, and feelings. Whatever attractiveness comes from mystery can only last so long — sooner or later we need to know what makes the other person tick if there is to be any kind of relationship.

Don't become intimidated by the concept of self-disclosure, thinking that it consists exclusively of sharing your deepest thoughts and feelings. While this type of personal sharing certainly is important under the right circumstances, simply sharing some of the many facts you know and opinions you hold is equally important and valuable. . . .

LISTENING

In conversation silence is sometimes golden. You have probably had the pleasant experience of talking with people who gave you their total attention, who were genuinely interested in what you had to say. It's likely that you left such conversations remarking to yourself about what a fabulous communicator these persons were, only to realize later that you did practically all the talking. Your partner's behavior here illustrated an important point: Sometimes the best communicator is one who mostly listens.

There are two reasons why listening can be valuable. First, it's often true that people like to hear themselves talk. This isn't always just an act of egotism. There's nothing wrong with sharing an accomplishment you're proud of or discussing a subject with which you're intensely involved. If you're genuinely interested in what a speaker has to say at times like these, it may not be necessary to add your thoughts to the conversation. Simply let the other person share, and enjoy it.

A second situation in which listening is valuable occurs when your partner is confused or has a problem. In these cases it's often helpful for the other person to talk the dilemma out, while you remain for the most part empathetically silent.

There are really two styles of listening, each of which you can use in conversations.

Passive Listening. Often the only contribution you need to make to a conversation is what psychologist Thomas Gordon (1970) calls "door openers" — occasional short verbal messages to let your partner know that you're paying attention. Exclamations like "uh-huh," "oh," and so on might not be very original, but they suit the purpose well. Of course, it's possible to use door openers like these as a way of *pretending* to listen when your mind is really elsewhere, but that is not the intention here. On the contrary, you can often learn the most about someone else simply by giving him space to share. People are often reluctant to talk about themselves, and your utterances can serve as a signal that you want to know about them.

Active Listening. . . . The kind of response in which one reflects back thoughts and feelings, without adding any judgments or advice of his own, has been termed *active listening* (Gordon, 1970), and it consists of simply summarizing the speaker's comments in one's own words. It's a highly effective tool.

Active listening works well in two kinds of situations. First, like passive listening, it's an invitation for the other person to go on talking. By paraphrasing your partner's comments you're in effect saying, "Yes, I understand that . . . what happened next?" A second use of active listening is illustrated in the scene [just described]. Paraphrasing can be a tremendously helpful device for helping people clear up their own confusion. People often are capable of finding answers for their own problems, and active listening gives them a way of sorting out the ideas that, unvocalized, can be confusing. . . .

SUMMARY

. . . If you think of each person as an island, then the ability to [communicate] comfortably and well becomes a kind of bridge, allowing us to join our island to others and share something of ourselves with different people and in turn learn more about them. A good series of interpersonal bridges is clearly important, for it's only through contact with others that we can establish relationships. On the other hand, don't hold onto the unrealistic expectation that you'll find a lasting relationship — or even a pleasant interlude — at the end of every bridge you build. It's simply not realistic to expect that you'll be interested in everyone you meet or that they'll all respond to your overtures. Instead, think of your ability to communicate successfully as a "batting average" — a percentage of successfully completed attempts to reach others. These skills . . . should help you increase that average, so that you find yourself involved in more and more satisfying relationships.

REFERENCE

Gordon, T. *P.E.T.: Parent effectiveness training: The tested new way to raise responsible children*. New York: Wyden, 1970.

Scripting

"What am I supposed to say?" "I can never think of the right words." "I'm not good at spontaneous responses." If these words sound familiar, scripting may solve the problem. Scripting provides guidelines for focusing and stating one's thoughts and words in assertive situations, in which it is difficult to think clearly and make sense of what is happening. These situations may involve unfamiliar problems, moderate anxiety levels, the need for a quick response, or a conflict message. Scripting uses a set of components that can be adapted for creative and spontaneous assertive responses in almost any situation.

Scripting involves three steps: (a) focusing on relevant elements of the situation, (b) deciding which of these elements should be expressed verbally, and (c) forming an assertive "script" or verbal statement. The most useful way to learn scripting is to practice until it is second nature. However, people have been known to use scripting successfully with much less practice. For example, one man returned from work to pick up his car at a local garage and found that uncontracted-for work had been done on the car at added cost. The man had not yet memorized the components of scripting, but had a list of them in his second car. He explained that he would be back in a few minutes, went outside to the car, consulted his list, and wrote a script for the situation. Script formulated, the man went back inside and assertively communicated his refusal to pay for that work for which he had not contracted. Scripting is not a magic formula that helps people always to get their way, but it is helpful for deciding what one wants to say.

FOCUS ON RELEVANT COMPONENTS

The situational components most relevant to assertion are (a) the behavior the assertor reacts to, (b) the feelings of the assertor, the effects that the behavior has on him or her, and the feelings of others involved, (c) the behavioral changes or preferences of the assertor, and (d) possible positive and negative consequences. In the case of the garage: (a) the customer reacted to being charged for services for which he had not contracted, (b) some of the customer's feelings may be anger, frustration, or disappointment with the service given; a possible effect might be that the customer will be late for dinner because of the problem and the mechanic may feel that he or she has been helpful in identifying and correcting the problem with the car, (c) the customer may want the mechanic to charge only for those services for which he had originally contracted or he may wish to negotiate a fair price in view of the lack of contract and the work done, and (d) the customer may decide to use the mechanic again if he does not have to pay for the extra services and to take the case to the Better Business Bureau if the mechanic insists that he pay for the extra services. In this example, the customer may decide that the potential positive consequences to himself would be communicating his position to the mechanic in an assertive way and not having to pay for uncontracted-for services. He may decide that the potential negative consequences would be the mechanic's anger, time lost by negotiating with the Better Business Bureau, and the need to look for a new garage.

After becoming aware of and focusing on the components of the assertive situation and organizing them into a meaningful pattern, the assertor can understand more about what is happening and decide what to do about it.

An exploration of short- and long-term consequences involves such things as looking at the power dynamics in the situation. People may decide not to assert themselves after looking at their own power or lack thereof and the possible consequences. If the assertor has no power or if the personal risks are too high, he or she may choose not to be assertive. If the risks to others are too high, he or she may decide to overlook something. For example, if another has had an extremely difficult day or is dealing with a difficult personal problem, one may decide not to be assertive over a relatively minor issue.

CHOOSE COMPONENTS TO BE EXPRESSED VERBALLY

Once a person has examined the consequences of being assertive and has decided to go ahead, the next step is to choose which components to talk about. Many people help themselves remember the four elements of an assertive response by using the acronym DESC, focusing on the first letter of the action words *describe, express, specify,* and *consequences* (Bower & Bower, 1976, p. 90). The acronym can be expanded by adding the words *explain, empathize,* and *consider*. More specifically, DESC means to:

1. *Describe* the situation or the behavior of people you are reacting to.

2. *Express* your feeling reaction to the situation or behavior, *explain* what other effects the person's behavior has on you (including thoughts, beliefs, or values), and *empathize* with how the other person feels.

3. *Specify* the behavior you would prefer from the other person or what you would like or need in the situation. (One preference may be to *negotiate* a different way of acting in the situation, rather than for you simply to decide alone what the preferred behavior should be.)

4. *Choose* the positive and negative *consequences* you are prepared to carry through if the preferred behavior does or does not happen, *consider* the potential positive and negative consequences to you of being assertive in the situation, and *consider* the consequences of your assertive response to the other people involved.

One can, of course, use all the components; for example, "When I breathe in smoke (describe), I get headaches and feel frustrated (express) because I cannot concentrate on what is going on in class (explain). I realize that those of you who smoke may have difficulty concentrating if you cannot smoke (empathize). I would like to negotiate some kind of solution (specify). If you will negotiate with me, I think we can make this a good place for all of us to learn; if you will not negotiate, then I am prepared to push for stronger rules on smoking in classrooms here (choose) in order to protect my ability to learn. I realize that some people may not feel good about my speaking out on this and my asking you to spend some time problem solving, but it is very important to me, and I hope that we can work this out quickly and to everyone's agreement (consider)."

Obviously, using all the components results in a short speech. A more useful and manageable approach is to express only one or two of the components verbally. Some components frequently used alone are: express ("I enjoy being with you," "I don't like that") and specify ("I want you to stop eating," "I don't lend my books," "I'd like more time to think about that"). Some "most used" combinations include: describe, specify, and choose for dealing with strangers or when one's legal rights are violated and describe, express, explain, empathize, and specify (negotiate) with friends. Using the first combination, the idea is to get a point across without becoming vulnerable to attack or offering another person an easy way out. For example, when having difficulty returning a malfunctioning television one could say: "The warranty on this television states that it is protected for another six months. I would like you to honor this warranty and repair my television without charge. If you can help me, we can complete this transaction quickly. If you cannot I would like to speak to the manager." To add your feelings ("I feel hurt that you are giving me such a difficult time") or to offer further explanations increases your vulnerability needlessly. The second combination is useful with friends, who are more disposed to understand and sympathize with the problem, and may be offended if consequences are mentioned ("When you arrive fifteen minutes late I feel frustrated, because I could have used that time to get more work done. The time we chose may be a bad one for you. I would like to decide on a time when we can both be on time for lunch"). At this point, talking about consequences would be overkill.

Even in the case of an overbearing salesperson, it is important to start with the least amount of assertion necessary and to bring up consequences only when it becomes appropriate to be more blunt or firm. When consequences are expressed, it is important that they not be perceived as an attempt to coerce. Consequences are the action one is already prepared to take, and stating them is an information-sharing process. For example, if a person is often late to the office, has been confronted with this behavior repeatedly, and nothing has changed, the employer can either fire the person or tell the person what the consequences will be if the behavior does not change and then give the person a chance to change the behavior. Stating consequences lets the other person know the level of frustration that has been reached and the action one is prepared to take.

FORM AN ASSERTIVE SCRIPT OR VERBAL STATEMENT

After identifying the assertive components in a situation and choosing which to express verbally, a person can write an assertive "script" for the situation. A good way to develop a script is to complete a set of typical lead-ins for each component, such as:

Describe: When you . . . When I . . . When . . .

Express: I feel . . . (*Explain:* Then . . . *Empathize:* I understand that you . . . You may feel . . .)

Specify: I would prefer . . . I want . . . I would like . . .

Choose: If you do . . . If you do not . . . (*Consider:* I realize . . .)

Once the script has been developed, its quality can be tested by asking these questions:

Describe. Is it objective, specific, simple, and concrete? ("When you look at the same spot on the wall for five minutes at a time . . .") Or is it evaluative ("When you act so dumb . . ."), general ("You always talk in that boring way . . ."), complicated ("You seem to look away and not really focus on me, you look into space and you hardly blink or say anything that you . . ."), or abstract ("It's just a feeling I have that you're not paying attention to me")? Does it describe behavior and not intentions, motives, or attitudes?

Express. Are feelings acknowledged or "owned" by the assertor? ("*I* feel," not "*you make me feel*"). Is it as calm and constructive as possible (do not attack), specific ("I feel angry," not "I feel funny"), expressive of a feeling ("I feel," not "I feel that you"), and directed toward a particular behavior or event, not a person or some global situation?

Explain. Is it concise, clear, relevant, and objective?

Empathize. Is it concise, concrete, and congruent with the obvious words and feelings of the other person in a way that recognizes his or her side of things?

Specify. Is it explicit and does it ask for small, observable behavioral changes or only one or two reasonable and realistic changes? Is the script specific about what behavior one is willing to change and does it leave the way open to negotiation, if desired? Occasionally it may be helpful to generate a list of alternative behaviors to help arrive at a joint solution.

Choose. Does the script emphasize the positive and possible and stress a willingness to carry out the consequences, which should be explicit and appropriate to the behavior? Is it clear to the other person that the information is being shared to let the other person know his or her choices and not to threaten?

SUMMARY

Scripting is a very useful assertion tool. It provides guidelines for focusing one's thoughts and words in assertive situations. Scripting involves (a) focusing on situational components most relevant to assertion, (b) choosing which of these components should be expressed verbally, and (c) forming an assertive "script" or statement. Some useful scripting aids are the acronym DESC, the use of typical lead-ins, and the guideline questions for testing the quality of an assertive script. Assertion is not all monologue and includes communication skills such as free information, active listening, and self-disclosure. With practice, the assertor can use scripting components selectively to form spontaneous and creative verbal assertive statements in situations as they occur.

Communication Triads: Practicing Verbal Assertion Skills

Goals

    I. To learn to recognize and identify some important elements of assertive verbal communication.

    II. To practice verbal communication skills useful for assertive responses.

Group Size

No more than thirty participants, preferably a number divisible by three.

Time Required

Two hours.

Materials

Newsprint, felt-tipped markers, and masking tape for the facilitator.

Process

    I. The facilitator announces the goals of the activity and gives a short

Adapted from pp. 31-33 of *A Handbook of Structured Experiences for Human Relations Training* (Vol. I, Rev.). J. William Pfeiffer and John E. Jones (Eds.). La Jolla, CA: University Associates, 1974.

lecturette on verbal communication skills, demonstrating the various techniques involved, listing them on newsprint, and answering any related questions.

II. The facilitator tells participants to form groups of three and to designate one group member as the speaker, one as the listener, and the third as referee/observer.

III. The facilitator explains:

"There will be three rounds; within each round each participant will have an opportunity to practice the communication skills involved in that round. Round 1 will involve the skills of self-disclosure: the I-message (speaker) and open-ended questioning (listener). The designated listener is to begin by asking an open-ended question to which the speaker is to respond with self-disclosure. The listener is to follow with another open-ended question and so on. The referee/observer's job is to see that both the speaker and the listener act within their roles and to take notes on what helps and hinders assertive communication between the two communicators. You have five minutes for this phase of round 1."

IV. The facilitator announces the end of round 1, phase 1, and asks the referee/observers to report on their observations within their groups and the groups to briefly discuss the interaction that has just taken place and the helping and hindering behaviors observed. (Three minutes.)

V. The facilitator leads a general discussion of what was learned from the phase. (Three minutes.)

VI. Phases 2 and 3 of round 1 are run in the same way, with each member of each triad taking new roles at the beginning of each phase so that all members have taken all three roles by the end of the round.

VII. The facilitator announces:

"Round 2 will involve the skills of describing an experience and active listening. The speaker is to begin by describing an experience he or she has had to which the listener is to respond with active listening. If the speaker finishes describing one experience, he or she is to continue with another. The referee/observer's job is the same as in round 1."

VIII. Steps IV through VI are repeated.

IX. The facilitator announces:

"The third and final round will involve the skills of giving free information and responding to free information/asking for clarification. The listener is to begin by asking a question to which the speaker will respond with some free information. The listener may then respond to the free information or ask a clarifying question to which the speaker is to respond with free information, and so on. The referee/observer's job remains the same."

X. Steps IV through VI are repeated.

XI. The facilitator leads a general discussion of learning from the total experience and asks for suggestions on ways these skills might be applied to the back-home situation.

Variations

I. Pairs may be used instead of triads, with partners sharing their reactions and observations and policing each other on the rules.

II. The speaker and listener in each round may practice both skills at the same time. Using this approach, a "price of admission" is required; i.e., in round 1 each of the two conversants must practice self-disclosure before they can ask an open-ended question; in round 2 each must practice active listening before they can describe an experience; and in round 3, each must respond to free information or ask a question of clarification before they can offer free information.

III. A round may be run focusing on one skill, such as active listening.

IV. A list of controversial topics may be brainstormed at the beginning of the experience to aid participants in selecting topics of discussion and to provide the opportunity to deal with more difficult communication areas.

V. The experience may be limited to one round by eliminating Steps VII through X. Within this round, the speaker in each phase chooses one from among the six communication skills to practice. The listener chooses a complementary skill from the list to practice, and the referee/observer's job remains the same as in the original version. Directions in Step III must be changed accordingly.

Assertive Words: Creating Verbal Scripts

Goals

  I. To develop appropriate verbal assertive responses to assertive situations.
  II. To apply a useful formula for developing assertive scripts.

Group Size

No more than twenty-eight participants, preferably a number divisible by four.

Time Required

One and one-half hours.

Materials

  I. Newsprint, felt-tipped markers, and masking tape for the facilitator.
  II. A pencil and a copy of the Assertive Words DESC Form for each participant.

Process

  I. The facilitator announces the goals of the experience and asks participants to brainstorm a list of assertive situations, which the facilitator posts on newsprint.

II. The facilitator gives a brief lecturette on the DESC script, demonstrates how to develop a DESC script for one of the posted situations, and answers any questions for clarification.

III. The facilitator distributes the Assertive Words DESC Form and pencils and directs participants to form groups of four and to apply the DESC script to as many of the posted situations as they can in the fifteen minutes allotted to them.

IV. The facilitator leads a group discussion of the scripts participants have created and of any problems or questions.

V. The facilitator directs participants to each select a personal assertion situation, to return to their small groups, and with the group's help, to create a script for each selected situation. (Thirty minutes.)

VI. The facilitator leads a group discussion of the scripts participants have created and any problems or questions.

VII. The facilitator asks for ideas from the group as to how the DESC script will be useful to participants in their daily lives.

Variations

I. Instead of responding to posted situations, participants can be given one-sided prototype dialogues. Each situation should be described in such a way that the appropriateness of an assertive response to the situation is obvious. Several lines to which the participants can reply should follow each description. Participants can then use the DESC script as a guide in developing responses to each stimulus line of the dialogue.[1]

II. Prototype dialogues as described in Step I can be tape recorded. The tape can be stopped after each stimulus line, while the participant gives a response.[1]

III. Participants can use the "unabridged" Assertive Words DESC Form, by inserting the EXPLAIN and EMPATHIZE components after the EXPRESS component:

EXPLAIN what other effects the other person's behavior has on you. Then . . .

EMPATHIZE with how the other person feels. I understand that you . . . (You may feel . . .)

and by adding the CONSIDER component after the CHOOSE component:

CONSIDER the consequences of your assertive response to the other people involved in the situation and yourself. I realize . . .

---

[1]Variations I and II are based on material found on page 32 of *Assert Yourself! How To Be Your Own Person*, by Merna Dee Galassi and John P. Galassi. New York: Human Sciences Press, 1977.

ASSERTIVE WORDS DESC FORM

Instructions: Write one or two sentences in each of the spaces below, corresponding to the situation you have chosen. Then, choose the words you would like to say in the situation you have chosen.

D ESCRIBE the other person's behavior or the situation being reacted to specifically and objectively.

When you . . . (When . . ., When I . . .)

E XPRESS your feeling reaction to the other person's behavior or the situation in a nonevaluative way.

I feel . . .

S PECIFY one or two behavior changes you would like the person to make. (Ask for agreement.)

I would prefer . . . (I want . . ., I would like . . .)

C HOOSE the consequences you are prepared to carry through. Tell the person what you can do for him or her if the agreement to change is kept (positive consequences).

If you do . . .

If necessary, tell the person what you will do if the agreement is not kept (negative consequences).

If you don't . . .

Adapted from p. 126 of *Asserting Yourself: A Practical Guide for Positive Change*, by Sharon A. Bower and Gordon Bower, copyright © 1976, by permission of Addison-Wesley Publishing Company, Inc., Reading, Mass.

Chapter Six

Nonverbal Assertion

Even though a person feels assertive, or intends to be assertive, or uses an assertive verbal message, that person's incongruent nonverbals can confuse the receiver of the message. Nonverbal assertion focuses on the physical and paralinguistic cues through which participants express themselves.

Nonverbals can be broken into visual and vocal elements. Visual elements include: eye contact, facial expression, body posture and movement, distance from the other person, touch, and appearance. Vocal elements include: loudness or volume, fluency, speed and rhythm, tone and inflection, pitch, articulation, tone or resonance, extraneous sounds — uh, uh-huh, ah, umm, swallows, coughs, sighs — and timing of responses.

One of the main reasons nonverbal assertion is taught after verbal assertion is that it is generally designed to accompany or enhance verbal behavior and it plays a variety of roles in relation to the spoken word. Nonverbal behavior can reflect what was said as well as accent it; it can enhance and regulate the flow of what is being said; and it can even substitute for it. Of course, nonverbal messages can also contradict verbal ones (Knapp, 1972). Nonverbals that are not perceived as assertive by the listener can cancel an assertive message or send a confusing double message.

Nonverbals Are the Music

Nonverbals are the music that accompanies verbal assertion; the goal is to reiterate, support, and enhance the verbal message. No matter how assertive or appropriate a statement is, if the accompanying nonverbal language is incongruent, the "music" can drown out the words. For example, three types of nonverbals can accompany the statement "I don't want to do that": (a) speaking in a very soft, whining tone of voice, pulling away from the other person, shifting from one foot to another, wringing one's hands, and looking at the floor; (b) using a strong, steady tone of voice and taking a firm, comfortable stance on two feet with hands relaxed at the sides and good eye contact; or (c) speaking in a raised and haughty tone of voice, leaning toward the other person, pointing a finger, and glaring at him or her. The same verbal message can be made to appear nonassertive, assertive, or aggressive simply by varying nonverbals (see Table 4).

Cultural Differences

Nonverbals are culturally bound, and those described in this book are derived from American culture. Subcultures may not be equally represented. For example, blacks use some different nonverbals than do whites, and males and females may be perceived differently when they demonstrate the same nonverbal behavior. In the United States, a tense male voice may identify a man as older, more unyielding, and cantankerous; a tense female voice may identify a woman as younger, more emotional, feminine, high strung, and less intelligent (Addington, 1968, p. 502).

Steps to Nonverbal Assertion

Sometimes, simply putting oneself in an assertive posture and using an assertive tone of voice and eye contact can help one feel more assertive. To practice nonverbal assertion, one can learn to (a) recognize and describe perceived assertive, nonassertive, and aggressive nonverbal behaviors in others; (b) modify one's own nonverbal behavior on the basis of useful feedback from others or observation of one's own; (c) practice appropriate behavior; and (d) solicit feedback from others on the new behavior. So many factors are involved in nonverbal behavior that no set of rules can be used for all situations. The best way to tell whether one is giving an assertive message is to solicit specific, descriptive, useful feedback and to monitor one's own behavior closely.

OVERVIEW OF THE CHAPTER

The chapter contains a lecturette, "Nonverbal Elements of Assertive Communication," and two structured experiences: "Nonassertion/Aggression/Assertion" and "Nonverbal Triads." The lecturette discusses some of the most cited dimensions of nonverbal communication (eye contact, facial expression, gestures and posture, and vocal elements) and gives pointers on how to use them to communicate assertively.

"Nonassertion/Aggression/Assertion" helps participants identify nonverbal behaviors they associate with assertion, nonassertion, and aggression

Table 4. Nonverbal and Verbal Behavior Associated with Nonassertion, Assertion, and Aggression

	NONASSERTION	ASSERTION	AGGRESSION
Emotion	Internalize Fear/anxiety/guilt/depression/fatigue/ nervousness/hurt	State all as they occur Confidence, self-esteem	Externalize "Secondary" to fear/guilt/hurt or "buildup" to inappropriate anger/ rage/hate or misplaced hostility/ righteousness/superiority
	Temperature below normal Not verbally expressed	Temperature normal Tone normal	Temperature above normal Expressed loudly and explosively
Nonverbal	Downcast, averted, darting or teary eyes Shifting of weight, slumped body, round shoulders, head down, shuffling walk	Open, direct, not staring eye contact Standing comfortably but firmly on two feet, steady, straight	Glaring, narrowed, expressionless eyes Leaning forward, stiff, rigid posture
	Wringing of hands, biting lips, adjusting clothing, nervous gestures,	Hands loosely at sides, relaxed	Clenched fists, jerky movements, finger pointing, hands on hips
	Pleading, monotone, apologetic, mumbling, whining, hesitant, giggly tone of voice	Strong, steady, firm, clear tone of voice	Raised, snickering, haughty tone of voice
General Posture	Moving away, self-effacing, dependent	Moving toward, facing up to situations, standing up for self, independent or interdependent	Moving against, other-effacing, counterdependent
Verbal	Rambling statements Qualifiers (maybe/I wonder if you could/ only/just)	Concise statements "I" statements (I think/I feel/I want)	Clipped, interrupting statements Threats (you'd better/if you don't/ watch out)
	Fillers (uh/well/you know) Negatives (don't bother/it's not really important)	Cooperative words (let's/how can we resolve this) Empathic statements of interest (what do you think/what do you see)	Calling names, demanding, accusing Put-downs (come on/you must be kidding) Judgmental, sarcastic, evaluative comments (should/bad), Sexist or racist terms

Based on "Assertion Theory" by C. Kelley in *The 1976 Annual Handbook for Group Facilitators*. J. William Pfeiffer & John E. Jones (Eds.). La Jolla, CA: University Associates, 1976.

and compare their associations with those of others. It requires participants to engage in some physical movement. "Nonverbal Triads" is designed to help participants practice and receive feedback on nonverbal behaviors to accompany assertive responses in situations of their choice. Participants portray the three response styles for each situation and receive feedback on the accuracy of the portrayal. This structured experience also trains participants to recognize the three response styles and to give accurate feedback.

PROFESSIONAL CONSIDERATIONS

One way to study vocal cues is to use a tape recorder. Participants can be encouraged to record their voices on tape while talking on the phone or to others at home.

A mirror or videotape can be used to practice nonverbal visual cues. Videotape playbacks are especially interesting with the sound off.

People who have been nonassertive for long periods of time in response to a particular situation may feel that they are being aggressive when practicing a nonverbal assertive response. It is important to mention this to participants, as well as to give accurate feedback on how the participant is coming across, until he or she becomes accustomed to this new level of expression.

Participants may also be reticent about practicing nonverbal assertion because they are somewhat shy or inhibited or because they do not know how to change nonverbal behavior. One way to help participants give themselves freedom to express themselves is to have them imagine several moves or gestures they have wanted to make in the group but have not made for one reason or another. Give participants "permission" to make these moves or gestures for ten to fifteen minutes, with the caution that they must not injure anyone else. The facilitator can lead a discussion of the nature of the behaviors chosen and the risks involved for the person choosing them (Osborn & Harris, 1975).

Participants may not be conscious of their nonverbal behaviors, and so must be made aware of them before they can change them.

When doing "Nonverbal Triads" it is important that participants name the *specific* behavior they are observing and tell what that behavior communicates to them. Many times participants will begin with vague descriptions: "She overdid it," "She moved a lot." The facilitator may need to insist on specific descriptions of nonverbal behavior and what message that behavior conveyed.

In "Nonverbal Triads" participants sometimes need to have the point clarified that the nonassertive and aggressive nonverbals are being portrayed, not in order to practice these styles for future use, but because this gives the participants a way to discriminate among them in the future. Sometimes participants are mistaken in their perception of their own nonverbal behavior as it relates to the assertion continuum. The most common mistake is for participants to believe themselves to be portraying aggression, when others perceive them as clearly assertive. Direct and accurate feedback is the best way to overcome problems of faulty self-perception.

Nonverbal Elements of Assertive Communication

Sometimes it's difficult to pin down the exact, observable behaviors that can show you how to express yourself more effectively. . . . Some visual, vocal, and verbal traits play a large part in effective assertive communication.

VISUAL ELEMENTS

"Actions speak louder than words" may be an overworn phrase, but it's still true. If you mean what you say, your nonverbal behavior will back up your statements. On the other hand, the most assertive words will lose their impact if expressed in a hesitant, indirect manner. . . .

Eye Contact

Inadequate eye contact is usually interpreted in a negative way as anxiety, dishonesty, shame, boredom, or embarrassment. Even when they are not aware of a person's insufficient eye contact, others will often react unconsciously to it by either avoiding or taking advantage of the person exhibiting it. Don't go overboard and begin to stare down everyone you meet — this will be just as distracting as the other extreme — but do be sure to keep your gaze direct.

If it is necessary, you can gradually begin to increase your eye contact by first directing your glances toward different parts of the other person's face, such as the forehead, mouth, or chin. From a distance of four feet or so it's impossible to tell whether this kind of behavior is any different from an actual eye-to-eye look.

Excerpted and adapted from "Elements of Assertive Communication," pp. 47-53 of *CONFIDENCE IN COMMUNICATION: A GUIDE TO ASSERTIVE AND SOCIAL SKILLS*, by Ronald B. Adler. Copyright © 1977 by Holt, Rinehart and Winston. Reprinted by permission of Holt, Rinehart and Winston.

Facial Expression

In the typical assertiveness training group, one or two participants will express confusion as to why they have such trouble being taken seriously. They claim to use the appropriate language, keep eye contact, stand at the proper distance, and so on. When asked to demonstrate how they usually express themselves, the problem often becomes apparent: Their facial expression is totally inappropriate to the message. Many communicators, for example, verbally express their dissatisfaction while smiling as if nothing were wrong. Others claim to share approval or appreciation while wearing expressions more appropriate for viewing a corpse. After one student demonstrated his behavior in job interviews, the reason for his lack of success became obvious. Although he claimed to feel confident about his abilities, his clenched jaw and miserable expression advertised a tense job candidate. The problem in each of these examples is the same: In order for you to be taken seriously your facial expression should match the other parts of your message.

Gestures and Posture

Like facial expressions, your movements and body positioning can either contribute to or detract from the immediacy of a message. Fidgeting hands, nervous shifting from one foot to another, or slumped shoulders will reduce or even contradict the impact of an assertive message. On the other hand, gestures that are appropriate to the words being spoken and a posture that suggests involvement in the subject will serve to reinforce your words. Watch an effective storyteller, interviewer, actor, or other model and note the added emphasis they give to a message.

Recognizing the importance of these actions doesn't mean that you should begin to act in an exaggerated way to make your point. The ridiculous sight of a person with waving arms or a jabbing finger can be just as distracting as a zombielike pose. The point here is to loosen up enough to let your gestures suit the words they accompany.

Body Orientation

Another way of expressing your attitude is through the positioning of your body in relation to another person. Facing someone head on communicates a much higher degree of immediacy than does a less direct positioning. In fact, a directly confronting stance in which the face, shoulders, hips, and feet squarely face the other [can sometimes] be interpreted as indicating an aggressive attitude. (To verify this impression, think of the stance used by a baseball player who is furious with an umpire's decision or a Marine drill instructor facing a recruit.) Observation for assertive models will show that the most successful body orientation for most settings is a modified frontal one, in which the communicators are slightly angled away from a direct confrontation — perhaps 10 to 30 degrees. This position clearly suggests a high degree of involvement, yet allows the occasional freedom from total eye contact. . . .

Distance

Choosing the correct distance between yourself and another person is an important ingredient of assertion. Anthropologist Edward Hall (1959, 1969) has outlined four distinct distances used by Americans in differing situations. *Intimate distance* ranges from the surface of the skin to about 18 inches. As its name implies, it is appropriately used for private purposes: expressions of affection, protection, and anger. *Personal distance* runs from 18 inches to approximately four feet, and is used with people we know well and feel relaxed with. As Hall states, this is the range at which we keep someone "at arm's length," suggesting that while there is relatively high involvement here, the immediacy is not as great as that which occurs within intimate distance. *Social distance* ranges from four to 12 feet, and is generally appropriate in less personal settings: meeting strangers, engaging in impersonal business trans- actions, and so on. This is the range at which job interviews are often con- ducted, customers approached by sales people, or newcomers introduced to us by a third party. We often accuse someone who ought to be using social distance but instead moves into our personal space of being "pushy." Finally, Hall labels as *public distance* the space extending outward from 12 feet. As its name implies, public distance is used in highly impersonal settings and occa- sions involving larger numbers of people: classrooms, public performances, and so on. Be sure you are using the appropriate range for the messages you want to express.

VOCAL ELEMENTS

[Nonverbal assertion does] not focus on *what* you say, but rather on *how you say it*. To understand how the voice conveys messages, recall a time when you have overheard a muffled conversation going on behind a wall or a closed door. You almost certainly had a good idea of the type of feelings being exchanged even though you could not understand the words being spoken or see the visual behavior of the communicators. Let's take a look at four ways that your voice can convey assertiveness.

Loudness

The volume of your voice says a great deal about your feelings at the moment. There are two ways in which loudness affects the immediacy of your communication. First is the basic volume you use — the way you speak most of the time. You may, for instance, have the habit of talking so softly that others find it hard to understand you. Whatever the reasons for such a quiet tone, the impression it often creates is one of timidity and uncertainty. On the other hand, you might talk so loudly that other listeners become uncomfortable around you. Excessive volume usually suggests aggressiveness, anger, or boorishness, even when you have no such feelings.

Unlike the people who always express themselves at an inappropriate volume, others speak too loudly or softly only at certain critical times. For instance, you might find your normally pleasant voice change into a shout when you are angry. Or you might almost entirely lose your voice when you are upset. Needless to say, either of these extremes will usually diminish the effectiveness of your message.

Rate

Some speakers talk too rapidly and others too slowly. A speedy delivery often conveys a sense of nervousness or aggression, while an overly hesitant manner often appears to indicate uncertainty.

The average rate of speech is between 100 and 120 words per minute, thus providing a gauge against which you can measure your own speed. . . .

Fluency

In addition to speaking at a proper rate and volume, another important vocal factor is the absence of disfluencies: unnecessary sounds such as "um," "er," "ya know," as well as other distracting vocal mannerisms such as repetitious and long pauses. You might already be aware of using certain disfluencies in your speech. If not, try asking others who know you well whether you use any. . . .

Affect

The affective ingredients of your voice include both your tone and inflection. These elements are major tools for expressing your feelings. Think of the number of messages you could convey with a single sentence such as "I hope you will call me," just by changing the tone. These simple words could communicate excitement, hopefulness, affection, sarcasm, anger, or disinterest, depending on the variations in pitch chosen by the speaker.

In addition to varying the tone, notice how many more shades of meaning could come from stressing different words:

"*I* hope you will call me." (*They* don't want you to call, but I do.)

"I *hope* you will call me." (I doubt that you will, but I'd like it.)

"I hope *you* will call me." (I don't care about anybody's call but yours.)

"I hope you *will* call me." (I know you're able, but I hope you'll choose to.)

"I hope you will *call* me." (Don't just send a postcard, but phone me!)

"I hope you will call *me.*" (Don't call anyone but me.)

You can probably think of additional meanings for this sentence by combining tone and emphasis in other ways.

Many communicators reduce the immediacy of their messages by underplaying the affective dimension. Speaking in a monotone will soon bore almost anyone. Using the same pattern of inflection to express every thought can be irritating. Try to become aware of the tones and inflections you use and see whether they get your message across most effectively. . . .

VERBAL ELEMENTS

Don't Overqualify Statements

Often we are apprehensive about how a message will be received, and in order to soften its impact we qualify our thoughts or feelings. Qualifiers are words or phrases that discount the immediacy of a message:

— "You probably will think I'm being touchy, but . . ."

— "I hope you don't mind, but . . ."

— "I hope I'm not bothering you, but . . ."

— "I may be wrong, but . . ."

The common element in all these qualifiers is the word "but," which serves to discredit everything in the sentence that precedes it. In fact, when used often enough, the mere sound of "but" serves as a warning that the forthcoming thought will totally contradict what has already been said: "John, I've really enjoyed going out with you, but I want to have a change." "We've found your work here quite satisfactory, but our budget forces us to let you go." "The paper you wrote in this course had several good ideas, but I graded it as a D for the following reasons . . ."

Other qualifiers include:

— *just* (as in "I just wanted to talk to you for a few minutes," or "There's just one problem . . .")

— *kind of, sort of* (as in "I was kind of unhappy about what you said about me," or "I sort of hope you can keep the noise down.")

— *little* (as in "There's a little problem I need to talk about," or "I wish you could try a little harder to be on time.")

— *any type of apology* (such as "I'm sorry to bring this up," or "I hate to ask this favor.")

You can see from these few examples that in overusing qualifiers you become your own worst enemy, discounting everything you've said before the other person even responds.

Remember: You have the right to appear foolish, to be unsure of yourself, to express your feelings, and to act independently of the approval of others. Don't apologize for yourself: There's nothing wrong with your thoughts! Take yourself seriously, and others will start to do the same thing.

This suggestion doesn't mean that you should totally remove qualifiers from your language. Of course there are times when you ought to apologize for your actions or express your uncertainty, but don't overdo it or your image will suffer, both in your own eyes and in the eyes of others. . . .

SUMMARY

Some points to remember when communicating assertively are to maintain appropriate eye contact, keep a distance that suits the occasion, suit facial expression to words, make suitable gestures, and not fidget or show other distracting mannerisms. It is best to maintain an alert, not tense, posture, a direct but not confrontive stance, a suitably loud voice, a fluent, medium rate of speech, and appropriate tone and inflection. The message should be clear and expressed in complete sentences with no qualifiers, discount messages, and distracting vocal sounds. Assertive visual, vocal, and verbal traits help to send a more effective assertive message.

Nonassertion/Aggression/Assertion:
Nonverbal Components

Goals

    I. To experience and differentiate the nonverbal components of assertive behavior from those of aggressive and nonassertive behavior.

    II. To increase awareness of one's own assertive behavior.

Group Size

    Ten to fifty participants.

Time Required

    Approximately thirty minutes to one hour.

Materials

    Newsprint and a felt-tipped marker.

Process

    I. The facilitator asks participants to call out their associations to the word "assertiveness" and records their responses on newsprint.

Adapted from pp. 36-38 of *A Handbook of Structured Experiences for Human Relations Training* (Vol. VI). J. William Pfeiffer and John E. Jones (Eds.). La Jolla, CA: University Associates, 1977.

II. The facilitator tells each participant to think of the most nonassertive individual he or she has ever seen and to imagine the behavioral characteristics associated with that person. The facilitator then directs the participants to mill around, each acting out nonverbal nonassertive behavior.

III. After one or two minutes, the facilitator directs the participants to "freeze" in a fixed position depicting nonassertive behavior, to look around at the other people, and to identify the similarities in their behavior.

IV. The facilitator elicits comments about the nonverbal manifestations of nonassertiveness and lists these on newsprint. (Usually the comments will include the behavioral components of eye contact, body posture, facial expression, and interaction distance.)

V. After all responses are recorded by the facilitator, participants are directed to change from nonassertiveness to aggressiveness. Again, they are told to think of the behavior of the most *aggressive* individual they have ever encountered and to use the room in any way they want in order to role play the aggressive behavior nonverbally. The only stipulation is that there be no physical abuse or destruction of property.

VI. At the end of one or two minutes, the facilitator instructs the participants to remain in a "frozen" position depicting aggressive behavior and to look around the room and observe similarities in the behavior of the other members.

VII. The facilitator then elicits comments about the similarities of the observable nonverbal behaviors that are related to aggressiveness and records the comments on newsprint.

VIII. The facilitator describes the behavioral characteristics of an *assertive* person, focusing on the nonverbal components of assertive behavior.

IX. The facilitator directs the participants to think of a person they have observed who seems to fit best the description of an assertive person and to depict that person's behavior nonverbally.

X. After one or two minutes, the facilitator directs the participants to "freeze" as before and to observe and compare each other's behavior.

XI. The facilitator leads a discussion on the participants' comfort and familiarity with the nonassertive, aggressive, and assertive behaviors just experienced. The facilitator asks participants to name the differences between nonassertive, aggressive, and assertive behavior and lists these on newsprint. He or she may compare this listing to the original responses to the word "assertiveness" elicited in Step I and suggest that participants use these "body clues" to help them recognize what they are feeling and how they are acting in specific situations. Participants may be encouraged to think of ways they can move from aggressive or nonassertive behaviors to assertive behaviors.

XII. The facilitator gives a short lecturette on nonverbal assertion.

Variations

   I. If the group is large, part of the group can participate in the nonverbal activity, while the remainder can be process observers.

  II. Participants can be verbal while being nonassertive, aggressive, and assertive, and these components can be processed as well.

 III. Instead of asking participants to think of individuals and imagine characteristics associated with those individuals (Steps II, V, and VIII), the facilitator may wish to give more specific guidance, for example:[1]

   A. Think of a situation in which you have trouble asserting yourself. Close your eyes for a few seconds and picture yourself being nonassertive; then open your eyes.

   Now, get up and walk around the room. Let your shoulders droop. Look down at the ground. Now, stop. Feel the tension in your stomach. You may want to lean on something. Your feet are restless. You have the weight of the world on your shoulders. Feel the burden. You have no rights! Who would listen to you? Let yourself feel the anxiety, the pressure, the frustration of not being able to ask for what you want.

   Now, stop! Think for a few seconds about what that felt like. Then, clear your mind.

   B. Now, move into an aggressive stance. Think of a situation in which you would feel aggressive, perhaps something about which you've been holding back your anger for a long time. Now stand up. Clench your fists. Tighten your stomach. Narrow your eyes until they feel hard and cold. Stamp your feet, or plant them firmly on the floor. With your hands on your hips, march or stomp around thinking, "I'll get even with them. They'll be sorry. They'd better look out!"

   Now, stop and think for a few seconds about how that felt. Then, clear your mind.

   C. Now assume an assertive stance. Stand up straight, shoulders back, head up. Look directly ahead. You are erect but also comfortable, relaxed, attentive, and balanced. Stand there and think to yourself, "I'm about to enter a situation feeling good about myself, knowing

[1] Excerpted from the book *The New Assertive Woman* by Lynn Z. Bloom, Karen Coburn, and Joan Pearlman. Copyright © 1975 by Lynn Z. Bloom, Karen Levin Coburn, and Joan Crystal Pearlman. Reprinted by permission of DELACORTE PRESS.

what my rights are, and believing I have the right to do what I intend to do. I'll be able to handle it suitably. I feel comfortable and strong about this."

Now, stop and think for a few seconds about how that felt. Then, clear your mind.

Nonverbal Triads: Recognition and Congruence

Goals

I. To learn to recognize and identify nonverbal assertive, nonassertive, and aggressive behaviors.
II. To practice giving specific feedback on nonverbal behavior.
III. To develop congruence between verbal assertive messages and accompanying nonverbal behavior.

Group Size

From twelve to twenty-eight participants.

Time Required

One and one-half to two hours.

Materials

Blank paper and a pencil for each group.

Process

I. The facilitator announces the goals of the experience, gives a short

---

This activity is based on material on p. 159 of *The New Assertive Woman*, by Lynn Z. Bloom, Karen Coburn, and Joan Pearlman. New York: Delacorte Press, 1975.

lecturette on nonverbal and verbal congruence, and asks participants to form three to four groups of four to seven members each. Paper and a pencil are given to each group.

II. Each group is told to choose an assertive situation (samples may be given) and to develop a verbal assertive response to that situation. When the groups are ready, the facilitator gives the following instructions:

> "You have twenty minutes to develop three role plays based on the situation your group has chosen. You must use the same or similar verbal response in each of the three role plays, but portray different nonverbal behavior in each. One role play is to show, nonverbally, an assertive response to the situation, a nonassertive response, and an aggressive response. The same person may play the central role three times, or roles can be rotated, giving more participants a chance to receive feedback on their nonverbal behaviors. Although all members of a group do not have to act in the role play, each member should be actively involved in the development of the role play and the coaching of those playing the roles."

III. The facilitator asks participants to form one large group. Each group's role plays are presented in random order, with no announcement of which is intended to demonstrate assertive, nonassertive, or aggressive behavior. After each of the three role plays, the facilitator leads a discussion of the types of nonverbal responses (nonassertive, assertive, aggressive) identified by the observing participants, and the specific nonverbal behaviors that prompted that identification. The group then reveals which type of response the role play was intended to portray. The facilitator leads a brief discussion of any other observed behaviors that portrayed a particular response and of other behaviors that might have been included to make the portrayal more clear. (Thirty to forty minutes.)

IV. The facilitator announces that techniques for accurately identifying and expressing nonverbal behaviors will be practiced on a more personal and individual level now and asks each participant to choose an assertive situation that he or she would like to work on and to develop an assertive verbal response to that situation.

V. The facilitator asks participants to form groups of three and gives these instructions:

> "Each participant is to repeat his or her verbal assertive response three times, each time using a different accompanying nonverbal response (nonassertive, assertive, aggressive). The responses are to be presented in random order, without announcing which nonverbal behavior is being portrayed. After each response, the other two members of each group are to identify the response they thought was being portrayed and describe the specific behaviors that led

them to their conclusions. The person practicing the behaviors then reveals which of the three behaviors he or she was attempting to portray. Group members may discuss which behaviors seemed congruent with that response and what might have been added to make the response even more congruent. If a specific response was not correctly identified, the participant may wish to practice his or her response again." (Ten to fifteen minutes.)

VI. The facilitator asks the groups to report on their experiences and leads a general discussion of ways that participants can practice the skills of nonverbal assertion and congruence.

Variations

I. The role plays and practice can be done without words, as "silent movies," if participants wish to concentrate more heavily on body postures and facial expression.[1]

II. Instead of practicing responses to actual situations, participants can practice Step V using a sample list of assertive statements, for example:

No, I don't want to go to a movie tonight, but thank you for inviting me.

It's my turn to be waited on next.

I like your direct way of talking to me.[2]

---

[1] Based on material presented on p. 127 of *The Assertive Woman*, by Stanlee Phelps and Nancy Austin. San Luis Obispo, CA: Impact Press, 1975.

[2] Based on material presented on p. 111 of *Assertive Training for Women*, by Susan M. Osborn and Gloria G. Harris. Springfield, IL: Charles C Thomas, 1975.

Chapter Seven

Cognitive Assertion

Feelings are reactions to thoughts, which are reactions to situations[1] (Ellis, 1962). If the meaning we give to events determines our feelings, it is important to develop realistic, productive thoughts. Cognitive assertion is the ability to think rational and realistic thoughts appropriate to the assertive situation. It involves "self-talk" (what one is telling oneself in an assertive situation). A person may know how to say something assertive and how to be nonverbally assertive, but may diffuse the motivation to be assertive by telling himself or herself that such behavior is not possible or correct or will bring terrible consequences. Cognitive assertion is especially important in difficult situations in which a person must sustain assertive behavior for a longer length of time and has a greater chance to change his or her mind.

Cognitive assertion is usually developed through rational-emotive techniques and theory (Ellis, 1962) and behavior modification techniques.[2] Basically, cognitive-assertion techniques involve identifying and interrupting irrational or counterproductive thoughts and replacing them with more realistic or useful thoughts.

ORIGINS OF NEGATIVE SELF-TALK

Negative self-talk may be of one's own invention or it may have been learned through the past modeling of others, from deductions made from interactions with others, or through advice or messages from others. Many counterproductive or erroneous beliefs are reinforced by society. One of the reasons asser-

---

[1] Physical pain is one exception to this statement.

[2] According to Schmidt (1976a, p. 72) cognitive restructuring "draws heavily from two areas of psychotherapy which have been demonstrated to be useful: rational-emotive therapy developed by Albert Ellis and behavioral therapy originated by B. F. Skinner and amplified by Arnold Lazarus and Joseph Wolpe."

tion has been particularly useful to women is that women seem to have internalized those messages encouraging them to be quiet and nonassertive. Sometimes these messages become so much a part of a person's belief system that they even affect one's beliefs in one's rights. "It is common for a person who has been aggressive in a given situation to feel some guilt as a result of his behavior. It is less widely recognized that the assertive person also experiences such guilt produced by conditioning. The institution of society has so carefully taught the inhibition of expression of even one's reasonable rights that one may feel badly for having stood up for himself" (Alberti & Emmons, 1974, p. 6). These dynamics are shown in Table 5.

COGNITIVE ASSERTION AND CONFIDENCE IN RIGHTS

Cognitive assertion and confidence in one's rights may overlap if "shoulds" have affected not only one's behavior in certain situations but also one's belief in one's rights. Since both involve changes in self-talk, cognitive-assertion techniques can be used effectively to help build confidence in ownership of an assertive right that has been affected by "shoulds." Confidence in rights, however, is a prerequisite to assertion and is based on building confidence more than on challenging self-talk. Cognitive assertion techniques are necessary only in specific situations in which negative self-talk exists. Cognitive assertion tends to focus on what one "should" do in the situation (obligation) and on what will happen as a result of being assertive (consequences). When such thoughts are not based in reason or are not useful, they can make it difficult for a person who has a right to be assertive to be so when appropriate.

Galassi and Galassi (1977) point out the differences among thoughts about rights and responsibilities (confidence in rights); thoughts about how one should behave or appear to others; and thoughts about probable consequences of behavior (cognitive assertion). In their example, they apply each type of thought to the ability to express personal opinions assertively and give examples of challenges to each type:

> *Thoughts about rights and responsibilities:* I'm not smart enough, attractive enough, old enough, experienced enough, etc., to be entitled to express an opinion on that subject. *Challenges:* Is it true that I need to have special group membership in order to be entitled to express an opinion? Of course not. Everyone is entitled to his/her opinions. It is possible that special group membership could give me more experience or knowledge about the subject. Nevertheless, I am still entitled to my opinion, and I have the right to express it in an assertive manner.

> *Thoughts about how I should behave or appear to others:* If I voice my opinion and I am wrong, then how will I look? *Challenges:* I don't have to look any particular way to other people. What's so awful about being wrong? I can't always be right. No one is. If I am wrong, at least I'll know it, and I'll be able to rethink my opinion. Besides, most opinions are subjective and are not necessarily right or

wrong. I'd rather be able to express my opinion than to sit there like a bump on a log and feel inhibited.

Thoughts about possible consequences: If the other person disagrees with my opinions, he/she won't like me, and then we'll get into an argument. *Challenges:* What evidence do I have that supports this belief? People can often disagree with each other on matters without disliking each other. No two people and no group of people can always agree on everything. If the other person doesn't like me for my views, that's up to him/her. I have a right to express them as long as I do it assertively. Why does a disagreement have to result in an argument? All I plan to do is to assert my position and listen to what the other person has to say. If I feel that he/she is becoming aggressive, I can always break off communication by saying something such as, "Well, I understand your point of view, but I am still going to stand by my own views. Perhaps we could discuss it further at another time," or "I prefer that we do not discuss this any further since it seems that we have reached an impasse on this matter." (p.143)[3]

METHODS TO OVERCOME COUNTERPRODUCTIVE THOUGHTS

The methods most frequently used to combat erroneous or counterproductive thoughts are to use reason or to stop or arrest the thought or to use a combination of these two techniques. McMullin and Casey (1975, p. 46-51) list some other methods a person can use to promote cognitive assertion:

1. Keep a record of the most powerful challenges you have used and how potent they are for you (on a scale of zero to ten).
2. Go out and prove that an irrational thought is untrue.
3. Practice ten minutes a day arguing with yourself in a mirror as though the person in the mirror had said the irrational thought and you are challenging him or her.
4. Ask people who handle a situation well what they say to themselves to act assertively or imagine what someone you respect would think.
5. Unrealistic or counterproductive thoughts usually have payoffs. It is sometimes helpful to challenge those payoffs as well as the thoughts.
6. Instead of countering a thought with words, replay the situation objectively in your mind, without labels or interpretations.
7. Use covert rehearsal (described in Chapter Ten) to prepare for situations in which you anticipate difficulty by imagining yourself countering possible counterproductive thoughts.
8. Create a list of thoughts that cause problems. Write three challenges to each one, and read the list once a day.

---

[3] Reprinted from p. 143 of *Assert Yourself! How To Be Your Own Person*, by Merna Dee Galassi and John P. Galassi. Copyright © 1977 by Human Sciences Press, 72 Fifth Avenue, New York, NY 10011. Used with permission.

Table 5. How Socialization Messages May Negatively Affect Assertion

SOCIALIZATION MESSAGE	EFFECT ON RIGHTS	EFFECT ON ASSERTIVE BEHAVIOR	HEALTHY MESSAGE
Think of others first; give to others even if you're hurting. Don't be selfish.	I have no right to place my needs above those of other people.	When I have a conflict with someone else, I will give in and satisfy the other person's needs and forget about my own.	To be selfish means that a person always places her/his needs above other people's. This is undesirable human behavior. All healthy people have needs and strive to fulfill these as much as possible. Your needs are as important as other people's. When there is a conflict over need satisfaction, compromise is a useful way to handle the conflict.
Be modest and humble. Don't act superior to other people.	I have no right to do anything which would imply that I am better than other people.	I will discount my accomplishments and any compliments I receive. When I'm in a meeting, I will encourage other people's contributions and keep silent about my own. When I have an opinion which is different than someone else's, I won't express it; who am I to say that my opinion is better than another's.	It is undesirable to build yourself up at the expense of another person. However, you have as much a right as other people to show your abilities and take pride in yourself. It is healthy to enjoy one's accomplishments.
Be understanding and overlook trivial irritations. Don't be a bitch and complain.	I have no right to express anger or even to feel anger.	When I'm in a line and someone cuts in front of me, I will say nothing. I will not tell my boyfriend that I don't like his constantly interrupting me when I speak.	It is undesirable to deliberately nit pick. However, life is made up of trivial incidents and it is normal to be occasionally irritated by seemingly small events. You have a right to your angry feelings, and if you express them at the time they occur, your feelings won't build up and explode. It is important, however, to express your anger assertively rather than aggressively.

Help other people. Don't be demanding.	I have no right to make requests of other people.	I will not ask my friend to reciprocate babysitting favors. I will not ask for a pay increase from my employer.	It is undesirable to incessantly make demands on others. You do have a right to ask someone else to change their behavior if their behavior affects your life in a concrete way. A request is not the same as a demand. However, if your rights are being violated and your requests for a change are being ignored, you have a right to make demands.
Be sensitive to other people's feelings. Don't hurt other people.	I have no right to do anything which might hurt someone else's feelings or deflate someone else's ego.	I will not say what I really think or feel because that might hurt someone else. I will inhibit my spontaneity so that I don't impulsively say something that would accidentally hurt someone else.	It is undesirable to deliberately try to hurt others. However, it is impossible as well as undesirable to try to govern your life so as to never hurt anyone. You have a right to express your thoughts and feelings even if someone else's feelings occasionally get hurt. To do otherwise would result in your being phony and in denying other people an opportunity to learn how to handle their own feelings. Remember that some people get hurt because they're unreasonably sensitive and others use their hurt to manipulate you. If you accidentally hurt someone else, you can generally repair the damage.

Reprinted from Patricia Ann Jakubowski, "How Socialization Messages May Negatively Affect Assertion," in Edna I. Rawlings and Dianne K. Carter (Eds.), *Psychotherapy for Women*, 1977, pp. 149-151. Courtesy of Charles C Thomas, Publisher, Springfield, Illinois.

9. Rather than challenging problem thoughts, simply concentrate on a series of rational thoughts.
10. Models can talk about their fears and anxieties as they enter a practice situation, state challenges as they cope with the situation, and subsequently give themselves rewarding self-statements.
11. Challenges can be followed by thoughts, images, or activities that provide positive reinforcement.

Even after the act of assertion is over, a person can reinforce counterproductive thought habits by criticizing his or her assertion or by feeling guilty, fearful, or anxious about it. "What you think and how you feel about your own behavior determines your continued success in assertiveness. . . . if you wish to be successful with assertiveness you will have to work on thinking thoughts that commend the behavior. . . . the better you feel about what you did the more apt you are to do it again" (Paris & Casey, 1978, p. 35).

OVERVIEW OF THE CHAPTER

The chapter contains a lecturette, "Talking to Oneself," that explores the importance of cognitive assertion, examines counterproductive or erroneous thoughts that are based on notions of obligation or fear of consequences, and gives challenges to those thoughts. The causal relationship between thoughts and feelings is explored briefly. An explanation of thought stopping[4] is included, and steps are presented for deciding whether a thought is realistic and useful.

The structured experience "Have To, Choose To" helps participants examine some thoughts about obligations in order to determine whether these thoughts are realistic or useful and to help participants recognize their own power and the option to be more assertive. The structured experience helps participants practice thought stopping. In the structured experience "Right Thinking," participants practice identifying negative self-talk in an assertive situation, develop challenges to that self-talk, and covertly practice these challenges.

PROFESSIONAL CONSIDERATIONS

Cues that may indicate when one is acting on misconceptions are listed by

---

[4]Joseph Wolpe (1958) is generally credited with the introduction of the thought-stopping technique (Gambrill & Richey, p. 129; Galassi and Galassi, p. 36; Lange & Jakubowski, p. 144). Wolpe (1973, p. 213), however, states that "Thought-stopping was introduced by J. G. Taylor in 1955 . . . ; but, unknown to him, it had already been advocated by a largely forgotten writer, Alexander Bain (1928)."

Galassi and Galassi (1977, p. 34): "(a) if you are rehearsing and you don't feel comfortable after successive rehearsals, (b) if you know what you would like to say but your speech is hesitant or faltering, or (c) if you find yourself becoming increasingly aggressive or hostile," these are keys that you should examine your self-talk in the situation.

Negative self-talk often has served some helpful purpose for the participant, or it may have been the only way that the person has known how to think. When the trainer and other participants challenge these thoughts, they should be supportive and offer possible options, but it is ultimately up to the participant to decide whether to change. Also, one should never presume to know what the other person is thinking, but simply respond to whatever thoughts the person identifies. As Lange & Jakubowski (1976, p. 97) point out, "When members discover effective challenges they usually experience a gut reaction," so challenges should make emotional as well as intellectual sense to participants.

Meichenbaum (1975) suggests two interesting techniques for helping participants get in touch with negative self-talk in an assertive situation: (a) clients close their eyes and "run movies through their heads" of recent assertion situations they have experienced, paying attention to their thoughts, images, feelings, and behaviors in the situation; and (b) clients are videotaped while role playing the assertive situations and view the tape immediately afterward. During the viewing they reconstruct the thoughts they had during the role play.

When thought stopping is being developed, negative self-talk may occur more often at first and then quickly die out. Thought stopping should be used every time the thought occurs or not at all. If you are unsure whether to use it in a particular situation, use it (Fensterheim and Baer, 1975).

A negative thought that does not diminish through use of techniques presented in this chapter may have been held for a long time and the client may need special help in a one-on-one situation.

According to the Galassis, cognitive assertion may need to be practiced frequently — at first, as many as fifty times a day (Galassi & Galassi, 1977, p. 36).

Fensterheim & Baer (1975, p. 110) point out that "The thoughts you may think you have under control can re-emerge under three conditions: (a) when you're very tense for whatever reasons, (b) when you're fatigued, and (c) when you're physically ill." When they do emerge, continue with thought stopping so they do not become habitual again.

Talking to Oneself

Sometimes we know what we want to say and can use the correct body language to accompany the words, but still seem unsure about using our skills in an assertive situation. This may be due to what we are thinking — self-talk or internal dialogue — while we are behaving assertively. *Self-talk that makes assertion difficult is usually either erroneous (irrational) or counterproductive. Self-talk that supports assertion is sometimes termed cognitive assertion.*

Besides thinking that we are not entitled to basic human rights, whether generally or specifically, two other types of thoughts can prevent us from behaving assertively: *thoughts of obligation* (I have to, he should) and *thoughts about fearful consequences* (I couldn't survive that, she'll kill me).

THE CONNECTION BETWEEN THOUGHTS AND FEELINGS

Although cognitive assertion focuses on changing thoughts, it indirectly changes feelings too, because emotions generally result from assumptions, evaluations, or interpretations (thoughts). When these thoughts are erroneous or counterproductive, they can trigger self-defeating emotions such as despair, rage, depression, guilt, anxiety, or feelings of worthlessness. When these thoughts change, the resulting emotions also change. For example, if an employee repeatedly arrives late a supervisor can think: "This is annoying to me. I have to expend extra energy to work without this person. I need to talk with him about this problem and see to it that whoever fills this job arrives on time." The probable accompanying feelings would be frustration, annoyance, or irritation. The supervisor can also think: "That person has to know that I need him here on time. He's probably testing me to the limit. This is terrible." The probable accompanying feelings would be rage, hostility, or indignation. Although many people would say: "That person is making me furious," in reality these people are making themselves furious through their own internal

128

dialogue. Different feelings can result from different thoughts, and they can be self-defeating when they are based on erroneous or counterproductive thoughts. Self-defeating emotions usually can be changed by identifying, challenging, and replacing one's self-talk.

IDENTIFYING NEGATIVE SELF-TALK

The problem with counterproductive thoughts or beliefs is that they are so habitual we seldom stop to ask whether they are realistic or not, and so we continue to consider them good reasons for avoiding assertive behavior. It sometimes helps to check out negative self-talk in a situation by (a) becoming aware of what we are saying to ourselves; we often become so accustomed to self-talk we are no longer aware of it; (b) defining each word in our thoughts in order to know *exactly* what we mean; (c) reversing roles, i.e., checking to see if it would make sense for someone else to think in this way (it sometimes helps to ask what other people think about our way of thinking); (d) looking for evidence that supports our belief and checking the degree to which we believe we would be affected if it were true; and (e) questioning how effective the belief is in helping one to act assertively. If the negative internal dialogue seems realistic and useful, there may be a good reason to forego being assertive; if, as happens in many cases, the internal dialogue proves to be faulty, it is important to counter those thoughts.

A common theme of counterproductive beliefs is that they are extreme or absolute, generally dealing with such concepts as "must," "everyone," "no one," "always," "perfection," "tragedy," etc. When analyzing your own beliefs, it is helpful to be sure that you are not drawing conclusions when evidence is lacking or even contradictory, exaggerating the meaning of the event, disregarding important aspects of the situation, oversimplifying events as good/ bad, right/wrong, or overgeneralizing from a single incident (Lange & Jakubowski, 1976).

CHALLENGES TO NEGATIVE SELF-TALK

How does a person begin to challenge counterproductive thoughts? These suggestions may help:

1. List any counterproductive thoughts occurring in the situation. What do you consider yourself or others obligated to do? What are the possible and probable consequences of being assertive?

2. Develop a list of challenges or counterbeliefs (positive self-talk) to the negative thought. These should be based on reality, useful, believable and

believed, directed toward one's thoughts rather than toward one's feelings or emotions, and as powerful or persuasive as possible.

3. Once you have identified counterproductive thoughts and have developed challenges to those thoughts, practice substituting the challenges until they are second nature in real life.

Some examples of counterproductive beliefs and challenges to those beliefs follow.[1]

Obligations

Thought: A person should be liked, loved, or approved of almost all the time by all the people who are significant to him or her.

Specific Example: "I shouldn't express appropriate anger because my friends don't like that."

Possible Challenges: (a) It is nice to be approved of by every significant person but it is not necessary; (b) if someone I would like to have approve of me does not, I can try to find out exactly what the person does not like about my behavior and then I can decide whether I want to change it; (c) if I decide that the rejection is not based on inappropriate behavior on my part, I can find others I can enjoy being with; (d) I can decide what I want to do instead of adapting or reacting to what I think others want; (e) you cannot please everyone; and (f) I approve of myself.

Thought: A person should be perfect and not make mistakes — or at least have real competence or talent.

Specific Example: "I have to play perfect tennis."

Possible Challenges: (a) I would like to be perfect or best at this task, but I do not *need* to be; (b) what I do does not have to be perfect in order to be good or even successful; (c) success does not determine my worth as a person; (d) I will be happier if I attempt to achieve at a realistic level; (e) it is impossible for anyone to be perfect; and (f) if I insist that I must be perfect, I will also always worry or be unhappy; if I do what I want to do and enjoy it as well as I can, I will feel happier and perform better.

Consequences

Thought: People who harm others are bad, wicked, or villainous persons, and one should severely blame or hurt them for their acts.

Specific Example: "That person pushed ahead of me in line; I think I'll give him a piece of my mind."

---

[1]These counterproductive beliefs and the challenges to them are based on "Ten Irrational Ideas," taken from pp. 127-136 of HOW TO LIVE WITH A NEUROTIC AT HOME AND WORK, by Albert Ellis. Copyright © 1975 by Albert Ellis. Used by permission of Crown Publishers, Inc.

Possible Challenges: (Lange & Jakubowski, 1976, p. 131.) "(a) I can tell people firmly and directly what they are doing that has negative consequences for me . . .; (b) [hurting a person] costs me, too . . . seldom does it facilitate correction or change [without creating new problems]; (c) just because I think something is wrong doesn't mean it is wrong; (d) I (or others) may have behaved obnoxiously, unfairly, or incompetently, but that doesn't mean that I (or others) always will; (e) [people] can recognize and work to correct [their mistakes]."

Thought: If a person is treated unfairly by another, there is nothing that person can really do.

Specific Example: "The steak I ordered is cooked wrong and my vegetables are cold, but I guess you just can't get a decent meal any more."

Possible Challenges: (a) I can let people know that I do not like the way they are treating me; (b) I can search for some ways of changing things that will be more to my liking; (c) I believe in my right to receive what I pay for; and (d) I can reserve judgment until I give the person involved a chance to correct the mistake.

Thought: When things do not go the way a person would like them to go, life is awful, terrible, horrible, or catastrophic.

Specific Example: "If I lose my job, I'll die."

Possible Challenges: (a) I don't like what's happening; I'm frustrated or upset by it, but I can live through it; (b) I can work to make my life the way I want it to be, as much as possible; (c) I do not need to overreact to this.

THOUGHT STOPPING

One other technique that has proven helpful in eliminating negative internal dialogue is "thought stopping" (Wolpe, 1973), a technique for controlling unwanted thoughts or images through negative self-reinforcement — specifically through shouting the word "stop" aloud in the practice setting when the thought or image occurs and eventually simply shouting "stop" silently to oneself.

Thought stopping is very useful, but it is even better to follow the thought stopping with a productive or pleasant thought or to use it to arrest a counterproductive belief and then to substitute a challenge. Using this technique, you would recognize a counterproductive thought in your stream of consciousness, shout "stop" silently, and then immediately replace the thought with a more productive or pleasant one or with a challenge. Obviously, this technique takes practice because it involves not only learning a new skill but breaking an old habit. Some negative self-talk is of one's own invention, but many times it has been learned through messages from others, through the past modeling of others, or from deductions made as a result of interactions with others.

SUMMARY

Sometimes we know what to say and how to act but stop short of being assertive because of erroneous or counterproductive thoughts — predominantly thoughts of obligation (shoulds, have tos, musts) and thoughts of consequences (catastrophes, ogres). These thoughts, in the form of assumptions, evaluations, or interpretations, are formed in reaction to a situation, and emotions are in turn generated as a result of these thoughts, so changing our thoughts in a situation usually changes our feelings as well.

If internal dialogue is not realistic and useful, challenges can be developed and used with thought stopping to replace or counter it. Thought stopping can also be rewarded by substituting pleasant images or words. Positive self-talk is considered cognitive assertion because it involves expressing ourselves assertively in our thoughts, which in turn promotes assertive action.

Have To, Choose To: Developing Assertive Thought Patterns

Goals

I. To examine some thought patterns that may keep people from being assertive.

II. To practice the technique of thought stopping.

III. To develop more assertive thought patterns.

Group Size

No more than fifteen dyads.

Time Required

One and one-half to two hours.

Materials

I. A pencil and blank paper for each participant.

II. Newsprint and felt-tipped markers for the facilitator.

Adapted from "I Have To - I Choose To" and "I Need - I Want" in Susan M. Osborn and Gloria G. Harris, *Assertive Training for Women*, 1975, pp. 124-125. Courtesy of Charles C Thomas, Publisher, Springfield, Illinois.

Process

I. The facilitator states the goals of the activity and gives a brief lecturette on cognitive assertion.

II. The facilitator distributes a pencil and blank paper to each participant and directs participants to make lists of all the things they have to do in their lives, by completing the statement "I have to _____" ten times, if possible. (Five to ten minutes.)

III. The facilitator instructs participants to go back and write beside each response "or else _____", completing the statement with an explanation of who or what makes them do each thing they have to do. (Five to ten minutes.)

IV. The facilitator explains that "I have to _____" statements often are based on socialization messages, irrational beliefs, or undefined fears rather than on fact. Many "I have to _____'s" are considered negative self-talk because the person who thinks in this way denies his/her power to choose in situations in which there is, in fact, a choice. Negative self-talk promotes nonassertive or aggressive response styles.

V. The facilitator explains that an "I choose to _____" statement is a sign of a sense of freedom and responsibility for oneself and one's choices and is called positive self-talk.

VI. The facilitator directs participants to choose partners with whom to share their lists, and, with their partners' help, to change as many of their statements from "I have to _____" to "I choose to _____" as possible. (Ten to twenty minutes.)

VII. The facilitator asks participants, with the help of their partners, to write beside each "I choose to _____" response "because _____", completing the statement with an explanation of what motivates them to choose each item. (Ten to twenty minutes.)

VIII. The facilitator tells participants to report on their experiences to this point and answers any questions they may have.

IX. The facilitator explains the technique of "thought stopping" as a means of changing negative self-talk to positive self-talk. The facilitator asks participants to practice the technique of thought stopping in the following way:

One person begins by repeating an "I have to _____" statement from his or her partner's list until the partner interrupts by yelling in a commanding voice "STOP" while clapping his or her hands and immediately reading the corresponding "I choose to _____" statement. The first person again reads an "I have to _____" statement, and so on down the list. After the list has been completed, partners reverse roles. (Ten minutes.)

X. When each partner has practiced thought stopping with his or her list, the facilitator asks participants to practice reading some of the "I have to _____" statements silently to themselves while imagining yelling "STOP" and clapping, and then silently reading the corresponding "I choose to _____" statement. (Five minutes.)

XI. The facilitator indicates that participants can use these techniques in assertive situations by becoming aware of the "I have to _____" statements involved and by practicing silent thought stopping followed by "I choose to _____" statements.

XII. The facilitator asks participants to choose situations in which they would like to be more assertive, to look for any "I have to _____" self-talk involved (What am I telling myself I have to do in this situation?), and, with their partners' help, to change this talk to "I choose to _____" (What choices am I making, or can I make, that I am not taking responsibility for in this situation?) if possible. (Ten to twenty minutes.)

XIII. The facilitator asks participants to spend five minutes practicing thought stopping using the statements developed in Step XII.

XIV. The facilitator directs participants to discuss with their partners situations in which they can practice these techniques in their daily lives.

XV. The facilitator asks participants to report in the large group on the different types of situations in which they plan to use the new techniques.

Variation

Following Step XIII, the facilitator can explain that, besides looking at the things one is *already doing* with a sense of power and choice, it is possible to look at the things one would *like to be doing* in this way using positive self-talk (goals, dreams, aspirations, etc.).

The facilitator asks participants to make lists of some of the things they want or want to do in their lives by completing the statement "I want _____" or "I want to _____" ten times if possible. The facilitator asks participants to share their lists with their partners and to add to as many of these new items as possible the words: "The way I can get what I want is _____" followed by definite assertive action plans.

Right Thinking: Challenging Dysfunctional Beliefs

Goals

    I. To examine the concept of rational or useful beliefs.
   II. To develop skill in challenging dysfunctional beliefs.
  III. To build assertive thought patterns.

Group Size

    Up to ten groups of three members each.

Time Required

    One hour and fifteen minutes.

Materials

    I. A pencil, blank paper, and a copy of the Right Thinking Work Sheet for each participant.
   II. Newsprint, felt-tipped markers, and masking tape for the facilitator.

Process

    I. The facilitator states the goals of the activity and gives a brief lecturette on

---

This activity is based on the ideas of irrational beliefs and of challenging those beliefs developed by Albert Ellis (1962; 1973) in his rational-emotive therapy.

erroneous or counterproductive thoughts.

II. The facilitator gives some examples of assertive situations and asks participants to volunteer some fears ("ogres") the subject in each situation might have, to identify any of these fears that may qualify as dysfunctional beliefs, and to suggest some counterbeliefs or "challenges" to those dysfunctional beliefs.

III. The facilitator instructs participants to choose assertive situations of their own that they would like to work on, to imagine themselves in the situations, and to determine what they are afraid will happen if they are assertive and what dysfunctional beliefs they may hold in the situation. (Ten minutes.)

IV. The facilitator gives participants paper and pencils and asks them to make lists of the ogres involved in their situations, for example:

If I tell her how I really feel . . .

> she won't like me any more.
>
> I'll feel terrible.
>
> she might tell other people negative things about me.
>
> I might lose my job.
>
> I'll never be able to face her again.

V. The facilitator gives participants copies of the Right Thinking Work Sheet and tells them to form groups of three to share their lists and to help each other develop lists of challenges or counterbeliefs for as many of their ogres as possible, using the work sheet questions as guidelines. (Fifteen to twenty minutes.)

VI. The facilitator points out the importance of recognizing dysfunctional beliefs in assertive situations and immediately replacing them with challenges. He or she tells participants to spend several minutes imagining themselves in the assertive situations again, getting in touch with and imagining their fears or ogres, and practicing pushing the fears back by repeating the corresponding challenges to themselves. (Five to ten minutes.)

VII. The facilitator asks participants to discuss in their small groups ways in which they can use the challenge technique they have learned to deal with dysfunctional beliefs in their daily lives.

VIII. The facilitator directs participants to share with the large group some of the ways in which they plan to use what they have learned from the activity.

Variations

I. In Step V one person can read one of his or her ogres aloud and the other two members of the triad can read the corresponding challenges. The group members can then reverse roles: two members can read ogres and the third respond with his or her corresponding challenges.

II. Thought stopping, as used in the "Have To, Choose To" activity, can be practiced in Step V.

III. The following sequence can be used at the beginning of the experience or after Step V to help illustrate the principles involved in cognitive assertion and changing irrational beliefs:[1]

A. The facilitator states the goals of the activity and asks participants to imagine themselves in unpleasant assertive situations, to imagine the situations in detail in order to make them seem as realistic as possible, and to face and experience their uncomfortable feelings fully.

B. As the participants feel increasingly anxious, hostile, depressed, embarrassed, etc., the facilitator tells them to force aside their strong negative emotions until only mild negative feelings are being experienced. The facilitator continues to remind participants to force aside or reduce their strong feelings.

C. When the participants have reduced their feelings, the facilitator asks participants to reconstruct the statements they repeated to themselves in order to reduce their strong emotions.

D. The facilitator leads a discussion of how participants used their thoughts to change their feelings and how this technique can be applied in assertive situations.

IV. The experience can be based on "shoulds rather than on "ogres."

---

[1]Adapted from pp. 98-100 of *Responsible Assertive Behavior*, by Arthur J. Lange and Patricia Jakubowski. Champaign, IL: Research Press, 1976. Used with permission.

RIGHT THINKING WORK SHEET

A. Is this a realistic belief? What evidence do I have that this may or may not happen?

B. Even if this is a realistic belief, is it as terrible an occurrence as I am imagining? How would I handle this if it happened?

C. Is holding this belief helping me to act the way I want to act in this situation?

D. How would I feel if I were the other person? What do other people think would be the logical consequences of being assertive in this situation?

E. What challenges might I use to counter this fear, for example:
   Fear: She won't like me any more.
   Challenges: You don't have to be liked by everyone; if she doesn't like you just because you say this particular thing, is this the kind of friend you want to have?; I have said similar things to her in the past, and she has accepted them well.

Chapter Eight

Integration

This chapter focuses on integrating each of the separate assertion skills into one total assertive response and practicing them together in an approximation of real life. Integration has been the focus of assertion training since its origin. In fact, Flowers and Booraem (1975, p. 30) state: "Rehearsal and practice (of responses to various interpersonal situations) are the first key to assertion training. Many groups advertise themselves as assertion training; however, if there is no rehearsal, whatever else the group is, it is not an assertion training group."

Integration techniques are firmly embedded in behavior modification principles. Behavioral rehearsal is "by far the most commonly used assertive training technique" (Rimm & Masters, 1974, p. 93). It is a role-playing procedure in which assertive behavior is practiced, usually while one is acting out a real-life situation. It is sometimes defined as a combination of role play with modeling, feedback, shaping, and other techniques. Wolpe (1973) calls behavioral rehearsal a later term for his role-playing technique described in 1958 as "behavioristic psychodrama." Wolpe included modeling and shaping with role play. Lazarus (1966) first used the term "behavior rehearsal" to describe a technique in which modeling and constructive criticism accompany role play. Behavioral rehearsal is defined here as role play, sometimes accompanied by techniques such as modeling and role reversal, for the purpose of acquiring a skill to be used in a real-life situation. The important thing is to rehearse until the behavior practiced can be transferred to the real-life situation.

Integration follows verbal, nonverbal, and cognitive skills because it combines these three core skills (as well as the preparatory skills) after they have been practiced separately. If a trainer is able to work with one small group of people, the sequence can be more flexible. The trainer can have a member role play the scene and then practice one aspect of behavior (verbal, nonverbal, or cognitive) that needs particular work, then rehearse again. However, a small trainer-to-participant ratio is rare, so the structured approach is used more frequently.

Once people have begun to practice assertion in real-life situations, it is important that they manage their environments so that they continue to be positively reinforced. This is essential in order to transfer assertive behavior to their own lives. Adler (1977) suggests several types of positive reinforcers that can be useful in the back-home situation in addition to the social reinforcers already mentioned (attention, recognition, approval, praise): (a) other types of social reinforcers, such as affection, conversation, smiles, or other ways people act that the assertor finds desirable; (b) tangible or material reinforcers such as an ice cream cone or new clothes; (c) desirable activities like going to a movie; and (d) intrinsic feelings of satisfaction, pride, accomplishment, or relief. Adler (1977, pp. 133-135) includes some guidelines for choosing reinforcers. The reinforcers "should be important to you . . . should be more powerful than any benefits which come from acting in your old, unsatisfying ways, . . . should not be so important that you . . . would suffer greatly by failing to earn it, . . . should not be one that will lose its effectiveness through use [1] . . . should be accessible, [and] should be available as soon after the desired behavior as possible."

OVERVIEW OF THE CHAPTER

This chapter contains a lecturette on behavioral rehearsal, "Putting It All Together," which includes a discussion of modeling and role reversal, shaping and positive reinforcement, evaluation or processing, feedback, and goal setting. There are two structured experiences, "Behavioral Rehearsal" and "Escalation." The latter uses a hierarchy of practice situations, arranged in small steps from low to high anxiety level. The assertor begins by practicing only one or two assertive statements and ends by practicing being assertive in a highly anxious, but still successful, situation.

PROFESSIONAL CONSIDERATIONS

Participants should be told that trying a difficult assertion without preparing well involves some risk. It is also important to let the assertor take responsibility for final choice of a response to the situation.

Participants have a tendency to focus on what was done wrong rather than what was done right. It is important that participants understand shaping and positive reinforcement and guard against the tendency to overload others with advice or with too many requests for changes.

Generally, before beginning to rehearse any behavior, participants should know what rights are important in that situation, have confidence in those

---

[1] One can use several different reinforcers on the same project to keep this from happening.

rights, examine the verbal components of the situation, know what they want to say, know what nonverbal language they wish to use, and know what self-talk they want to use.

Participants should describe the situation they want to practice as specifically and concretely as possible. This saves time and helps ensure transferable practice. The questions who, what, when, where, and how are useful for setting up the scene, as well as for determining the specific way the assertor wants to act. The question why should be avoided; it tends to lead to psychologizing and away from practice. Behavioral rehearsal is role play with the goal of developing new skills as opposed to developing insight or catharsis.

If the participant is having difficulty with a scene, it should be stopped for discussion. Continuing when someone is anxious or upset or is demonstrating inappropriate or dysfunctional behavior is not constructive. Some means of coping with the problem can be worked out. On the other hand, if a client shows only slight hesitancy or is approximating the desired behavior, unobtrusive prompting can be used to give him or her support and encouragement. The prompting can be "any kind of direct instruction, cue, or signal given to the client during the rehearsal of a scene [either] verbally or with sign language" (Liberman et al., 1975, p. 70).

If a situation chosen for behavioral rehearsal proves to be very difficult, the assertor should be directed to practice a somewhat easier version of the same situation (Flowers & Booraem, 1975):

> Easier situations are rehearsed before harder ones to maximize the chances of real world success. . . . The client should be encouraged to pick interactors whom s/he perceives as easier to deal with before s/he tries to role play with interactors whom s/he perceives as more difficult. It should always be emphasized that being picked as an easy or hard interactor . . . is not a value judgement. . . . In fact, a group member picked as the hardest person to practice with in one scene is often picked as the easiest in another, even by the same client. (p. 30)

Some things to remember about behavioral rehearsal:

1. Stick to one problem in one situation. Do not try to solve everything at once.

2. Stick with the problem that was originally decided on, i.e., stay on track.

3. Choose a recent situation or one that is likely to occur in the near future.

4. Keep the role-play segment no longer than one to three minutes.

5. Responses should be kept as short as possible.

6. Remember that the assertor is the ultimate expert on what the assertive situation is like and what the best assertive response for himself or herself is in that situation (Lange & Jakubowski, 1976, p. 158). Role players should be chosen on the basis of who the assertor feels could play the parts best.

Besides individual problems, behavioral rehearsal can be used to practice stock situations or to practice special application areas such as making requests, giving compliments, etc. It is important to choose themes that are of interest to all participants for maximum involvement and participation.

An appropriate number of behavioral rehearsals for one segment or for one situation varies from three to ten. Unless the situation being rehearsed is short, it should be broken into segments that are practiced in the order in which they occur.

Behavioral rehearsal can be practiced in front of a mirror or with the assertor taking both roles, simply changing physical position to indicate which role is being played (Bloom, Coburn, & Pearlman, 1975).

Some participants have difficulty believing that role playing will be of help to them in real-life situations. Adler (1977) makes the point that behavioral rehearsal is like a football team analyzing the opposing club's probable strategies as well as one's own strengths and weaknesses: "The value of such practice becomes clear once the real game has started . . . behavior rehearsal can help you experience the *general* situations that you'll encounter later, so that you'll get a basic idea of how to handle them comfortably and naturally" (p. 70).

The token system of feedback can be used. This involves having observers give or show tokens to role players to show when they think a response is nonassertive (blue), assertive (white), or aggressive (red) (Flowers, 1975). This technique does not interrupt the role play, keeps everyone — including the "silent" members — involved, and helps observers "hear" how other members perceive the role play. Also, the process reinforces the assertor, gives people the opportunity to express differences of opinion, provides ongoing feedback, and provides a way of discriminating among assertive, nonassertive, and aggressive behavior (Paulson, 1975). One disadvantage of the token system is that, without further discussion, participants may not be able to articulate what specific behaviors caused them to show the token they showed. Specific feedback is important for a person who is trying to decide what to change in his or her behavior. According to Flowers and Booraem (1975):

> One important side issue of the use of tokens is that when the entire group except for one member judges a behavior as assertive (white tokens) and one member judges it as aggressive (red token), the red token giving member . . . often becomes the targeted client at this point. The leaders should not allow the group to attack the client who is different, but should find out what behaviors that client labels as assertive and slowly encourage that client to engage in behaviors that push the limits of . . . discrimination of appropriate behavior. (p. 31)

With training clients who have already practiced the elements of verbal, nonverbal, and cognitive assertion, modeling seems to be a sometimes enhancing (Freedman, 1971) but seldom necessary intervention. In training, modeling seems most appropriate when: (a) a person demonstrates inappropriate behavior and it is easier to show the correct behavior than to explain or prompt (especially useful for nonverbal or complex behavior) or (b) a client is not responding at all or does not seem to know how to begin. Modeling is also a good way to expand one's repertoire of assertive responses. Some things to remember about modeling are the following:

1. Attention is necessary for learning. Since modeling is learned vicariously through watching and listening, the assertor must know which behaviors to pay attention to and to remember (Bandura, 1971), so it sometimes helps to have a group discussion on what the model did that made the response especially assertive or to have the trainer point out some of these behaviors.

2. Bandura (1971, p. 689) states that "close examination of research findings reveals that similarity [of the model to the observer] has, at best, weak effects on modeling." Modeling is more influential when the observer views the model's behavior as desirable and as having positive consequences. The assertor remembers the responses better if he or she has a chance to practice the model's behavior (Steel & Hochman, 1976).

3. An experiment (Ullman, 1968) has shown that the model should not be too far ahead of the clients' abilities because it makes it too hard for the clients to be like the model and to be reinforced for success.

The "Behavioral Rehearsal" structured experience provides one way, but not the *only* way, to practice this standard technique.

Participants have a tendency to become involved in their own roles as hasslers in the "Escalation" activity. Sometimes a hassler who is supposed to hassle twice will keep hassling unless someone stops him or her. Because the experience is supposed to be successful for the assertor, it is important to emphasize the rules strongly so that the hassler does not overpower the assertor. The role of the partner-coach must be emphasized strongly, because he or she controls the type and amount of feedback the assertor receives, helps the assertor decide what behavior to improve, and stops hasslers who are not following role guidelines.

Participants tend to want to sit down once the assertor has interacted with them in the "Escalation" line. The assertor should stand because it is usually more difficult to assert oneself standing up, and he or she can also receive better feedback on nonverbal behavior in this position. So that others remain standing, it is usually helpful to point out that standing provides a solid feeling of support to the assertor and that this falls away when people sit down.

In "Escalation," it is important to remind people that it is highly unlikely that they will ever have to go to the lengths they must go to in dealing with the high person on the hierarchy. Also, "Escalation" emphasizes a successful experience and some clients may feel that this is unrealistic, but "appropriate assertiveness . . . *usually* is successful" (Rimm & Masters, 1974, p. 100) and the more experiences of success that a person has had — even in behavioral rehearsal — the easier it should be to withstand a failure.

In addition to the reasons listed in the lecturette, role reversal may also be useful because it gives the assertor a chance to play the role of the other person and "act out her worst fears of how the other person can respond to her" (Bloom, Coburn, & Pearlman, 1975, p. 174).

Putting It All Together

Various skills are necessary to prepare for assertion: self-confidence, the ability to identify rights, and confidence in one's rights. Other skills come into play during the actual assertive act: verbal, nonverbal, and cognitive. Each of these skills can be learned and practiced separately, but all must ultimately be brought together and integrated into one assertive act, which constitutes a skill in itself and requires practice.

When practicing assertion, you should usually proceed gradually through a series of small steps. A practice sequence may include practicing preselected assertion situations, practicing segments of a real-life situation, then practicing the entire real-life situation. From this point, you can practice some aspects of the situation in real life and, finally, assert yourself in the actual situation.

AVAILABLE TECHNIQUES

Behavioral Rehearsal

Integration and practice of all the assertion skills is the end goal of assertion training, and a number of techniques, including behavioral rehearsal,[1] are available to practice assertion. Behavioral rehearsal is a role-playing procedure (acting out a real-life situation) in which you practice behaviors that are to become part of your skill repertoire. The goal of the role play is to develop your skills, not provide insight or catharsis (Jakubowski, 1977). Other people you choose act out the roles of whoever else is involved in the real-life situation. You (as the assertor) briefly describe the situation and the other person(s) involved and brief other group members who will play the parts of the other people. You then practice speaking and responding as you wish eventually to do in the real-life situation. Some possible situations include asking for a raise,

---

[1]See the introduction to this chapter for an explanation of the origin of the term.

dividing the housework, setting a child's curfew, or dealing with a sales clerk. Chairs or small props can be set up to symbolize the real setting.

There are several advantages to role playing: (a) it reduces your anxiety and develops courage and confidence (Bloom et al., 1975); (b) it helps you to foresee and plan for unexpected behaviors on the part of other people involved; (c) it is the closest you can come to practicing the actual assertion situation; (d) it gives you a chance to observe your own behavior in a safe environment, to receive feedback from others, and to rework unsatisfactory behavior. A side benefit is that you learn through observing other group members. Because behavioral rehearsal is so basic a technique, it has been modified in many different ways and used in conjunction with other techniques of behavior modification or behavior therapy. All of these techniques except modeling and role reversal are general assertion techniques that can be used to develop all areas of assertion skills.

Modeling

Modeling (Bandura, 1968) is demonstrating behavior for an observer that the observer wishes to learn. When you wish to practice assertion in a specific situation, other group members or the trainers may have some skills for dealing assertively with that particular situation and may be willing to briefly take your place to model how they would assert themselves. Some other ways to practice modeling are through filmed, videotaped, audiotaped, or imaginary fantasy models. Modeling helps you become involved at a low risk level, adds to your response repertoire, provides concrete examples of how to behave in the situation, and sometimes reminds you of behavior patterns you have not used for some time or strengthens your confidence in responses for which you have not been rewarded in the past.

Role Reversal

During role reversal (first described by Moreno [1953] as a psychodrama technique) role players exchange roles for a brief time. Whereas modeling involves showing you some alternative models for being assertive in the situation, role reversal is generally used to help a supporting role player represent his or her role. You, as the person most familiar with the others involved in the real-life situation, can help make those playing supportive roles more convincing. Sometimes a verbal description of these other people is not enough. For example, a person playing the boss may respond in a more dictatorial way than the real boss actually does, so the quickest and most useful approach is to have you and the role player reverse roles so that the secondary player may grasp the role more accurately. Role reversal provides an efficient, graphic way of helping those in supporting roles, allows you to understand the outlook of other people in the situation, and gives you a feeling of greater control.

Shaping and Positive Reinforcement

Shaping is a way to develop a desired behavior by rewarding or positively reinforcing every small step toward the desired behavior and refraining from punishment or negative reinforcement of those behaviors that do not approximate the desired response. The idea is to begin by rewarding you for anything that resembles the desired assertive behavior and then to reinforce each closer approximation to the desired behavior by focusing on the positive aspects of your assertive behavior. For example, if you rehearse asking for a raise, you may begin the rehearsal with good eye contact and appropriate words, but aggressive hand gestures and a loud voice. According to the principles of shaping, you would be positively reinforced for good eye contact and appropriate words. This reinforcement might occur simply by having your attention called to the assertive behaviors or by your being praised for these behaviors or by your being given some tangible recognition such as a token or a point. Types of positive reinforcement that are most practical to use in the training situation are attention, recognition, approval, or praise. Vicarious reinforcement — being reinforced through watching others being reinforced — is also useful.

Shaping emphasizes the positive and successful elements of your assertive behavior, building self-confidence and a positive self-image; allows a gradual behavior change, both a realistic and pragmatic approach that helps motivate you to continue to practice assertive behaviors; and helps you to focus repeatedly on those elements that make up an assertive response. Positive reinforcement, like shaping, emphasizes the positive and successful elements of your assertive behavior and builds your self-confidence and positive self-image, motivates you to continue to practice assertive behaviors, strengthens your assertive behavior, and gives you permission to feel good about that behavior (Steel & Hochman, 1976). Positive reinforcement and shaping are more than just behavioral-rehearsal techniques; they can be used to learn most assertion skills.

You may ask how you will know what to change about your behavior if only the good is emphasized. One answer is that anything that resembles the desired behavior is reinforced, which increases usage of that behavior.

Evaluation or Processing, Feedback, and Setting Goals

Some other techniques — evaluation (or processing), feedback, and goal setting — used to teach assertion skills also help you to approximate the desired behavior.

Evaluation is discussing (processing) what has been happening in the group by using specific questions as the focus for discussion: What behaviors did you see? What helped convey an assertive response? What are some other ways of handling the situation?

Feedback is giving others information about how their behavior has been perceived by you or the effect it has had on you. To be most helpful, this information should be specific, observable, useful, and objective. Evaluation and feedback are used at all levels of assertion, but are especially important when practicing assertion and integrating assertion skills. The important thing when giving feedback or doing evaluation is to focus on the positive. The behavioral rehearsal should be stopped at intervals so that the assertor can receive positive reinforcement and feedback to help him or her decide what to do differently before practicing the situation again. The assertor is best able to decide what behavior to change from one behavioral rehearsal to the next. Only if the assertor is undecided or needs more information is it necessary for other participants to give suggestions.

Setting goals involves deciding what specific behavior you wish to learn or improve. Goals should depend on you and not on the other people involved in the situation. For example, there is a difference between "to tell the other person I want him to stop asking me questions while I am on the phone" and "to get the other person to stop asking me questions when I am on the phone." Practice should be aimed at your actual goal rather than at one that someone else has chosen. Then feedback can be used to give you clear direction. Evaluation and feedback help group members focus on how well their goals have been met, on what they are doing, on what remains to be done in order to reach the goals, and on whether new goals need to be set. Generally, only one or two possible changes or new goals should be worked on at a time. You and the trainer usually discuss the feedback and set the new goals.

Evaluation teaches group members questions to ask and what to look for when analyzing any assertive act, provides an opportunity to compare behavior with goals, and gives information to apply to the next practice session. Feedback gives observers an opportunity to share information they have gathered, provides confirmation of or adds to the assertor's own understanding of the behavior, and involves everyone in the practice process. Setting goals helps the assertor to understand specific action steps must be taken to reach the goal of assertive behavior and helps focus on those steps, gives a target, and gives a measure of progress.

SUMMARY

Integration and practice of skills is the core of assertion training. The main practice technique is behavioral rehearsal, a role-play procedure in which you practice behaviors and new skills that are to become part of your repertoire. Supportive techniques include modeling and role reversal, as well as the more general assertion techniques of shaping, positive reinforcement, evaluation, feedback, and setting goals. Each of these techniques has unique advantages when used correctly and appropriately. Practice and integration of all assertion skills is the bridge from the training session to real life.

Behavioral Rehearsal: Integrated Practice of Assertion Skills

Goals

I. To practice integrating verbal, nonverbal, and cognitive assertion skills.
II. To simulate a real-life assertion situation and increase the ability to respond assertively in that situation.

Group Size

No more than thirty participants.

Time Required

One to one and one-half hours.

Materials

I. A copy of the Behavioral Rehearsal Questionnaire and a pencil for each participant.
II. Newsprint, felt-tipped markers, and masking tape for the facilitator.

Process

I. The facilitator announces the goals of the activity and asks for a volunteer who has a particular ongoing assertion situation that he or she is interested in working on in the group.

II. The facilitator asks the volunteer to briefly describe the situation, including the people involved, the physical setting, the specific interactions that take place, and the assertive response he or she wishes to make.

III. The facilitator tells the volunteer to choose participants to play the roles of the various people involved in the situation and to role play a small section (one to three minutes) of the interchange involved in the situation with the other participants. If the volunteer does not feel comfortable practicing the desired assertive response, he or she can simply role play his or her normal behavior in the situation and have a volunteer or the trainer model an assertive response in the situation before attempting it.

IV. If, after this segment, the volunteer feels that another participant is not playing his or her role as the real character would play it, he or she is directed to either coach the participant briefly or reverse roles with that person for a short time. If there are several possible reactions on the part of the characters involved in the situation to assertion on the part of the volunteer, the most desirable outcome is role played first.

V. The role-play segment is repeated and the facilitator asks participants and the volunteer to describe those behaviors which seemed assertive on the part of the volunteer. The facilitator asks the volunteer what behaviors he or she would still like to practice in the situation segment. The facilitator gives the volunteer a copy of the Behavioral Rehearsal Questionnaire and directs him or her to use it as a guide in thinking about possible changes.

VI. The role-play segment is repeated. When the volunteer seems confident in this segment of the interchange, a larger segment of the situation may be practiced, following Step V guidelines.

VII. The facilitator divides participants into groups of three, four, or five and distributes copies of the Behavioral Rehearsal Questionnaire and a pencil to each participant.

VIII. The facilitator explains that assertive situations participants have trouble with in their lives will be practiced in the small groups. Each participant will have twenty minutes to practice his or her situation. The facilitator posts the sequence of the activity as follows:

A. Volunteer chooses partner to direct the role play.

B. Volunteer describes situation and chooses people to act out the roles involved.

C. Volunteer role plays small section of situation with participants.

D. Partner stops the role play and checks with the volunteer to see if participants are being realistic in their roles; if they are not, the volunteer gives more background or a short role reversal is practiced.

E. Partner asks for positive assertive behaviors observed by participants and by the volunteer him- or herself.

F. Partner caucuses with volunteer on Behavioral Rehearsal Questionnaire to decide what areas need more work or whether to go on to the next section.

IX. Before the groups begin, the facilitator emphasizes that the idea is to have a series of successful assertive experiences and that group members are to describe *positive* behaviors they observe in the volunteer and give *positive* feedback or suggestions.

X. At the end of each twenty minutes, a new volunteer practices his or her situation, using Steps A through F.

XI. The facilitator asks for reactions and questions from the participants regarding the rehearsals that have been completed and leads a discussion of what has been learned, with an emphasis on back-home applications.

Variations

I. In Step V the facilitator may also ask for suggestions from the participants on behaviors the volunteer may want to practice in the situation.

II. If necessary and appropriate, the facilitator may model assertive behavior on the part of the volunteer in Step V or may direct a participant to do so.

III. The facilitator may give the participants different colored tokens to display during the role play as feedback to the volunteers on their behavior. Participants are instructed to show one color token when they feel that the volunteer is being assertive, a second color when they feel the volunteer is being nonassertive, and a third color when they feel the volunteer is being aggressive. At appropriate intervals, the facilitator may instruct participants to discuss why they are displaying a certain color token.

IV. Index cards describing various assertion situations can be used. Each volunteer draws one of the cards and role plays that situation, or a situation is read from a card and participants take turns volunteering to play the roles described. Volunteers may also choose situations they would like to practice from the stack of cards.[1]

---

[1]Based on Larry Kiel, *The Assertive Game*. Paper presented at the St. Louis Chapter of the Association for the Advancement of Behavior Therapy, Washington University, St. Louis, November 1973.

BEHAVIORAL REHEARSAL QUESTIONNAIRE[2]

1. Did you feel confident and good about the assertion you displayed?

2. Did you stand up for your own rights without violating the rights of others?

    a. What rights were you standing up for in the situation?

    b. On a scale of 0-10, 10 being very confident, 0 being not confident, how much confidence did you feel in owning your rights in the situation?

3. Did you say and do what you wanted to say and do?

    a. Did you speak directly, objectively, and nonapologetically, stating what you wanted?

    b. Were your voice and body calm and firm?

4. Did you tell yourself positive things as you were being assertive?

5. Were you aware of the consequences to yourself and to the other person of being assertive in the situation? Were you willing to face and/or act on those consequences?

6. What steps would you now like to take regarding this situation?

---

[2]Some additional criteria for evaluating assertive behavior are listed in Figure 13 of "Assessment Procedures for Assertive Behavior," Part III, Chapter Twelve, of this text.

Escalation: An Assertion Activity

Goals

I. To allow participants to experience success in communicating while under stress.

II. To enable participants to practice communicating effectively in stressful situations.

Group Size

Any number of groups of six or eight participants each.

Time Required

One to two hours.

Materials

I. A pencil and paper for each participant.

II. Appropriate Escalation Role Sheets for each participant.

Adapted from pp. 127-129 of *A Handbook of Structured Experiences for Human Relations Training* (Vol. VI). J. William Pfeiffer and John E. Jones (Eds.). La Jolla, CA: University Associates, 1977. The term "escalation" is borrowed from McFall and Marston (1970). The technique is common in behavior therapy. See, for example, Rimm and Masters (1974, pp. 93-103) and Lange and Jakubowski (1976, pp. 108-111).

Process

I. The facilitator introduces the experience and outlines its goals.

II. He or she leads the participants in brainstorming a list of typical stressful situations. (Five minutes.)

III. The facilitator gives a lecturette defining assertion and presents some specific guidelines for formulating an assertive response.

IV. The facilitator distributes pencils and paper and says that each participant is to record a hypothetical situation from the list or actual stressful situation that he or she would like to practice responding to. The facilitator says that each participant should also write down an assertive response that he or she would like to be able to make in the situation described. (Ten minutes.)

V. Participants are directed to choose partners and to share with their partners what each has written. (Ten minutes.)

VI. The dyads are directed to form groups of six to eight participants each.

VII. The facilitator says that one participant from each group is to volunteer to be first to practice his or her situation and desired response with the members of his or her group. (Five minutes.)

VIII. The facilitator directs the members of each group other than the volunteer and his or her partner to stand in a line. The facilitator explains that these people will serve as "hasslers" to create a stressful situation. The person on the left is designated the "mild hassler," and the roles are escalated from left to right so that the member on the right will serve as the most intense "hassler."

IX. The facilitator then explains the roles (volunteer, partner, and hasslers) to be played by the group members and gives each person an appropriate role sheet (or the roles could be posted).

   A. Each volunteer is to describe the stressful situation that he or she has written about, then stand in front of and respond to each hassler, in turn, with the assertive response that he or she has expressed a desire to be able to make.

   B. The volunteers' partners are to be sure that they understand the situation and response and are to offer suggestions for making the response as specific and assertive as possible. They accompany the volunteers as they proceed from one hassler to the next. The partners (a) make sure that the hasslers follow their role guidelines; (b) lend support to the volunteers by their presence; (c) solicit *positive* feedback from the group members on the volunteers' performance after each new hassler has been dealt with; and (d) confer with the volunteers, following each solicitation of feedback, on one or two things the volunteers would like to do or could do to improve their responses to the next hassler.

C. Each hassler is to play the role of antagonist in the situation described by the volunteer and is to remain true to that situation without expanding or adapting it. Each hassler is to play the role with the degree of intensity assigned to him or her; "mild" hasslers may ask one question or make one statement, and so on. (Hasslers in the far right position are cautioned not to hassle indefinitely.) Finally, *all hasslers are to ensure a successful experience for the volunteer by allowing the volunteer to "win" each encounter as he or she progresses along the line of hasslers.*

X. The role play is conducted. (Approximately twenty minutes.)

XI. The members of each group discuss the activity in terms of what helped and what hindered their volunteer in making an effective assertive response and the degree to which the experience brought about an increase in his or her confidence and skill in communicating the response. Other volunteers and their partners take turns within groups as time allows.

XII. The total group reassembles, and subgroups report on their discussions. The facilitator then leads the total group in processing the experience.

Variations

I. "Canned" situations can be used instead of ones brainstormed by the group members.

II. The activity can be performed by one group initially, to serve as a demonstration for the total group. It can then be performed by many groups simultaneously.

ESCALATION ROLE SHEETS

Role of Hasslers

1. Do not exaggerate or change the situation.
2. Hassle no more (nor less) than your position in line calls for (low, medium, high).
3. Make the experience successful for the volunteer.

Role of Partner

1. Caucus with volunteer on situation.
2. Stand beside volunteer as volunteer describes situation to hasslers.
3. Stand beside volunteer going down line.
4. Make sure hasslers stay within their guidelines.
5. Caucus with volunteer after each turn with a hassler on positive behaviors observed, and keep the group reaction positive.
6. Give one helpful suggestion after each interaction or elicit one from volunteer on one thing to do differently with next hassler.
7. Make the experience successful for the volunteer.

Role of Volunteer

1. Caucus with partner on situation to be played.
2. Briefly summarize situation to group.
3. Interact with hassler #1.
4. Caucus with partner on positive behaviors observed.
5. Hear positive behaviors observed by group.
6. Caucus with partner on one thing to do differently with next hassler. Repeat Steps 3 through 6 down the line.

COMPONENTS
OF ASSERTION
ACCESSORY SKILLS

Chapter Nine

Special Application Areas

Special application areas are categories of situations for which specific supplementary skills and guidelines have been developed. These areas include different types of interactions (requests, compliments, criticism, etc.) and different types of people or situations (consumer, job, family, etc.).

Some assertion trainers have stated that, since assertion is situation specific, special application areas are the real focus of assertion training. However, although most people may have problems with specific situations (rather than with all situations), some general techniques are involved in assertion that can be applied to all situations and that are transferable to a great variety of new situations. Once these core skills have been mastered, the focus can change to the use of accessory assertion skills for special application areas. To deal with special applications requires refinement of basic skills, and it means improving what has already been learned.

Special applications are important to practice because some situations can be understood or handled more easily when more is known about them. For example, it is easier to carry on a conversation in a group when one knows more of the skills specific to group conversation; dealing with anger or protecting oneself against subtle forms of aggression is easier if one understands some of the dynamics of anger and how one can protect oneself from attack assertively. In terms of protective skills, "almost all situations can be handled with more direct, assertive statements, however some persistent persons continue to nag or persevere, rage on or annoy to the point where certain of these [protective] responses may be appropriate" (Lange & Jakubowski, 1976, p. 115).

Participants are encouraged in assertion training to isolate their problem areas and to choose situations from those areas for practicing assertion skills. When studying special application areas, participants can concentrate as a group on appropriate areas to learn additional techniques. Most of the special application skills focus on verbal — and rarely on nonverbal or cognitive — assertion.

Much of the assertion literature has sections devoted to special application areas. Those who wish to study the recommended guidelines in specific areas can refer to the appropriate literature referenced in Table 9 in Part IV of this book, in which special application areas are annotated. Areas most discussed in the literature are communication, personal development, social relations, the work setting, consumer relations, personal protection, close relationships, sex, and children. The potential areas of application are virtually unlimited.

OVERVIEW OF THE CHAPTER

This chapter contains four lecturettes and five structured experiences, selected on the basis of usefulness to a wide variety of clients and as a sample of the diversity of special application areas. Some lecturettes are designed to accompany specific structured experiences; others are not.

"Conversation Skills for Groups" is designed to accompany the structured experience "Conversation Circle." Both focus on group conversations — how to initiate or join, how to change the topic or content (participation level), and how to end the conversation and leave the group. These skills build logically on the interpersonal communication skills practiced in Chapter Five's, "Communication Triads": self-disclosure, open-ended questioning, active listening, giving and responding to free information, and describing an experience.

Two structured experiences focus on one's relationship with significant others ("Interaction Constellation") and/or people to whom one is close ("Positive Assertion"). The first provides a graphic analysis of one's relationships to determine assertive, nonassertive, and aggressive behavior patterns and to change these to more assertive ones. "Positive Assertion" emphasizes that assertion is not always a response to conflict but may involve such things as giving and receiving compliments, or sharing positive feelings about a person with that person. This structured experience focuses on one's actions that please a friend or someone close and on what one likes about that person's actions. A method of verbally sharing and contracting for more pleasure is included.

The title of the lecturette "Assertion on the Job" speaks for itself. "Dealing with Anger" presents a model for understanding anger and some guidelines for dealing with one's own anger and that of others. The structured experience "What's the Threat?" is designed to accompany "Dealing with Anger" and help participants apply the anger model to specific situations.

"Protective Skills" presents some controversial techniques by which to defend oneself when attacked. Some trainers teach these and similar skills as the main assertion skills to be used in all assertion situations, even when the need for such defensive techniques is not apparent. "Protective Skills" discusses the subject in a constructive, responsible, and useful way.

"Stations" provides a way to practice any special application area the participants choose.

PROFESSIONAL CONSIDERATIONS

Participants sometimes find it more difficult to express positive or caring feelings than to refuse requests or use protective skills.

When teaching protective skills, it is important to emphasize that they should be used only when necessary and should never be repeated by rote so that what the other person is saying is simply "tuned out."

Keep guidelines for each special application area clear, concise, and few in number.

Some typical guidelines for practicing "extra" skills for special situations are:

Making Requests:

1. Be direct.
2. No justification is necessary, although explanations usually help.
3. No apology is necessary.
4. Do not take a negative response personally.
5. Be prepared to hear "No" as well as "Yes," and respect the person's right to say it.

Refusing Requests:

1. Simply say "No." You may give a reason, but you are not obliged to justify your response.
2. Ask for time to think the request over.
3. Ask for more information/clarification.
4. Take responsibility for your decisions.
5. If pressured, you may repeat your "No," but you do not have to give a reason or justify your answer.

Conversation Skills for Groups

In a conversational situation, people are often at a loss to know how to initiate or break into conversations. Once the conversation has begun, it is important to know how to keep it going. Two useful skills are changing the content and changing the topic of the conversation. Also, it is important to know how to end a conversation or how to move from one conversation level to another. It is useful to know how to initiate, maintain, and end conversations assertively.

There are at least eight ways of initiating conversations:

- Ask a question or make a comment on the situation or mutual activity that you are *both* involved in.

- Compliment the other person on some aspect of his or her behavior, appearance or some other attribute.

- Make an observation or ask a casual question about what the other person is doing.

- Ask if you may join another person or ask him to join you.

- Ask another person for help, advice, an opinion, information.

- Offer something to someone.

- Share your personal opinion or experience.

- Greet the person and introduce yourself.

Many examples could be listed under each category depending upon the context, person involved and so forth. . . .

For each type listed, you could make a comment, ask a question, or do both. For example, you could offer an opinion, explain briefly why you feel that way, and then ask the other person what s(he) thinks. These variants entail different degrees of commitment from the listener. For example, if you offer a

Excerpted and adapted from IT'S UP TO YOU, by Eileen D. Gambrill and Cheryl A. Richey. Copyright © 1976 by Eileen D. Gambrill and Cheryl A. Richey. Reprinted with permission of Les Femmes Publishing, Millbrae, California.

comment, no response may be required. However, if you ask a question, a direct request is made. Different types of initiating statements also offer varying amounts of information about yourself. If your initiating remark consists of a question, you do not offer much of your own thought, but you do convey that you are interested in what the other person has to say and, in addition, provide him with an opportunity to speak. If you make a comment, offer some reasons why you have said this, and also ask the person for her opinion, then you offer something of yourself in addition to providing an opportunity for her to speak. The information you provide about yourself offers a natural source of questions for the other person. Be sure to wait for an answer if you ask a question. Some people make the mistake of asking one question after another, which gives the impression that they are not really interested in what others think because they don't even bother to wait for an answer. . . .

When initiating conversations, it is important to remember several points:

1. *Be positive rather than negative.* When initiating a conversation, it is better to express your comment in a cheerful way than to sound depressed or bored. . . .

2. *Be sure your comment is in context.* Make sure your comment relates to a situation or that you share enough of your thoughts so that s(he) knows what you are referring to.

3. *Be as direct as possible.* Look directly at the person and voice your intentions. . . .

4. *Try to be helpful.* Attempt to ease the other person's discomfort. . . .

5. *Take advantage of your sense of humor.* People enjoy laughing and it will be a point in your favor if you can make them laugh. . . .

6. *Don't make your opening remarks too long.* Allow others to respond to your first comments before making others. . . .

7. *Ask yourself how you would respond to a remark.*

8. *Ask open-ended questions.* Open-ended questions require more than a yes or no reply. They encourage others to offer more information. . . .

9. *Note free information that is offered and react to this.* . . .

10. *Don't try to initiate conversations with people who are deeply engrossed with some other person or activity.* A high level of engrossment may mean that the person will not be open to engaging in conversation. . . . However, one never knows for sure if a person is open to conversation until you try to start one with him or her. . . .

11. *Don't give up too easily.* You may have misinterpreted the reserved or cautious response of someone as rejection of your initiating attempts. Often people are cautious about starting conversations with strangers. . . .

12. *Getting rebuffed is not the end of the world.* . . .

Your comment might have been appropriate but still you may receive a minimal or negative reply. Perhaps the person did not hear you or misinterpreted your comment. Perhaps s(he) is in a sullen mood and would rebuff any overture. Be sure to give yourself a compliment such as, "Well, it was really good that I tried!" for attempting to exert more influence over your social environment and learn what there is to be gained, if anything, from the attempt that failed. . . .

Encouraging and Responding to the Initiation of Others

It is important to respond appropriately to the initiation attempts others make. Once you are in a situation where there are people you would like to meet, it is possible that they will attempt to make contact with you. You can facilitate their attempts by appearing open and receptive to initiations and by responding in a positive manner. There are a number of nonverbal behaviors that can enhance your appearing sociable and inviting, including directness of eye contact, smiling frequently, and a relaxed body posture. . . .

Breaking into Ongoing Conversations

. . . It is also necessary to know how to get into an ongoing conversation so you can express yourself fully. To enter a fast-moving conversation, you may have to initiate your comments during a brief pause or hesitation. If you wait for a long pause, you may not be able to get a word in and the topic could change before you get a chance to share your ideas. This does not mean that you interrupt others while they are still talking, but rather, that you speak up quickly after they have finished their statement. Interrupting others indicates that you do not care about what they are saying and are only concerned with your own ideas. Therefore, instead of interrupting, it is important that you learn to identify when there is a *natural pause* in the conversation, when the person stops to breathe or collect his thoughts after a statement. Even a very talkative person must occasionally stop talking. . . .

It is also helpful to know how to enter the conversation when the opportunity does not present itself. You could raise your voice slightly. Even a slight increase functions as a signal to others that you want to speak. It is not necessary to yell or scream. The content of your speech may also be helpful. Questions ("I don't understand what you mean by . . ."), opinions, and the use of the person's name are often good ways to enter a conversation. It is difficult for someone to continue talking nonstop if distracted by the use of his name, for example, "Ralph, I agree with what you're saying because . . ."

When attempting to break into conversation, what you do with your body can be just as important as what you say with words. Moving your body toward the other person, for example, sitting forward in your chair, or standing closer to the other person, may engage his attention. It is more likely that others will offer you an opportunity to talk if you sit in a visible location than if you sit crumpled in your chair fading into the shadows. Your hands can be used as expressive tools to distract and gain attention. Hand gestures can signal others that you wish to speak or a light touch on the arm or shoulder can communicate your readiness to speak.

The techniques for gaining entry into a conversation can be used when you want to enter a group of people who are talking, for example, at a party. First approach the group and position yourself as if you were a part of the group. Listen for a while so you know what is being discussed, and then gain the attention of the others by offering an opinion about what is being discussed or share an experience. . . .

Once a conversation is initiated and a number of comments have been exchanged, you can do several things to encourage a longer and more interesting discussion. . . .

Maintaining Conversations

Changing the content or specific topics can provide a refreshing lift to any conversation, even between old friends. . . .

Changing the Content of Conversations

You may want to change the content of conversation within the confines of the original goal. . . . Examples of several general conversational content areas are . . . :

1. *Discussion of feelings, assumptions, or impressions of each other. . . .*

2. *Share personal thoughts and opinions about a subject. . . .*

3. *Engage in a mutual exchange of facts; share objective information about a subject. . . .*

4. *Share fantasies, dreams, images, goals or desires. . . .*

5. *Share recent activities. . . .*

6. *Share past experiences. . . .*

7. *Share humorous events, tell funny stories, laugh at yourself. . . .*

Changing the Topic of Conversation

In addition to changing the . . . content area of a conversation to maintain an enjoyable exchange, you can also introduce new topics. You can change the topic of conversation without modifying . . . general content of an exchange. For example, if the . . . general content involves sharing recent activities, specific topics could include what you did last weekend, the book you recently finished, and so on.

There are a variety of ways to introduce new topics. An ideal time to introduce a new topic is generally during a brief pause in the conversation which serves as a natural break between one topic and the next. You might say: "Yesterday I read in the paper that . . ."; "Have you heard about . . ."; "I've been wanting to tell you about . . ." Sometimes the relationship between several topics exists only because the mention of one happens to remind you of the other. You might say, "Speaking of . . . do you think . . ." or "That reminded me of the time when . . ." or "I know it doesn't seem related, but that reminded me of . . ."

Another way to change the topic of conversation is simply to say that you would like to discuss something else. If you become bored or irritated when talking about some topic, then you should change it. You could express your desire directly and perhaps give a reason. . . .

Preparation can increase your ability to introduce different topics of conversation. . . .

Once you have listed and itemized some topics that you can readily introduce, enjoy talking about, and can elaborate upon, you can use this list as a reminder before engaging in conversations. Remember to begin with relatively "safe" topics, those you feel comfortable discussing. . . .

ENDING CONVERSATIONS

Increasing your social contacts also involves having to terminate conversations and arrange for future meetings more often. It is important for your conversational enjoyment to learn how to end conversations that you do not enjoy, prolong those which are pleasurable, be skillful in arranging for future meetings with people whom you would like to see again, and be firm in refusing requests for later meetings that you are not interested in.

The appropriate way to end a conversation is somewhat dependent upon whether you both remain in the same place, for example, during a party or intermission at a concert, or whether you can leave the situation, as in a conversation struck up on the street or in a store. In either case, you may see someone else whom you would like to talk to and say, "Excuse me, I see someone that I'd like to say hello to." If you can leave the situation, in addition to actually starting to move away, you could say, "Excuse me. I have to go now," or "Well, I think I'll continue my walk." It's a good idea to start your exit immediately. For instance, you could stand up, get your coat, and ease your way toward the exit. If you remain where you are and continue to talk, s(he) may not believe that you really want or need to leave. If you have invited people over to your home and feel that you would like to end the evening, perhaps because of tiredness or other commitments, you could offer a statement that implies your intent as well as indicates your enjoyment of the evening. You could say, for example, "I've really enjoyed this evening. I'd like to get together again soon."

Given that you do not wish to continue an exchange, you should remain politely firm. If the other person attempts to prolong an interaction by saying, "I'll walk with you," you might say, "No, I would prefer to walk by myself." There is no need to be harsh or rude in order to be firm. That is, one can be assertive without being aggressive. Don't allow yourself to be pressured into continuing an encounter when you do not wish to do so nor allow yourself to be "talked into" arranging a future meeting with someone when you would rather not. . . .

Many people feel that it is impolite to maintain one's preferences in the face of repeated requests to alter them. On the contrary, exerting pressure upon someone is impolite. It is impolite to badger you and to be insensitive to your preferences.

Arranging for Future Contacts

Pleasurable interactions may be lost by neglecting to arrange for future contact. You may not know how to contact a person again. In other situations, someone may be in a given place at certain times, for instance, you both may have an evening class together. If this is not the case, then some minimal information must be exchanged. You could, for example, share how much you enjoyed the conversation, say that you would like to get together again, and offer your phone number and name, that is, write it down. You are then in a stronger position to request information, such as a name, phone number, and possibly an address. Some people are reluctant to give out their phone numbers but may be willing to accept yours. . . .

SUMMARY

Initiating conversations or breaking into ongoing conversations, maintaining conversations through changing the content or the topic of the conversation, and ending conversations or moving from one conversation to another are extremely useful assertion skills in situations in which people are communicating with one another. Many people do not realize that these skills can be learned, believing that some are natural-born talkers while others are destined to feel inadequate and uncomfortable in conversational situations. Conversation skills can be improved through knowledge and practice of some of the basic skills involved. This improvement should, in turn, make communication with others more enjoyable and rewarding.

Assertion on the Job

Of all the tests that reveal your power to be assertive, your handling of love and work reveal the most.

To be assertive in either area, you must possess an active orientation and set goals that enhance your self-esteem. But in the close relationship of love, your aim should be openness, communication, and sharing of your whole emotional being. Feelings come first. In the job, the assertive emphasis reverses. Doing comes first. Feeling comes second. The aim is achievement and accomplishment. Because of this, relations with people at work tend to be superficial rather than intimate. The stress in the feelings you express there is more on appropriateness than openness.

In pursuit of job goals, you remain an individual, relating to, but separate from, others. The work itself becomes an extension of yourself, expressing something of you — your style, your speed, the way you meet on-the-job problems. The more assertive you are in relation to work and the more willing to show "this is me," the more satisfactions you gain. When the structure of the job or your own psychological blocks prevent this, dissatisfaction, resentment, and alienation occur.

Assertion on the job involves five basic skills:

1. *An Active Orientation.* You must think through your work goals, the steps you must take to achieve them, and how, in doing this, you can utilize your talents to the fullest possible extent.

2. *Ability to Do the Job.* Interferences, obstacles, and blocks sometimes arise in the work situation because you have not mastered the skills you need for your particular job. In addition, you may have problems with self-control. You may possess bad work habits, lack discipline and the ability to concentrate.

Excerpted and adapted from the book DON'T SAY YES WHEN YOU WANT TO SAY NO, by Herbert Fensterheim and Jean Baer. Copyright © 1975 by Herbert Fensterheim and Jean Baer. Reprinted by permission of the David McKay Company, Inc.

3. *Control of Your Anxieties and Fears.* Inappropriate emotional reactions interfere with work performance. General tensions can produce fatigue, irritability, and poor judgment. Fear of a specific work situation may lead to avoidance of the very task needed to get your job done — and may keep you from achieving your work goal.

4. *Good Interpersonal Relations on the Job.* Lillian Roberts, a noted personnel counselor, once told me, "Most people get fired because they can't get along with other people." You must be able to relate to peers, subordinates, and superiors; make requests and ask favors; say no when necessary; handle put-downs.

5. *The Art of Negotiating the System.* This requires a knowledge of the job society and the specific skills that will enable you to work within, through, or against it to achieve your particular goals.

THE UNASSERTIVE JOB TYPES — FROM THE PIGEON TO THE EXPLOITED

Within the office framework many personalities exist desk by desk — some lively, some quiet, others efficient or inefficient, lazy or hardworking. One group is linked by the common quality of unassertiveness. I divide those who lack job assertiveness into six basic categories.

1. *The Pigeon.* You're good at your work, liked and respected by all, but get nowhere on the job. . . .

2. *The Person in the Background.* You do an excellent job, but nobody knows it. . . .

3. *Your Own Worst Enemy.* You substitute aggression for assertion. . . .

4. *Always the Bridesmaid/Best Man.* Because you don't mobilize yourself to work properly, you don't fulfill your potential. . . .

5. *The Complainer.* Your problem is passivity. You constantly gripe about work demands, the office environment, the way people speak to you or act toward you. . . .

6. *The Exploited.* Smiling sweetly, you say yes to every request. . . .

Most people realize the economic importance of their jobs. They know the way they earn their daily bread determines where and how they live, the schools their children attend, the clothes they buy, the income that will enable them to purchase a Florida condominium when they retire.

However, they fail to take this knowledge a step further. They *do not think through the role of the job in their lives*, evaluate what they want to give to the job and get from the job. As a result, they do not gain what they really want and feel dissatisfied with what they do get.

Depending on such factors as temperament, age, learned attitudes toward work, available work opportunities, goals in life in general, the job means different things to different people. The decision of the kind of job you want to get and keep and the way you want to behave and perform on the job is one only you can make. Failure to make this decision often leads to unfortunate consequences such as frustration, boredom, unhappiness. Because vocation is such a major life area, these consequences may affect every other aspect of your existence.

Whatever decision you make about the importance of work in your life, whether you work on the assembly line in a Detroit auto plant, as a middleman in a middle-league firm, or earn a six-figure income as an industry head, self-assertion is vital to any job situation. Here is a seven-point guide to help you achieve it.

Think Through Your Job Goal

Many people lack assertion because they have not formulated their goals. Many possible job goals and combinations of job goals exist.

Some reality-oriented goals include:

1. *The job is simply a place where you earn your living.* You put up with your 9:00 to 5:00 stint so that you can collect a paycheck and meet your bills. You will work overtime for extra pay, but you want the right to choose whether you work overtime on any specific occasion. . . .

2. *You want to make as much money as you can.* For this goal, you will sacrifice pleasure, leisure, relationships. You will accept pressures, worries, and do anything you have to do to earn a huge income. . . .

3. *You want glory, status, prestige.* You willingly undertake responsibilities to get that exalted title. . . .

4. *You want the work to be rewarding to you, to be in terms of your own interests and skills.* Many people never achieve this goal because they start in the wrong field and never have the guts to leave. . . .

You cannot always prevent yourself from starting in the wrong field, but once you discover that you have, shift before it's too late.

5. *You want personal growth and a feeling of movement through life from the job.* Often this goal involves constant challenge and a high level of anxiety.

6. *You want to make a social contribution, to do meaningful work.* You yearn to make the world a better place in which to live, help the underprivileged, fulfill a civic obligation by working for the government, or change society by opposing the government. For you, the main thrust of work comes from implementation of a principle.

These are just a few of the possible goals. Some are incompatible. Usually you cannot make a lot of money and have complete job security. Some can be combined. By determining your major goal, you can think through your main job thrust.

But there are also neurotic goals that do not relate to reality.

Some neurotic goals include:

1. *The need to be needed.* You have to feel indispensable. If you leave, everything will collapse — a theory that rarely proves true. . . .

2. *The need to be liked rather than respected.* Many unassertive people become very concerned about whether or not people like them. They fear that if they say no to a request (no matter how unreasonable), stand up for themselves, succeed in a difficult project, speak up firmly, other people will not like them. Maybe they won't. But in a work situation, *respect matters far more than liking.* . . .

3. *The need to master impossible situations.* Some people reason that if a work situation doesn't come off satisfactorily, it must be their fault. They must remain in the situation until they conquer it; to leave is a cop-out. . . .

4. *The need to be the good child, to win approval.* You are confused between *task orientation*, where you put the emphasis on doing the job well, and *ego orientation*, where you use the job to prove something about the kind of person you are. With the latter approach, you become more vulnerable, more sensitive to stress and disruption, and oriented away from the objective realities of the job itself.

5. *The need to have the world feel sorry for you.* Without awareness, you set up such impossible job conditions that everyone says, "Poor you." Thus, you gain the reinforcers you want — sympathy and concern — but not the reinforcers that would best serve your professional interests. . . .

Take the Active Approach to Getting the Job That Is Right for You

Knowing your job goal is not enough. You want to achieve it. Let's assume that having thought through your goal, you decide to look for a new job. . . .

Some important action steps would include:

1. *Plan your overall strategy.* Learn the arts of job-hunting and resume-writing. A number of good books exist on this subject. . . .

2. *Gather necessary information.* Use the public library or the library of a trade association to find out about companies where jobs might exist. Talk with friends and friends of friends who have knowledge they can pass on to you.

3. *Find out where the jobs actually are.* In addition to reading want ads and visiting employment agencies, don't overlook trade associations and professional organizations and employment centers operated by your college or alumni club. These can serve as information sources.

4. *Master the art of performing well at the interview*. If you feel you will have difficulty with certain questions . . . practice your answer *before* you go for the interview. . . .

5. *Make direct, assertive approaches to possible employers*. Find the right person at the place you'd like to work and try to set up an appointment. . . .

The active approach may enable you to get a better job. More important, this technique makes you feel more in command of yourself. You respect yourself.

Make Sure You Have the Skills to Maintain Your Present Job

When you start a job, you rarely know everything you need to know. Or you may be skilled in the main part of the job, but not in other subsidiary areas. Active acquisition of any technique needed will improve your morale and the quality of your work. . . .

1. *Learn skills that will help you move on to a higher job if that's your aim*. Pick them up on the job, from reading, self-teaching, or courses. Acquiring these — plus letting people know about your new knowledge — makes promotion more probable.

2. *Take an active orientation to your working environment to make it optimal for you*. Don't be afraid to ask for a chair with a straighter back or a newer typewriter. If people constantly barge into your office, keep the door closed as a do-not-disturb signal. . . .

3. *Use self-control on bad habits that interfere with work:*
(a) Identify the habit you want to change.
(b) Prepare a specific program for changing this behavior.
(c) Set as your intention something that you can reasonably accomplish — soon. Aim for a series of successes.
(d) Examine the situation to see if you can make the unwanted act harder to perform and the desired act easier to perform.
(e) Establish the desired habit. Positive reinforcers, in terms of praise from friends or giving yourself presents, help.
(f) Monitor yourself. Keep charts. If you see you are performing the wanted behavior more and the unwanted behavior less, you will feel encouraged.

Learn to Control General Anxiety on the Job

In the job situation constant tension produces many effects. It may cause you to have difficulty concentrating on your work, impair judgment so that you make incorrect decisions, make you so unstable and hypersensitive that slight things annoy you to an extraordinary degree. In this way, it interferes both with your output and your relations with co-workers, bosses, and subordinates. Tension consumes energy and can lead to extreme fatigue at the day's end; insomnia at night; physical ills, such as illness stemming from low physical resistance; and can contribute to psychosomatic disorders like high blood pressure or gastric ulcers. . . .

Learn to Control the Specific Anxiety You Have Learned to Associate with a Specific Job Task

In addition to the overall tensions you experience on the job, you may also fear certain clearly defined situations . . . In the job setting, these fears can lead you to perform poorly, lose your job, and often keep you from ever showing up at the office. . . .

Master the Art of Good Personal Relations on the Job

The kind of work you do and your ability to perform it represent only a portion of your professional picture. A major share of your success or failure on the job, plus your own satisfaction, depends on relations with others. . . .

When relating to others on the job:

1. *Make it easy for people to do what you want them to do.* For example, in asking for a raise, do anything possible that will simplify the situation so the boss can say "yes."

   (a) Give your chief the reasons you deserve a salary increase. Don't make him hunt for them. . . .
   (b) Make sure you know office policies about raises (they are usually reviewed when the budget for the upcoming year is prepared). If you ask for one when it is not due, you run up against the Standard Operating Procedure barrier.
   (c) Do homework. If you can't screw up your courage to make the pitch for more pay, try role-playing with a close friend or spouse. . . .

2. *Speak up* — to praise others, to keep others from putting you down, when you're right or wrong, and to protect your own position. Usually these situations involve the use of feeling talk, saying no, and just plain talking up for yourself, and occur in four circumstances:

   (a) As a superior, you must give feedback. Employees want to know what you think of their work. You can praise or criticize constructively, but let them know your opinion in a positive way. . . .
   (b) You must stand up for yourself. When you deal with other people, they either deliberately or inadvertently will do things that affect you, your work, your company standing. By communicating your feelings, you prevent them from putting you down. . . .
   (c) As a subordinate, you can say no to a superior. . . . Some people in

power positions never want to hear the word "no," but most bosses are human and will respond when you put your negative properly. Your no response must include the reason why.... In the job situation your no answer must relate more to the factual aspects of the matter involved than what you feel. ... By saying no, you don't always win your case, but the matter becomes open to discussion and negotiation....

(d) As an independent, in business for yourself, you must speak up for the money your services are worth....

3. *Define your problem behaviors in job interpersonal relations and deliberately work to change them.* Try to reduce the anxiety connected with them, or actually change your pattern....

(a) Practice problem situations beforehand. Be prepared. Don't expect some divine angel to come to your aid on the spot. Competence often decreases anxiety....

(b) You can't prepare for everything in advance. You must be able to think creatively on your feet and communicate your thoughts so that they get through to others.... You can train yourself....

4. *Recognize that other people have feelings too.* All the reactions of co-workers do not center around you. They are independent of you, and possess their own thoughts, feelings, problems....

Negotiate the System

Having the behavioral skills is necessary, but not sufficient. You must know where and when to apply them. This means a knowledge of the business system in general and your own job situation in particular. You have to learn to keep abreast of changes within your company and determine whether they provide a threat or opportunity for you. If you're ambitious, you must work in an area where your work shows....

1. *Keep your job goal in mind.* Just because an opportunity comes up does not mean you have to take it. It may actually lead you away from your goal. Or the opportunity may cause you to see your present situation in a different way....

2. *Know how to deal with the prejudices you face.* Sometimes you can discuss them. Sometimes you must fight....

3. *Know when to quit.* Sometimes the system is too inflexible or lacks the potentiality for fulfilling your goals.... Sometimes, the system doesn't work for you because your goals or the job situation has changed.... Finally, in operating in the business world, always ask yourself two questions:

Where do you want to go?

What do you have to do to get there? ...

SUMMARY

Assertion on the job involves five basic skills: (1) an active orientation, (2) the ability to do the job, (3) control of your anxieties and fears, (4) good interpersonal relations on the job, and (5) the art of negotiating the system. Once you have thought through your job goal and know what you want from your work, decide which of these skills you need to develop further in order to help you reach your goal.

Dealing with Anger

Anger is the first emotion human beings experience and the last one we learn to manage effectively. As early as four months of age, the human infant's vague feelings of distress differentiate into recognizable anger; for many of us, a lifetime is spent in denying, suppressing, displacing, or avoiding this troublesome emotional experience. Because anger usually occurs within an interpersonal context, it is a frequent group phenomenon and presents a management challenge to all concerned.

Anger happens when we perceive an external event (object or person) as threatening or when we experience the frustration of unmet expectations. Although anger seems to be a response to something outside of us, it most often is an intrapersonal event: we make ourselves angry. But because anger is so unpleasant and human beings are so adept at projection, we usually attempt to locate the source of our anger outside ourselves with statements such as "You make me angry," "You have irritating habits," "You bother me."

ANGER AND THREAT

When we perceive an external event as threatening to our physical or psychological well-being, a cycle of internal movements is initiated. As the perception is formed, assumptions are made internally about the possible danger of the threat. The assumption is then checked against our perceived power of dealing with the threat. If we conclude that the threat is not very great or that we are powerful enough to confront it successfully, a calm, unflustered response can occur. But if we conclude that the threat is dangerous or that we are powerless to handle it, anger emerges in an effort to destroy or reduce the personal threat and to protect our assumed impotency. The anger cycle can be graphically represented. (See Figure 7.)

Reprinted from John E. Jones and Anthony G. Banet, Jr., "Dealing with Anger," pp. 111-113 of *The 1976 Annual Handbook for Group Facilitators.* J. William Pfeiffer and John E. Jones (Eds.). La Jolla, CA: University Associates, 1976.

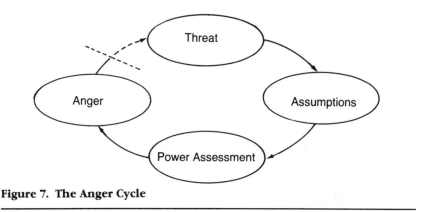

Figure 7. The Anger Cycle

Resentment and Expectations

In the Gestalt view, anger is resentment, an experience accompanying a demand or expectation that has not been made explicit. Unanswered demands or unmet expectations are frustrating; they become another kind of threat, which trips off the anger cycle within us.

Maladaptive Expressions of Anger

Unlike most other feelings, anger has no specific body organs for expression.[1] Physiologically, anger is accompanied by an increase in blood pressure and muscle tightness; psychologically, there are impulses to say aggressive words, strike out, commit violence. But the expression of anger can be so terrifying and threatening that, rather than express it outwardly, we sometimes turn it inward, against ourselves. This short-circuiting of the anger cycle produces distortions of another magnitude; anger turned inward is experienced as guilt; guilt produces feelings of depression, incompetence, helplessness, and, ultimately, self-destruction.

   Another common way to short-circuit the anger cycle is to vent the feeling, not at the perceived threatening event, but at someone or something else that is convenient. We are angry at the traffic jam, but we snap at an innocent spouse. The children consistently refuse to meet our expectations, but we kick the dog. We are angry at the group leader, but we complain about the food. Such displacement of angry feeling serves to ventilate but not to resolve: the anger cycle still lacks closure. When displacement becomes generalized to the system, the government, or the state of Western culture, we begin to see the whole world as hostile and we develop a wrathful, attacking behavior style.

---

[1]Bodily responses during anger and in sexual arousal are nearly indistinguishable; the only difference is that in sexual arousal, rhythmic muscular movement, tumescence, and genital secretion or ejaculation may occur.

Expression of anger can lead to violence; turning it inward produces depression. Displacement is ultimately ineffective and can damage innocent third parties. Repeated failure to close the anger cycle can produce a hostile, cynical, negative view of reality. And even though anger usually occurs in an interpersonal context, it is not an interpersonal event, but self-generated. We make ourselves angry, and there is no one else who can honestly be blamed. Suffering the anger often seems to be the only alternative.

DEALING WITH PERSONAL ANGER

The obvious way to eliminate anger from our lives is to become so personally secure that nothing threatens us. Short of that level of self-actualization, the procedures described here may help.

Owning anger. Acknowledging anger and claiming it as our own behavior is a helpful first step. It increases self-awareness and prevents unwarranted blaming of others. Turning blame and attribution into "I" statements locates the anger where it actually is — inside us. This procedure can help develop a sense of personal power.

Calibrating the response. Anger is not an all-or-nothing experience. It ranges from relatively mild reactions such as "I disagree," "I don't like that," and "I'm bothered," through medium responses such as "I'm annoyed," "I'm pissed off," and "I'm irritated," to intense reactions such as "I'm furious," "I'm enraged," and "I feel like hitting you." Learning to differentiate between levels of anger helps us to assess accurately our capacity for dealing with it.

Diagnosing the threat. What is frightening about the perceived threat? What do I stand to lose? Anger happens because we quickly assume that the situation is dangerous — so quickly that we frequently do not know why the stimulus is threatening. Diagnosing the threat frequently reveals that it is simply a difference in values, opinion, upbringing, or styles of behaving.

Sharing the perceived threat is a way to make the internal anger cycle a public or interpersonal event. It diffuses the intensity of feeling and clarifies our perceptions. It permits us to receive feedback and consensual validation.

Forgiveness involves letting go of the anger and cancelling the charges against the other — and ourselves. Forgiving and forgetting cleans the slate and is a way of opening yourself to future transactions. Forgiveness is a magnanimous gesture that increases personal power.

DEALING WITH ANOTHER'S ANGER

In interpersonal situations, we often respond to another person's anger, whether or not we have occasioned it, by threatening or frustrating behavior. It frequently happens that we receive another's anger just because we happen to be there. Laura Huxley, in her aptly titled book *You Are Not the Target* (1963), views the anger of another as negative energy that is dumped on us, just as ocean waves dump their energy on the beach.

Anger from another has high potential for hooking us into what is essentially someone else's problem. If we view another's anger as threatening, we start the anger cycle in ourselves, and then we have our anger to deal with, as well as the other person's. To be angry because someone else is angry makes no sense, but it frequently happens anyway. Contagion is a usual by-product of intensity.

Anger from another, if responded to appropriately, can increase interpersonal learning and strengthen a relationship. The following steps may be helpful.

Affirm the other's feelings. An old Jules Feiffer cartoon devotes nine panels to one character building up his anger toward another. Finally, he verbally confronts the other with "I hate you, you son of a bitch!" The other character replies, "Let us begin by defining your terms." To *affirm* another's anger is to acknowledge that you are receiving it and to express a willingness to respond. To *disallow* another's anger usually heightens its intensity.

Acknowledge your own defensiveness. Let the other person know what you are feeling. Acknowledge that your own tenseness may lead to miscommunication and distortion. Develop an awareness of the impact of received anger on your body.

Clarify and diagnose. Give and request specific feedback. Distinguish between wants and needs. Check expectations. Discover together who owns what in the situation. When interpersonal needs and wants are out on the table, the resolution of anger becomes more probable.

Renegotiate the relationship. Plan together how similar situations will be dealt with in the future. Contracting to practice new behavior may help eliminate the sources of friction. Acknowledge regret and exchange apologies if that is warranted. Agree on a third-party mediator to help if the two of you are getting nowhere.

Anger does not disappear if we refuse to deal with it; it continues to grow within us. If we deal with anger directly, the discomfort and unpleasantness are compensated by the new learning and self-strengthening that occur. If we deal with it indirectly, we easily trap ourselves into polarization, passivity, "gunnysacking," name-calling, blaming, gaming, and viewing ourselves and our adversary as weak and fragile. Anger is not the worst thing in the world. It is a powerful source of energy, which, if creatively and appropriately expressed, leads to personal growth and improves interpersonal functioning. . . .

REFERENCE

Huxley, L. *You are not the target*. New York: Farrar, Straus & Giroux, 1963.

Protective Skills

RISKS OF PROTECTIVE SKILLS

One of the most controversial issues in assertion training is the use of specific structured techniques for situations where the individual is being *unfairly* criticized, manipulated, pressured, or taken advantage of by someone else. The concerns about teaching and using these various protective skills are these:

The individual can overuse these verbal techniques to the disadvantage of the assertor and recipient — in both superficial and intimate relationships.

These structured techniques, if used alone, will not foster closer relationships between individuals.

Being the recipient of some of these protective techniques can be very frustrating.

If the assertor and the recipient do not work out a more equitable communication system and understanding, the communication and the relationship between the individuals may cease to exist as a result of using these techniques.

It is debatable as to what constitutes *unfair* criticism, pressure, manipulation, etc. By quickly turning to these procedures, the individual may become so defensive that he will not hear or respond to appropriate messages of concern.

To some extent, each of these concerns is valid; consequently, these protective techniques must be used with a considerable amount of caution . . .

Excerpted and adapted from pp. 147-155, 157-160, 162-166 of *Assertion Training*, by Sherwin B. Cotler and Julio J. Guerra. Champaign, IL: Research Press, 1976. Used with permission.

Open Communication

Whenever one feels that he is being treated unfairly or unjustly, a clear, honest statement of that fact is the single most assertive act a person can make. The clear, honest statement of one's needs or feelings in a relationship is the common denominator throughout all of the protective as well as the social approach procedures. . . . In most situations, an honest, clearly worded statement will be an effective and sufficient assertion. . . .

There are a number of situations . . . where it is both appropriate and necessary to use some protective skills. These are very powerful techniques which can cause a temporary or permanent break in the communication or the relationship itself. Consequently, they should only be used *after* the honest communication has failed and the other person persists in victimizing, not listening, or not respecting the client. . . .

These defensive techniques . . . are verbal defenses which are intended to protect the individual but not insulate him from feedback and communication; one must learn to discriminate when criticism is constructive and when it is destructive. . . .

It is a controversial issue whether it is appropriate or constructive to give people "programmed" ways of responding to intimates when there is friction between them. We know that it is possible to train individuals to effectively shield themselves from the unfair criticisms of another. However, if these techniques are used in all situations, whether the criticism is just or unfair, the individual can become so tightly defended that no one will be able to affect the person. Closer relationships will gradually cease to exist, and the individual will perhaps remain more isolated than before. This is a real danger. Consequently, it will be emphasized once again that these protective skills are to be used only as a last resort and only after other more open, positive efforts have failed.

Terminating Protective Measures

Once the decision is made to use a protective technique, the individual also has the responsibility to listen for changes in the communication. If the unjust interaction is terminated, then the assertive individual should immediately cease his use of the defensive technique and resume more open communication. On the other hand, if the unjust interaction is again resumed, the defensive technique should also be repeated. Knowing when to start and when to continue using the technique is as crucial as knowing how to use it. . . . In most instances this start-stop procedure is necessary before a more equitable communication system is established. In the case of a nag, the nagging person does not immediately cease nagging. Instead the process fluctuates where the nagging ceases for awhile, then resumes, and then ceases again later. During these lulls . . . the honest communication should be repeated.

The primary goal in the use of these techniques is to interrupt a destructive and unjust interaction pattern, replacing it with a fair and mutually respectful communication. In our assertion groups, we encourage our clients to use negotiation and contracting as a primary tool for this. Once the destructive interaction is terminated, both parties can negotiate for a mutually satisfactory contract. In a customer-salesman relationship that may mean, as the assertor, you do not buy the product but agree to take the individual's business card for future reference. In an intimate relationship, the negotiation and contracting is usually more complex, but both parties can strive to give the other person as much as possible without negotiating away individual values, rights, and dignity.

Consequences of Teaching Protective Skills

When these protective skills are first employed, the recipient of the interaction — the person who is doing the nagging, criticizing, pressuring — is likely to feel some frustration in not being able to affect the individual in the desired manner; consequently, the communication will probably stop. In most cases, this break in the communication system is only a temporary one and resolves itself in a more equitable interaction when the other person recognizes that the assertor is able to stand up for his rights and protect himself.

However, in some cases, the other individual may not wish to adopt a more equitable relationship. Consequently, if both individuals hold their ground, there may be a more permanent break in the relationship ultimately resulting in a divorce, loss of friendship, or loss of a job. Because of this possibility, it is very important in learning these protective techniques that a person be aware of the possible consequences of his actions so that he can choose whether or not to act defensively. If, under the circumstances, the person chooses not to respond to unjust criticism with the use of verbal assertion he may still be taught how to reduce much of the anxiety present by utilizing a procedure such as systematic desensitization.

Many individuals, however, do choose to respond when subjected to unfair circumstances. It is, perhaps, not very surprising that once individuals begin to realize that they have some rights in this world and that their own dignity need not be negotiated away, they view the termination of this inequitable relationship as a rewarding outcome rather than as a punitive consequence . . . In many cases a more permanent break in the relationship can be avoided by . . . both of the concerned parties simultaneously (e.g., husband-wife, student-teacher, child-parent, boss-employee) learning assertive skills. . . .

With all the precautions in mind, people do tend to improve their appropriate assertive skills with the addition of these defensive techniques. Those who have been trained in the use of these defensive procedures have, for the most part, maintained their previous relationships and have also established new relationships. Consequently . . . the techniques . . . have been constructive rather than destructive. . . . With practice comes the sophistication to be able to appropriately and fairly discriminate when to use and when not to use the protective techniques. The assertor will have much lower anxiety in these situations; consequently, he will be less likely to distort what is being said and will be less likely to hear an "attack" statement where one is not intended. With practice and sophistication, the assertor will have less need to resort to a "protective shield" and, instead, will rely more heavily on open, honest, and clear communication.

As a final note . . . sometimes . . . an inordinate amount of time is spent in learning how to put off others and to protect oneself in assertion situations. Although this is an important and necessary part of the assertion training process, . . . a greater amount of time should be spent learning how to foster closer, more meaningful relationships. It is perhaps true that before an individual is willing and able to get very close to another person, he first must feel able to protect himself. However, defenses alone are not enough. As John Stevens (1971, p. 34) stated, *"The walls that keep out arrows and spears also keep out kisses and roses."* . . . Protective skills alone are . . . not conducive to the overall goals of assertion training. . . . It is of the utmost importance to remember that building greater self-esteem and closer, more mutually pleasurable relationships is the ultimate goal of assertion training.

With these cautions as an introduction, let us examine some specific techniques with which individuals can protect themselves from being taken advantage of by others when the situation calls for this. These protective skills include broken record, selective ignoring, disarming anger, and sorting issues. . . . Fog and negative inquiry are two additional techniques . . . however fog has a strong passive-aggressive flavor and . . . requires the individual to say something he does not really believe. . . . And negative inquiry places strong self-concept demands upon the assertor.

As can be readily noticed, some of the techniques are similar in their content and their purpose. Which technique is chosen is often a matter of personal style. In some cases, one or more techniques can be combined and used simultaneously in the interaction. . . .

PROTECTION ONE: BROKEN RECORD

Of the various protective techniques used, the broken record is probably the most basic. The broken record can be used by itself, or as a component of several of the other techniques to follow. In addition to being potentially useful in situations where a person is defending himself from being nagged, criticized, or pressured, the broken record can also be used in situations where the assertor is requesting something for himself.

The broken record is essentially the continuous repetition of the clear statement of the assertor's feelings or main point. No other issues are attended to in the conversation other than the point being made by the assertor. In effect, the individual sounds like a "broken record," repeating over and over again his position in as concise a statement as possible. In many conversations, side issues are brought in by the other individual to distract or anger the person. To respond to these side issues can escalate the conversation to the point where all clarity of the main point is lost. With the use of the broken record, one point is covered at a time and all side issues are saved for later discussions. . . .

This technique can also be effectively and appropriately used in situations where the assertor is making a request. The procedure is the same as before. The assertor returns the conversation to the main point whenever irrelevant issues are introduced or he is being ignored. The person using the broken record does not necessarily repeat the same sentence over and over again. As long as the conversation is on the relevant topic, there is no reason to restate the original sentence. If, on the other hand, a side issue is brought up, the original sentence stating one's position is then repeated.

Because conversation continues and negotiation and contracting are possible using this technique, the other person is not as likely to become frustrated. Also, this technique is not necessarily intended to end a conversation as some of the other protective techniques are designed to do. . . .

In using the broken record and the other protective skills to follow, there are two important points to remember. First of all, if you are defending yourself using one of these techniques, it may be necessary to stay with the technique for several responses until the other individual gets tired and begins to back off. Although you may be able to stop a negative interaction with just one broken record response, the likelihood is that you will need to use this protective shield at least three times in succession before the other person stops. In some cases you will need more than three responses; consequently, you should practice giving eight to twelve responses in order to overlearn this defensive stance. In most cases, however, about three responses will do it. As an example, one large encyclopedia company instructs its door-to-door salespeople to break off the sales pitch if the potential customer says "No" three times without giving any extra information to work on.

Secondly, if you are asking for some need of yours to be filled (e.g., asking someone next to you to put out a cigarette that is bothering you), you must be prepared to make the request at least two times. It is amazing how many requests are turned down on asking the first time and then agreed to on the second request. . . .

PROTECTION TWO: SELECTIVE IGNORING

Selective ignoring is the discriminatory attending and nonattending to specific content from another individual. That is, the assertor does not reply to unfair or abusive interactions, but instead replies only to statements that are not destructive, guilt-producing, or unjust. The verbally abusive individual is met with silence when he is being unjust. Not only does the assertor remain totally silent through the unfair interactions, but his nonverbal cues must also be controlled. Head-nodding in particular is a reinforcing, nonverbal cue to a speaker. Those who have had public speaking experience will recall how comfortable it is to speak to an audience that is smiling and head-nodding in approval. The rationale for the effectiveness of this technique is that the assertor extinguishes the responses of the other person. That is, the assertor no longer resists the interaction, but simply removes the reinforcement. This technique is relatively easy to use under high anxiety states in that it requires no defensive speech. However, the effectiveness of the technique involves sophisticated discriminations of when to attend and when not to attend to specific information. The assertor does try to continue an ongoing conversation, but responds selectively to the information given. . . .

The selective ignoring technique (or, for that matter, any of the other defensive techniques) does not guarantee a change in the other person's behavior, even though this is often the result. These techniques are intended to protect the recipient of an unjust interaction. A high pressure salesperson, for example, may remain a high pressure salesperson; he simply will not be able to sell to more assertive clients.

PROTECTION THREE: DISARMING ANGER

Disarming anger can be an extremely useful protective technique — in some cases, it may even save the person's life. This technique involves an honest contract offered by the assertor to another individual who is exhibiting high amounts of anger and who may, in fact, be bordering on physical violence. The contract that the assertor tries to work out is an agreement stating that the assertor will talk about whatever issue the other person wants, but only after some of his anger dissipates. Essentially, this is a negotiation for a cooling off period so that both parties can think more clearly and hopefully resolve the issue at hand. This contract is offered whether or not the accusations being made are true or false. Even if the accusations are true and the assertor does eventually apologize, there is no reason why this individual should be made to look or feel like a worthless, stupid human being in the process (or be physically assaulted). As part of the technique, the assertor does not reply to name-calling or other side issues. The assertor also does not escalate the interaction by screaming back. In effect, he uses a broken record offering the contract, "I will talk about whatever you want, but first calm down." In this case the assertor must be able to sit patiently through the individual's initial bursts of anger. (In extreme cases when one's physical safety is at stake, getting away from the situation for awhile may be a wiser choice if this is possible.) It is also important that the assertor is able to appear reasonably relaxed throughout this part of the interaction; consequently, . . . it may be necessary to desensitize oneself to screaming as well as to the anger in the screaming.

Disarming anger is not intended to negate or invalidate the other individual's anger. The intention is to use the technique in order to facilitate communication — not to terminate it. . . . Whenever a person's anger is very high, his ability to listen and incorporate new information seems to be diminished. Trying to talk with such an angry person can be frustrating, useless, and risky. If some technique is not used here, the danger exists that both individuals will become extremely angry — possibly to the point where verbal or physical abuse is escalated. Although some anger and a raised voice may be very appropriate at times, . . . people have the right not to be abused by extreme anger regardless of the reason. The intent of this technique is to disarm *extreme, unreasonable anger*. Although many constructive communications can be made in anger (Bach & Wyden, 1968), for this to occur the fighting must be "fair," where communication is honest, direct, and specific; where name-calling is eliminated; where issues are not stored; and where the ultimate aim is to clear the air rather than to emerge as the "winner."

Disarming anger can be a useful addition to a person's ability to cope with other people. . . .

PROTECTION FOUR: SORTING ISSUES

Occasionally, in the course of an interaction, more than one message or issue will become sandwiched together. Unless these issues or messages are sorted out and dealt with separately, the individual may begin to feel confused, anxious, and guilty. Consequently, it is to the assertor's and the recipient's advantage to deal with these different issues separately. . . .

For example, a person may associate your willingness to loan him your car with your willingness to be his friend. Oftentimes, when two or more issues are sandwiched together and are not properly sorted, the individual goes away feeling guilty or anxious. By attempting to sort the various issues at hand, the assertor is better able to discriminate just what is being asked or implied by the other individual so that he can then formulate an appropriate response without leaving things unresolved or "up in the air."

Sorting issues is a more complex procedure to practice because more verbal response may be required than with some of the other techniques.

Situations that can benefit from this procedure typically occur less frequently, and the sandwiching of different issues may be more subtle than overt criticism, nagging, or anger: "If you loved me, then you would. . . ." "I thought you appreciated the favor I did for you — how could you. . . ." "Don't you care about this job? Why is it you. . . ." However, when the need does arise for sorting issues, this procedure can be very useful. . . .

SUMMARY

Broken record, selective ignoring, disarming anger, and sorting issues are four powerful defensive skills which cause the user to walk the fine line between assertion and aggression. They should be used with extreme caution, only as a defense against unjust interaction, only after all more constructive skills have been tried, and only until the unjust interaction can be changed to a more constructive communication.

REFERENCES

Bach, G. R., & Wyden, P. *The intimate enemy*. New York: William Morrow & Company, 1968.

Stevens, J. *Awareness: Exploring, experimenting, experiencing*. Moab, UT: Real People Press, 1971.

Conversation Circle: Improving Social Skills in Groups

Goals

   I. To develop assertive group conversational skills.

  II. To learn to recognize and identify assertive group conversational skills.

Group Size

From fourteen to thirty participants.

Time Required

One and one-half hours.

Materials

    I. Newsprint, felt-tipped markers, and masking tape for the facilitator.

   II. A 3″ x 5″ card for each participant with a topic from the Conversation Circle Subject List written on each card.

  III. A Conversation Circle Skills Sheet and a pencil for each participant.

Process

   I. In advance of the meeting, the facilitator prepares one 3″ x 5″ card for each participant; each card has one topic from the Conversation Circle Subject List written on it.

II. The facilitator explains the goals of the experience and gives a brief lecturette on group conversational skills.

III. The facilitator distributes a Conversation Circle Skills Sheet, a pencil, and a subject card to each participant.

IV. The facilitator divides the participants into groups of from seven to ten members and explains that during the next twenty minutes participants are to:

A. Talk to other participants, but talk only about your own topic as noted on your subject card or about topics that have been introduced into the conversation by other participants.

B. Practice each of the skills listed on the Conversation Circle Skills Sheet at least once.

C. Maintain groups of from seven to ten members each throughout the activity, that is, if one or two members of one group join a second group, one or two members of the second group should terminate their conversations shortly thereafter to join another group.

V. The facilitator answers any questions participants have and monitors the activity.

VI. The facilitator asks participants to form groups of four to five to discuss the following questions:

1. Which of the conversation skills did you practice? Which were easy? Which were difficult?

2. What useful words or ways of acting did you discover that helped make one or more of the conversation skills effective?

VII. The facilitator asks participants to summarize and share the results of the discussion in Step VI and posts the results.

VIII. The facilitator directs participants to contract with their small group (Step VI) on a specific way they will use one of their learnings in a back-home group situation.

Variation

The Conversation Circle Skills Sheet can be revised to focus on other types of group situations. Participating in meetings, for example, might incorporate the following skills: introducing an agenda item, resisting interruptions, summarizing, disagreeing, or agreeing.

CONVERSATION CIRCLE SKILLS SHEET

Four group conversational skills are described below. Practice each skill at least once during the twenty-minute practice period. Note in the spaces provided any words or ways of acting you observe that you may find particularly useful in your own conversations.

A. OPENERS — initiating a conversation or joining an ongoing conversation.

B. TRANSITIONS — changing the topic of a conversation. (When it makes sense or when you are motivated to do so, i.e., when you are bored, etc.)

C. MOVERS — changing the content (participation level) of a conversation. (Moving a conversation from one of the following levels to another: facts/thoughts/personal experiences/feelings/fantasies/jokes/etc.)

D. CLOSERS — ending a conversation and moving on.

CONVERSATION CIRCLE SUBJECT LIST

clock	nail	map
rug	chair	book
wall	picture	doorknob
fork	lamp	ring
light bulb	stone	road
hair	shoe	television
water	paper	brick
peanut	ice cube	guitar
blue	plate	sand
sun	yarn	wood

Positive Assertion: Reinforcing and Changing Behaviors in Close Relationships

Goals

    I. To learn to express positive feelings assertively, especially in close relationships.

    II. To practice using contracting skills in assertion.

Group Size

No more than thirty participants.

Time Required

Forty-five minutes to one hour.

Materials

A Positive Assertion Work Sheet and a pencil for each participant.

Process

    I. The facilitator announces the goals of the activity, explains that many

---

Adapted from the book DON'T SAY YES WHEN YOU WANT TO SAY NO, by Herbert Fensterheim and Jean Baer. Copyright © 1975 by Herbert Fensterheim and Jean Baer. Used by permission of the David McKay Company, Inc.

people see assertion only as a response to uncomfortable situations, and says that many people also have difficulty being assertive when they feel positively about something.

II. The facilitator gives each participant a copy of the Positive Assertion Work Sheet and a pencil and instructs participants to complete the form. (Ten to fifteen minutes.)

III. The facilitator leads a discussion of positive assertion and the contracting process.

IV. Participants are told to form pairs to develop assertive ways of sharing what they have written with the person they have written about and of contracting with that person for change. (Ten to fifteen minutes.)

V. The facilitator leads a discussion of what participants have learned about themselves and about positive assertion and contracting and answers any questions.

POSITIVE ASSERTION WORK SHEET

A. List ten things a friend or someone close to you does that please you:

1.

2.

3.

4.

5.

6.

7.

8.

9.

10.

B. List three things that you would like this person to do more often. In answering this question and the next, please be POSITIVE and SPECIFIC. How often did he or she do each of these things in the last seven days? How important is each of these things to you?

1.

It was done   Do you consider it:

_____ times   _____ very important

in the last   _____ important

seven days   _____ not too important

Adapted from Marital Counseling Inventory by Richard B. Stuart and Freida M. Stuart. Copyright © 1972 by Behavior Change Systems. Available from: Research Press, 2612 N. Mattis Ave., Champaign, Illinois 61820.

2.   It was done   Do you consider it:

____ times   ____ very important

in the last   ____ important

seven days.   ____ not too important

3.   It was done   Do you consider it:

____ times   ____ very important

in the last   ____ important

seven days.   ____ not too important

C. Please list three things that this person would like you to do MORE OFTEN, again being positive and specific. How often have you done each of these in the last seven days? About how often has this person asked you to do each of these things during the last seven days?

1.   I did it ____   This person asked me

times in the   to do this ____ times

last seven   in the last seven

days.   days.

2.   I did it ____   This person asked me

times in the   to do this ____ times

last seven   in the last seven

days.   days.

3.   I did it ____   This person asked me

times in the   to do this ____ times

last seven   in the last seven

days.   days.

D. List some ways you might share some of list A with the person you have written about.

E. List some ways you might negotiate a contract in which both you and this person can agree to work on new behaviors. The rules for drawing up a contract designed to bring about behavioral change are:

1. *The contract involves both people.* Each has responsibilities, and each receives desired rewards as he or she fulfills these responsibilities. Each person receives something he or she wants from the other.

2. *The contract must be acceptable to both parties.* Each must be willing to accept the specific responsibility in return for the specific rewards.

3. *In negotiating the contract, the people involved set limits on what can and cannot be negotiated.* In this way, change is facilitated by avoiding impasse areas.

4. *The behaviors involved in the contract are specific, positive, observable, and countable.* Do not use behaviors such as "improve our friendship." Do use such desired behaviors as "the number of times she initiates a conversation with me." Although it is not always possible to have countable behaviors, try to find them. Avoid unobservable behavior such as thoughts or feelings. The change in these will follow from the change in observable actions. Always stress the behaviors you want to *increase* rather than those you want to *decrease*.

5. *The contract should be written in detail* so that it makes clear the responsibilities and rewards of each person. This avoids confusion about the original agreement at a later date. Whenever possible, keep track of the target behaviors with graphs, charts, points, or tokens.

6. *Each person should rate the behavior of the other.*

7. *In advance, set times for deciding on the extension or renegotiation of the contract.*

Contracts make good intentions workable. The situation is avoided in which one person claims, "Here I am doing my share, but my friend gives me nothing in return. I carry the whole burden. It isn't fair." Although it may seem like a cold and businesslike form to use within a close relationship, a contract can actually increase warmth and openness.

Interaction Constellation: Developing Assertive Interaction Patterns with Significant Persons

Goals

I. To explore and clarify interaction patterns with significant persons in one's life.

II. To examine ways of developing or maintaining assertive interaction patterns with significant persons in one's life.

Group Size

No more than thirty people.

Time Required

One hour.

Materials

I. Newsprint, felt-tipped markers, and masking tape for the facilitator.

II. A pencil and a copy of the Interaction Constellation Work Sheet for each participant.

Adapted from pp. 30-33 of ASSERTING YOURSELF: A PRACTICAL GUIDE FOR POSITIVE CHANGE, by Sharon A. Bower and Gordon Bower, copyright © 1976, by permission of Addison-Wesley Publishing Company, Inc., Reading, Mass.

Process

I. The facilitator introduces the goals of the activity, distributes the Interaction Constellation Work Sheet and a pencil to each participant, and asks participants to complete Part A of the work sheet. (Five to ten minutes.)

II. The facilitator leads a discussion of and posts responses to Part A, encouraging participants to edit and add to their responses during the discussion.

III. Participants are told to complete Part B of the work sheet. (Ten minutes.)

IV. The facilitator instructs participants to form groups of three or four to discuss their work sheets by responding to the following questions:

1. With whom are you able to solve problems to the satisfaction of both of you? You do not feel "put down" by him or her. You feel there is mutual trust, admiration, give-and-take. Have you drawn circles to reflect this?

2. What are the assertive behaviors that help you achieve a feeling of balance with these people? (Ten minutes.)

V. The facilitator asks participants to share assertive behaviors discussed in Step IV with the large group and posts the behaviors.

VI. Participants are told to complete Part C of the work sheet. (Five to ten minutes.)

VII. The facilitator tells participants to discuss their work sheets in their small groups, responding to the following questions:

1. If you had drawn these constellations of circles six months ago, would they have looked the same? If not, do you feel the changes "just happened" or did you (and the other person) *make* them happen? If you made them happen, how did you do it?

2. What behaviors can you maintain or initiate (use the posted list as a guide) to help you approach your "perfect constellation" and promote more assertive interaction patterns? (Ten minutes.)

VIII. The facilitator instructs participants to share behaviors discussed in Step VII with the large group and posts the behaviors.

IX. The facilitator tells participants to formulate attainable action steps toward achieving their "perfect constellations" and participants share these steps briefly in the large group.

Variations

I. The facilitator may wish to incorporate a lecturette on protective skills to help participants focus on alternative methods of dealing with dominant persons.

II. Participants can role play their typical behavior with significant people in their lives whose relationships with them they have a hard time "categorizing," and receive feedback from their partners on behavior patterns and potential changes.

III. A "live" diagram may be done in which participants explore their interaction constellations with other participants by placing themselves in the center of the floor and positioning significant others from the group in relation to horizontal and vertical axes until the constellation "feels" right. The constellation can then be recorded on paper and discussed further.

INTERACTION CONSTELLATION WORK SHEET

Part A: Definitions

1. If you feel that another person is *equally* as important as you, how do you define "equally important"? If you feel that someone is *more* important than you, how do you define "more important"? If you feel that someone is *less* important than you, how do you define "less important"?

2. If you feel that someone is of *equal status* with you in a relationship, what do you mean by "equal status"? If you feel that someone holds a *dominant* position in your relationship, what does "dominant" mean to you? If someone is *subordinate* in your relationship, what does "subordinate" mean?

3. What does a "close" relationship with another person mean?

Part B: Circles

1. Keeping your definitions in mind, draw and label circles on the following page to show how you see yourself in relation to the significant people in your life: mother, father, brother, sister, colleague, employer, friend, mate, children. Observe the following rules in drawing your circles:

   a. SIZE *Bigger* = you consider the person *more* important than you.

   Smaller = you consider the person *less* important than you.

   Same size = you consider the person to be *equally* as important as you.

   b. POSITION (Vertical space)

   Above you = you consider the person to be in a dominant position.

   Below you = you consider the person to be in a subordinate position.

   On the same plane = you consider the person to hold a position equal to yours.

   c. *DISTANCE* (Horizontal space)

   Far away from you = you consider the relationship to be distant (not close or intimate, but not necessarily unfriendly).

   Near you = you consider the relationship to be friendly.

   Overlapping position = you consider the relationship to be warm, close, and intimate.

Picture your significant relationships by drawing your circles here:

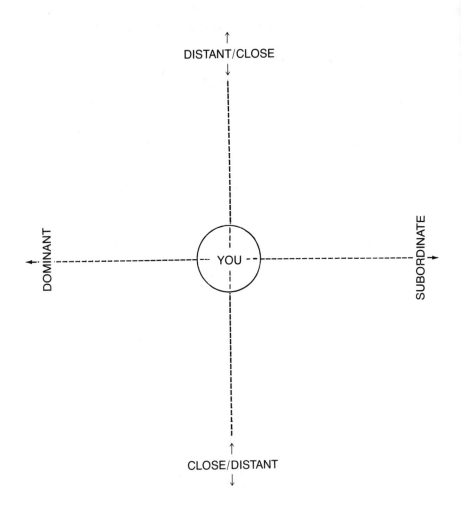

2. Elaborate on your picture of your significant relationships, following these instructions:

For those people toward whom you typically react passively (doing too little too late), fill in the circles with this snail-like design:

For those people toward whom you typically react aggressively (doing too much too soon), fill in the circles with this warlike design:

For those people toward whom you typically react assertively (solving problems easily without bad feelings), fill in the circles with this flowered design:

If you interact in more than one way with a person (both passively and aggressively), draw that person's circle both ways:

What other combinations of behaviors do you observe in yourself when interacting with a friend? The following pictures suggest a combination or alternation of interaction patterns:

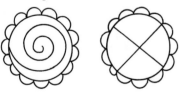

Part C: Perfect Constellations

Which circles would you like to change? In size? position? distance? What would a "perfect" picture look like? On the page below, draw your "perfect constellation" of significant relationships. (Draw significant others the ideal size, in an ideal position, the ideal distance from you.)

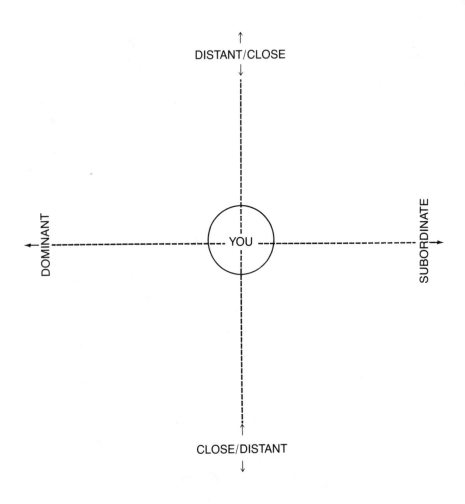

What's the Threat?: Dealing with Anger Assertively

Goals

I. To understand the function of anger.

II. To practice assertive ways of dealing with anger.

Group Size

No more than fifteen dyads.

Time Required

One and one-half to two hours.

Materials

I. Newsprint, felt-tipped markers, and masking tape for the facilitator.

II. A pencil, blank paper, and a copy of the What's the Threat Questionnaire for each participant.

Process

I. The facilitator distributes the What's the Threat Questionnaire, paper, and pencils and instructs participants to complete it privately in preparation for the activity. (Ten minutes.)

This activity is based on pp. 111-114 of *The 1976 Annual Handbook for Group Facilitators*. J. William Pfeiffer and John E. Jones (Eds.). La Jolla, CA: University Associates, 1976.

II. Participants are told to choose partners and to discuss with those partners one or two of their responses and anything they may have learned from completing the questionnaire about the way in which they tend to view or deal with anger. (Five to ten minutes.)

III. The facilitator presents a short lecturette on anger, including the anger cycle and steps to take to express anger.

IV. The facilitator tells participants to think about the kinds of things that usually make them angry and to each choose a real situation in which they would like to learn to express their anger more appropriately.

V. Participants are asked to share their situations with their partners and, with their partners' help, to identify the threat involved in the situations and to role play sharing those threats in sensitive, assertive ways with those involved. The following guidelines are posted:

A. Acknowledge your anger.

B. Gauge how much anger you are feeling.

C. Diagnose the threat.

D. Share the perceived threat in a nonthreatening way, use "I" statements, and ask for help and clarification.

E. Release the anger when the interaction is completed. (Ten to twenty minutes.)

VI. The facilitator asks participants to share what they have learned from the experience and any questions that have arisen.

VII. The facilitator asks participants to choose new partners, to each think of a situation in which they have trouble responding to another's anger, and to role play responding to that anger in a sensitive, assertive way. The following guidelines are posted:

A. Affirm the other's feelings.

B. Acknowledge your own defensiveness.

C. Clarify and diagnose.

D. Renegotiate the relationship. (Ten to twenty minutes.)

VIII. The facilitator asks participants to share what they have learned from the experience with the large group.

IX. The facilitator directs participants to discuss with their partners some specific ways in which they can use what they have learned.

Variation

As a last step, or instead of role playing, participants can practice dealing with anger situations within the group. The facilitator can direct participants to rehearse, sharing the threat involved in the anger they actually have felt, feel, or could feel toward someone in the room if the person acted in a certain specified way. Time is then allotted for each participant to approach the other person actually involved and to share the threat with him/her. (If more than one person wants to share with the same person, each waits in line.) After sharing their feelings with the other persons, participants make themselves available to others by remaining alone and standing until approached. At the end of the time period, participants return to their partners to discuss the experience. The facilitator leads the group in a discussion of the experience.

WHAT'S THE THREAT QUESTIONNAIRE

How do I express and respond to anger:

1. Do I usually keep quiet when I'm angry?

2. Do I usually walk away from the other person when I'm angry?

3. Do I simmer for days and then vent my anger in a big blowup?

4. Do I appear to feel hurt when I'm actually angry?

5. Do I take out my anger on someone other than the person at whom I'm angry?

6. Do I express my anger directly and firmly, but without labeling the other person?

7. When someone else is angry with me, can I respond directly and effectively, with composure? Can I listen, try to understand their grievance?

8. Do I feel hurt and withdraw when someone is angry with me?

Excerpted from the book THE NEW ASSERTIVE WOMAN, by Lynn Z. Bloom, Karen Coburn, and Joan Pearlman. Copyright © 1975 by Lynn Z. Bloom, Karen Levin Coburn, and Joan Crystal Pearlman. Reprinted by permission of DELACORTE PRESS.

Stations: Practicing Assertive Approaches
to Special Application Areas

Goals

   I. To learn some guidelines for being assertive in special application areas.
  II. To practice being assertive in special application areas.

Group Size

     An unlimited number of participants; a number of facilitators corresponding to the number of special application areas to be practiced.

Time Required

     Forty minutes to two hours and ten minutes.

Materials

   I. Newsprint, felt-tipped markers, and masking tape for the facilitator.
  II. A 3" x 5" card for each participant for each special application area to be practiced. Each card contains guidelines for the special application area being practiced.
 III. Blank paper and a pencil for each participant.

Process

   I. In advance of the meeting, the facilitator prepares one 3" x 5" card for each participant for each special application area; each card contains guidelines for the special application area being practiced. These guidelines can be found in the pertinent special application area literature (see lecturettes in this chapter and reference chart in Table 9, Part IV of this book). Sample guideline cards:

Making Requests	*Refusing Requests*
1. Be direct.	1. Simply say "No" with no apology. You *may* give a reason, but you are not obliged to justify your response.
2. No justification is necessary, although explanations usually help.	2. Ask for time to think the request over.
3. No apology is necessary.	3. Ask for more information/ clarification.
4. Do not take a negative response personally.	4. Take responsibility for your decision.
5. Be prepared to hear "No," as well as "Yes" and respect the person's right to say it.	5. If pressured, you may repeat your "No," but you do not have to give a reason or justify your answer.

II. A facilitator announces the goals of the activity and states that in addition to the assertion skills participants already have learned, some additional guidelines are helpful for specific types of situations. He or she posts a list of the special application areas to be practiced in thirty-minute intervals. (These areas are chosen in advance by the facilitator(s) and may include making requests, refusing requests, giving criticisms, receiving criticisms, giving compliments, receiving compliments, using protective skills, and/or any other appropriate situation involving an interaction between two people.) A facilitator must be available for each application area that is to be covered.

III. The facilitator announces that participants are to form groups according to the special application area they are most interested in practicing. The facilitator may wish to designate certain areas of the room as practice sites for special applications by posting signs in advance.

IV. A facilitator takes his or her place at each station, asks the participants to brainstorm a list of situations in which it is difficult to practice the skills necessary for that particular application area, and posts these situations.

V. The facilitator explains the guidelines for being assertive in that particular application area, demonstrates how to apply these guidelines using one or two of the posted situations as examples, and gives each participant a corresponding 3" x 5" card containing the guidelines presented.

VI. Each facilitator instructs each participant to choose a partner and to practice role playing several of the posted situations, or situations of their own choosing, using the guidelines presented. (Fifteen minutes.)

VII. Participants are told to report to their small groups on the experience, and each group discusses any questions that have come up. (Five minutes.)

VIII. The lead facilitator announces each thirty minutes that participants may rotate to a new station or stay at their present station, depending on their choice of practice area. Steps IV through VII are repeated for each thirty-minute period. (Facilitators may rotate for each round or stay at the same station throughout the activity.)

IX. The facilitator asks participants to choose partners and to discuss how they can use the techniques they chose to practice in their daily lives.

Variations

I. Participants can use predesigned lists of typical situations rather than brainstorm their own lists at each station.

II. Participants may stay in one large group and choose a new partner for each round to practice a set series of special-application-area skills.

III. Participants may volunteer their own guidelines, culled from their own personal experience, and these can be added to the guideline cards.

IV. Special application areas can focus on role or setting (children, job, intimate, consumer, etc.) or on assertion skill area (self-confidence, identification of rights, confidence in rights, etc.) rather than on type of interaction (requests, criticisms, etc.).

V. In an ongoing group, a questionnaire can be given to participants at a previous session to determine special application areas that the participants would like to practice.

Chapter Ten

Special Needs

Special needs skills are those necessary under special circumstances. For example, participants occasionally encounter a particularly difficult situation in which they are overly anxious or feel the need to develop assertion skills at a more gradual pace. In these situations, a person may find it difficult to be assertive — even though the person has preparatory and core assertion skills. Special needs techniques are appropriate in these cases to enhance other assertion skills. Also, in some therapy situations, anxiety may be so high that the client cannot learn assertion skills. In the latter case, special needs skills sometimes fall under the category of preparatory skills. This chapter focuses on the ability to use special needs techniques when necessary.

The special needs techniques presented here offer ways to reduce anxiety that has not been dispelled by learning preparatory and core assertion skills and to approach being assertive at a more gradual pace. Areas of special need, if they exist at all, do not become apparent until the core skills have been established because assertion is taught in a hierarchical sequence, i.e., participants are encouraged to practice easier situations before more difficult ones. One of the interesting things about anxiety reduction is that to begin assertion training, one must have reasonably low levels of anxiety, but if a person has these low levels, assertion training reduces anxiety even more, as well as "secondary reactions" to tension and anxiety ("fear of loss of control, fear of the anxiety itself, or an overwhelming feeling of helplessness in the face of tension"; Lazarus, 1972, p. 37).

All assertion techniques reduce anxiety to some extent because:

1. Even if one is feeling anxious, assertion gives an appropriate format for expressing these feelings, thus dissipating them.

2. Erroneous beliefs can cause a person to overreact to situations that are not in themselves anxiety producing. Self-confidence, confidence in rights, and cognitive assertion skills all tend to reduce the chance that one will feel such anxiety.

3. Knowing that one has the skills with which to respond to a situation helps reduce anxiety. Theory and integration as well as verbal, nonverbal, and cognitive skills help build the confidence necessary to be assertive.

4. Taking action tends to inhibit anxiety.

Special needs skills for reducing anxiety generally take a longer time to learn than do other techniques. Special techniques for this purpose include relaxation, the Subjective Units of Discomfort Scale, covert rehearsal, covert modeling, covert reinforcement, and systematic desensitization.

Relaxation

The progressive relaxation technique was developed by Jacobsen (1938) and modified for use in training by Wolpe (1958, p. 135): "The essence of the method is to give ... intensive and prolonged training in the practice of relaxation, and then to ... keep relaxing all muscles not in use (differential relaxation)." It is the systematic tensing and relaxing of muscle groups.

Subjective Units of Discomfort Scale

The Subjective Units of Discomfort Scale (SUDS; Wolpe & Lazarus, 1966, p. 73) is a method whereby participants set up a discomfort scale from 0 (most relaxed they could possibly be) to 100 (most tense they could possibly be). Every gradation within the scale is treated as a subjective unit of discomfort, and the participant is taught to keep a running measure of his or her anxiety levels by assigning numbers on the scale to his or her anxiety level at any particular time.

Participants are asked to imagine scenes in which they are completely calm and relaxed and to give those situations 0 scores and then to imagine the most tense, anxiety-producing situations possible and to assign the situations ratings of 100. The idea is to monitor SUDS level until the person is relaxed enough to express himself or herself. When expressing negative feelings or dealing with certain powerful people, one may appropriately have a higher SUDS level. Some discomfort is usually normal in such circumstances; the idea is not to reach 0, but simply to reduce SUDS levels as much as possible while responding assertively. The SUDS scale can be used to put difficult situations in proper order on a hierarchy, to list anxiety-producing situations that participants want to work on, or to monitor changes in levels of anxiety.

Covert Methods

Covert rehearsal, covert modeling, and covert reinforcement involve imagining scenes rather than acting them out. In *covert rehearsal* (Cautela, cited in Rathus & Nevid, 1977), the assertor breaks a scene down into manageable segments and imagines responding assertively to each segment. If the assertor is unable to imagine being assertive, *covert modeling* is used, in which the assertor imagines someone else or a succession of people being assertive in the situation and then tries again to imagine being assertive.

Covert reinforcement involves thinking of a positive image, word, or anything that invokes pleasure, immediately following the image of a successful assertive response. Cautela (cited in Kanfer, 1975) suggests attaching a verbal cue such as "reinforce" to the image to permit easy recall. Once one is able to imagine the scene easily, the behavior can be practiced and reinforced overtly.

Systematic Desensitization

Systematic desensitization (Wolpe, 1973) involves constructing a hierarchy of progressively more anxiety-provoking scenes and imagining confronting these scenes while practicing or substituting a response incompatible with anxiety — relaxation, fantasy, curiosity, anger, etc. — in order to systematically desensitize oneself. *In vivo* desensitization is using the same technique with actual situations. Opinions are mixed in the assertion literature as to whether desensitization should be carried out without the help of a therapist or professional. Fensterheim and Baer (1975, p. 264) caution: "This is a rather technical procedure and if not performed correctly there is some danger the [fear] can get worse." However, Kahn and Quinlan (1967) report that "do it yourself" desensitization kits were found to be almost as successful as those administered by therapists. Adler (1977, p. 103) states that systematic desensitization is "usually used under the supervision of a professional, [although] recent research suggests that it can be used successfully by individuals on their own. . . . If you do experience difficulties you should consult a trained professional for help." Such a difficulty may consist of an inability to stop the fantasies or an inability to reach the top of the hierarchy.

A desensitization hierarchy is constructed by defining the fear, making a list of fear-producing scenes, and rank ordering the scenes in terms of level of anxiety produced.

Adler (1977, p. 104) presents a useful description of client-controlled systematic desensitization: take the hierarchy list and find a quiet place; relax for a minute and look at the first item; visualize the scene vividly, holding the picture in your mind without drifting to another scene; picture yourself in the situation for up to twenty seconds. Notice how you are acting. If you can hold the image for twenty seconds without any anxiety, relax and enjoy that feeling for a minute and then picture the scene again; after relaxing another minute, repeat the process with the next item. Continue until you are able to imagine yourself remaining calm in the highest SUDS setting. Picture each scene calmly twice before moving on. If you experience anxiety, immediately stop picturing the scene and relax. Take a full minute to experience calm, and then try picturing the scene again. If you become anxious as soon as you picture a scene, return to the previous item, and consider whether you need to insert an intermediate step as a transition or to break a difficult scene into parts and imagine each part. No more than three items should be covered in a session. As a rule, an effective hierarchy consists of between ten and twenty steps, spread so the gap between each is small enough to be crossed comfortably.

Bower and Bower (1976, pp. 60-61) describe an adaptation for trainers: "After instructing students to imagine the first scene in their hierarchy, have them raise a finger if they feel any anxiety. When [they] raise fingers tell them to stop visualizing scene one. Then instruct them to visualize the comfort zone. Ask [them] to raise a finger when they feel relaxed. Instruct them to again visualize scene one and to raise a finger when they feel anxious. Continue alternating between the comfort zone and the first zone. When the majority can visualize the first scene without experiencing anxiety, ask them to visualize scene number two and raise a finger if they experience anxiety [etc.]." Imagine each scene twice, even if there is no anxiety.

OVERVIEW OF THE CHAPTER

The chapter contains two lecturettes, "Covert Techniques" and "Coping with Stress," and two structured experiences, "Covert Rehearsal/Reinforcement" and "Relaxation." "Covert Techniques" describes covert rehearsal, segmenting, covert modeling, and covert reinforcement and gives participants practice in visualizing — a prerequisite for covert techniques. "Covert Rehearsal/ Reinforcement" provides practice of the four covert techniques, which are less threatening and less anxiety producing than overt techniques.

"Coping with Stress" explores some origins of stress, discusses the stress-reduction technique of progressive relaxation, and gives some basic relaxation guidelines. "Relaxation" guides the participants through the SUDS and progressive-relaxation techniques.

PROFESSIONAL CONSIDERATIONS

When practicing relaxation, participants should not make their muscles so tense that it hurts or feels like a muscle will be strained. It is a good idea to have participants consult a physician before practicing this technique if they have had any back trouble, muscle strain, or respiratory problem or if they have any doubt about their medical readiness.

In terms of the sequence in which muscle groups are to be tensed, Wolpe

(1973, p. 104) states: "There is no necessary sequence for training the various muscle groups in relaxation, but the sequence adopted should be orderly."

As an indication of total time needed for relaxation procedures, Adler (p. 96) suggests ten sessions of about thirty minutes and suggests two practice sessions per day. Practice with each of the fifteen muscle groups when beginning; as you advance you can begin tensing and relaxing larger and larger groups of muscles at a time. This will reduce the time it takes to relax until eventually you will be able to relax all muscles on command.

When relaxation is practiced, lights should be dimmed. It usually helps to have participants who wear contact lenses remove them before closing their eyes.

Suggestions for how long to relax following tensing of each muscle or muscle group range from twenty to sixty seconds.

Some possible problems when teaching relaxation include:

1. *Distractions*. Try to monitor the environment.

2. *Unpleasant sensations, including tingling, floating, or dizzy feelings*. Rosen (1977, p. 66) suggests: "Remain still [and] notice how the sensations can lessen in their intensity and blend into more comfortable feelings of relaxation." Point out that these sensations are not unusual.

3. *Muscle jerks or spasms*. Bernstein and Borkovec (1973, p. 46) advise: "Mention that spasms are very common and often occur prior to sleep. Point out that such spasms are noticeable during a session because a client is awake, focusing on his/her muscles and probably not used to experiencing deep relaxation in a waking state."

4. *Cramps*. Reduce the time for tensing muscles and use less force when tensing muscles.

5. *Disrupting thoughts*. Rosen (1977, p. 68) suggests: "Concentrate on your breathing [or] call to mind an alternative and pleasant image."

6. *Feeling sleepy*. Try to stay awake.

Covert techniques require an ability to invoke images.

When constructing a hierarchy, Flowers (1975) recommends that items not be more than ten SUDS units apart.

When practicing desensitization, it is best to imagine scenes with as much detail as possible and to master each scene in the hierarchy before proceeding to the next.

For covert modeling, Paris and Casey (1978) comment that it is best to imagine the model being assertive but not so much more assertive than the assertor that it seems unrealistic. The scene should be something the assertor feels he or she can do with some practice.

Sometimes it is not in the best interest of the client to relax when tense. Participants should check to see if it is more appropriate for them to relax or if they are experiencing useful tension and should simply assert themselves.

In the "Relaxation" structured experience, the long-term goal is to be able to do the entire sequence. The facilitator may not be able to use the entire sequence (SUDS and relaxation and covert reinforcement) in a beginning session, due to participants' ability levels.

The "Covert Rehearsal/Reinforcement" and "Relaxation" structured experiences describe one way, not the only way to practice these standard techniques.

Covert Techniques

If no one is available to practice an assertion situation with you or if your anxiety level is too high, overt behavior rehearsal will be impossible. . . . In such cases you can use the alternative method of *covert rehearsal* to practice your goal. Covert rehearsal . . . practice is carried out privately through visualization. The basic steps . . . are as follows: First, set a specific behavioral goal. Next, seek models to get a clear idea of how you might carry out the behavior. The actual practice of the behavior is done in your mind by picturing yourself behaving in the desired way, and then imagining how the other people involved in the scene would respond.

There is no question that this method works. . . . Competitive skiers . . . mentally practiced racing techniques, competitiveness, and memory in order to cut down on skiing errors and increase competitiveness. The results were impressive: One college team won its league championship, a number of individual contestants improved their performance over previous levels, and after a few sessions of . . . behavioral techniques, the U.S. Olympic Nordic Cross Country Relay skiing team turned in its best performance ever (Suinn, 1976).

The key to success in covert behavior rehearsal is *clear visualization*. In order for the process to work you must be able to vividly picture yourself in the target scene, as if you were actually there. Simply observing yourself as you would a movie actor is not as effective as actually seeing the sights, smelling the odors, and hearing the sounds you would encounter in real life. The effect of clear visualization can be dramatic. . . . One swimmer . . . reported that the scene actually changed from black and white to color as she mentally dove into the pool and experienced the cold temperature of the water in her rehearsal scene. The electromyograph responses of a skier as he went through the course in his imagination also indicate the impact of these methods: the needle

Excerpted and adapted from *CONFIDENCE IN COMMUNICATION: A GUIDE TO ASSERTIVE AND SOCIAL SKILLS*, by Ronald B. Adler. Copyright © 1977 by Holt, Rinehart and Winston. Reprinted by permission of Holt, Rinehart and Winston.

jumped into activity as the athlete began his race, peaking at points that corresponded to the muscle bursts that occur as the contestant hit his jumps and rough spots on the course. One professional skier actually moved his boots while skiing the course in his mind. In the same way you should be sure that your images are almost as realistic as if you were there in person.

You can increase your ability to visualize clearly by picturing each scene as I describe it. Start by seating yourself comfortably in a quiet spot, close your eyes, and listen. Actually let yourself experience the situation. . . .

PRACTICE SCENE 1

You are driving your car on a crowded city freeway. It's midday, and the temperature is in the high eighties. Your windows are open, and you can feel the hot, dirty air blowing around your body. There is a strong smell of exhaust fumes, and the noise of the traffic fills the air around you. The sky overhead is sunny, but there is a brownish tinge of smog around the horizon. Your car radio is tuned to a news broadcast, and the announcer is presently delivering the weather forecast: more sun, heat, and smog.

All around you are autos, trucks, and buses. As they move, the sunlight occasionally reflects off a piece of chrome or paint. You are driving in the fast lane, and the feeling is almost as if you are being swept along by the vehicles around you. At the moment you are being followed by a large truck. Suddenly the driver pulls up to only a few feet behind you and flashes his lights, signaling you to move over or speed up. . . . Simultaneously, the lane to your right opens up and you change lanes and give the driver the go-ahead.

Let yourself relax a moment and prepare to apply the same procedures to Scene 2.

PRACTICE SCENE 2

You have purchased a shirt or blouse from a local merchant, only to find that the size was incorrectly labeled and that the item is consequently too small. You have just walked into the store to return the item. The door closes behind you, and the sounds of the street are replaced by the noise of the cash register and other customers talking with salespeople. Notice the difference between the artificial indoor light and the bright sun outside. Feel the difference in the air temperature against your skin. Look around the store and notice the racks of clothes. What items do you see on each one? What colors and patterns do you see? Feel the weight and notice the texture of the item in your hand. What color and pattern is it?

Now the salesperson walks toward you. What expression is she wearing? How do you feel? Now you hold the item up and state your problem. Listen to the sound of your voice and hear the exact words you use to explain yourself. What tone of voice do you speak with? Are you talking quickly or slowly? What is your posture and facial expression?

Now the clerk responds. Listen to her exact words, and observe the nonverbal messages she sends. How do you feel now? Go ahead and listen to your response, letting the conversation run its course, paying close attention to exactly what takes place and how you react.

Three additional techniques — segmenting the situation, covert modeling, and covert reinforcement — can be useful in covert rehearsal. To segment the situation is to break down the assertive act into small, manageable segments. For example, if you are placing a difficult phone call, the first segment would be to stand up, the second would be to walk toward the phone, the third would be to pick up the phone, the fourth would be to dial the number, etc. It is easier and more productive to master a skill in small steps. You can also increase the frequency with which you practice the skill; approach people with whom you have less difficulty being assertive first and work your way up to more difficult encounters; and attempt more and more challenging situations.

Covert modeling is useful if you have difficulty even *imagining* yourself being assertive. Begin by imagining someone else being assertive in the situation and then practice imagining yourself being assertive in the same situation.

Covert reinforcement is a method of reinforcing assertive covert rehearsals or of rewarding yourself mentally for assertive behavior. First, select a pleasurable scene that gives you a good feeling. Next, imagine yourself enacting the first segment of your assertive situation. Then say the word "reinforce" to yourself, and immediately imagine your pleasurable scene. Practice this segment ten times and move on to the next segment until you have practiced the entire scene.

After you have covertly practiced each segment of the assertive behavior you want to practice ... think about how you performed. Decide which behaviors you handled especially well, and which one or two could use improvement. After you have an idea of how you could handle yourself better, review the scene mentally again with the added improvement and repeat the evaluation process. Finally, when you are ready, go ahead and practice the scene with overt behavior rehearsal.

If this process of covert rehearsal still sounds far-fetched, consider how often we use it in everyday thoughts, though usually for destructive ends. How many times have you failed in some important way — perhaps a job interview, a social occasion, or an athletic contest — by predicting that it would be a disaster. Catastrophic expectations such as these have a way of becoming self-fulfilling prophecies by obsessing you to such a degree that you end up behaving in the horrible way you anticipated. Covert rehearsal uses the same principles to achieve positive ends, helping you to visualize yourself behaving successfully.

SUMMARY

... Behavior rehearsal can be conducted either overtly or covertly. In the latter case ... the target scene is reviewed in the communicator's mind instead of being acted out publicly. Covert rehearsal involves practicing assertion privately through visualization. The method has been proven quite effective, especially when rehearsing situations with higher anxiety levels or when rehearsing alone. Three helpful and compatible techniques are segmenting the situation, covert modeling, and covert reinforcement. Once a situation has been practiced covertly, it should be practiced overtly before attempting to carry it out in real life.

REFERENCE

Suinn, R. Body thinking: Psychology for Olympic champs. *Psychology Today*, 1976, *10*(2), 38-43.

Coping with Stress

A frequent complaint of nonassertive people is that they feel they are "too emotional," or they "can't control" their emotions. In distressing social situations their emotions take control. But at one time or another, all of us must deal with stress. To become a person who can act assertively when you want to, you must learn how to cope successfully with conflicts. There are some specific techniques for learning to relax and for desensitizing yourself to anxiety which help most people to improve their ability to handle tense situations.

HOW EMOTIONS CAN KEEP YOU FROM BECOMING ASSERTIVE

A learned emotional reaction (such as social anxiety) has four aspects: the environmental situation, your bodily reactions, your overt (observable) behavior, and your covert (silent) behavior. For example, suppose the *situation* is your Downer insulting you; your *physical reactions* may be shallow breathing and heart palpitations, your *overt behavior* may be withdrawn shyness, and your *covert behavior* may be saying sentences to yourself such as "I can't stand it" or "I'm too weak to talk back" or "I'm a coward," or seeing yourself as a helpless victim submitting to an all-powerful person. (See Figure 8.)

The important thing to keep in mind is that your emotional reaction is a learned reaction — the current situation provokes this reaction because it resembles a past situation where you felt anxiety or humiliation. Old emotional reactions, partly revived from memory, cause mild physiological reactions along with an "interpretation" of what is happening, what you predict will happen, and how you feel about it. This interpretation — which depends largely upon your emotional training and emotional habits — shapes the be-

Excerpted and adapted from pp. 46-52 of ASSERTING YOURSELF: A PRACTICAL GUIDE FOR POSITIVE CHANGE, by Sharon A. Bower and Gordon Bower, copyright © 1976, by permission of Addison-Wesley Publishing Company, Inc., Reading, Mass.

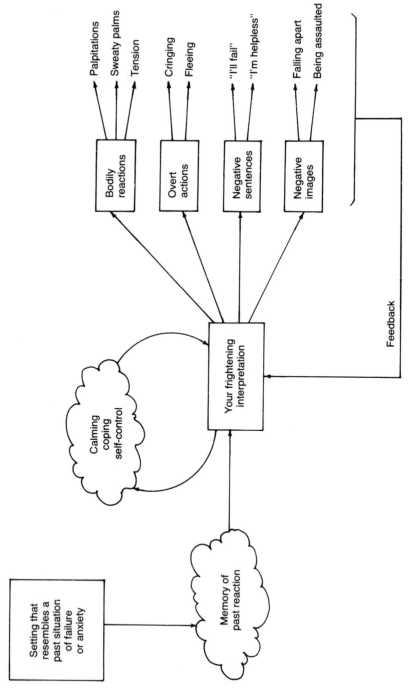

Figure 8. Dynamics of a Learned Emotional Reaction

havior you then display. You may feel physical signs of tension. You may adopt a cringing posture. You may say negative sentences to yourself ("I'm weak, helpless, exhausted, stupid"). You may be assailed by negative images — of some metaphor to the current scene ("I see myself as a sniveling puppy trying to stand up to an enormous bulldog"), or of a feared outcome or consequence of the current scene ("I see the person screaming at me, then leaving for good"), or of yourself ("I'm a weakling") and the other person ("He has nerves of cold steel"). Note that there is a feedback loop from these emotional behaviors to the interpretation. For example, in some cases noticing signs of slight tension can cause even further anxiety in an accelerating spiral.

How, then, can you change your emotional reactions? You do it by practicing certain coping skills. . . .

Before describing a technique for controlling tension let's look more closely at what happens to you when you experience an emotion. . . . Examine your physical signs of arousal as you picture your problem scene. You may note . . . physical signs . . . such as blushing, pounding heart, tremors, and feelings of weakness.

Since you were remembering yourself in a moderately threatening scene, you probably noticed . . . a few signs, indicating the mild tension and other reactions that most people feel when anxious. The important point is not to overreact and interpret any of these signs as an emotional attack. A blush does not mean you are hopelessly shy, nor a dry mouth that you can't speak up forcefully. Emotions are not debilitating *per se* — the same physical signs are associated with joy or delight, yet ecstatic people have no trouble speaking out.

We are familiar with occasions when people blow things up out of proportion. It happens when your physical reactions and your negative self-statements get into a feedback loop so that each system fuels the fire of the other one. . . .

Effective people attribute the tension to the slightly stressful situation and carry on, knowing they will be all right once underway. But others tell horror stories to themselves, about their disabilities and likely failure. These increase . . . tension and exaggerate the physical signs of arousal. Seeing these increased physical signs sets off another cycle of increasingly frightening self-evaluations, ending with the strong urge to flee from the situation. . . .

LEARNING TO RELAX

One good way to keep your emotions from getting the best of you and to relieve the tensions of a stressful life style is a process known as progressive relaxation.[1]

---

[1] A standard reference is Edmund Jacobsen, *Progressive Relaxation*. Chicago: University of Chicago Press, 1938.

We would all like to be able to turn off our inner tensions at the end of the day. The search for a method to overcome nervous tension has been pursued by doctors, scientists, and common folk. If you ask people how they control tension, you will hear a smorgasbord of home recipes: hot baths, massage, diets, hot milk, exercise, reading, transcendental meditation, television, hypnotic suggestion, and drugs. . . .

Muscle relaxation controls emotions to a great degree. . . . By relaxing muscles which tense up during negative thinking, it is possible to turn off the worrying brain that prevents you from enjoying life.

Learning to relax takes practice. But after devoting 30 minutes a day for at least a month to practicing, most people do learn to progressively relax their muscles. And the practice really pays off. . . . One individual put it this way: "Learning to control my tensions by relaxing has helped me enjoy the moment I'm living now, instead of dreading the moment I think I have to live tomorrow."

How to Practice Relaxation

Muscle tension is specific and physical. Experience it so you can learn to control it. Try this experiment: make a tight fist and notice the feelings from the fist muscles as you tense them. That is the sensation of tension. Now, let your fist become limp: the feeling as your hand loosens is relaxation. Now try to produce the same experiences with other parts of your body. For instance, make as big a smile as you can, squinching up your face — feel the tension in the jaw, lips, and throat. Now, let it go and feel the sensations of relaxation. . . .

You can learn to identify the different sensations of tension and relaxation in various muscle groups. With repeated practice sessions, you can learn to monitor, identify, and control even small tensions such as those in the neck, eye muscles, or forehead. As you monitor, you can catch yourself at almost any moment during your workday with some excess tension; once you detect a tense muscle, you can deliberately let it go and experience relaxation. For example, many people have unnoticed tension in their eyes (squinting), or in their forehead (wrinkling of forehead when concentrating), in their shoulder muscles while they are writing or reading, or in their neck muscles when walking or sitting. Your goal is to detect and eliminate such muscle knots. You can record progressive relaxation instructions on a tape recorder, then play the tape whenever you want to practice. . . . If hearing yourself on the tape is bothersome, ask a friend to record the exercise. When you are ready to practice, prepare the setting. Select a quiet room, darken it, take the telephone off the hook, and lie down on a sofa, bed, or floor. If you feel cold, put a light blanket over you. Lie down, turn on the tape recorder, close your eyes, and follow the instructions.

Relaxation is pleasurable, so try to practice it once or twice a day for 30 minutes. Continue the exercises for as many weeks as you like. Think of the relaxation exercises as you would think of jogging or physical exercise: it is generally worth working at it whenever you can — even for a period less than 30 minutes. The instructions can be abbreviated for a 10 or 15 minute relaxation session.

A good way to help bring instant relaxation into your daily life is to associate a verbal command with the reaction of going into the relaxed state. As you listen to the tape and feel yourself becoming more relaxed, take a big breath, then exhale and silently say the magic words, "Relax. Let go and relax!" Your calming words will become associated with the physical state of deep relaxation. Then you can start to practice relaxing your muscles throughout your whole working day. As you sit at work, at lectures, in your car, at the movies, as you walk or stand, attend periodically to your physical state. If you do detect some tense muscles, take a deep breath, exhale and say to yourself, "Relax! Let go and relax!" and repeat it over several times. Try in those moments of attention to place yourself into your accustomed state of deep relaxation while keeping your eyes open. Be on the lookout for areas of subtle muscle tension; these are focal points for emotional tension. You can feel a lot freer, happier, and less high-strung and nervous if you can detect and eliminate these pockets of muscle tension.

Covert Rehearsal/Reinforcement: Preparing for Difficult Assertion Situations

Goals

I. To reduce anxiety about difficult assertion situations.
II. To practice assertion using a low-threat technique.

Group Size

No more than thirty participants.

Time Required

One hour.

Materials

Blank paper and a pencil for each participant.

Process

I. The facilitator announces the goals of the activity, gives blank paper and a pencil to each participant, and instructs participants to make lists of things that give them pleasure or make them "feel good." These can be places, sights, sounds, smells, or a combination, such as a soft rain on a warm afternoon, running on the beach, the smell of new books, or the sound of children laughing. (Five to ten minutes.)

II. Participants are told to take turns reading two or three of their favorite items off their lists. They are encouraged to add any new items they think of as the other participants read their lists.

III. Participants are told to put their lists aside, then to select situations in which it is particularly difficult to be assertive, but in which they wish to be assertive and are willing to accept the consequences of being so. (Five minutes.)

IV. The facilitator asks the participants each to choose a partner, and with the partner's help to break their situations down into very small segments. For example, if the situation is to place a difficult phone call, the first segment might be to stand up, the second to walk toward the phone, the third to pick up the phone, the fourth to dial the number, etc. (Ten minutes.)

V. Participants are to take turns closing their eyes while their partners read the first action segment of the situation aloud. The participant whose eyes are closed is to imagine himself or herself completing the first action segment in the chosen situation (covert rehearsal) and is to follow that image immediately by remembering one of the items from his or her list of pleasures (covert reinforcement). The partner should then read the next action segment in the chosen situation; again the participant is to imagine the segment and follow that image immediately with an image from his or her pleasures list. If at any point the participant cannot imagine him- or herself performing a segment of the action sequence, he or she may imagine someone else being assertive in the action segment (covert modeling). (Five to seven minutes.)

VI. The facilitator informs participants that they are to exchange roles with their partners once they have practiced the entire chosen situation. The new participant then practices his or her own sequence.

VII. The facilitator answers any questions participants may have, explains that this technique may be used to rehearse any difficult assertion situations as a "warm up" to behavioral rehearsal, and says that the principle of covert reinforcement can be used in an assertion situation, or after one has been assertive, to reinforce oneself.

VIII. The facilitator asks participants to discuss with their partners specific ways in which they might use this technique in a back-home situation and then leads the group in a discussion of some of these back-home applications.

Relaxation: Calibrating and Reducing Anxiety

Goals

   I. To practice calibrating anxiety levels.
  II. To practice relaxation techniques useful in reducing anxiety.

Group Size

No more than thirty participants.

Time Required

Forty-five minutes to one hour.

Materials

Blank paper and a pencil for each participant.

Process

   I. The facilitator announces the goals of the activity, gives each participant blank paper and a pencil, and asks each participant to imagine a situation in which he or she has the least anxiety or discomfort possible, to make a note of that calm scene or situation at the bottom of the paper, and to mark a zero beside that situation.

II. The facilitator then tells each participant to imagine a situation in which he or she has the greatest anxiety or discomfort possible, to make a note of that situation at the top of the paper, and to mark a 100 beside that situation.

III. The facilitator tells each participant to choose a situation in which being assertive produces a great deal of anxiety and to assign a number between 0 and 100 to the situation corresponding to their discomfort or anxiety level in that situation, using the scale established by the other two situations noted on paper (SUDS).

IV. The facilitator tells participants to share their calm scenes with the group and to note any calm scenes others mention that are also calm scenes for them.

V. The facilitator answers any questions that have come up and leads a discussion of the experience thus far.

VI. Participants are told to assume comfortable positions in chairs or on the floor. The facilitator then leads them in tightening (5-7 seconds) and then releasing or relaxing (20-30 seconds) each set of muscles in the body, one by one, following the instructions in Step VII. The tightening and relaxation of each set of muscles should be repeated from two to five times. As participants develop their relaxation skills, the muscles can be tightened and relaxed by major groups. The facilitator may wish to use the following outline of major muscle groups as a guide:

Major Group I
a. dominant hand and forearm
b. dominant biceps
c. nondominant hand and forearm
d. nondominant biceps

Major Group II
a. forehead
b. cheeks and nose
c. jaws
d. lips and tongue
e. neck and throat

Major Group III
a. shoulders and upper back
b. chest
c. stomach

Major Group IV
a. thighs and buttocks

      b. calves

      c. feet

VII. The facilitator leads the group through each set of muscles as follows:

Tense the muscles in your hand and forearm and hold this position for a few seconds . . . Now relax the muscles and exhale smoothly and evenly while thinking, "I am calm and relaxed" or "relax" . . . Imagine your calm scene . . . Now repeat this sequence . . . Now tense your biceps . . . Hold this position for a few seconds . . . Now relax the muscles and repeat, "I am calm and relaxed" or "relax" while imagining your calm scene . . . Continue to breathe smoothly and evenly. (Twenty to thirty minutes.)

VIII. The facilitator asks participants to imagine themselves being assertive in their chosen anxiety-producing situations and to monitor their anxiety levels by assigning numbers from their anxiety scale to the discomfort felt.

IX. Participants are instructed to work toward keeping their anxiety at a lower level by following any rise in discomfort or anxiety with thoughts of their calm scene, the words "relax" or "I am calm and relaxed," or body tensing and relaxing accompanied by smooth and even breathing. (Usually, the words and the calm scene are not strongly enough associated with the muscle relaxation to induce immediate results until the participants have practiced regularly over a period of time, using progressively larger groupings of muscles. Thus, beginners may have to use the tense-and-relax method to lower their anxiety-scale levels in the situation.)

X. The facilitator leads a discussion of the experience in the large group and asks for reports of changes in discomfort level and methods used to induce those changes.

XI. Participants are asked to discuss specific ways in which they intend to use the techniques they have learned to increase their ability to be assertive in difficult situations. (The facilitator may wish to suggest that one way to begin building this skill is to learn to monitor and assign anxiety-scale numbers to discomfort levels in various day-to-day situations and to practice relaxation techniques on a regular basis.)

Variations

I. In Step VII the facilitator can have participants practice relaxing by tensing their bodies into tight balls, then stretching them out as far as possible, and finally simply sinking limply into a chair or onto the floor.

II. The relaxation techniques can be used before beginning practice of a difficult scene, or to monitor anxiety levels and keep relaxed while practicing.

III. The discomfort-level scale can be used to help participants construct a hierarchy of assertive situations and to practice their skills by beginning with a situation that has a low anxiety level and gradually moving up the hierarchy.

IV. In an ongoing workshop, this structured experience may be practiced in segments, adding a new segment with each practice. (Segment one: Steps I through V; Segment two: Steps VI and VII; Segment three: Steps VIII through XI.) Any one of these segments can also be run separately, providing participants already have the necessary skills.

V. The participant may wish to make a tape recording of Step VII in order to practice with the relaxation guidelines at home.

VI. As participants become more skilled at relaxing, they may be instructed to pay attention to particular muscles or muscle groups that they are tensing in Step VIII, and to use this information to selectively focus on and relax these muscles in Step IX.

PART II

FORMS
FOR
ASSESSMENT

Introduction to Part II

The three assessment forms included in this section are designed to help assertion clients assess their own areas of difficulty and to aid trainers in focusing the training.

The "Assertion Vignettes Matrix Form" requires participants to visualize each of sixteen assertive situations and to rate their anxiety about each one. The form is designed to separate the participants' assertion difficulties into categories. It was developed by Cotler and Guerra (1976), based on their findings that most assertive situations can be placed into one of four categories (Cotler & Guerra, 1976, pp. 9-10): "social approach or request responses with strangers and situational relationships, social approach or request responses with friends and intimate relationships, protective or refusal responses with strangers and situational relationships, and protective or refusal responses with friends and intimate relationships" and that most participants' difficulties fall into one or two of the four categories.[1]

By using the "Assertion Vignettes Matrix Form," participants are usually able to narrow their focus to the category in which they need the most practice. Participants may wish to verify that this is truly the category needing work by focusing on two or three assertion situations they are currently having difficulty with and noting in which one of the four categories those situations fall or by using the "Sixty Assertive Situations" form.

On this form participants rate themselves as usually assertive, nonassertive, or aggressive in each of the "Sixty Assertive Situations" and select five of the situations on which to work in the training session. Space is provided to record specific data concerning each of the five situations. The form contains seven special application categories that can be used to determine areas of general interest in the group or what special application skills to work on. "Sixty Assertive Situations" also can be used in conjunction with the "Assertion Vignettes Matrix Form" because it is divided equally into approach and response items that can be applied either to friends or strangers.

---

[1]Various other ways of categorizing assertive situations are available in the literature.

The "Assertion Skills Check List" form is designed to assess participants' skills in ten areas. Participants determine their desire to do more work in specific skill areas versus their satisfaction with their levels of competence in the areas. Each skill area is subdivided into: (a) knowledge and understanding of the principles involved; (b) skill level; and (c) actual use or application of the skill in one's own life. The "Assertion Skills Check List" can be very helpful to the facilitator who is designing an event, especially if he or she is running an advanced assertion workshop and is unsure about which areas to concentrate on.

Two other assessment forms are included in this book: the "Assertion Response Discrimination Index" (Chapter One) helps participants discriminate among assertive, nonassertive, and aggressive verbal responses, and the "Assertion Self-Assessment Table" (pp. 318) serves approximately the same purpose as the "Sixty Assertive Situations" form.

A number of assessment forms are available in the literature: "Assertiveness Inventory" (Adler, 1977, pp. 9-12), "Assertiveness Inventory" (Alberti & Emmons, 1974, p. 117), "Female Assertiveness Inventory" (Baer, 1976, pp. 69-71), "Questionnaire: Blocks to Acting Assertively" (Bloom, Coburn, & Pearlman, 1975, pp. 131-135), "Assertion Inventory" (Gambrill & Richey, 1976, pp. 158-159), "Check List of Possible Topics for Your Assertion Training Group" (Lange & Jakubowski, 1976, pp. 218-220), "Assertiveness Inventory" (Liberman, King, DeRisi, & McCann, 1975, pp. 146-149), "Assertive Behavior Assessment for Women" (Osborn & Harris, 1975, pp. 193-196), and "AQ Test" (Phelps & Austin, 1975, pp. 5-8). Many are similar in that they list a series of assertive situations that the client must rate in terms of his or her own assertion ability in various situations. A number of assessment forms are cited in the review of specific books in Part IV of this text. Other assessment forms, some especially useful for screening purposes, are described in "Screening Procedures" and "Assessment Procedures for Assertive Behavior" in Part III, Chapter Twelve.

Assessment forms may be used before, during, or after assertion training — before to define assertion problems and areas of difficulty; during to monitor progress, develop skills, and identify assertive situations to practice; after to determine what changes have occurred and in what areas participants need further work.

Assertion is built on incremental learning and experiences of success. Participants should not begin practice with very difficult situations; less difficult situations chosen should still be challenging, however. It is more difficult to build confidence after a large failure than to build confidence slowly with successful experiences.

If a participant checks *all* situations on a form as difficult or responds nonassertively or aggressively in all situations, the trainer should explore the possibility that this person has more than situational assertion needs and that he or she may need more intensive help than can be provided in the training setting.

Assertion Vignettes Matrix Form

The following vignettes are grouped according to four categories of assertion. As you read each situation, visualize yourself in the situation, visualize handling the situation in what you feel is an appropriate assertive manner, and decide if you are experiencing high, medium, or low levels of difficulty (or anxiety) during this visualization process. Then place the appropriate letter next to each situation indicating whether you would experience high anxiety or difficulty (H), medium anxiety or difficulty (M), or low anxiety or difficulty (L) in the situation described.

   I. Initiation, approach or request situations with strangers, passing acquaintances, or work relations.

_____ A. *Eye Contact*

   You are beginning to talk with someone of the opposite sex whom you do not know very well. You are standing at a comfortable distance from the other person, and you are looking directly at the person's eyes as you begin to talk. Visualize that scene. Now visualize the same scene again, but this time visualize yourself smiling, if you did not do so before, or visualize yourself keeping a straight face if you were smiling in the first scene.

_____ B. *Self-Praise*

   Think of four positive qualities you have. Now visualize yourself describing these qualities to someone you are just meeting for the first time.

_____ C. *Introducing Yourself*

   You are in a group meeting where most people do not know one

Adapted from pp. 9-22 of *Assertion Training*, by Sherwin B. Cotler and Julio J. Guerra. Champaign, IL: Research Press, 1976. Used with permission.

another. You are sitting in your chair and the leader of the group asks each of you to tell the others what you do for a living and to describe some of your hobbies. Visualize that scene.

Now visualize that you are asked to do the same thing, but this time you are asked to stand and come to the front of the room before making your introduction. As you visualize this scene, imagine that the person one seat away from you is walking toward the front of the room and that it will soon be your turn. Then imagine that this person finishes with his introduction and it is now your turn to stand up, go to the front of the room, and address the audience.

_____ D. *Conversations*

You are at a party and there are several people present whom you have never met before. You notice one person to whom you are attracted, and you decide you would like to get to know this person better. You walk over to the individual, introduce yourself, and begin talking. Visualize yourself in this situation and picture what happens.

Decide if you knew how to start the conversation and reflect on how anxious you were in visualizing this scene.

Now visualize that the person you are interested in meeting is standing and talking with a small group of people. Your task is now to visualize yourself walking over to this group and becoming a part of the conversation so that you can get to know the person better.

Now imagine that you are talking with someone at this party when you notice an old friend come in whom you have not seen for a long time. You want to terminate your present conversation and go over and see your old friend. Imagine yourself terminating the conversation and going over to meet your friend.

II. Initiation, approach or request situations with friends or persons close to you.

_____ E. *Compliments* (Part I)

Visualize yourself complimenting a friend. The compliment can be on the way the friend is dressed or some other nice thing you have observed him/her doing.

_____ F. *The Neighbor* (Part I)

You are doing some work around your house and you realize that you are missing a tool to complete your job. You do not want to buy it at a store right now, and you remember that your neighbor has that tool. Visualize that you are now at your neighbor's house asking for the temporary loan of the tool.

_____G. *The Neighbor* (Part II)

Now assume that you are the neighbor who loaned the requested tool. However, several weeks have gone by, and you now need the tool yourself. You go next door and ask that the tool be returned. Visualize that scene.

_____H. *The Nonverbal "Warm Fuzzy"*

Imagine yourself sitting next to a friend toward whom you feel very positive. Without using any words, convey a warm positive feeling to this individual.

III. Response, acceptance, or refusal situations with strangers, passing acquaintances, or work relations.

_____I. *In the Restaurant*

You are in an expensive restaurant and have ordered a steak cooked the way you like it best. However, when the steak is brought to your table, it is not cooked the way you ordered it. You therefore refuse the steak and state that you would like to have it cooked the way you originally asked.

Did you know how to assertively refuse the improperly prepared steak and remind the waiter/waitress of your original order? Is your anxiety very high at this point?

_____J. *Salesperson*

Picture yourself answering your front door one evening and being confronted by a rather pushy salesperson who is trying to sell you a product. Although this is a product that you have purchased in the past (e.g., magazines, cookies, insurance), you do not have the interest or money to buy this product now. Assume that you cannot just shut the door — instead you must communicate to the person by what you say and how you say it that you are not interested.

_____K. *Refusing to Donate*

While you are at work one afternoon, a secretary from one of the other offices whom you do not know very well approaches you. The secretary tells you that one of your co-workers has just had a baby. The secretary is taking up a collection of $2 from each person in order to buy a nice gift for the new mother and baby. Your working interactions with the new mother have been very unpleasant over the past year. Reflecting on this for a moment, you feel that you do not wish to contribute to this collection fund, even though you can well afford the $2. Your task is to politely refuse the request of the secretary who is standing before you and knows nothing about your previous interactions and feelings concerning the new mother.

_____L. *Anger*

You are busy at work when an employee from another department comes in, screams at you in a very angry voice, and calls you names such as "stupid" and "incompetent." The person accuses you of making an error that proved to be very costly and embarrassing to him/her. At this point, you are not even certain if you made the error, but it is extremely difficult to tell just what happened as long as the person is screaming and carrying on in this manner. Visualize how you would handle this situation, what you would do and say to the other person, and your anxiety level.

IV. Response, acceptance, or refusal situations with friends or persons close to you.

_____M. *Compliments* (Part II)

Imagine that a friend is complimenting you. How to you respond to this praise?

_____N. *Confidential Information*

You have been talking with someone who has given you some confidential information about Pat, a friend of yours with whom you work. Before this information was given, you agreed to keep the information confidential until the person could personally talk with Pat and discuss the matter. It is now the next day and Pat approaches you. Pat knows that you have discussed the situation with the other person and wants to know what was said. Your task is to try to keep this information confidential, as you have agreed to do. Pat is making statements such as "If I am really your friend, you will tell me what was said," "I have told you information like this before under similar circumstances," and "You really are against me, too." Visualize how you would handle this situation.

_____O. *Criticism*

Picture yourself being confronted by a friend or relative who seems to enjoy criticizing people — especially you. You have concluded that this particular individual is not really trying to help you, but, instead, engages in this activity to obtain a one-up position. You have told this individual before that you do not appreciate this behavior and that you would like it stopped. However, the person is now at it again. Visualize the situation. Did you know how to verbally stop the criticism? Was your anxiety very high?

_____P. *The Party*

There is a party tonight that you would like to attend, but you know that you cannot because you have work you must do at home. Your friends call and tell you the party will be no fun without you. Your task is to refuse the invitation. Visualize how you would handle the situation.

ASSERTION VIGNETTES MATRIX RESPONSE SHEET

Directions: Count the number of items marked high (H), medium (M), or low (L) within Sections I, II, III, and IV of the Assertion Vignettes Matrix Form and enter the totals in the appropriate blanks below. Those sections in which the greatest number of high or medium scores appear indicate the areas in which it is probably especially difficult for you to be assertive.

	Dealing with a stranger, acquaintance, or work relationship	Dealing with a friend or person close to you
An initiation, approach, or request situation	Section I (A,B,C,D) High _____ Medium _____ Low _____	Section II (E,F,G,H) High _____ Medium _____ Low _____
A response, acceptance, or refusal situation	Section III (I,J,K,L) High _____ Medium _____ Low _____	Section IV (M,N,O,P) High _____ Medium _____ Low _____

Sixty Assertive Situations

The purpose of this form is to help you determine some specific situations in which you would like to be more assertive.

PART I

Directions: The following sixty items describe some typical assertion situations. Indicate with a check mark in the appropriate blank whether you would rate your usual response to each item as nonassertive, assertive, or aggressive.

If you consider your usual response to a situation to be somewhat nonassertive *and* somewhat assertive or somewhat assertive *and* somewhat aggressive, place the check mark in the space *between* the appropriate columns.

If you are *usually* assertive in a particular situation, but are nonassertive or aggressive in the *same* situation with a *specific person, type of person, topic*, or *a particular setting*, mark nonassertive or aggressive for that item.

If you consider yourself to be assertive in every situation described, mark those in which it is more difficult for you to be assertive or add some situations in which you are *not* usually assertive to the list.

Nonassertive **Assertive** **Aggressive**

—————————— 1. You give a compliment.

—————————— 2. You tell a person that you like or are attracted to him/her.

—————————— 3. You tell a person you love him/her.

Many of these situations are common in the literature, e.g., see Gambrill & Richey (1976).

Nonassertive

Assertive

Aggressive

——— ——— ——— 4. You tell someone good things about you or your accomplishments.

——— ——— ——— 5. You ask for clarification of something you do not know or understand.

——— ——— ——— 6. You admit that you are nervous or afraid.

——— ——— ——— 7. You admit that you are wrong.

——— ——— ——— 8. You express your opinions or feelings when they are different from others being expressed.

——— ——— ——— 9. You interact with authority figures or people important to you.

——— ——— ——— 10. You give appropriate criticism.

——— ——— ——— 11. You approach and join a conversation.

——— ——— ——— 12. You change the topic of a conversation.

——— ——— ——— 13. You leave a group conversation.

——— ——— ——— 14. You go somewhere alone (movie, party, etc.) or are the only "single" in a group.

——— ——— ——— 15. You tell your partner in a sexual relationship how you like and do not like to be touched.

——— ——— ——— 16. You ask a person to do something with you (go to a movie, go for a walk, come over for coffee).

——— ——— ——— 17. You ask for a date.

——— ——— ——— 18. You end an unsatisfactory relationship.

——— ——— ——— 19. You ask for information you need from professionals or strangers.

——— ——— ——— 20. You ask for help from a salesperson.

——— ——— ——— 21. You ask for a better table in a restaurant.

——— ——— ——— 22. You ask a doctor what is wrong with you and why.

——— ——— ——— 23. You return unacceptable merchandise.

——— ——— ——— 24. You ask a favor.

——— ——— ——— 25. You ask for help or advice.

Nonassertive

Assertive

Aggressive

___ ___ ___ 26. You ask to borrow something.

___ ___ ___ 27. You ask someone to return something you have loaned.

___ ___ ___ 28. You ask someone not to smoke.

___ ___ ___ 29. You ask for a raise.

___ ___ ___ 30. You apply for a job.

___ ___ ___ 31. You receive a gift.

___ ___ ___ 32. You accept a compliment.

___ ___ ___ 33. You resist an unfair demand.

___ ___ ___ 34. You respond to a personal question.

___ ___ ___ 35. You respond to an unfair remark or criticism.

___ ___ ___ 36. You respond to a sexist or racist remark.

___ ___ ___ 37. You stand up for yourself when attacked.

___ ___ ___ 38. You tell a person he/she is doing something that bothers or offends you.

___ ___ ___ 39. You respond when someone takes credit for something you did.

___ ___ ___ 40. You receive justified criticism.

___ ___ ___ 41. You tell a person who has called that you are too busy to talk.

___ ___ ___ 42. You interrupt or terminate a conversation with a wordy person.

___ ___ ___ 43. You respond to someone who has interrupted you.

___ ___ ___ 44. You accept an invitation to a party or get-together.

___ ___ ___ 45. You refuse an invitation to a party or get-together.

___ ___ ___ 46. You refuse a date.

___ ___ ___ 47. You refuse sexual advances from someone with whom you do not want such a relationship.

___ ___ ___ 48. You refuse a salesperson's offer of help.

___ ___ ___ 49. You refuse to buy from a salesperson who pressures you.

Nonassertive **Assertive** **Aggressive**

———— ———— ———— 50. You send back unacceptable food in a restaurant.

———— ———— ———— 51. You accept a free demonstration of an appliance in your home.

———— ———— ———— 52. You refuse to pay for services for which you did not contract.

———— ———— ———— 53. You object when someone cuts in front of you in line.

———— ———— ———— 54. You ask people in a theater to stop talking, kicking your chair, etc.

———— ———— ———— 55. You do not have the time to give a person the help or advice he/she is asking for and tell the person so.

———— ———— ———— 56. You refuse a request.

———— ———— ———— 57. You refuse to loan your car, money, books, etc.

———— ———— ———— 58. You refuse to contribute to a worthy cause.

———— ———— ———— 59. You respond to a fellow employee's idea in a meeting.

———— ———— ———— 60. You refuse to grant a raise, time off, etc., to an employee.

PART II

Directions: In the spaces provided below, enter specific information about five of the situations you just rated with which you have *moderate* difficulty. (Do not choose the most difficult situations.)

Item Number	Specific Person or Type of Person Involved	Specific Setting, Topic, or Emotion Involved	Other Specific Information
_____	_____	_____	_____
_____	_____	_____	_____
_____	_____	_____	_____
_____	_____	_____	_____
_____	_____	_____	_____

Note: "Sixty Assertive Situations" can be used to classify problem situations into the following categories:

General Category

Initiation, Approach, or Request .... Items 1-30

Response, Acceptance, or Refusal .... Items 31-60

Specific Category

Positive Assertion .... Items 1-4, 31-32

Vulnerability/Self-Respect .... Items 5-10, 33-40

Conversation .... Items 11-13, 41-43

Friendship/Relationship .... Items 14-18, 44-47

Consumer .... Items 19-23, 48-54

Requests/Responses .... Items 24-28, 55-58

Job .... Items 29-30, 59-60

Assertion Skills Check List

The following check list will help you to focus on assertion skills you would like to build at this time. Within each skill area, you will have the opportunity to indicate your interest in (1) acquiring more knowledge and understanding of the principles involved, (2) acquiring more skill, or (3) actually using or applying the skills in your own life.

Directions: Place the appropriate letter in the blank space in front of each item to indicate whether you:

A. Definitely want more work in the area

B. Could use more work in the area if time permitted

C. Are satisfied with your level of development in the area

When you have finished, transfer the letter scores to the appropriate boxes below. The results will show in which areas you desire more work and which you consider to be sufficiently developed.

	Theory	Self-Confidence	Identification of Rights	Confidence in Rights	Verbal Assertion	Nonverbal Assertion	Cognitive Assertion	Integration	Special Application Areas	Special Needs
1. Knowledge and Understanding										
2. Skill										
3. Application										

THEORY

_____ 1. I know the rationale for assertion and understand the basic assertion concepts.

_____ 2. I am able to apply the basic assertion concepts and rationale to assertive situations and to discriminate among nonassertive, assertive, and aggressive responses.

_____ 3. I apply the basic assertion concepts and rationale and discriminate among nonassertive, assertive, and aggressive responses in appropriate real-life situations.

SELF-CONFIDENCE

_____ 1. I know about self-confidence and understand how to build it.

_____ 2. I believe in my own self-worth and am able to raise my confidence when necessary.

_____ 3. I use my skills to maintain and raise my self-confidence in my own life.

IDENTIFICATION OF RIGHTS

_____ 1. I know what the basic human rights are and understand how to identify them in situations.

_____ 2. I am able to identify the basic human rights involved in situations.

_____ 3. I use my skills to identify the basic human rights in appropriate real-life situations.

CONFIDENCE IN RIGHTS

_____ 1. I know the philosophy underlying basic human rights and understand how to build confidence in these rights.

_____ 2. I believe that basic human rights belong to me, as well as to other people, and am able to raise my confidence in these rights when necessary.

_____ 3. I use my skills to maintain and raise my confidence in basic human rights in my own life.

VERBAL ASSERTION

_____ 1. I know what verbal assertion is and understand how to be verbally assertive.

_____ 2. I am able to develop and use assertive statements.

_____ 3. I develop and use assertive statements in appropriate real-life situations.

NONVERBAL ASSERTION

_____ 1. I know what nonverbal assertion is and understand how to be nonverbally assertive.

_____ 2. I am able to identify and demonstrate assertive body posture and other assertive nonverbal behaviors (tone of voice, facial expression, etc.) in assertive situations.

_____ 3. I use assertive body posture and other assertive nonverbal behaviors in appropriate real-life situations.

COGNITIVE ASSERTION

_____ 1. I know what cognitive assertion is and understand how to be cognitively assertive.

_____ 2. I am able to formulate and think positive assertive thoughts in appropriate situations.

_____ 3. I formulate and think assertive thoughts in appropriate real-life situations.

INTEGRATION

_____ 1. I know and understand how to integrate verbal, nonverbal, and cognitive assertion skills.

_____ 2. I am able to use verbal, nonverbal, and cognitive assertion skills simultaneously.

_____ 3. I use verbal, nonverbal, and cognitive assertion skills simultaneously in appropriate real-life situations.

SPECIAL APPLICATION AREAS

_____ 1. I know and understand how to apply accessory principles in specific situational areas (requests, anger, sensuality, criticism, etc.).

_____ 2. I am able to use accessory skills appropriate for dealing with specific situational areas.

_____ 3. I use accessory skills for specific situational areas in appropriate real-life situations.

SPECIAL NEEDS

_____ 1. I know and understand how to reduce my anxiety in assertive situations.

_____ 2. I am able to reduce my anxiety when necessary and appropriate in assertive situations.

_____ 3. I use my anxiety-reduction skills when necessary and appropriate in real-life situations.

PART III

PROFESSIONAL CONSIDERATIONS

Introduction to Part III

Chapter Eleven presents "Workshop Design Considerations" in detail. Participant entry needs, group size, length and goals of programs, group composition, and implementation guidelines are discussed, as well as design components to include in a training program. Sample designs for one-hour, three-hour, one-day, three-day, and advanced two-day events are presented, utilizing lecturettes, structured experiences, and assessment forms from Parts I and II of the book.

The four articles in Chapter Twelve are intended to give the assertion trainer an understanding of some current theoretical, research, assessment, and ethical positions.

Alberti and Emmons (1974) wrote the first book devoted entirely to assertion training. In the article reprinted here, "Issues in Assertive Behavior Training," written in 1977, Alberti "calls into question some earlier assumptions," briefly explores the history of assertion theory and research, and discusses current work and the state of the art. He then turns to current issues in assertion practice and ethics, providing a concise and useful fish-eye view of assertion today.

Arthur Lange and Patricia Jakubowski have teamed up on several significant projects recently. Their books, reviewed in Part IV of this book, were published in 1976 and 1978, and an assertion film featuring presentations by both was released in 1978. They are the authors of two articles included here: "Ethical Considerations" and "Screening Procedures." The first explores the ethical responsibilities of trainers in regard to their own skill level, advertising and screening procedures, training procedures, research conducted with assertion training groups, and transfer of assertion skills to the back-home setting. "Screening Procedures" is an in-depth discussion of screening techniques, criteria, issues, and difficulties.

John and Merna Galassi, both actively involved in the assertion field, put together the comprehensive and useful "Assessment Procedures for Assertive

Behavior." The Galassis present a short review of the state of the art; list, categorize, and discuss the potential uses and drawbacks of various assertion instruments for use before, during, or after assertion training; and describe their own "Assertion Self-Assessment Table," a procedure for constructing one's own inventory.

A rapidly growing field, assertion is finding application potential and client enthusiasm in many settings. Issues have surfaced faster than the theoretical base has grown; practice continues to outpace research. In this very active field, Alberti, Lange, Jakubowski, and the Galassis provide some refreshing stability.

Chapter Eleven

Workshop Design Considerations

Writers, researchers, and practitioners do not agree entirely on which skills belong in an assertion training program or on the sequence in which these skills should be included. In this book, all skills classified as assertion skills by prominent writers and researchers are divided into ten categories according to a useful and functional training sequence. However, the entire sequence cannot always be covered in a limited time period, and it may not make sense for every group of participants to cover the entire sequence. What the trainer decides to include depends on several important considerations. Some considerations, such as physical facilities, available materials, and location, are fairly straightforward. Others, such as entry needs of participants, group size, group composition, number of trainers, length of program, and goals of the program, merit a brief discussion. This chapter focuses on these major design considerations, presents model designs for a one-hour presentation, for three-hour, one-day, and three-day workshops, and for an advanced two-day workshop, and gives some general implementation guidelines.

WHAT TO CONSIDER

Entry Needs of Participants

For training purposes, clients must be identified early who have more general, more intense, or a greater number of assertion needs than can be accommodated in a particular training event. These needs can be identified through proper advertising, screening, or assessment procedures conducted during the first session of an ongoing workshop. (These issues are dealt with in detail in the "Readings on Professional Issues" chapter of this text.) The idea is to find the best match between setting (training or therapy) and participant to maximize learning conditions. If a participant has more, or very different, types of problems than other participants do, he or she may not be able to keep up in the training event or may slow others down.

Group Size and Availability of Trainers

The number of participants who can be accommodated and number of trainers available are closely tied to the type of structure that will be used. Methods the trainer can incorporate are somewhat affected by all three factors.

Larger groups (twenty-five or more) must be structured tightly if only one or two trainers are available, because people in larger groups have a tendency to misinterpret instructions and to become sidetracked. Also, the trainer cannot monitor discussions closely for depth of disclosure and the sensitivity with which disclosures are being received. Because individualized attention is almost impossible in large groups, generally a lecture or an experiential lecture (using hypothetical, rather than real, situations to practice) interspersed with question-and-answer periods works best.

Medium-sized groups (fifteen to twenty-five participants) with one or two trainers, or larger groups that can be divided into smaller groups (six to fifteen) with one trainer per small group plus one or two lead trainers, still need to be structured tightly, although somewhat less than a large group with one trainer. In this setting, a regular assertion training format may be followed, but time guidelines and a *moderate* amount of experiential structure must be adhered to in order to keep the group on track and assure practice time for everyone.

Informal group discussion can be combined with structured experiences in small groups in a more fluid pattern. The structure can be adapted more easily to the changing assertion needs of participants in the small-group format because it is easier for everyone to be heard and there is no need to coordinate activities with other groups in the same room.

A summary of general guidelines for setting up sessions according to group size is outlined in Table 6.

Length and Goals of the Program

Program length and program goals are so interrelated that one determines the other to a great extent. If only so much time can be allotted, then only certain goals can be achieved within that time frame. Conversely, if the goals are specified, then a general time frame is dictated by those goals.

It is important to keep learning goals and training objectives clear and manageable in any training event. If a client requests one hour of assertion training, the trainer must be able to state clearly what can and cannot be done within that time frame. When planning events, trainers must be able to gauge the amount of time needed to meet the stated goals and objectives.

Table 6. General Guidelines for Setting Up a Workshop According to Group Size

GROUP SIZE	STRUCTURE	METHOD
Six to fifteen participants One or two trainers	Single group activity, with some practice in subgroups Flexible time periods and design	Informal discussion Structured experiences and practice in total group or subgroup Lecturette in total group
Fifteen to twenty-five participants One or two trainers or Twenty-five or more participants with one trainer per fifteen participants, plus one or two lead trainers	Small-group activities with reporting of results to the large group Tighter structure Less flexible time lines More set format or design	More structured discussion periods Structured experiences and practice in small groups Lecturette in total group
Twenty-five or more participants One or two trainers	Mostly large group Tightest structure	Lecture Experiential lecture Question and answer Hypothetical situations

Generally, the trainer should translate goals into "desirable outcomes" or in some way avoid guaranteeing particular outcomes from the event. The trainer cannot *make* the participant learn, although the structure and guidance he or she provides helps participants who are motivated to learn. Possible desirable outcomes from assertion training are here defined as an awareness of, interest in, knowledge of, skill in, and application or real-life use of any of the ten skill areas discussed in this book: Theory, Self-Confidence, Identification of Rights, Confidence in Rights, Verbal Assertion, Nonverbal Assertion, Cognitive Assertion, Integration, Special Application Areas, and Special Needs. Thus, within each skill area, emphasis can be placed on any of five levels of skill development:

1. Awareness that the skill exists.
2. Interest — motivation to learn more about the skill.
3. Knowledge, including an understanding of the skill concepts and guidelines.
4. Proficiency in the skill.
5. Application of the skill in appropriate real-life situations.

Five popular time frames and suggested corresponding goals are shown in Table 7. Model designs for each of these five time-frame/goal combinations are presented later in this chapter. Awareness of, interest in, and knowledge of any skill are important for constructive continued use of that skill; they

Table 7. Goals and Feasible Time Frames

TIME FRAME	GOALS
One hour	Awareness of and interest in all ten skill areas Knowledge of Theory
Three hours	Awareness of and interest in all ten skill areas Knowledge of Theory and Verbal Assertion Some skills in Theory and Verbal Assertion
One day	Awareness of and interest in all ten skill areas Knowledge of Theory, Verbal, Nonverbal, and Cognitive Assertion and Integration Skill in Theory, Verbal, Nonverbal, and Cognitive Assertion and Integration
Three days; six three-hour sessions; or two days with a one-day follow-up session	Awareness of and interest in all ten skill areas Knowledge, skill, and application of Theory, Self-Confidence, Identification of Rights, Confidence in Rights, Verbal, Nonverbal, and Cognitive Assertion, and Integration
One to three days (Advanced)	Review of previously learned skills (Theory through Integration) Awareness, interest, knowledge, skills, and application of Special Application Areas and Special Needs

facilitate learning the skill itself; and they help people feel confident to practice the skill. They also provide incremental learning steps toward the final goal, application. Reaching these goals prepares the way for assertion, whether a follow-up session is scheduled or whether the workshop is simply an introduction to assertion for those wishing to explore their commitment to it.

A knowledge and understanding of theory are necessary to use assertion skills constructively and to generalize to situations other than those practiced in the training setting. So in a one-hour time frame only these goals (awareness, interest in all areas, knowledge of theory) are pursued.

When more time is available, as in a one-day time frame, core skills (verbal, nonverbal, and cognitive) are added to the design, with the understanding that the participants are sufficiently proficient in the three preparatory assertion areas (self-confidence, identification of rights, and confidence in rights) when they arrive. A larger time frame (three days) permits the addition of these preparatory skills to the training design.

A one-to-three-day time frame permits advanced training in various accessory assertion skills (special applications and special needs), assuming that participants have already developed the preparatory and core skills.

When participants have time to return to their home settings between sessions as in a two- or three-day workshop, application of various skills can be stressed. Opportunities for practice are greatest when the sessions are spaced over several weeks. A continuous program, on the other hand, allows less chance for practicing applications but gives more intense practice and eliminates the need to re-establish a climate of group trust with each new session and to remind participants of what they did in previous sessions. When application is not possible, however, participants should be told of techniques and potential hazards involved. Application is vital; without it, assertion training is only an interesting exercise.

Goals are also somewhat interrelated with entry needs of participants and with group size. For example, groups of twenty-five or more with one or two trainers are virtually limited to one-hour or three-hour time frames and corresponding goals, because experiential lecture and question and answer are not appropriate methods to develop assertion skills. In this case, the group size prescribes a general time frame and goals. On the other hand, participants are assumed to be proficient in the preparatory skills in the one-day model and in preparatory and core skills in the advanced model.

Obviously, a chief variable here is whether the participants have enough background to begin at the level indicated.

Group Composition

Similarities and differences among group members should be managed in a way that maximizes learning opportunities. A first consideration is whether the participants will be strangers to one another, acquaintances, or members of an intact group. Generally, it is easier for strangers to be open about their assertion difficulties and they are more willing to work on them in the group setting. If the participants are acquaintances or an intact group, it must be determined whether they feel that they can involve themselves in the learning process. A potential advantage of intact groups is a common language and a knowledge of common problem situations.

A second consideration is the background or culture of those involved — i.e., the degree of dissonance or consonance that exists in terms of background beliefs, occupation, etc. Some dissonance in this area can enhance learning by providing a multiplicity of viewpoints; too much dissonance can mean a lack of relevance or ability to understand others.

The participant difference discussed most often is the male/female differ-ence, because men and women, in general, have been socialized differently in terms of assertion. In general, men have been encouraged to be assertive or aggressive in Western society, women to be nonassertive. One view is that women do better in groups in which they relate only to women because they have been so socialized in relation to men that they continue to show the same dysfunctional behaviors when in training groups with men. Others believe that the presence of men helps create a more realistic practice situation for both sexes; that in the training setting there is a tendency for each to give support and encouragement to the other — a strong reinforcer; and that each side has a chance to understand the problems of the other and the origins of these problems.

Most assertion participants, male or female, come to the training session with nonassertive, rather than aggressive, behavior patterns. Thus, the differ-ences are not as great as they might seem at first glance. One workable compromise is to allow participants to form groups according to their own needs and to encourage or allow same-sex groups to form during the early stages of skill practice, moving into mixed-gender groups in the core-skills or integration phases. When male/female group composition is being consid-ered, the advantages and disadvantages of heterogeneity or homogeneity may need to be weighed with each group of participants, topic, level of develop-ment, etc.

In summary, several factors merit special consideration in assertion train-ing design: entry needs, group size, availability of trainers, structure, method, goals, time limits, and group composition. The relationships among these factors (except group composition, which is more independent) are di-agrammed in Figure 9. When any of the factors connected by two-pronged arrows have been determined, the factors on the opposite ends of these arrows have been defined or limited to some extent. The diagram can help the trainer pinpoint crucial limitations for a particular training project.

The broken arrow describes limits only in the case of large groups, when methods are limited to lecture, experiential lecture, and question and answer, and thus goals are limited to awareness, interest, and knowledge. For smaller groups, the blocks connected by the broken arrow can be determined inde-pendently of one another.

The dynamics of Figure 9 can be demonstrated by two examples:

Assertion training in an experiential lecture format is requested by a client system. If an experiential lecture method is plugged into the model, all other factors are determined to some extent, since the broken arrow is operative (Figure 10).

Assertion training is requested by a client system for a three-day time block for people with no previous assertion training (Figure 11).

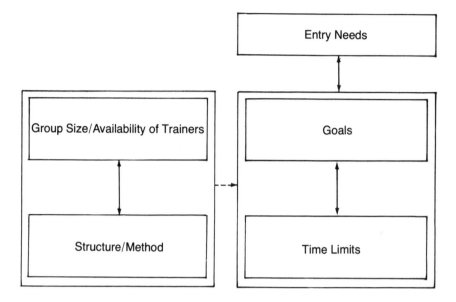

Figure 9. The Relationships Among Group Design Factors

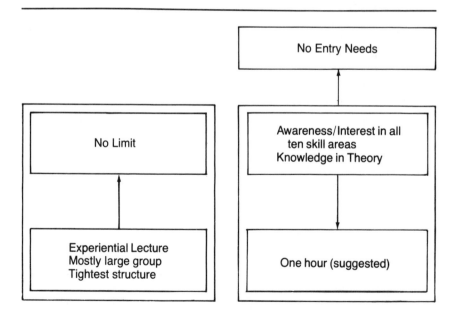

Figure 10. Training Using an Experiential Lecture Format

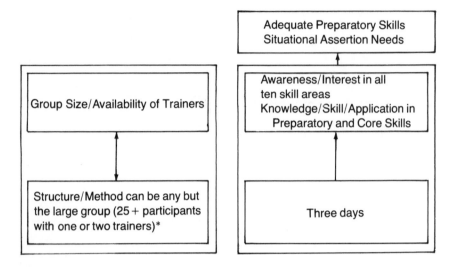

Figure 11. Training in a Three-Day Time Block for Clients with No Previous Training

WHAT TO INCLUDE IN A TRAINING EVENT

It is useful to include several elements in a training design: (a) an introduction of the staff, (b) some means of breaking the ice or getting acquainted and of learning participants' expectations, (c) a statement of the preannounced goals of the event, (d) a statement of what participants can do to get the most out of the event, (e) an overview of the major elements, sequence, and logic of the event (i.e., the design[1]), (f) a program designed to accomplish the stated goals based on a skill-development model (Figure 12), (g) some goal setting for back-home application and some planning of how to implement these goals, and (h) an evaluation of the event for the facilitator's benefit.

The skill-development model (Figure 12) shows that participants can cycle through up to five levels of skill development in each skill area, from awareness through application, depending on the goals of the event. Skill areas are connected by the total workshop design and the theoretical "big picture" that explains why the next skill area is being covered at this particular point in the design and helps participants understand where they have been and where they are going.

---

*Large groups are one of two exceptions. The chart works only for goals of awareness, interest, and knowledge.

[1]"Goals, Roles, Norms, and Overview," a sequence of opening activities that follows an icebreaker as a standard feature in workshops by John E. Jones, University Associates, Publishers and Consultants.

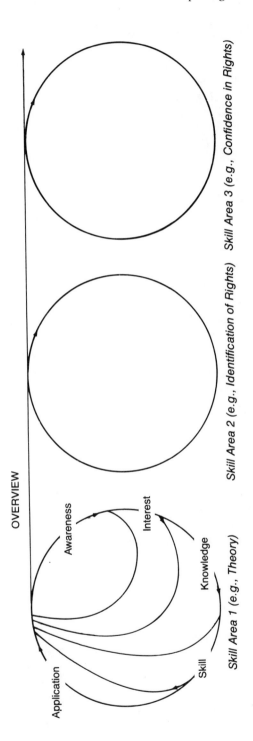

Figure 12. The Skill-Development Model

Although there are no hard-and-fast rules, different methods are generally used to develop different levels of skill. Readings, lectures (with examples), experiential lectures, discussion, films, structured experiences[2] with appropriate goals, and paper-and-pencil instruments are used most often to develop *awareness, interest*, and *knowledge*. Technique-based structured experiences, behavior modification techniques, and rational-emotive techniques are used to practice *skills*. "Homework," journals, records, or back-home assignments are used to develop the *application* level.

For example, when teaching a skill, the trainer might:

1. Give a definition of the skill and a presentation of its theoretical base through a brief lecturette (awareness).

2a. Give an example of assertion problems caused by lack of the skill and have group members give examples, or

2b. Conduct a short structured experience designed to raise awareness and interest (interest).

3. Give a more extensive theoretical base and some guidelines for skill practice (knowledge).

4. Model or demonstrate how to apply these guidelines to hypothetical situations and answer any participant questions (knowledge).

5. Help group members practice, model, or demonstrate applying the guidelines in hypothetical, or real, other-owned situations (skill).

6. Have group members practice applying the guidelines to real individually owned situations in a one-on-one or small-group structure (skill).

7. Discuss and contract with participants ways to transfer the skill to the real world, and debrief the experience with them (application).

Some useful guidelines for incrementing practice activities include: moving from covert toward overt practice and from directed toward improvised practice (Rich & Schroeder, 1976); moving from high structure toward low structure, and from one-on-one-specific situations or skills toward group-specific situations or skills (Egan, 1976); and moving from hypothetical situations or real, other-owned situations toward real, individually owned situations.

SAMPLE DESIGNS

Some sample designs are presented here to show some of the ways in which the activities in this book can be combined or the trainer may wish to incorpo-

---

[2]The activities in this book are written according to an experiential model, i.e., participants engage in an activity or experience, share their reactions and observations, integrate this data, arrive at some generalizations, and apply the generalizations. Thus, a structured experience may cycle participants through several levels of the skill-development model.

rate activities he or she has collected or invented. The sequence of events in the designs follows the framework presented in the introduction to this book. Time frames and goals from Table 7 are used.

A One-Hour Presentation

Brief staff introduction

Lecturette: "Assertion Theory" (Chapter One)

Lecturette: An overview of assertion skills and the skill sequence presented in the introduction to this text

Periodic question-and-answer and discussion periods

Optional short film presentation

Recommendation of books and opportunities for further training

Objectives

   I. To give a basic outline of the ten assertion skill areas.

  II. To stimulate interest in these skill areas.

 III. To introduce some principles and dynamics of assertion theory.

Process

   I. The facilitator introduces himself or herself and any other staff members.

  II. The facilitator gives lecturettes on "Assertion Theory" and on assertion skills and the skill sequence found in the introduction to this text, giving specific examples.

 III. At various points during the lecturette, the facilitator invites questions, takes time to answer them, and asks participants to share reactions or observations with each other or with him or her.

 IV. A short film on basic assertion principles may be shown.

  V. The facilitator recommends specific assertion literature and further training programs.

A Three-Hour Presentation

Brief staff introduction (five minutes)

Structured Experience: "Yes-No" and Lecturette: "Assertion Theory" (Chapter One; forty-five minutes)

Brief statement of preannounced goals of the event (five minutes)

Overview of content of training event (five minutes)

Coffee break (ten minutes)

Structured Experience: "Assertive Words" and Lecturette: "Scripting" (Chapter Five; one and one-half hours)

Lecturette: An overview of assertion skills and the skill sequence presented in the introduction to this text

Discussion of back-home applications, recommended books, and opportunities for further training (five minutes)

Objectives

 I. To outline the ten assertion skills.

 II. To stimulate interest in the assertion skills.

 III. To introduce some principles and dynamics of assertion theory and verbal assertion.

Process

 I. The facilitator introduces himself or herself and any other staff members.

 II. The facilitator leads participants in the "Yes-No" structured experience, using the "Assertion Theory" lecturette in Step IX of the structured experience.

 III. The facilitator states the goals of the event, gives a brief overview of the training design, and announces a coffee break.

 IV. The facilitator leads participants in the "Assertive Words" structured experience, using the "Scripting" lecturette in Step II of the structured experience.

 V. The facilitator gives a lecturette on assertion skills and the skill sequence found in the introduction to this text.

 VI. The facilitator suggests ways to apply what has been learned to the back-home setting and recommends specific assertion literature and further assertion training programs.

A One-Day Workshop

Brief staff introduction (five minutes)

Participants get acquainted and share expectations (thirty minutes)

Brief statement of goals of the event (five minutes)

Overview of content of training event (five minutes)

Lecturette: An overview of assertion skills and the skill sequence presented in the introduction to this text (ten minutes)

Coffee break (ten minutes)

Structured Experience: "Yes-No" and Lecturette: "Assertion Theory" (Chapter One; forty-five minutes)

Structured Experience: "Assertive Words," eliminating its Steps III and IV, and Lecturette: "Scripting" (Chapter Five; one hour); Assessment Form: "Sixty Assertive Situations" (Part II of this text; ten minutes)

Lunch

Lecturette: "Nonverbal Elements of Assertive Communication" (Chapter Six; ten minutes) and Structured Experience: "Nonverbal Triads," Steps V and VI only (Chapter Six; twenty-five minutes)

Structured Experience: "Have To, Choose To," eliminating its Steps XII and XIII, and Lecturette: "Talking to Oneself" (Chapter Seven; sixty minutes)

Coffee break (ten minutes)

Structured Experience: "Behavioral Rehearsal" (Chapter Eight; one hour)

Setting goals for back-home applications (ten minutes)

Recommended books and opportunities for further training (five minutes)

Objectives

I. To outline the ten assertion skills.

II. To stimulate interest in the assertion skills.

III. To introduce some principles and dynamics of assertion theory, verbal assertion, nonverbal assertion, cognitive assertion, and integration.

IV. To provide an opportunity for practicing skills in the areas of theory, verbal assertion, nonverbal assertion, cognitive assertion, and integration.

Process

I. The facilitator introduces himself or herself and any other staff members.

II. Participants take turns sharing their names, something about themselves, and their expectations for the training event.

III. The facilitator states the goals of the event and gives a brief overview of the training design.

IV. The facilitator gives a lecturette on assertion skills and the skill sequence found in the introduction to this text, then announces a coffee break.

V. The facilitator leads participants in the "Yes-No" structured experience, using the "Assertion Theory" lecturette in Step IX of the structured experience.

VI. The facilitator leads participants in the "Assertive Words" structured experience, eliminating its Steps III and IV and using the "Scripting" lecturette in Step II. Following Step II of the structured experience, the facilitator distributes the "Sixty Assertive Situations" form and pencils and asks participants to choose five situations that are moderately difficult for them and to list these situations in Part II of the form. The facilitator distributes the DESC form prior to Step V of the structured experience.

VII. The facilitator announces a lunch break.

VIII. The facilitator gives the "Nonverbal Elements of Assertive Communication" lecturette.

IX. The facilitator leads participants in the "Nonverbal Triads" structured experience, using only its Steps V and VI.

X. The facilitator leads participants in the "Have To, Choose To" structured experience, eliminating its Steps XII and XIII and using the "Talking to Oneself" lecturette in Step I of the structured experience. He or she announces a coffee break at the end of the activity.

XI. The facilitator leads participants in the "Behavioral Rehearsal" structured experience.

XII. The facilitator leads participants in a discussion of specific ways to use their new learnings in back-home settings.

XIII. The facilitator recommends specific assertion literature and further assertion training programs.

A Three-Day Workshop

Day I

Brief staff introduction (five minutes)

Structured Experience: "Boasting" and Lecturette: "Improving Your Self-Esteem" (Chapter Two; forty-five minutes)

Participants get acquainted and share expectations (twenty minutes)

Brief statement of goals of the event, what participants can do to get the most out of the experience, and an overview of its major elements (fifteen minutes)

Coffee break (ten minutes)

Lecturettes: "Assertion Theory" (Chapter One) and an overview of assertion skills and the skill sequence presented in the introduction to this text (fifteen minutes)

Assessment Form: "Sixty Assertive Situations" (Part II of this text; ten minutes)

Structured Experience: "Basic Human Rights" and Lecturette: "What Are My Rights?" (Chapter Three; one hour)

Lunch

Lecturette: "Developing a Belief System" (Chapter Four; ten minutes)

Structured Experience: "Rights Circle" (Chapter Four; one hour)

Coffee break (ten minutes)

Structured Experience: "Communication Triads," eliminating its Step IX, and Lecturette: "Communication Skills" (Chapter Five; one and one-half hour)

Contracting for back-home applications or "homework" (ten minutes)

Day II

Sharing results of back-home applications (ten minutes)

Structured Experience: "Assertive Words" and Lecturette: "Scripting" (Chapter Five; one and one-half hours)

Coffee break (ten minutes)

Structured Experience: "Nonassertion/Aggression/Assertion" and Lecturette: "Nonverbal Elements of Assertive Communication" (Chapter Six; forty minutes)

Structured Experience: "Nonverbal Triads" (A) and Lecturette based on Table 4: "Nonverbal and Verbal Behavior Associated with Nonassertion, Assertion, and Aggression" (Chapter Six; thirty minutes)

Lunch

Structured Experience: "Nonverbal Triads" (B) (sixty minutes)

Coffee break (ten minutes)

Structured Experience: "Right Thinking" and Lecturette: "Talking to Oneself" (Chapter Seven; one hour and fifteen minutes)

Structured Experience: "Behavioral Rehearsal" (A) (Chapter Eight; twenty-five minutes)

Contracting for back-home applications (ten minutes)

Day III

Sharing results of back-home applications (ten minutes)

Lecturette: "Putting It All Together" (Chapter Eight; ten minutes)

Structured Experience: "Behavioral Rehearsal" (B) (one hour)

Coffee break (ten minutes)

Structured Experience: "Escalation" (Chapter Eight; one hour)

Lecturette: "Coping with Stress" (Chapter Ten; ten minutes)

Structured Experience: "Relaxation" (Chapter Ten; twenty minutes)

Lunch

Practice in the following special application areas:

Making Requests (twenty minutes)
Refusing Requests (twenty minutes)
Giving Criticism (twenty minutes)
Receiving Criticism (twenty minutes)

Coffee break (ten minutes)

Structured Experience: "Positive Assertion" (Chapter Nine; forty-five minutes)

Summary of the workshop (fifteen minutes)

Setting goals for back-home applications (twenty minutes)

Recommended books and opportunities for further training (ten minutes)

Objectives

I. To outline the ten assertion skills.

II. To stimulate interest in the assertion skills.

III. To introduce some principles and dynamics of assertion skills from theory through integration.

IV. To provide an opportunity for practicing skills in these areas.

V. To provide an opportunity to apply the skills in a real-life situation.

Process (Day I)

I. The facilitator introduces himself or herself and any other staff members.

II. The facilitator leads participants in the "Boasting" structured experience, using the "Improving Your Self-Esteem" lecturette in Step IV of the structured experience.

III. Participants take turns sharing their names, something about themselves, and their expectations for the training event.

IV. The facilitator states the goals of the event, suggests some behaviors that could be helpful for maximizing learning, gives a brief overview of the training design, and announces a coffee break.

V. The facilitator gives lecturettes on "Assertion Theory" and on assertion skills and the skill sequence found in the introduction to this text.

VI. The facilitator distributes the "Sixty Assertive Situations" form and asks participants to choose five situations that are moderately difficult for them and to list these situations in Part II of the form.

VII. The facilitator leads participants in the "Basic Human Rights" structured experience, using the "What Are My Rights?" lecturette in Step I of the structured experience.

VIII. The facilitator announces a lunch break.

IX. The facilitator gives the lecturette "Developing a Belief System."

X. The facilitator leads participants in the "Rights Circle" structured experience, then announces a coffee break.

XI. The facilitator introduces the "Communication Triads" structured experience, eliminating its Step IX and using the "Communication Skills" lecturette in Step I of the structured experience.

XII. The facilitator helps participants to create individual contracts to apply their knowledge, monitor their assertive behavior, etc., before the next session.

Process (Day II)

I. The facilitator leads a discussion of participants' results from the contracts of the previous day.

II. The facilitator leads participants in the "Assertive Words" structured experience, using the "Scripting" lecturette in Step II of the structured experience, then announces a coffee break.

III. The facilitator leads participants in the "Nonassertion/Aggression/Assertion" structured experience, using the "Nonverbal Elements of Assertive Communication" lecturette in Step XII of the structured experience.

IV. The facilitator leads participants in Steps I through III of the "Nonverbal Triads" structured experience, giving a lecturette based on Table 4: "Nonverbal and Verbal Behavior Associated with Nonassertion, Assertion, and Aggression" in Step I of the structured experience and distributing copies of the table.

V. The facilitator announces a lunch break.

VI. The facilitator leads participants in Steps IV through VII of the "Nonverbal Triads" structured experience, then announces a coffee break.

VII. The facilitator leads participants in the "Right Thinking" structured experience, using the "Talking to Oneself" lecturette in Step I of the structured experience.

VIII. The facilitator leads participants in Steps I through VII of the "Behavioral Rehearsal" structured experience.

IX. The facilitator helps participants to create individual contracts to apply their knowledge, monitor their assertive behavior, etc., before the next session.

Process (Day III)

I. The facilitator leads a discussion of participants' results from the contracts of the previous day.

II. The facilitator gives the lecturette "Putting It All Together."

III. The facilitator leads participants in Steps VIII through XIII of "Behavioral Rehearsal," then announces a coffee break.

IV. The facilitator leads participants in the "Escalation" structured experience.

V. The facilitator gives the lecturette "Coping with Stress."

VI. The facilitator leads participants in Steps VI, VII, and XI of the "Relaxation" structured experience.

VII. The facilitator announces a lunch break.

VIII. The facilitator gives brief guidelines for practicing four special application areas in pairs (each participant is to take half the practice time allotted to each application area) in the following order: making requests; refusing requests; giving criticism; and receiving criticism. (Participants may be asked to brainstorm a list of practice topics within each area, or they may wish to use stock situations.) At the end of the four practice sessions, the facilitator announces a coffee break.

IX. The facilitator leads participants in the "Positive Assertion" structured experience.

X. The facilitator summarizes the events of the workshop.

XI. The facilitator leads participants in a discussion of and contracting for specific ways to use their new skills in back-home settings.

XII. The facilitator recommends specific assertion literature and further assertion training programs.

A Two-Day Advanced Workshop

Day I

Brief staff introduction (five minutes)

Structured Experience: Variation I of "Introductions" (Chapter Two; thirty minutes)

Brief statement of goals of the event, what participants can do to get the most out of the experience, and an overview of its major elements (fifteen minutes)

Recap Lecturettes: "Assertion Theory" (Chapter One) and an overview of assertion skills and the skill sequence presented in the introduction to this text (ten minutes)

Coffee break (ten minutes)

Structured Experience: "Assertion Response Discrimination Index," Variation II (Chapter One; forty minutes)

Recap Lecturette on preparatory assertion skills (Chapters Two, Three, and Four; ten minutes)

Structured Experience: "Rights Fantasy" (Chapter Four; one hour)

Lunch

Recap Lecturette on core assertion skills (Chapters Five, Six, Seven, and Eight; ten minutes)

Assessment Form: "Assertion Skills Check List" (Part II of this text; fifteen minutes)

In-depth work on needed skills (one hour and twenty minutes)

Coffee break (ten minutes)

Lecturette: "Coping with Stress" (Chapter Ten; ten minutes)

Structured Experience: "Relaxation" (Chapter Ten; forty-five minutes)

Contracting for back-home applications (ten minutes)

Day II

Sharing results of back-home applications (ten minutes)

Structured Experience: "Interaction Constellation" (Chapter Nine; one hour)

Coffee break (ten minutes)

Structured Experience: "What's the Threat?" (Chapter Nine; one and one-half hours)

Assessment of special-application-area needs (ten minutes)

Lunch

Lecturette: "Covert Techniques" (Chapter Ten; ten minutes)

Structured Experience: "Covert Rehearsal/Reinforcement" (Chapter Ten; one hour)

Coffee break (ten minutes)

Structured Experience: "Stations" (Chapter Nine; one hour and twenty-five minutes)

Setting goals for back-home applications (ten minutes)

Recommended books and opportunities for further training (five minutes)

Objectives

    I. To review the principles and dynamics of assertion skills from theory through integration.

    II. To provide an opportunity to review knowledge, skills, and applications of assertion skill areas from theory through integration.

    III. To introduce a basic outline of special application areas and special needs.

    IV. To stimulate interest in learning special applications and techniques for special needs.

    V. To introduce some principles and dynamics of special application skills and techniques for special needs.

VI. To provide an opportunity for skill practice in these two areas.

VII. To provide an opportunity for application of these skills.

Process (Day I)

I. The facilitator introduces himself or herself and any other staff members.

II. The facilitator leads participants in the "Introductions" structured experience, using Variation I, followed by Steps V and VI of the structured experience.

III. The facilitator states the goals of the event, suggests some behaviors that could be helpful for maximizing learning, and gives a brief overview of the training design.

IV. The facilitator gives a lecturette summarizing and supplementing the major points in the "Assertion Theory" lecturette, gives a brief summary of assertion skills and the skill sequence, and announces a coffee break.

V. The facilitator introduces Variation II of the "Assertion Response Discrimination Index," followed by Step V of the structured experience.

VI. The facilitator gives a lecturette summarizing and supplementing the major concepts and dynamics of preparatory assertion skills.

VII. The facilitator leads participants in the "Rights Fantasy" structured experience.

VIII. The facilitator announces a lunch break.

IX. The facilitator gives a lecturette summarizing and supplementing the major concepts and dynamics of core assertion skills.

X. The facilitator distributes the "Assertion Skills Check List" form and asks participants to complete all but items I and J. Participants are polled for areas they wish to concentrate on.

XI. The facilitator provides an appropriate structure for work in those areas indicated by the check lists, then announces a coffee break.

XII. The facilitator gives the lecturette "Coping with Stress."

XIII. The facilitator leads participants in the "Relaxation" structured experience.

XIV. The facilitator helps participants to create individual contracts to apply their knowledge, monitor their assertive behaviors, etc., before the next session.

Process (Day II)

I. The facilitator leads a discussion of participants' results from the contracts of the previous day.

II. The facilitator leads participants in the "Interaction Constellation" structured experience, then announces a coffee break.

III. The facilitator leads participants in the "What's the Threat?" structured experience, using the "Dealing with Anger" lecturette in Step III of the structured experience.

IV. The facilitator posts a list of some special application areas and asks participants to add to the list and then to indicate which one or two areas each of them wishes to develop knowledge, skill, and application in at this time.

V. The facilitator announces a lunch break.

VI. The facilitator gives the lecturette "Covert Techniques."

VII. The facilitator leads participants in the "Covert Rehearsal/Reinforcement" structured experience, then announces a coffee break.

VIII. The facilitator leads participants in the "Stations" structured experience based on the results of the assessment conducted in the previous three-hour session (Step IV above), keeping the rounds to twenty-five minutes each.

IX. The facilitator leads participants in a discussion of specific ways to use their new knowledge in back-home settings.

X. The facilitator recommends some specific assertion literature and further assertion training programs.

An advanced assertion workshop also could be run with the focus on *any* of the preparatory or core skill areas, as long as participants have already had some basic training in them. Another possibility would be to focus on just one special application area.

IMPLEMENTATION GUIDELINES

Implementation guidelines for individual assertion skills are in the introductions and lecturettes to the appropriate chapters. Some general guidelines and considerations are presented here.

Three categories of general assertion techniques should be utilized:

1. *Positive Reinforcement, Shaping, and Hierarchies*. Give the client positive reinforcement for any change in the direction of the desired behavior. It is important that the client have a successful experience, which builds confidence and lessens anxiety. Reward small steps toward the large assertion goals. To this end, use a hierarchical approach when selecting practice situations, i.e., practice easier situations before more difficult ones with as many gradations as necessary to provide for incremental learning.

2. *Evaluation or Processing and Feedback*. When processing an experience, see that activities are debriefed or discussed and that useful observations and pieces of information are exchanged.

Specific, objective, solicited and immediate feedback should be given to clients describing modifiable behaviors to help them understand how to become more assertive. Again, work on one or two changes at a time. Videotapes, films, and audiotapes are helpful, but participants also must develop skill in giving feedback to other participants and in describing behaviors they react to in others in real-life assertion situations (see Chapter Eight).

Participants also need to be taught how to receive feedback. Receiving feedback involves (a) hearing the feedback, (b) asking for clarification and consensual validation (others' observations of the same feedback given by a single participant), and/or (c) deciding which feedback they agree with and what behavior changes they are willing to practice on the basis of that feedback.

3. *Goal Setting and "Homework."* Participants must be encouraged to focus on specific, obtainable, positive, measurable, and observable assertion goals. Participants can work toward these goals in training sessions and then apply what they learn to back-home situations. Journals, logs, or records of behaviors observed in oneself or others, as well as other "homework" and self-assigned tasks, can be used to accomplish this transfer of learning. These "transfer of learning" techniques can be used to identify situations, behaviors, or relationships participants want to work on; to self-monitor assertive behavior; or to keep a record of progress toward goals.

Contracting, self-reinforcement, and use of a support person or group are useful techniques to help participants transfer the reinforcement they receive in the training setting to real life to maintain assertive behaviors they have learned. When participants use external self-reinforcement, "it is always better [if they] make the . . . reinforcer a social event rather than an object (such as a stereo) because the reinforcer itself will give the client a chance to be assertive" (Flowers & Booraem, 1975, p. 31).

Adler (1977) suggests the following ways for participants to develop specific goals for themselves:

1. Observe a live or symbolic model (characters in books or films or public figures) and focus on some desirable ways this person asserts himself or herself that you might want to, and realistically could, model yourself after.

2. Ask family or friends for alternatives.

3. Ask professionals (teachers, counselors, etc.) for ideas.

4. Look in assertion books for ideas.

5. Use your idealized self-image (Suskind, cited in Adler, 1977). Visualize yourself possessing all the assertive traits you find desirable and translate these into specific behavioral goals.

One interesting method for reporting the results of back-home applications in longer workshops is "mini-modeling" (Lange & Jakubowski, 1976, p. 185). Participants demonstrate their behavior in the back-home situation, rather than simply reporting it (assuming the back-home application had to do with a behavior that can be modeled). If a participant has been assertive in the situation, the behavior provides a good model for others. If the participant was unable to be assertive, other group members can be asked to model some possible assertive responses to the situation.

Flowers and Booraem (1975, p. 30) suggest that participants report successful experiences first. This "sets a tone of success in the group" and gives positive reinforcement. Another advantage of this approach is that it gives more open-ended time to participants who experienced problems and who may need the extra time to analyze their situations and to look at some alternative approaches. If a client has made a mistake, or has had a bad experience, the facilitator should be prepared to help him or her deal with and analyze the situation and continue working toward assertive behaviors. It is also helpful to include some time during each session of an ongoing group for participants to discuss new assertion situations in their lives.

Some factors that make the transfer of learning from the training setting to everyday life difficult are lack of motivation, failure to learn in the training setting, insufficient length or intensity of the training event, lack of support for learning outside the group, lack of cognitive knowledge or understanding about one's learnings, and moving too quickly or abruptly into a new and different "you" (Simpson, cited in Egan, 1976).

Some of the techniques discussed here — positive reinforcement, shaping, evaluation and feedback, and goal setting — are discussed in more depth in Chapter Eight.

Within-session assignments also can be used to practice application of assertion skills. When a climate of trust, involvement, and openness has been created, the group provides a supportive environment in which participants can practice their skills by dealing assertively with problems that come up between group members or by expressing themselves assertively within the group.

Participation in all training activities should be voluntary, with participants having the option of requesting "time out" for themselves. Confidentiality should be established as a norm in all groups because participants often discuss or practice dealing with real-life situations.

Participants should be made aware of the potential negative (as well as positive) outcomes of assertion training and of ways to deal with or avoid them:

1. "Pendulum" behavior may occur (Chapter One).
2. Assertion "overkill" may occur (Chapters One, Four, and Five).
3. Friends and relations may have a difficult time adjusting (Chapter One).
4. Assertion does not always "work" (Chapter One).
5. If the person(s) being addressed do not know how to respond assertively, their rights may be ignored inadvertently in the process (Chapter One).

6. If clients desire to learn assertive behavior with children, the trainer should consult books on this subject (see Part IV and Bibliographical Sources).

The assumption has been made that the trainer using this book has skills as a facilitator of experiential learning. Whatever his or her background, the assertion trainer should act within the limits of his or her knowledge, training, and capabilities and should be clear on the role he or she intends to play in the assertion group.

Lange and Jakubowski (1976) offer some useful guidelines:

Trainers should be experienced in group work, be prepared to handle unexpected psychological dynamics, and have adequate supervisory backup personnel available. In regard to specific preparation to do assertion training, [it is recommended] that prospective trainers go through a three-stage sequence before conducting their own groups: (1) be a participant in a group with an experienced leader, (2) co-lead a group with an experienced trainer with supervision by that person outside the group, and (3) lead a group alone or with another 'trainer in training' with supervision by an experienced trainer. (p. 202)

The design models presented in this book are meant as examples or points of departure. Recommended time limits are rough estimates; it may be possible to speed up a design or necessary to slow it down, depending on the entry needs and learning rates of the participants. It is important to choose or create a model that maximizes and focuses the learning for the participants in the existing setting with the existing time limits involved, as well as to choose a system the trainer believes in.

Whatever approach one uses, one should remind participants that, although assertion training can help them gain knowledge and skills and begin to apply those skills in specific situations, the process of being assertive must be carried on throughout life. New assertion situations are constantly occurring in our lives, and participants must continue to apply the general principles and skills learned to specific situations they encounter.

Chapter Twelve

Readings on Professional Issues

Issues in Assertive Behavior Training

Assertive behavior training has nearly "come of age".... Increasingly sophisticated research has provided significant depth of understanding of those dimensions of the process which are of demonstrable value, and has called into question some early assumptions. It is no longer sufficient for the practitioner to claim to "do assertiveness training." An up-to-date, ethically responsible approach demands that the professional operate with an awareness of theoretical perspectives, current research, and issues of ethics and practice. Indeed, each responsible facilitator of assertiveness in others must continually seek to answer the question "What is it about my practice of AT [assertiveness training] which makes it *legitimate* for me to offer it as a service to clients?"...

THEORETICAL ISSUES

The concept of assertiveness training has its roots in behavior therapy, notably in the work of Andrew Salter, Joseph Wolpe, and Arnold Lazarus, and was developed initially as a treatment procedure for clients with neurotic social anxiety.

Andrew Salter has commented upon the potential of assertion training in offering help for a wide range of client conditions. His 1949 book *Conditioned*

Alberti, Robert E., "Issues in Assertive Behavior Training," in Alberti, R. E. (Editor), ASSERTIVENESS: INNOVATIONS, APPLICATIONS, ISSUES. San Luis Obispo, California: Impact Publishers, Inc., 1977. Reprinted by permission of the publisher.

Reflex Therapy, now a classic in behavior therapy, presented detailed procedures for increasing "excitatory" behavior and decreasing "inhibitory" behavior. Salter introduced his then-revolutionary therapeutic concepts with the terminology of Ivan Pavlov, the Soviet physiologist who discovered *excitation* and *inhibition* as the key elements in the animal organism's capacity to be expressive emotionally.

Salter went on to present the essence of modern behavior therapy, including procedures for deconditioning anxiety, developing assertive responses, overcoming sexual dysfunction, treating addictions, freeing creative energy, and eliminating stuttering — all this in 1949! Although he never used the word *assertion* in his early work, AT clearly owes its foundation to Andrew Salter's *excitatory* model. He has remained steadfast in his dedication to Pavlovian principles, and his considerable success as a therapist — active in New York City today — has resulted directly from his consistently effective efforts to free clients of inappropriate inhibition.

Disinhibition, in the Salter-as-derived-from-Pavlov model, involves a *re-learning* process directed toward deliberate *excitatory* behavior. Repeated excitatory actions result in increased freedom and awareness of excitatory *feelings*, and a corresponding decrease in inhibitory actions and feelings. Thus, Salter's behavior change procedures (using now-common AT methods of exhortation, behavior rehearsal, relaxation-and-suggestion) lead to changes in neural activity (per Pavlov's notion that excitation is a function of neural connections in the brain), which develops a new freedom of thought, feeling, and further behavior change. As Salter observes, Pavlov's term for "disinhibition" may be literally translated as "unbraking" — removing the brakes. Salter advocates unbraking behavior and freeing individuals to their fullest excitatory potential. An important criterion in Salter's definition of assertion is *honesty*.

First to use the term *assertive* in conjunction with openness in interpersonal behavior was Joseph Wolpe. His early work in deconditioning anxiety led to the concept of "reciprocal inhibition" — that the organism can unlearn anxiety through pairing of anxiety-evoking stimuli with anxiety-inhibiting responses. Key responses which inhibit anxiety are, according to Wolpe, relaxation and assertion. By teaching a client to relax while confronting stimuli which have produced anxiety, the anxiety response is weakened. Repeated confrontations of this type while relaxed can reduce the anxiety markedly — to effectively negligible levels. This is the paradigm involved in the *systematic desensitization* procedure.

Assertiveness, similarly, may be paired with an anxiety-inducing stimulus in order to inhibit and, eventually, overcome the anxiety, in Wolpe's model. By expressing non-anxious feelings — assertions of anger, pleasure, affection — the client weakens the anxiety response and thus encourages further assertions in the future. Sufficient practice of assertive responses — as all AT practitioners are aware — can effectively eliminate situation-specific anxiety, and often has carry-over into other social situations as well. Dr. Wolpe's work, like that of

Salter, continues to be highly influential in assertiveness training and behavior therapy in general.

As we began our work with assertiveness training, Mike Emmons and I were heavily influenced by a humanistic value system, and by our own early training in the model of Carl Rogers (1961). Thus, we drew from Wolpe's behavioral concepts, and from the notions of human rights and potential, and were perhaps first to present AT as a behavioral-humanistic procedure for helping persons to gain their "perfect rights." The concept of assertiveness as a contributor to self-esteem, although only a clinical observation at that time, was an integral part of our contribution. Moreover, we have consistently opted for a non-manipulative view of assertion, as contrasted with hurtful aggression. Finally, in part thanks to the influence of Mike Serber, with whom we had the good fortune to work for a time, we expanded the notion of positive and caring expression as a dimension of assertiveness. In fact, it has been observed that we include nearly all "good" feelings and behavior. Thus, it may be said that the major Alberti-Emmons contributions have been (1) to move AT from a be-havioral treatment for neurotic anxiety to a behavioral-humanistic approach to enhancing self-esteem; (2) to develop more systematic AT procedures, includ-ing emphasis upon non-verbal components in the feedback-coaching process; (3) to emphasize the notions of expanding the boundaries of human rights and expressing positive and caring feelings; and (4) to advocate ethical responsibil-ity and standards for professional AT facilitators.

Arnold Lazarus, for a time a colleague of Wolpe, has more recently begun to develop an approach to AT and other therapeutic procedures which he calls "broad-spectrum behavior therapy." He has broken the barrier of "purely scientific" behavior principles, and does a good deal of integrating of be-havioral and humanistic approaches. Lazarus' conception of assertiveness is somewhat more limiting, in that he prefers to deal only with standing up for rights under the rubric "assertive." The expression of affectionate and other positive feelings are part of Lazarus' "broader" term *emotional freedom*, in which he includes expressions of all forms of affective thoughts, feelings and behaviors.

Among the more recent approaches to theoretical conceptualization of assertive behavior is that of Richard McFall, whose rigorous application of experimental criteria has led him to the conclusion that assertion must be viewed in a situation-specific manner, and must be defined in terms of its behavioral referents. *Measurability* of behavior and its effects are among the strict criteria which McFall considers essential. One of the signal research psychologists working with assertive behavior training, McFall is responsible for the first experimental study of AT (McFall and Marston, 1970). His current concern is for an adequate *behavioral competence* definition of assertion, noting that until we can adequately define the concept in terms which are observable and measurable, our treatment/training procedures are form without substance.

Herbert Fensterheim, himself a practitioner of AT (and perhaps reluctant to characterize himself as a theorist), has offered a pragmatic challenge to McFall. Fensterheim and McFall engaged in a lively discussion which the editor witnessed during the 1975 meeting of the Association for Advancement of Behavior Therapy. In a personal communication to the editor, Fensterheim (1977) followed up that AABT discussion with the observation that, although McFall's approach has the distinct advantage of "observable, recordable, measurable behaviors" and statistical objectivity, it has "nothing to do with Assertion or with life in general." Fensterheim also notes that he currently relates assertiveness to the *learned helplessness* paradigm of Seligman and his associates, with self-esteem as the major positive reinforcer — assertiveness gains self-esteem, helplessness loses self-esteem.

Another theorist who supports the hypothesis of a learned helplessness relationship with assertiveness is Gosta Andersson, whose doctoral dissertation at the University of Gothenburg, Sweden, was entitled "Toward a Unifying Theory of Assertiveness." Andersson undertook an empirical study of the concept of assertiveness because of a conclusion that the concept, as a personality trait, had not been adequately studied. The author wished to test the assumptions in the popular *typological* view of assertiveness — that some *people* are "excitatory" or "non-assertive" — against the notion of assertiveness as one *dimension* of the person.

Andersson developed a test of assertiveness, administered it to some 380 subjects of varying ages and life roles, then performed extensive factor analytic studies of the resulting data. Two principal factors were derived: *assertiveness inhibition* — an avoidance of the expression of opinions and feelings; and *assertiveness expression* — an expression of opinions, feelings, and refusal behavior.

Finally, Andersson proposes a theoretical model of *assertiveness deficiency* (a function of inhibition score minus expression score), and relates that concept to *helplessness*. Comparisons with standardized personality test data led Andersson to observe that assertiveness deficiency is positively related to depression, anxiety, pessimism, feelings of insufficiency, expectancy of inability to control reinforcement, needs of affiliation, needs of succorance, and needs of nuturance. Moreover, as might be expected, assertiveness deficiency is negatively related to self-confidence and autonomy.

The Andersson model offers strong empirical support for the concept of assertiveness as a dimension of personality. However, it should be remembered that Andersson's approach began by considering only a binary option: trait *vs*. type. Further examination of the Andersson data in terms of situation-specific criteria could prove enlightening.

In his discussion of a dimension of assertiveness essentially overlooked by other theoreticians (and most practitioners as well), Donald Cheek (1976) presents a strong argument for including the ethnic/cultural identity of the client as a component in AT theory. Noting that "there can be no therapy developed for someone you basically do not understand," Cheek challenges theoreticians and practitioners to discard theoretical assumptions developed from white-only populations. He considers the *intent of the communicator* to be the principal criterion for defining assertive behavior, and urges consideration of the social-cultural context in the labeling process.

How then do we reconcile these divergent theoretical positions? *Is* there a "unifying" theory? Is it important for the practitioner to have such a theory? The issues are complex, and the current state of the art/science of assertive behavior theory leaves them unresolved. As a general perspective, perhaps we can agree that:

1. Assertiveness is a characteristic of *behavior*, not of *persons;*

2. Assertiveness is a *person-and-situation-specific*, not a universal, characteristic;

3. Assertiveness must be viewed in the *cultural context* of the individual, as well as in terms of other situational variables;

4. Assertiveness is predicated upon the ability of the individual to *freely choose* his/her action;

5. Assertiveness is a characteristic of *socially effective, non-hurtful* behavior.

RESEARCH ISSUES

Since research involves empirical investigation of theoretical hypotheses and variables of method and practice, the issues of research are nearly identical to those of theory and of practice. Nevertheless, it is useful to consider separately the concerns which are stimulating controlled studies of AT and its component constructs.

Preparation of this section has been made immeasurably easier by virtue of an excellent report of research issues in AT by Alexander Rich and Harold Schroeder (1976). Indeed, the interested reader is urged to study their very comprehensive paper for details, since only the barest outline will be presented here.

Definition of the concept of assertiveness again appears as a key issue. How shall we research a concept which is undefined? Indeed, how is it taught if undefined? Operational definitions which may satisfy our needs for training formats are simply inadequate as variables against which to collect quantifiable data. Without quantification, outcome studies are extremely difficult, at best. Yet, *can* we legitimately quantify human behavior? The debate goes on.

Trait vs. situation-specific concepts of behavior have been the source of another continuing controversy in the psychological literature for decades, and assertive behavior has recently been in the center of this dialogue. Greater specificity, of course, offers greater measurability, and contributes to objective evaluation. An increasing volume of research, moreover, concludes that no generalized trait of "assertiveness" exists.

Practitioners are skeptical, nonetheless. Too many clients appear with a broad constellation of non-assertive characteristics. And too many trainees emerge from clinical interventions with dramatically improved assertiveness in many areas of their lives. Perhaps resolution of this apparent conflict lies in two directions:

1. Experimental studies which evaluate behavior change are (of necessity in the current state of the art of behavioral measurement) carefully controlled to allow as few variables as possible to contribute to the outcomes. It is tempting to speculate that the very nature of such measurement limitations in controlled *experimental* conditions *precludes* a generalization or transfer of training by trainees. Human behavior is subject to an axiom of the physical sciences, known as *Heisenberg's Uncertainty Principle*, which says, in effect, that *the very act of observation or measurement itself CHANGES a phenomenom, so that exact measures are not possible*. Moreover, if training is restricted to a very narrow range of skills (as is typically true under experimental conditions) it is not likely that trainees will generalize as readily as those exposed to a broadly-based training experience.

2. We draw heavily from large-sample statistical treatment of experimental data in behavioral studies. Individual changes over time tend to regress toward group means when viewed in this way. It is entirely possible that some clients have the necessary learning skills to effect their own transfer of assertive behavior training to a variety of situations, while others are limited to skills learned in the training situation.

The reader may wish to leave the door open on this issue until more definitive research data are available.

Methodology of assertive behavior training is a persistent issue related to the preceding two. If we cannot clearly define assertive behavior, it is difficult to determine how we shall teach it! Thus many approaches are subsumed under the name "assertiveness training" . . . and this very variety makes definitive research virtually impossible. Questions raised by practitioners are pertinent: Is AT primarily concerned with *verbal* or *non-verbal* procedures? Is it *training* or *therapy?* Who are the *clients?* What *settings* are appropriate? How *long* should interventions last? What *qualifications* are necessary for trainers/therapists?

The focus of training in AT is somewhat diffuse. Are we principally concerned with skill training? Anxiety deconditioning? Cognitive restructuring? All of the above? Once again the individual client is the key mediating variable, but most researchers are reluctant to perform N = 1 studies.

Measurement of assertive behavior and of training effects is itself a significant limitation for adequacy of research in AT. The general limitations of measurement of behavior and behavior change apply to AT, and are compounded by the shortcomings for other variables noted above.

Early research in assertive behavior training was primarily directed toward efficacy of techniques. Relative value of behavior rehearsal, video tape feedback, covert conditioning, homework, token feedback, bibliotherapy, scripts, coaching, non-verbal components, were all evaluated in terms of the inadequate criteria of assertiveness which are available. Current and future research directions will undoubtedly lead us out of the current fluid state, as we develop firmer conceptual models for the content and process of assertive behavior training.

ISSUES OF AT PRACTICE AND ETHICS

Practitioners, after all, are principally interested in those issues which are of direct relevance to practice. The reader is urged to carefully consider the preceding sections of this article as well. However, as we view AT practice, a number of key concerns emerge:

Client self-determination is a fundamental value in any change-oriented intervention. As facilitators, we recognize and teach the importance of assertiveness. In our enthusiasm for encouraging and coaching clients to *be* assertive, we must resist the temptation to deny the client's right to *choose* to assert or not to assert! It is our responsibility to coach the client in assertive skills; it is the client's responsibility to decide whether and when to use those skills.

Client choice is, in my opinion, the primary criterion against which all interventions should be weighed. The fact is, we know assertion does not always work, and clients should not be pushed into risk-taking by zealous facilitators who do not have to live with the consequences of such assertions.

We may pause to reflect on the comment of Alfred Sams of Bangalore, India, who wrote in response to his reading of *Your Perfect Right* that he liked our ideas, but in the "real world" *aggression works!* Alas, he is close enough to make us rest uneasily!

Facilitator understanding of what is happening is a key ethical issue. Indeed, one must characterize as unprofessional and unethical any facilitator who practices AT without at least a basic understanding of: 1) principles of learning and behavior, 2) anxiety and its effects upon behavior, and 3) limitations and potential dangers of AT. The professional *role* of the facilitator (e.g., teacher *vs.* social worker *vs.* psychotherapist) of course calls for both a differing *level* of intervention and differing facilitator skills. Clearly an important dimension of this issue is that the facilitator recognize his/her limitations and act accordingly.

Level of intervention, as noted above, is an issue which, like the others, affects all dimensions of AT. *Therapy*, the most intensive intervention, represents clinical efforts to assist persons who are severely inhibited by anxiety, or who significantly lack social skills, or who are controlled by aggression. *Training*, by contrast, is less intensive and is characterized by non-clinical interventions aimed at teaching assertive skills to those persons who require only encouragement and skill training. *Self-help*, of course, represents efforts by individuals to develop assertiveness on their own, and would include professionally prepared written materials or tapes designed to aid the process. Definition of these differences, identification of the level of intervention appropriate to each client's needs, and standards for the qualification of practitioners at each level are key issues in AT yet to be resolved. . . .

Monitoring facilitator effectiveness is a continuing problem for all types of change-oriented interventions. How do we know whether a facilitator is effective or not? How does one make appropriate referrals *without* knowing? *Certification* has long been considered a method for dealing with this problem. At least one task force of the Association for Advancement of Behavior Therapy decided that the problems of certifying qualified professionals outweighed the benefits. *Evaluative research* is always a desirable procedure, but may appear impractical for short term interventions, particularly in non-clinical settings. Notwithstanding difficulties in conducting adequate studies, *some follow-up is incumbent* upon the professional facilitator. *Educating consumers* holds perhaps the greatest promise, *if* we as practitioners would undertake to inform our clients sufficiently about the AT procedures we employ, the potentials, and the hazards. Clients themselves then become the best evaluators — as indeed they have always been — of our effectiveness. Nevertheless, we need to continue to look toward more adequate training programs (both pre- and in-service) for facilitators, continued research on dimensions of facilitator effectiveness, and a high standard of ethical behavior on the part of the facilitators.

Application to social issues is a dimension of AT which does not receive much attention ... Recent efforts in this area are developing impressive gains. . . .

In a conversation with a group of professionals who apply AT in a variety of settings, I raised this issue. We wondered together whether a "law and order" society would respond favorably (reinforce) to assertive requests by minority citizens for equal opportunity in jobs, housing, education, and civil and criminal justice. A Black woman in the group answered for all of us: "Whether or not we think society will provide these things, ethically it is our responsibility as AT facilitators to teach the skills necessary for these denied citizens to *make the assertive request!*" And, I might add, to work assertively *ourselves* to bring about the changes we believe in.

Ethical guidelines for the practice of AT should be adopted. Practitioners of AT include persons in many professional roles (teachers, social workers, managers, personnel and training officers, physicians, correctional personnel, psychologists, ministers, counselors, women's group leaders, nurses, and on and on). Nevertheless, some broad set of ethical guidelines is needed. . . . Although many persons who practice some form of AT are not otherwise engaged in rendering a "psychological" service, it is nonetheless true that the encouragement and facilitation of assertive behavior is essentially a *therapeutic* procedure. When we, in *any* professional role, engage in helping persons to change their behavior, attitudes, and interpersonal relationships, we are, in my opinion, obligated to act within an ethical framework.

A multidimensional model for viewing assertive behavior training may assist the practitioner in evaluating the appropriateness of his or her AT interventions:

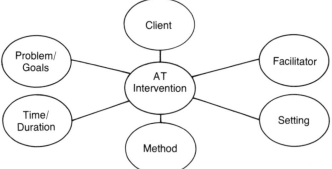

The dimensions may be characterized as follows:

Client: Who is seeking AT? Is the person a child or adult? Man or woman? Ethnic or Anglo? Hospitalized? Imprisoned? Aged? Is the client someone who can make an informed choice to try AT?

Problem/Goals: For what purpose is AT sought (or recommended)? Shyness? Severe inhibition? Supervisory skills? Anxiety reduction? Counter-condition aggression? Are the goals appropriate to an AT intervention?

Facilitator: Who is conducting AT? Self? AT trained professional? Mental health worker? Teacher? Community group leader? Untrained person? Does the facilitator have the skills, understanding, and ethical principles effectively and responsibly to carry out an AT intervention?

Setting: Where is AT being conducted? Home? School? Clinic? Hospital? Prison? Business? Does the setting provide a facilitative environment, freedom of client choice, supervision/evaluation of the facilitator?

Time/Duration: How long does the AT intervention last? A few minutes? An hour? A few hours? A day? A weekend? Intensive sessions over several weeks? Does the length of the intervention provide for a brief encouragement, a facilitative workshop, or an intensive long-term therapeutic effort?

Method: How is the AT intervention conducted? Pep talk? Behavior rehearsal? Modeling? Didactic presentation? Covert sensitization? Memorize scripts? Desensitization? Self-management training? Does the method represent a "programmed" facilitator technique, or is it tailored to client needs? Is care taken to encourage small successful steps, or are punishing consequences likely?

Each AT intervention, from the most casual use of behavioral rehearsal to the most intensive therapeutic treatment of anxiety, may be viewed within the six-dimensional framework suggested above. In so doing, the professional facilitator may carefully examine the appropriateness and ethical responsibility of the intervention. It is evident that the dimensions are related, and largely interdependent (e.g., time duration of intervention depends upon setting, client, etc.), but may be examined independently in each case. Care in selection of AT interventions according to these six criteria may considerably enhance the level of ethical responsibility in the practice of an important tool for behavior change. . . .

A FINAL NOTE

. . . Despite its impressive recent history and wide popularity, AT is still a very young and developing procedure. This article has raised at least as many questions as it has answered. . . .

As assertion practitioners continue to extend and share their observations, experiences, comments, ideas, opinions, and research new answers and new questions seem likely to contribute to the constantly expanding literature of assertive behavior training.

REFERENCES

Cheek, D. K. *Assertive black . . . puzzled white: A black perspective on assertive behavior*. San Luis Obispo, CA: Impact Press, 1976.

Fensterheim, H. Personal communication to the editor, January, 1977.

McFall, R. M., & Marston, A. R. Behavior rehearsal with modeling and coaching in assertive training. *Journal of Abnormal Psychology*, 1970, *76*, 295-303.

Rich, A. R., & Schroeder, H. E. Research issues in assertiveness training. *Psychological Bulletin*, 1976, *83*(6), 1081-1096.

Rogers, C. R. *On becoming a person*. Boston: Houghton-Mifflin, 1961.

Salter, A. On assertion. In R. E. Alberti (Ed.), *Assertiveness: Innovations, applications, issues*. San Luis Obispo, CA: Impact Press, 1977.

Ethical Considerations

A number of ethical issues regarding the training of assertion trainers, the process of training, the potential consequences of training for participants and others, and the researching of training groups warrant discussion. . . .

As with the encounter group movement, many people who are not academically or professionally trained are likely to be conducting assertion groups. Although academic credentials are not a guarantee of competence, we wish to express cautions to those persons who have had limited supervised experience in doing counseling, psychotherapy, or assertion training. First, the process of assertion training (particularly when the goal is personal growth, as opposed to more intensive psychotherapy) is not difficult to understand, but it is quite a complex procedure and requires practice with supervision to do it well. Essentially, our concern is that the participants may not profit from their experience and the trainers may not have a successful experience nor learn from it.

Second, the leaders in any psychologically focused group should be prepared to respond effectively to the variety of dysfunctional dynamics which might occur ranging from disruptions, attention-seeking, and gamey resistances to intense emotional reactions and withdrawals. Although the structured nature of much of assertion training minimizes the expression of interpersonal dysfunction within the group, participants still often engage in "gamey" or ineffectual behaviors in the group. The trainers not only need to know how to recognize such dysfunctions, but also must know how to respond to them. We have offered a number of suggestions for handling such behaviors. However, trainers should have previous experience in supervised group work before conducting a group alone. Trainers with little counseling or therapy experience also should have a more experienced person available for supervision and consultation.

Reprinted from pp. 273-283 of *Responsible Assertive Behavior*, by Arthur J. Lange and Patricia Jakubowski. Champaign, IL: Research Press, 1976. Used with permission.

Trainers should also assess their personal goals for doing assertion training as with any helping relationship. Probably everyone who leads groups seeks personal fulfillment through such work. Some leaders, however, may be seeking excessive recognition as a potent, "healthy," "together" person. For example, the "charismatic" leader described by Yalom & Lieberman (1971) may be more interested in having the group members leave with the thought, "Gee, she's really an amazing leader; she's so together" than with the thought, "I made some important changes for myself in the group today." We do not need to belabor the possible personal needs of trainers which might negatively affect the group process. Trainers should, however, look for their own tendencies to "show off" their assertiveness to the relatively nonassertive group members or to impress the group with their perceptiveness.

Before beginning the group, trainers have ethical responsibilities regarding two issues: advertising and screening participants. . . . Trainers have an ethical responsibility not only to adhere to a professional, informational mode of notifying people about the group, but also to exercise great care to avoid making unwarranted claims, for example, that assertion training will produce major personality changes, resolve marital problems, or enhance love life. Trainers are not selling toothpaste, but rather are offering professional services. We would also like to note the ethical responsibility trainers have for screening prospective group members. Screening has more than the functional purpose of increasing the likelihood of a good group; it allows trainers to responsibly exclude persons who are not seeking such an experience or who are in need of more intensive psychotherapy.

Either during a screening session . . . or at the outset of the first session, the trainers should clearly explain what is going to happen in the group (the focus on cognitive restructuring, personal rights, and rehearsal; the group procedures). The trainers also should explain what is not going to happen, for example, it will not be an encounter or sensitivity group focusing on interactions between members; nor will it be a heavily confrontational group; nor will it be a therapy group where deep intrapsychic dynamics, developmental patterns, and heavy investments in maintaining dysfunctional behavior would be the focus.

In most instances, participants initiate interest in joining an assertion group. However, we have seen persons, particularly within institutional settings, strongly pressured by a supervisor or friend into joining a group. At the screening session, this fact usually becomes apparent. It is important that the trainers communicate to both the candidate and the supervisor or friend that participation in the group must be voluntary. If pressured into the group, the person is likely to be resistive and have a negative effect on other participants. It is possible that the person is setting up a victim game which would be reinforced by being in the group under such conditions. Trainers may either refuse to allow such persons into the group, or establish an agreement directly with them on their assertion training goals. To support having someone in the group without his or her own commitment violates the very definition of assertiveness.

During the first session, the trainers should make a brief statement regarding confidentiality among group members. The message should essentially be that anything that is discussed in the group should stay in the group. It is all right to tell others about the specific exercises or how the group works on problem situations. No references should be made to specific individuals, even anonymously, nor to the specifics of a situation on which someone worked in the group. Some situations are not so personal that anyone would mind if others knew it was practiced in the group. Nevertheless, the blanket rule of confidentiality rules out the need for individuals to have to make such discriminations and seems to help participants be more comfortable working on highly personal situations.

Our primary ethical guidelines for trainer behavior during the group are to be direct and honest in whatever you do and to respect the personal rights of all group members. More specifically, trainers should explain not only what they are doing (e.g., when conducting an exercise), but also why they are doing it that way (using positive feedback at first so that the group's first interactions will be supportive; doing the exercises so that participants will learn various components of the rehearsal procedures to come; phrasing feedback during rehearsals in the form of suggestions so that the person working takes greater responsibility for deciding to make each change). In addition, trainers should avoid being provocative or negatively manipulative toward participants in an effort to elicit a particular response (unless of course it is part of a role play). Participants usually respond to such provocative techniques by withdrawing. For example, one participant wanted to work on not changing his mind as soon as someone else offered an alternative. He had two situations on which to work and selected one of them, whereupon the trainer attempted to convince him to work on the other (which he did). At that point, the trainer noted how easy it was to convince him, and the participant became embarrassed and probably angry, although he did not express it directly. There was no need for the trainer to create examples of nonassertiveness within the group, particularly when the participant had already chosen a situation to work on. The trainer was at least negatively manipulative and might have been supporting a "gamey" transaction to meet both his and the participant's dysfunctional needs for control and susceptibility, respectively. In another situation, a trainer asked a woman in the group if she wanted to continue working on a particular situation which she had just practiced several times. She said "OK, I guess," whereupon the trainer asked the same question with a somewhat critical tone. The woman became more anxious, paused, and said "If you think so." The trainer repeated his exact question several more times as the participant communicated increasing confusion and discomfort. The trainer finally asked her to say "Yes or No" and she said "No." The trainer later explained that he was trying to get her to recognize that her responses were not expressions of her own decisions, but rather adaptations to the trainer's wishes. In fact, however, he never explained to her what he was doing. The trainer also recognized later that he felt she was "acting" dumb by not understanding his repeating the question with greater emphasis on what *she* wanted to do.

Our interpretation of the interaction is that the trainer was not clear with the participant as to what he wanted and became angry when the participant became anxious and confused. In observing the interaction, we also believed the participant was shutting down as a protective behavior. A more effective way to deal with highly adaptive behavior in the group is to share your perception that the person may not be thinking of what she wants to do and then ask her if that is an accurate perception. Thus, a direct and open interaction could lead to an important refocusing of the participant's thinking in a noncritical, nonpressured context. Incidentally, the participant in this incident did not return to the group. Trainers do not have to "walk on eggs" in the way they respond to participants but mutual respect and direct, honest communication are crucial. Trainers *are* models.

Another issue regarding the process of assertion training has to do with the term manipulation. Some people react negatively to the use of "techniques" for more effective behavior as opposed to being "spontaneous." Moreover, some persons believe that they are being manipulative (and therefore bad) by assessing a situation and planning their behavior. Since some participants might resist intentionally trying to influence others for fear of being manipulative (and therefore bad), trainers should be able to discuss this issue and hopefully clarify the participants' thinking regarding the goodness or badness of manipulation. The term itself has come to take on a pejorative quality in our society. We believe, however, that attempts to shape another person's behavior in a positive direction or to influence interactions to turn out the way one would like are forms of manipulation *and* are not "bad." Actually, we are constantly attempting to manipulate ourselves and our world in all kinds of ways which we would not label manipulative. The critical issue, however, seems to be: Am I respecting my own personal rights *and the rights of others*. Thus, the real issue is not whether we consciously attempt to influence our world, but rather whether we are responsibly and ethically assertive as we attempt to exercise influence. On the other side of the coin, we have worked with participants who initially viewed assertion training as a way to get better at getting things from people with little regard for the personal rights of those people. We both spent considerably more time discussing the belief system issues regarding empathy and regard for the personal rights of others with these participants. Merely introducing such a different belief system is not enough to change a person's moral reasoning or belief system. Moreover, persons with a very rigid and insensitive perspective toward others often are quite fearful or angry and might best be helped in individual or group therapy. Assertion training might later be appropriate to help such a person begin to act on the newly developed belief system.

Assertion training can become manipulative in the negative sense when, for example, a person pays someone a compliment so that the person will pay him a compliment in return, or a person disagrees with his colleague so that the boss will be impressed. Recall that we defined assertiveness as a *direct, honest*, and *appropriate* expression of opinions, beliefs, needs, or feelings. These two examples were neither direct nor honest in the expression of needs. Unfortunately, it is not always easy to recognize what is actually prompting our own overt behavior or the behavior of others. We believe that through cognitive assessment procedures we can more easily recognize our own internal dialogs and what is prompting our behavior. At this point we also feel the need to reiterate a point made by Albert Ellis (personal communication) that we do not *have* to be assertive all the time nor do we have to be on guard in case we "fall back" into unassertive behaviors. Persons who make this mistaken belief have simply substituted a new "should" ("I *should* be assertive *always*"; "I *should* be *perfectly* assertive") which they can use to castigate themselves when they are not assertive. Thus, although we may choose to strive for being as assertive and interpersonally effective as we can be, we should not use assertiveness as a new absolute criterion for our OK-ness or not OK-ness.

Another area for ethical concern is the question of the legitimate definition of assertion training. . . . We believe it is important to define what assertion training is, not in order to exclude effective treatment modes nor to generate semantic conflict over terms. Rather, our concern is with the present popularity and proliferation of groups being labeled assertion training when they do not remotely represent the use of cognitive and behavioral principles and techniques. For example, we have learned of a person who calls her group assertion training and is actually doing something like advanced "feminine wiles" training. Confusion seems to exist between the process goals and the outcome goals of groups. Many treatment modes or group experiences may eventuate in more effective interpersonal communication; however, the procedures and group process vary considerably. We believe it is important for professionals to have a clearer understanding of what is legitimately labeled assertion training. Although combinations of cognitive and behavioral components may vary from trainer to trainer or group to group, we believe that clinical — as opposed to experimental — assertion training is a combination of these components. Trainers have an ethical responsibility to use psychological terminology appropriately; they should not conduct training groups under whatever label happens to be currently popular. Such "opportunism" is irresponsible to participants and to the profession. Admittedly, there is no recognized entity which passes judgment on what one may call his work, particularly if the person does not call it psychology or psychotherapy and is not a member of the American Psychological Association. The Committee on Scientific and Professional Ethics and Conduct of APA will make informal, educative efforts to inform members of inaccurate labeling of their work and, of course, take more formal action if the work is of questionable psychological value. The existence of a more formal committee would have its assets *and* its great liabilities. We believe that the members of the psychological and educational professions do have an ethical responsibility to clarify the labeling of their professional services. Caveat emptor is not enough.

Often in assertion groups, participants will reveal a number of psychological problems which are more appropriate for in-depth psychotherapy. As noted earlier, many psychological concerns include assertiveness components which are correctly dealt with in training groups. An ethical issue, however, emerges when trainers begin to do in-depth psychotherapy in what is offered as assertion training for personal growth. A most frustrating factor in explaining these ethical concerns is the problem of discriminating between assertion training (as a personal growth, learning, and therapy experience) and a more in-depth therapeutic procedure. Two directions might help to clarify the distinctions: the material attended to, and the manner in which the material is handled. Assertion training appropriately includes cognitive restructuring and behavior rehearsal procedures and several behavioral techniques such as relaxation and contracting.

An experienced therapist will also be able to recognize and interpret participants' psychological dynamics, historical origins of dysfunctional behaviors, or repression of feelings. If the trainers are offering an assertion training group for personal growth, these therapeutic practices are clearly going beyond such training. In effect, assertion therapy, rather than training, is being offered. If trainers decide they wish to pursue such psychological material utilizing additional therapeutic procedures, it is critical that participants be informed at the outset of the specific procedures to be used and that the group is also a therapy group. Assertion training may be used in conjunction with an assessment of the participants' behavioral-developmental patterns (e.g., in transactional analysis terms: assessment of games or scripts). Such procedures fit the third type of assertion training group which combines training with other procedures. Needless to say, in such groups, it is also important that the participants be advised of these procedures prior to joining the group.

We have shared our clinical observations with participants both within the group and individually when referrals seemed appropriate. For example, as a participant was working on speaking up in groups, it became clear that she was also not allowing herself to think. The trainer helped her identify some of the irrational thinking ("Never say anything stupid"), clarified her rights to express her opinions, and had her practice several situations. After the group, the trainer noted to the participant that she also seemed to keep herself from thinking and asked if she was aware of that. She agreed. The trainer asked if she could recall any support for not thinking as she was growing up. She did. The trainer suggested that if she wished to work on this, she might do so with a counselor. She felt there was something important to her shutting off and decided to work on it with a counselor. The trainer skillfully clarified what was appropriate for the assertion group and what was not. The trainer also was willing to make the confrontation and to recommend a source of resolution.

If the trainers wish to assess the impact of the group on its participants or to conduct other research, several ethical issues arise. First, participation in the research should be voluntary; it should not be contingent on doing the research if the group is offered as a service (as opposed to a research project). The participants should be informed of what they are required to do (without contaminating the data) for the project. They should be guaranteed anonymity beyond the researchers. If a no-treatment control group is offered, the trainers should be prepared to offer those persons training as soon as possible. The trainers should also share the individual results for that participant and the anonymous global results of the study with any participant who wants them.

Assertion training intentionally seeks behavior change for participants. Many of the participants' important relationships may have been based on their being unassertive in many situations. Helping persons change involves a number of ethical issues regarding the consequences of increased assertiveness to the participant as well as to significant others in that person's life.

It has already been noted that one should assess the consequences of being assertive; for example, in the work setting, possible consequences may be getting fired, demoted, or passed over for promotion or pay raises. Depending on the alternatives available, one might choose not to behave in a manner which, although assertive, would also lead to serious negative consequences. Trainers should make this issue clear and distinguish between such reasonable assessment and rationalizations which justify avoiding a situation that may result in negative consequences. With reasonable assessment, the person is choosing to behave based on reason; with rationalization, the primary motive is anxiety.

People are not assertive in a vacuum. Therefore, participants should always assess the likely consequences of their behavior. Trainers can make the point that one may choose not to stand up for one's rights when the consequences of such behavior outweigh the benefits of doing so. An important distinction can be made between individuals who reasonably choose not to be assertive (although they could be if they chose to) and individuals who avoid being assertive out of anxiety. . . .

Thus, the decision should be made out of reason and not out of anxiety. Such reasoning is not to be confused with "rationalizing" which sometimes accompanies avoidance behavior, i.e., "post hoc" reasons why avoidance made sense yet the actual motivating force for the behavior was anxiety. . . .

In some instances, participants have realized that several of their closest relationships have become disrupted as they increased their assertiveness. Often these relationships symbiotically required the participant to stay nonassertive; when the person changed, the relationship was out of balance. Trainers should be prepared to respond to participants who find they are losing some of their closest relationships. The participants (assuming they wish to continue such changes) can practice in the group discussing changes with the important people in their lives. Trainers should help participants assess what is happening in their relationships: Are others not liking the more assertive participant because of their own needs to perpetuate the earlier relationship, or is the participant behaving in ways that really are disruptive and does the participant wish to work on such behaviors? What does the participant think about this newly acquired assertive behavior?

The impact on others as one becomes more assertive is probably most serious in marriages, families, and other intimate relationships. Trainers should not only help participants assess the impact of their assertiveness on such relationships, but they should also help participants to deal with the reactions of intimates. We believe trainers have an ethical responsibility not to take a person out of an intimate living situation (especially children), teach that person to be assertive, and return the person to that "system" when others in that system are unprepared to handle these new behaviors. Clearly, we are not suggesting that such a person not seek or receive assertion training. Rather, the trainers should raise such concerns in the group and help participants to help others to understand their changes. Often the dialog carried on between intimates regarding the changes one of them is currently making helps to strengthen the relationship. In some cases, the relationship does not continue when a mutually satisfactory basis is not found.

Moreover, we believe trainers should be prepared to offer consultation, counseling, or make referrals for intimates seriously influenced by a participant's increased assertiveness. The trainer's role in such a consultation is to help the person explore how the participant's assertiveness is affecting him and to provide information to him on what assertiveness is about. Essentially, the message is that the participant is becoming more aware of her personal rights and working toward being more direct in expressing her thoughts, feelings, and needs. More subtly, we believe that such a consultation is reassuring; the person can better understand that assertion training is not a conspiracy against him, but rather a process that results in renegotiations within the relationship. The trainer might also discuss how to go about renegotiating in a way that allows both persons to feel OK about themselves.

At the same time, trainers should be alerted to several potentially negative outcomes of such a meeting: (1) the trainer might become too much of a spokesperson for the participant and thereby "rescue" him from expressing his own thoughts, (2) the other person might use the meeting to blow up or to make provocative accusations. Nevertheless, we believe that these consultations can be a very valuable experience for all involved and, therefore, support their occurrence and caution trainers to be sensitive to the fears and intentions of the others involved.

Our concern with changing someone who is functioning within a small system is even greater when the person has relatively little control in the system and the potential for negative reaction to assertiveness is great. Children and adolescents who are participating in assertion groups often cannot behave assertively without severe recriminations from their parents or other persons exercising control. The trainer's ethical responsibility here is to discuss these realities with the participant and to work on situations in such a way that the person can maximize the likelihood of being assertive at a level which minimizes the potential for punishment. Ideally, consultation with the entire family would be preferred but is not always available. We believe it would be highly unethical to train a young person to be assertive without realistic regard for the likely consequences.

SUMMARY

Trainers should be sensitive to the potential effect on others of the participants' increased assertiveness. This is not a caution to hold participants back in any way. Rather, we believe that trainers should: (1) be prepared to respond to participants' concerns about the effects of their increased assertiveness, (2) help participants to clarify for others how and why they are changing when they wish to explain, (3) be available for consultation or make referrals for close persons who recognize the changes in the participant, wish to understand more fully, and possibly make some changes in the way they have been relating to the participant, and (4) help participants to recognize and accept that some relationships are based on their being nonassertive and that these relationships are unlikely to change.

REFERENCE

Yalom, I., & Lieberman. M. A. A study of encounter group casualties. *Archives of General Psychiatry*, 1971, *25*, 16-30.

Screening Procedures[1]

Conducting screening interviews is one of the main ways in which trainers can assess whether a prospective group member is likely to benefit from assertion training. In addition, such screening interviews also enable the trainer to compose a more compatible group of individuals, to clarify purposes of the group, to start establishing therapeutic norms such as confidentiality, self-disclosure, giving support to others, and helping others, and to identify idiosyncratic assertion needs of the prospective members.

SPECIFYING SPECIFIC PROBLEM SITUATIONS

A first step in the screening process involves identifying specific situations in which a prospective group member has difficulty acting assertively. This helps the trainer ascertain whether the planned assertion training group will meet the person's needs. In the process, individuals become more active in delineating their problems and setting personal goals for change.

The individuals may be simply asked to describe specific situations in which they act nonassertively or aggressively, or they may complete one of the available paper-and-pencil assertion measures. The latter method often helps people become more aware of their assertion problems. Another method involves using the Wolpe-Lazarus Assertiveness Questionnaire (Wolpe & Lazarus, 1966) to identify and analyze an individual's problems in acting assertively. This questionnaire has been effectively used to identify assertive and nonassertive individuals (McFall & Marston, 1970; Eisler, Miller & Hersen,

Reprinted from pp. 293-303 of *Responsible Assertive Behavior*, by Arthur J. Lange and Patricia Jakubowski. Champaign, IL: Research Press, 1976. Used with permission.

[1] Parts of this chapter are taken from Jacubowski & Lacks (1975).

1973). The questionnaire consists of thirty questions which the trainer asks the prospective group member. Examples of these questions are:

Do you avoid complaining about the poor service in a restaurant or elsewhere?

If a friend unjustifiably criticizes you, do you express your resentment there and then?

Are you able to contradict a domineering person?

The person's answers on a paper-and-pencil assertion measure, the Wolpe-Lazarus Assertiveness Questionnaire, or to the trainer's request to simply describe specific problem situations are analyzed by the trainer and the assertion training candidate to determine nonassertive or aggressive patterns of behavior.

In analyzing these patterns, trainers need to keep in mind the conditions which can affect the ability to be assertive. MacDonald (in press) has noted that an individual's ability to be assertive in different situations depends on (1) the degree to which the other person is an intimate or a stranger, (2) the number of people present who will observe the behavior, (3) the status and sex of the other person, and (4) the extent to which one has time to prepare for assertive behavior. Additional conditions have been specified by Jakubowski & Lacks (in press): (1) whether one initiates the assertive encounter or instead is responding to the other person's initiated aggression or manipulation, (2) whether the situation calls for a type of assertive behavior one can enact, e.g., expressing affection, refusing requests, making requests, defending personal opinions, and finally, (3) whether the other person in the interaction controls significant reinforcers, such as the power to withhold affection, job raises, recommendations, etc. Those prospective group members who cannot identify specific problem situations are likely to be poor candidates for group assertion training.

IDENTIFYING CONDITIONS THAT PREVENT ASSERTIVE BEHAVIOR

When these patterns of nonassertive and aggressive behavior are identified, a next important step is to identify the causes of the nonassertion and aggression. Although there are many causes of nonassertion and aggression we see the following as four basic causes:

1. People may simply lack information or practice in acting assertively. In some cases, people may lack awareness of their own preferences, desires, and feelings.

2. People may not view their own or others' nonassertive, aggressive, and assertive behavior accurately. In such cases, they may feel unreasonably guilty after appropriate expressions of irritation because they inaccurately view it as

aggression, may inhibit spontaneous assertive behavior because they see this as aggressive, may react aggressively because they consider assertion as too weak and therefore nonassertive.

3. The belief system may be such that it does not support assertive behavior. For example, people may not believe that they or other people are entitled to express certain feelings, opinions, etc.

4. People may lack strategies for coping with their own excessive anxiety, anger, and guilt — feelings which interfere with their ability to act assertively.

In identifying the major causes of a person's nonassertion and aggression, the trainer can use such probes as: How are you most likely to act in this situation? If that failed, what would you do? What would you like to be able to say? What stops you from acting the way you'd like? How can you tell whether you've acted nonassertively or aggressively in this situation? What methods do you use to lower your anxiety in this situation?

While it is unlikely that during the screening interview a trainer will be able to do a full analysis of a prospective group member's problems in acting assertively, getting some sense of the chief causes of nonassertive and aggressive patterns can help trainers to better plan the assertion training experiences for an individual. It also helps the trainer determine whether an individual's needs are likely to be satisfied in a specific assertion training group. For example, when a person's basic problem is lack of information on how to act assertively, an assertion training group which emphasizes skill acquisition is likely to be more appropriate than one which emphasizes consciousness-raising. Or if the prospective group members mainly lack self-awareness of their needs and preferences, the trainer could develop a training program which includes more awareness-building activities.

OTHER FACTORS TO CONSIDER IN SELECTING MEMBERS

Situational vs. General Problems in Assertion. Alberti & Emmons (1974) differentiate between generally and situationally aggressive and nonassertive individuals. They caution against including generally aggressive or nonassertive individuals in assertion training groups until these persons have received therapy or possibly assertion training on a one-to-one basis. Before discussing their recommendation, we would like to clarify our understanding of assertion problems as "situational" or "general."

The available research evidence[2] does not support the view of assertion as

---

[2] For example, factor analysis of the Rathus Assertiveness Scale (Rathus, personal communication, 1973), Lawrence Assertive Inventory (Lawrence, 1970), the Assertion Inventory (Gambrill & Richey, 1975), and the College Self-Expression Scale (Galassi & Galassi, 1974) all revealed no general factors of assertion. Eisler et al. (1975) likewise supported the view that individuals who are assertive in one situation may not be assertive in a different interpersonal context.

a unitary and pervasive personality trait but rather that assertion is a situation-specific set of behaviors. Thus in a sense all assertion, nonassertion, and aggression can be considered as situationally determined. Some individuals are occasionally nonassertive or aggressive in a few specific situations while others have frequent problems across a vast spectrum of different types of situations. We see this latter group as generally nonassertive or aggressive. Our use of these terms does not imply a personality trait position.

Returning to Alberti & Emmons' caution about people who have general problems with assertion, it is our observation that some people are merely nonassertive or aggressive across many situations while other individuals have this problem *plus* other characteristics; for example, motor retardation, being unable to even imagine themselves acting assertively, being virtually out of contact with their feelings and preferences, or being extremely explosive. Sometimes a person's inability to act assertively is part of a much larger syndrome, like the "pampered child syndrome" (Rattner, 1971) in which individuals resent having to make their wants known to others, resent having to depend on others to figure out what their unexpressed needs are, and feel powerless to change their own passive-manipulative behavior patterns.

The upshot of all of this is that people who have general problems in assertion, which are complicated by some additional problems, would be more appropriately seen in therapy. These persons could receive assertion training after their more basic problems and ambivalences have been resolved. Generally nonassertive or aggressive individuals who are not so incapacitated by other complicated problems may be appropriately placed in group assertion training. However, as we will discuss later, these individuals may be better served by being in a homogeneous group composed of other persons who are also generally nonassertive or aggressive.

Motivation to Change. It is important to determine whether prospective members are really interested in changing their behavior and becoming more assertive. When members are very ambivalent about changing, they often end up spending a lot of group time simply discussing their ambivalence. In addition, the unmotivated or ambivalent group member may sabotage the assertion training group. For example, when a person is not interested in becoming employed and is in an assertion training group to acquire assertion skills to get a job, that person may end up sabotaging his own training. The entire group may also be hurt by one member's sabotaging efforts.

Commitment to Work. Another important consideration concerns assessing prospective members' willingness to actually work on changing their behavior through homework assignments, behavior rehearsals, etc. It is usually desirable to screen out those individuals who are merely curious about assertion training and are not committed to changing their behavior.

Willingness to Self-Disclose. It is important to ascertain that individuals are

willing to talk about those situations in which they have trouble acting assertively. When people report that it is difficult for them to be self-disclosive in
groups but that they are willing to do so, the trainer can ask them to consider
what would help make it easier for them to self-disclose. Individuals who
resent self-disclosing and strongly believe that others should be able to figure
out what they need would generally not be appropriate for assertion training
groups until they have resolved this issue.

Ability to Talk in Groups. People who are extremely uncomfortable during
the individual screening interview — who can barely be heard, who avoid eye
contact, who are vague and brief in their answers — stand a good chance of
being even more uncomfortable in the group setting. Such painfully shy
individuals usually would be more appropriately seen in individual assertion
training.

Realistic Expectations. It is important that the prospective members' expectations about the training group are appropriate. Individuals who hold
magical expectations of personality transformation or who expect an encounter experience are likely to be disappointed and possibly disruptive in the
training group.

Triadic Factors. Yalom & Lieberman's (1971) research in encounter groups
indicates that people may become "group casualties" when they have the
following three characteristics: (1) very low anxiety about being in the group,
(2) great vulnerability and low self-esteem, *and* (3) great motivation to change.
It is reasonable to believe that such individuals may prematurely disclose
deeply personal problems before a sufficient trust level has been established in
the group. Thus they would be unprepared for any negative group reaction. We
believe that these triadic factors are likely to be less important in assertion
training groups than in personal counseling and encounter groups. In assertion training groups, the emphasis is on skill acquisition rather than on
psychological probing and personal therapy. Also, the members in assertion
training groups are encouraged to provide positive feedback, support, and
information instead of negative confrontation and strong negative feelings.

Prior Bad Group Experience. When prospective members have had a
prior bad experience in a group, the trainer needs to ascertain whether their
bad experience was due to the leader or group — or whether the individuals
caused their own bad experience. For example, people who expect the leader
to be 100 percent attentive to all their needs, who cannot "stand" any confrontation, or who interpret any suggestions for improvement as unwarranted attacks
set themselves up to have a negative group experience. In selecting individuals
for assertion training groups, it is important to avoid those who are likely to
repeat their self-defeating pattern of behavior and end up having another "bad
group experience."

Other Issues. Individuals who see the trainer as a power figure to be
rebelled against, whose obvious anger is denied and covered by a thin veneer

of sweetness, who are highly manipulative, who have a borderline hold on reality, who are paranoid or psychopathic, who deny their obvious anger, who are overadaptive and take the position, "Just tell me exactly what I should do in the group and I'll do it," are generally poor candidates for group assertion training.

BALANCING THE GROUP

Sex Factors. Brumage & Willis (1974) found that single sex groups and mixed sex assertion training groups significantly improved their assertive behavior as measured by a paper-and-pencil measure of assertion (Rathus Assertiveness Schedule). The single sex groups improved more than those single sex groups which later added members of the opposite sex, which in turn improved more than the mixed sex groups. Group leaders rated the single sex groups as having greater cohesiveness and self-disclosure than the mixed sex groups. Our own experience with assertion training groups also supports these observations. Although the data are limited, it appears that having males and females in the same assertion training group will not reduce the overall effectiveness of the group experience; however, cohesiveness and self-disclosure are usually greater in single sex groups. Needless to say, when the assertion training group consists of members of both sexes, ideally there would be roughly equal numbers of males and females.

Age Factors. Age factors are usually not considered to be very important in encounter and personal counseling groups. However, in assertion training groups whose members are greatly different in age, group cohesiveness often suffers. In such groups, the members are likely to be dealing with very different assertion issues (e.g., trying to establish independence from parents vs. becoming more assertive at work), and the members frequently have trouble being supportive of each other's concerns. In general, it is better to have the group members in roughly similar age groups, where they are dealing with similar assertion issues. A side benefit is that the great homogeneity of members' problems makes planning the group experiences far easier.

Situational and General Problems. Mixing individuals who are extremely nonassertive with those who are extremely aggressive usually creates division within the group and may result in members dropping out. Likewise, mixing people who are generally nonassertive with those who have a few assertion issues also poses a problem. In such groups, generally nonassertive individuals often start emotionally withdrawing when the trainer does behavior rehearsals with the situationally nonassertive members. For example, in one group when a situationally nonassertive member practiced refusing a request, a generally nonassertive member crossed her arms, frowned, and turned her face away. This member felt that the person had no right to refuse the request in the first place. The trainer had to continually stop the process to deal with the issue of personal rights. In a sense, the generally nonassertive individual was still at the stage of learning the distinction between assertion, aggression, and nonassertion and accepting personal rights, while the other group members were ready to develop assertion skills through behavior rehearsal. In other cases, the group mixture of generally nonassertive and situationally nonassertive people may result in the generally nonassertive individuals devaluing themselves, feeling even more inadequate as they compare their slow progress with that of the more situationally nonassertive individuals, or becoming even more entrenched in their belief that assertive behavior is destructive.

Thus persons with general problems in assertion may be better served in a homogeneous group with others who share their problems. Trainers who mix general and situational persons need to be aware that this group composition is likely to result in some group management problems and may well be a disservice to the person with general problems in assertion.

SCREENING PROSPECTIVE GROUP MEMBERS
WHO HAVE CLINICAL PROBLEMS

For at least three reasons trainers need to know how to screen individuals who have clinical problems: (1) other therapists may refer their clients to a trainer for an assertion group, (2) trainers who are also therapists need to know the conditions under which assertion training may help their own clients, and (3) individuals may wish to join an assertion group for help with their clinical problems.

The assertion training case study literature has established that assertion training — often in combination with other therapeutic procedures — is a useful behavior change procedure for a wide variety of clinical problems:

Abdominal spasms (Lazarus, 1965)

Addictions (Salter, 1949, pp. 200-201)

Agoraphobia (Lazarus, 1966b; Rimm, 1973)

Asthma (Gardner, 1968; Wolpe & Lazarus, 1966, case no. 3)

Depression (Bean, 1970; Cameron, 1951; Katz, 1971; Lazarus & Serber, 1968; Piaget & Lazarus, 1969; Stevenson & Wolpe, 1960, case no. 3; Wolpe, 1958, case no. 2)

Dermatological problems (Seitz, 1953)

Hallucinations (Nydegger, 1972)

Headaches (Dengrove, 1968)

Marital problems (Fensterheim, 1972a; Eisler et al., 1974)

Phobias (Rimm, 1973; Lazarus, 1971; Cautela, 1966)

Sex problems (Edwards, 1972)

Urinary retention (Barnard, Flesher & Steinbook, 1966)

Unfortunately the case study literature does not explicitly address itself to an important assessment question: Under what conditions would these clinical problems be likely to benefit from assertion training? Let's take a mother who abuses her child. Under what conditions might assertion training be of help with this psychological problem? First, when a mother ricochets between nonassertive and aggressive behavior with her child. Second, when she nonassertively denies her own needs and feels like she is sacrificing herself for her child. Then, when she's drained, aggressively overreacting to the feelings of helplessness and inadequacy which are triggered when the child cries or is disobedient and seems to be demanding yet more of her. In summary, assertion training would be appropriate when the child abuse is at least partially caused by a mother's failure to accept and assert her own needs, to constructively express her anger and disappointment with her child and others, and to be assertive with her own parents and husband who may be highly critical of her and who therefore contribute to her feelings of inadequacy (Jakubowski, in press, a).

Since the assertion training case study literature does not explicitly describe these conditions, it is up to trainers to make this decision based upon their knowledge of the prospective member's assertion problems. Trainers can ask themselves: If the person were to act more assertively in certain specified situations, what changes would I expect to happen in the person's life, and are these changes likely to affect the person's presenting complaints? (Jakubowski & Lacks, in press). For example, if a trainer discovered that an alcohol-dependent client used alcohol in order to (1) escape from conflict situations with other people who are easily able to overpower the client; (2) indirectly express hurt and anger towards significant others; and (3) relax so that the client could express thoughts and feelings which ordinarily would have been suppressed, it would be reasonable that the client would benefit from assertion training (Jakubowski, in press, a). It could be anticipated that as a result of assertion training, the client would be able to effectively handle interpersonal conflicts and directly express hurt and anger. Thus, a major need for drinking alcohol would be reduced.

Using this approach in trying to ascertain whether a person's clinical problem would be likely to benefit from assertion training, is it likely that a widow *who seeks assertion training to ease her sadness* would benefit from such training? Not when her predominant concern is that she suffered a loss that no one else — except other widows — could appreciate; when she holds magical expectations about assertion training; when she cannot specify specific situations where she wants to become more assertive. Would a homosexual male *who wants assertion training to help him keep his lover* likely to be substantially helped? Again no — if the man has a history of his love relationships gradually deteriorating due to his increasing possessiveness, jealousy, and incessant demands for fidelity; when he demands that he be loved by everybody; when he refuses to do anything which would jeopardize others' approving of him. While such a man probably needs some additional assertion skills, it is unlikely that simple assertion would help him achieve his goal of keeping a lover forever. . . .

SUMMARY

One of the first assessment steps in assertion training involves ascertaining whether an individual's problems are appropriate for group assertion training. Making this determination usually involves various kinds of screening procedures, with the screening interview being an important procedure. Such interviews may also involve using various paper-and-pencil assertion measures. A critical issue for trainers of such groups is determining whether a particular individual's clinical or psychological problems are likely to benefit from assertion training. . . .

REFERENCES

Alberti, R. E., & Emmons, M. L. *Your perfect right: A guide to assertive behavior* (2nd ed.). San Luis Obispo, CA: Impact Press, 1974.

Barnard, G., Flesher, C., & Steinbook, R. The treatment of urinary retention by aversive stimulus cessation and assertive training. *Behaviour Research and Therapy*, 1966, *4*, 232-236.

Bean, K. L. Desensitization, behavior rehearsal, the reality: A preliminary report on a new procedure. *Behavior Therapy*, 1970, *1*, 542-545.

Brumage, M. E., & Willis, M. H. *How three variables influence the outcome of group assertive training*. Paper presented at the American Personnel and Guidance Association, New Orleans, April, 1974.

Cameron, D. E. The conversion of passivity into normal self-assertion. *American Journal of Psychiatry*, 1951, *108*, 98-102.

Cautela, J. R. A behavior therapy approach to pervasive anxiety. *Behavior Research and Therapy*, 1966, *4*, 99-109.

Dengrove, E. Behavior therapy of headaches. *Journal of American Society of Psychosomatic Dentistry and Medicine*, 1968, *15*, 41-48.

Edwards, N. B. Case conference: Assertion training in a case of homosexual pedophilia. *Journal of Behavior Therapy and Experimental Psychiatry*, 1972, *3*, 55-63.

Eisler, R. M., Hersen, M., Miller, P. M., & Blanchard, E. F. Situational determinants of assertive behaviors. *Journal of Consulting and Clinical Psychology*, 1975, *43*, 330-340.

Eisler, R. M., Miller, P. M., & Hersen, M. Components of assertive behavior. *Journal of Clinical Psychology*, 1973, *29*, 295-299.

Eisler, R. M., Miller, P. M., Hersen, M., & Alford, H. Effects of assertive training on marital interaction. *Archives of General Psychiatry*, 1974, *30*, 643-649.

Fensterheim, H. Assertive methods and marital problems. In R. D. Rubin, H. Fensterheim, J. D. Hendersen, & L. P. Ullmann (Eds.), *Advances in behavior therapy*. New York: Academic Press, 1972.

Galassi, J. P., & Galassi, M. D. Validity of a measure of assertiveness. *Journal of Counseling Psychology*, 1974, *21*, 248-250.

Gambrill, E. D., & Richey, C. A. An assertion inventory for use in assessment and research. *Behavior Therapy*, 1975, *6*, 547-549.

Gardner, J. E. A blending of behavior therapy techniques in an approach to an asthmatic child. *Psychotherapy: Theory, Research and Practice*, 1968, *5*, 46-49.

Jakubowski, P. Assertive behavior and clinical problems of women. In D. Carter & E. Rawlings (Eds.), *Psychotherapy for women: Treatment towards equality*. Springfield, IL: Charles C. Thomas, 1977.

Jakubowski, P., & Lacks, P. Assessment procedures in assertion training. *The Counseling Psychologist*, 1975, *5*(4), 84-90.

Katz, R. Case conference: Rapid development of activity in a case of chronic passivity. *Journal of Behavior Therapy and Experimental Psychiatry*, 1971, *2*, 187-193.

Lawrence, P. S. The assessment and modification of assertive behavior. (Doctoral dissertation, Arizona State University, 1970). *Dissertation Abstracts International*, 31, 1B-1601B (University Microfilms, No. 70-11, 888)

Lazarus, A. A. The treatment of a sexually inadequate man. In L. P. Ullmann & L. Krasner (Eds.), *Case studies in behavior modification*. New York: Holt, Rinehart and Winston, 1965.

Lazarus, A. A. Broad spectrum behavior therapy and the treatment of agoraphobia. *Behavior Research and Therapy*, 1966, *4*, 95-97.

Lazarus, A. A. *Behavior therapy and beyond*. New York: McGraw-Hill, 1971.

Lazarus, A. A., & Serber, M. Is systematic desensitization being misapplied? *Psychological Reports*, 1968, *23*, 215-218.

McFall, R. M., & Marston, A. R. An experimental investigation of behavior rehearsal in assertive training. *Journal of Abnormal Psychology*, 1973, *81*, 199-218.

Nydegger, R. V. The elimination of hallucinatory and delusional behavior by verbal conditioning and assertive training: A case study. *Journal of Behavior Therapy and Experimental Psychiatry*, 1972, *3*, 225-227.

Piaget, G. W., & Lazarus, A. A. The use of rehearsal-desensitization. *Psychotherapy: Theory, Research and Practice*, 1969, *6*, 264-266.

Rathus, S. A. A 30-item schedule for assessing assertive behavior. *Behavior Therapy*, 1973, *4*, 398-406.

Rattner, L. The pampered lifestyle. In A. G. Nikelly (Ed.), *Techniques for behavior change*. Springfield, IL: Charles C Thomas, 1971.

Rimm, D. C. Thought stopping and covert assertion. *Journal of Consulting and Clinical Psychology*, 1973, *41*, 466-467.

Salter, A. *Conditioned reflex therapy*. New York: Farrar, Straus & Giroux, 1949.

Seitz, P. F. D. Dynamically-oriented brief psychotherapy: Psychocutaneous excoriation syndromes. *Psychosomatic Medicine*, 1953, *15*, 200-242.

Stevenson, I., & Wolpe, J. Recovery from sexual deviations through overcoming of nonsexual neurotic responses. *American Journal of Psychiatry*, 1960, *116*, 737-742.

Wolpe, J. *Psychotherapy by reciprocal inhibition*. Palo Alto, CA: Stanford University Press, 1958.

Wolpe, J., & Lazarus, A. A. *Behavior therapy techniques*. New York: Pergamon Press, 1966.

Yalom, I., & Lieberman, M. A. A study of encounter group casualties. *Archives of General Psychiatry*, 1971, *25*, 16-30.

Assessment Procedures
for Assertive Behavior

The purpose of this paper is to discuss procedures for assessing assertive behavior which are useful to the assertion training practitioner. As is the case with other methods for modifying human behavior, progress in developing and refining the technique has outstripped progress in developing measures of assertive behavior and in evaluating the effects of the technique. The importance of assessment in the development and evaluation of an assertion training program is unquestionable.

Unfortunately, a number of methodological and conceptual difficulties exist in current assessment procedures. Among these difficulties are the lack of a commonly accepted definition of assertive behavior, the problem of differentiating aggressive behavior from assertive behavior, the relationship between anxiety and assertion, the lack of well-validated, paper-and-pencil measures of assertive behavior which are composed of subscales to measure different aspects of assertion, the cultural and situational relativity of assertion, our incomplete knowledge of the nonverbal components of assertion, and the lack of adequate *in vivo* behavioral measures. Since the above issues have been discussed in detail elsewhere (Bodner, 1975; Galassi & Galassi, 1976; Hersen, Eisler, & Miller, 1973; Jakubowski & Lacks, 1975), the focus of the paper is on answering the following question: Given the current state of the art, what assessment procedures are most useful to the assertion training practitioner? In order to answer this question, it is important first to adopt a common definition of assertive behavior and to recognize that the function and scope of assessment may vary depending on whether it is being used prior to, during, or after training.

Galassi, J. P., and Galassi, M. D., "Assessment Procedures for Assertive Behavior," in Alberti, R. E. (Editor), ASSERTIVENESS: INNOVATIONS, APPLICATIONS, ISSUES. San Luis Obispo, California: Impact Publishers, Inc., 1977. Reprinted by permission of the publisher.

Parts of this article have been reproduced, with permission from *Assert Yourself! How to Be Your Own Person*, Merna Dee Galassi and John P. Galassi, Copyright © 1977. Human Sciences Press.

NATURE OF ASSERTIVE BEHAVIOR

Assertion consists of a number of verbal, nonverbal, and paralanguage (tone of voice, inflection, etc.) behaviors. These behaviors are learned, and their purpose is to communicate an individual's wants, needs, opinions, etc. to others in a socially acceptable manner. Assertion is not conceptualized as a general or unitary personality trait (i.e., something that one has) but as a series of learned situation-specific behaviors (i.e., something one does). More specifically, assertion involves expressing a variety of behaviors (e.g., refusing requests, giving compliments, etc.) verbally, nonverbally, and through paralanguage to a number of people (e.g., friends, bosses, etc.). Table 8 illustrates this point in greater detail. Assertion occurs within a situation (e.g., private, public, etc.) that is embedded within a cultural context. One's behavior and therefore what is assertive and socially acceptable is affected by all of the above factors. Change in any one of the factors influences whether a given set of verbal, nonverbal, and paralanguage behaviors is judged to be assertive.

ASSESSMENT PRIOR TO TRAINING

Assessment for screening prior to training is designed to answer several questions. First, given a particular cultural context, what complex of behaviors (verbal, nonverbal, and paralanguage) does the potential trainee either have difficulty expressing or express infrequently, to what persons, and in what situations? Secondly, given the cultural context, what complex of behaviors does the potential trainee express in an aggressive manner, to what persons, and in what situations? Finally, what are the reasons (controlling variables) for the trainee's difficulties in assertion, and what components (e.g., modeling, behavioral rehearsal, cognitive restructuring, etc.) of an assertion training program would be most helpful to him/her?

Ideally, the first two questions are most adequately answered through behavioral observation of the trainee(s) in real life or in simulated (role-played) situations. Either the trainer or trained observers can rate the trainee's behavior in a variety of situations, either real or simulated (e.g., Galassi, 1973; MacDonald, 1974; McFall & Marston, 1970), which call for assertive behavior. In the typical role-played or behavior performance situation, the trainee is given a description of a situation which calls for assertive behavior. Then, he/she is asked to respond to statements that are delivered live or on tape by another person. The situation may require the trainee to initiate a statement or simply respond to the other person. In addition, the trainee may be asked to give one response or several responses. A typical simulated situation[1] is provided below.

---

[1] Excerpted from Galassi, M. D., and Galassi, J. P. *Assert Yourself! How to Be Your Own Person*. New York: Human Sciences Press, 72 Fifth Avenue, 1977.

You've gone to lunch at a restaurant. You've ordered a chef salad with thousand island dressing. However, when you get your salad, it has blue cheese dressing on it. You prefer thousand island. The waiter/waitress is approaching your area now.

Waiter/Waitress: Is everything okay?

Trainee:

Waiter/Waitress: I distinctly remember you ordering blue cheese dressing.

Trainee:

Waiter/Waitress: I have it written down right here on my slip — blue cheese.

Trainee:

Waiter/Waitress: All right, I'll be back in a few minutes.

In such situations, a baseline of the trainee's behavior can be recorded and deficiencies in the verbal, nonverbal, or paralanguage areas can be noted. The value of behavioral observation in pinpointing a trainee's strengths and weaknesses in self-expression is undeniable; however, it often is impractical to rely solely on behavioral observation as an assessment strategy, especially when the practitioner is concerned with screening large groups of trainees for assertion training.

ASSESSMENT INSTRUMENTS

As a result, many trainers find it useful to employ self-report questionnaires or inventories as preliminary screening devices in conjunction with one or more behavioral assessment interviews and/or observations. Most of the self-report inventories developed to date provide information only on the frequency with which a trainee believes that he/she asserts him/herself in situations which require such behavior. Some of the inventories provide information about the level of discomfort (anxiety) which accompanies self-assertion. Few of the inventories provide information on whether the self-expression is aggressive or not, the reasons for the lack of assertiveness, and the verbal, nonverbal, and paralanguage behaviors that are present or absent in a particular assertion. For the most part, the best of the currently developed inventories attempt to provide the practitioner with a general survey of the presence or absence of assertion with a variety of behaviors (e.g., refusing a request, expressing justified annoyance, etc.), persons, and situations. Assuming that the trainee's self-report is reasonably accurate, these inventories can provide the trainer with information on the frequency of the trainee's assertions and on the behaviors, persons, and situations which might be included in the trainee's program. Subsequently, interviews and/or behavioral observation of the trainee's performance in real life or simulated situations could be used to "flesh out" the content of the program.

The authors are aware of at least 17 inventories in various stages of development with the majority having been intended for use with college

Table 8. Assertion Self-Assessment Table

PERSONS

BEHAVIORS	Friends of the same sex	Friends of the opposite sex	Intimate relations, e.g. spouse, boyfriend, girlfriend	Parents, in-laws, and other family members	Children	Authority figures, e.g. bosses, professors, doctors	Business contacts, e.g. sales-persons, waiters	Coworkers, colleagues, and subordinates
Expressing Positive Feelings Give compliments								
Receive compliments								
Make requests, e.g. ask for favors, help, etc.								
Express liking, love, and affection								
Initiate and maintain conversations								

Self-Affirmation Stand up for your legitimate rights	Refuse requests	Express personal opinions including disagreement	Expressing Negative Feelings Express justified annoyance and displeasure	Express justified anger

students and/or adult populations. The existing inventories and question-naires include: the Action Situation Inventory (Friedman, 1971), the Adolescent Assertion Discrimination Test (Shoemaker, 1973 as cited in Bodner, 1975), the Adolescent Self-Expression Scale (McCarthy & Bellucci, 1974), the Adult Asser-tion Scale (Jakubowski & Wallace, 1975 as cited in Lange & Jakubowski, 1976), the Adult Self-Expression Scale (Gay, Hollandsworth & Galassi, 1975), the Assertion Inventory (Dalali, 1971), the Assertion Inventory (Fensterheim, 1971), the Assertion Inventory (Gambrill & Richey, 1975), the Assertiveness Inventory (Alberti & Emmons, 1974), the AQ test (Phelps & Austin, 1975), the College Self-Expression Scale (Galassi, DeLo, Galassi, & Bastien, 1974), the Conflict Resolution Inventory (McFall & Lillesand, 1971) which was designed explicitly to measure refusal behavior, the Constriction Scale (Bates & Zim-merman, 1971), the Lawrence Assertive Inventory (Lawrence, 1970), the modi-fied Rathus Assertiveness Schedule for the junior high level (Vaal & McCullagh, 1975), the Rathus Assertiveness Schedule (Rathus, 1973), and the Wolpe-Lazarus Assertiveness Questionnaire (Wolpe & Lazarus, 1966).

We are not aware of any published, standardized, paper-and-pencil inven-tories for the assessment of assertive behavior with children from elementary school through adolescence. Although Vaal and McCullagh (1975) demon-strated that a modified version of the Rathus Assertiveness Schedule (RAS) possessed a lower readability level than the original RAS and that it possessed acceptable test-retest reliability for junior high school students over a two-month period, validity data have not been presented for the inventory.

For older populations, Jakubowski and Lacks (1975) and Lange and Jakubowski (1976) have stated that the Adult and College Self-Expression Scales appear to be the most useful for measuring a wide variety of different types of assertive behaviors. Both measures were conceptualized according to the behaviors and person's model of assertion described earlier. Although neither of the scales provides subscale scores for assertion with particular behaviors or particular persons, inspection of individual items can provide the practitioner with useful information concerning which behaviors and persons to focus on during assertion training.

The 50-item College Self-Expression Scale (Galassi, DeLo, Galassi & Bas-tien, 1974) was designed to measure the frequency or degree of difficulty of engaging in a variety of assertive behaviors with such persons as same and opposite sex peers, parents and relatives, authority figures, business relations, and strangers. The behaviors tapped include asking favors, complimenting, initiating conversations, expressing positive feelings such as love and affection, refusing unreasonable requests, expressing justified annoyance and anger, and standing up for legitimate rights. A variety of situations were represented. Norms have been collected for almost 4,000 college students. Two-week test-retest reliability coefficients of .89 and .91 have been reported for two samples. Significant positive correlations have been found between the College Self-Expression Scale (CSES) and the Dominance, Intraception, Hetero-sexuality, Achievement, Defensiveness, Self-Confidence, Exhibition, Change, Favorable, and Autonomy Scales of the Gough Adjective Check List, while significant negative correlations were obtained between the College Self-Expression Scale and the Unfavorable, Succorant, Abasement, Deference, and Counseling Readiness Scales (Galassi, et al., 1974). The scale has been found to have little or no overlap with a measure of aggression (Galassi & Galassi, 1975).

In addition, Galassi and Galassi (1974) found that college students who seek personal adjustment counseling rate themselves as less assertive than both vocational-educational counselees and non-counseled college students. Significant but small correlations were obtained between student teachers' scores on the CSES and ratings of assertiveness by their supervisors and between dorm residents' scores on the CSES and ratings by resident hall assistants. Students who score low on the CSES have been differentiated from high scorers and from a combination of moderate and high scorers in a behavioral role playing test of assertiveness (Galassi, Hollandsworth, Radecki, Gay, Howe, & Evans, 1976). The ability of the scale to demonstrate change following assertion training has been demonstrated by Galassi, Galassi, and Litz (1974). Additional research by Lacks and Connelly (cited in Lange & Jakub-owski, 1976) indicates that the items are not significantly correlated with social desirability, that the scale takes a minimum amount of time to complete (average of 8.1 minutes, range 3-15), and is favorably received by respondents.

The 48-item Adult Self-Expression Scale[2] includes four original and 29 rewritten items from the College Self-Expression Scale. The items were de-signed to tap the expression of seven behaviors (expressing personal opinions, refusing unreasonable requests, initiating conversations, expressing positive feelings, standing up for legitimate rights, expressing negative feelings, and asking favors) in six interpersonal situations (with parents, the public, authority figures, friends, intimate relations, and in global situations in which the person is not specified). Reliability and validity studies (Gay, Hollandsworth, & Galassi, 1975; Hollandsworth, Galassi, & Gay, 1976) were conducted with a community college population (age 18-60), psychiatric patients, male prisoners, and adult students enrolled in evening classes at a technical institute and a university. Findings comparable to those for the College Self-Expression Scale were obtained. The relationship between the Adult Self-Expression Scale and be-havioral performance measures of assertive behavior has not been investigated to date.

With respect to the question of the quality and appropriateness of self-expression (aggressiveness), the existing instruments do not seem to tap this in

---

[2]A sample copy of the scale is available from ASES, P. O. Box 17174, Charlotte, North Carolina 28211.

either a systematic or comprehensive fashion.[3] Similarly, the inventories provide almost no information about the reasons for nonassertive or aggressive behavior. Nonassertive or aggressive behavior in a situation may occur for at least three reasons: appropriate responses are blocked due to the presence of anxiety in the situation; the trainee does not know what an appropriate response is for the situation; and the trainee is unsure of his/her rights or does not believe that he/she has the right to respond assertively in the situation.

The Assertion Inventory (Gambrill & Richey, 1975) is an exception to the last statement and does provide information concerning reason one. The scale attempts to differentiate the frequency of engaging in assertive behavior from the degree of discomfort which is involved in asserting oneself. For each of the 40 scale items, trainees indicate their degree of discomfort or anxiety as well as their frequency of engaging in the designated behavior. Of course, the presence of anxiety could be tapped through other paper-and-pencil inventories and the use of physiological measures. However, the equipment needed to measure many physiological responses would be costly and impractical for the practitioner, and existing paper-and-pencil measures of anxiety either lack the necessary situational specificity and/or are too time consuming to administer.

INDIVIDUALIZED ASSESSMENT

Given the methodological weaknesses and the lack of diagnostic information provided by existing inventories, the assertion training practitioner may find it advantageous to construct his/her own inventory. Described below is a procedure for constructing such an inventory. By having the trainee complete all of the steps, the practitioner can learn the frequency of the trainee's assertion with a variety of behaviors and persons, the situations in which the trainee is aggressive, the presence of debilitating anxiety, the trainee's knowledge of appropriate behavior, and whether or not the trainee feels that he/she understands his/her rights in given situations. This assessment procedure is designed to provide the practitioner with maximum flexibility in assessment, in the sense that behaviors and persons can be added or deleted at will; questions that are not of interest (e.g. aggressive behavior) can be omitted; and specific details of a situation can be added if desired (e.g. Do you express justified annoyance to your parents when you are alone with them at home? versus Do you express justified annoyance to your parents?). The assessment procedure, the Assertion Self-Assessment Table, and instructions for presenting it to trainees is provided in the following section.

---

[3]We have used the Buss-Durkee Inventory (Buss, 1961) to tap this dimension of self-expression. Although we have found this inventory to be somewhat helpful, it, like other measures of aggression, appears to lack the situational specificity which is so helpful in assessment and in planning a training program.

ASSERTION SELF-ASSESSMENT TABLE[4]

Assertive behavior involves directly expressing your feelings, preferences, needs, rights, and opinions without undue anxiety and in a manner which is neither threatening nor punishing to others. Assertion consists of numerous behaviors (e.g. refusing requests, giving compliments, etc.) directed toward various people (e.g. bosses, friends, etc.). Individuals differ in their ability to express these behaviors and in their ability to interact effectively with these persons.

Before learning more about behaving assertively, it would be helpful to determine how you presently express yourself. As with other skill training programs (e.g. speed reading), assertion training is enhanced if an assessment of the participant's skills is conducted prior to beginning the program. This assessment provides information that will be helpful in tailoring the program to meet your specific needs.

Now turn to the Assertion Self-Assessment Table (Table 8). Notice that the row headings list a variety of behaviors which represent three major categories of assertion: expression of positive feelings, expression of self-affirmation, and expression of negative feelings. The column headings list persons to whom those behaviors may be addressed. The persons represented are not inclusive of all people with whom you may interact. Some columns contain more than one person. In these instances, you should choose the person who is most relevant for you. For example, if you are married, you will be answering (in most cases) questions about your behavior with your spouse, rather than boyfriend/girlfriend. The darkened cells indicate situations which are unlikely to be relevant for most people. There may be other situations which are not applicable to you. Simply ignore those cells which do not apply.

The Assertion Self-Assessment Table will be used to evaluate frequency of assertions, presence of anxiety, areas of aggression, knowledge of appropriate behavior, and knowledge of personal rights. By completing Steps 1-6, you will determine how frequently you assert ten different behaviors with eight different persons. Your responses to Steps 7-12 will indicate whether or not you experience undue anxiety while expressing yourself, and Steps 13-19 will help you evaluate whether you are aggressive while expressing particular behaviors with given persons. Steps 20-22 will help you to determine your knowledge of situationally appropriate responses, and Steps 23-25 will enable you to determine your knowledge of personal rights that are involved in the situation.

---

[4]Excerpted from Galassi, M. D., and Galassi, J. P. *Assert Yourself! How to Be Your Own Person*. New York: Human Sciences Press, 1977.

Frequency of Asserting Yourself

Step 1. In reading the table, use the following question with each row and column heading:

Do I (*row heading*) to/from/of/with (*column heading*) when it is appropriate?

For instance, if you begin with the upper left hand cell, you would form the following question: Do I *GIVE COMPLIMENTS* to *FRIENDS OF THE SAME SEX* when it is appropriate?

Step 2. In answering the question for each cell, write in the word which best describes how often you engage in the behavior in that situation. Choose your answer from the words USUALLY, SOMETIMES, or SELDOM. For example, if you SELDOM give compliments to friends of the same sex when appropriate, you would write the word SELDOM in the upper left hand cell of the table.

Step 3. Now complete each cell in the table in the manner described in Steps 1 and 2.

Step 4. Look at the table and find the places where you answered with the words SELDOM and SOMETIMES. Are there one or more behaviors (e.g. making requests) for which you have given a number of SELDOM and SOME-TIMES answers? If there are, list those behaviors here.

We suggest that you devote special attention to these behaviors in your assertion training program.

Step 5. Again, look at the places where you have the words SELDOM and SOMETIMES. Are there one or more persons (e.g. intimate relations: spouses, boyfriends, girlfriends) for whom you have given a number of SELDOM and SOMETIMES answers? If there are, list those persons here.

We suggest that you devote special attention to these persons in your assertion training program.

Step 6. As you look at your SELDOM and SOMETIMES answers, you may find that they do not group into any particular behaviors or persons. This is not uncommon since people often have difficulty expressing only certain feelings to only certain people.

Presence of Anxiety

Step 7. To assess whether you experience any discomfort or undue anxiety when you express yourself, use the following question with each row and column heading:

When I (*row heading*) to/from/of/with (*column heading*), do I become very nervous or unduly anxious?

For instance, if you begin with the upper left hand cell, you would form the following question: When I *GIVE COMPLIMENTS* to *FRIENDS OF THE SAME SEX*, do I become very nervous or unduly anxious?

Step 8. For each cell, answer the question with either a YES or NO. If you answer YES, write YES in the cell. If you answer NO, it is not necessary to write NO in the cell. For example, if you become very nervous when you compliment a friend of the same sex, write YES in the upper left hand cell.

Step 9. Now complete each cell in the table in the manner described in Steps 7 and 8.

Step 10. Look at the table and note where you entered the word YES. Are there particular *behaviors* for which you have given a number of YES responses? If there are, list those behaviors here.

Step 11. Again, look at your YES answers. Are there particular *persons* for whom you have given a number of YES responses? If there are, list those persons here.

Step 12. You may find that your YES answers do not group under any particular behaviors or persons. This is not uncommon since people often experience anxiety only when expressing certain feelings to certain people.

Evaluation of Aggressive Behavior

Step 13. If you are considering assertion training because you feel that your behavior is aggressive at times, complete Steps 14 through 19. If this is not a concern of yours, skip to Step 20.

Step 14. As you may be aware, aggression can be expressed directly and include such behaviors as threats, hostile remarks, name calling, and ridicule, or it can be expressed indirectly and include such behaviors as sarcasm and malicious gossip. To determine whether you behave aggressively, at times, use the following question with each row and column heading:

Am I aggressive when I (*row heading*) to/from/of/with (*column heading*)?

For instance, if you are reading the lower right hand cell (last cell in the table), you would form the following question: Am I aggressive when I *EX-PRESS JUSTIFIED ANGER* to *COWORKERS?*

Step 15. In answering the question for each cell, *shade* in those cells for which you report behaving aggressively in that situation.

Step 16. Complete each cell in the table in the manner described in Steps 14 and 15.

Step 17. Look at the table and note the cells you have shaded. Are there one or more *behaviors* for which you have shaded a number of cells? If there are, list those behaviors here.

We suggest that you devote special attention to these *behaviors* in your assertion training program.

Step 18. Again, note the cells you have shaded. Are there particular *persons* for whom you have shaded a number of cells? If there are, list those persons here.

We suggest that you devote special attention to these *persons* in your assertion training program.

Step 19. You may find that your shaded cells do not group under any particular behaviors or persons. This is not uncommon since people often are aggressive only when expressing certain behaviors to certain people.

Knowledge of Appropriate Responses

Many times people experience problems in expressing themselves because they do not know what would constitute a socially appropriate response in a particular situation.

Step 20. Look at those cells which you have *identified* as ones in which you infrequently assert yourself, you feel unduly anxious, or you have a tendency to behave aggressively. For these cells *only*, answer the following question:

Do I know what would constitute an appropriate and assertive response when I (*row heading of identified cell*) to/from/of/with (*column heading of identified cell*)?

For instance, if the last cell in the table were one of your identified cells, you would form the following question: Do I know what would constitute an appropriate and assertive response when I *EXPRESS JUSTIFIED ANGER* to *COWORKERS?*

Step 21. Complete each *identified* cell in the manner described in Step 20.

Step 22. List those cells in which you feel uncertain about what constitutes an assertive response.

We suggest that you devote special attention to *learning to discriminate appropriate responses* for these situations in your assertion training program.

Knowledge of Personal Rights

Problems in self-expression also can result when people are not sure that they have the right to assert themselves in a situation or are not sure of their rights in general with respect to the other individual(s) involved.

Step 23. Look at those cells which you have *identified* as ones in which you infrequently assert yourself, you feel unduly anxious, or you have a tendency to behave aggressively. For these cells *only*, answer the following question:

Do I know my rights in those situations in which I (*row heading of identified cell*) to/from/of/with (*column heading of identified cell*)?

For instance, if the last cell in the table were one of your identified cells, you would form the following question: Do I know my rights in those situations in which I *EXPRESS JUSTIFIED ANGER* to *COWORKERS?*

Step 24. Complete each *identified* cell in the manner described in Step 23.

Step 25. List those cells in which you feel uncertain about your rights.

We suggest that you devote special attention to *learning about your rights* in these situations in your assertion training program.

This completes the Assertion Self-Assessment Table.

A Footnote for Trainers

Assuming reasonable accuracy of the trainee's answers, the Assertion Self-Assessment Table alone or in conjunction with behavioral observation and/or clinical interviews should provide ample information about the most relevant content to include in an assertion training program for a given trainee as well as suggest the components of an assertion training package that will be most beneficial to a given client (e.g. relaxation and behavioral rehearsal for anxious trainees, cognitive restructuring for trainees who are uncertain about their rights, etc.).

ASSESSMENT DURING TRAINING

Assessment during training is designed to answer at least three questions. First, what specific aspects of an assertive response (verbal, nonverbal, and paralanguage) does a trainee need to develop and refine during training? What progress is the trainee making with respect to these aspects from session to session? Finally, to what extent are the trainee's skills in assertion transferred to and maintained in his/her environment?

A behavioral observation method of assessment would appear to be of prime importance in answering many of these questions. Figure 13 presents a set of criteria[5] that can be used in a behavioral observation assessment strategy. The criteria are designed to be used by both the trainer and the trainee to evaluate the adequacy of the trainee's performance in the role-played or behavioral performance interactions that typically are included in assertion training programs. The use of these criteria has been discussed extensively elsewhere (Galassi & Galassi, 1977). As a result, only a few important points will be restated.

First, the criteria are designed to facilitate the assessment of the verbal, nonverbal, and paralanguage aspects of a trainee's response. The topography of these components will vary depending on the behavior being expressed, the cultural context, etc. For example, it is appropriate to raise one's voice when expressing justified anger, but a loud voice seems inappropriate when express-

---

[5]These criteria also can be used in any pretraining screening that may be conducted using behavioral observation of the trainee in real life or simulated situations which call for assertive behavior.

1. Determine the anxiety experienced by the trainee in the situation:

    Suds score*

    Eye contact

    Relaxed posture

    Nervous laughter or joking

    Excessive or unrelated head, hand, and body movements

2. Evelute the verbal content:

    Did the trainee say what he/she really wanted to say?

    Comments concise and to the point?

    Comments definitive, specific, and firm?

    No long-winded explanations, excuses, or apologetic behavior

    "I" statements and "feeling talk"

3. Evaluate how the message was delivered:

    Almost immediately after the other person spoke

    No hesitancy or stammering

    Appropriate loudness, tone, and inflection

    No whining, pleading, or sarcasm

4. Decide whether the trainee was pleased with his/her behavior.

Figure 13. Criteria for Evaluating Assertive Behavior

---

ing love and affection. Trainers can adapt these general criteria to the requirements of the situation in which the trainee finds him/herself. Secondly, we have found it useful to evaluate the trainee's performance in four major areas: the degree of discomfort or anxiety experienced, verbal content of the response, the manner in which the message was delivered, and the satisfaction expressed by the trainee with his/her performance.

Question three can be answered by teaching trainees to use the criteria in everyday interactions and by teaching them to record their behavior between sessions. The trainee can record his/her behavior with respect to the frequency of occurrence and the quality of the behavior as judged by the trainee using the assertive behavior criteria above. For example, if a trainee is practicing how to refuse requests between sessions, then he/she can record each time a situation occurred which called for refusal behavior.

---

*The Suds score refers to the Subjective Unit of Disturbance Scale score developed by Wolpe (1969). Trainees are instructed to rate the level of anxiety that they felt in situations calling for assertive behavior on a subjective scale which ranges from 0, completely relaxed, to 100, extremely anxious.

The trainee would record whether he/she refused the request as well as the adequacy of the refusal as judged on the criteria listed in Figure 13. If a validity check on the trainee's recordings is desired, then help can be enlisted from a friend or relative of the trainee who has access to the trainee's behavior in situations which call for refusal. By reviewing the trainee's records at each session, a trainer can determine the progress that is being made and institute any modifications in the training program which might be indicated from the records and from a discussion with the trainee.

If a more scientific demonstration of change is desired, then a trainer could employ a single subject research design such as the multiple baseline design (Hall, 1971). Assume that prior to training, it has been established that a trainee has difficulty refusing requests, giving compliments, and initiating conversations. The trainee could be taught to record the occurrence/nonoccurrence of these behaviors for a period of time (e.g. one week) before training in order to provide a baseline or pretreatment level against which comparisons during and after training could be made. Training might begin by teaching the trainee only to initiate conversations. During this time period, the trainee would be encouraged to initiate conversations in real life but not be concerned about refusing requests or giving compliments. The trainee would continue to record the occurrence/nonoccurrence of all three behaviors. As soon as the trainer noticed an increase in initiating conversations that was maintained for a period of time (e.g. one week), he/she would initiate training on the second behavior. Once change was obtained on the second behavior, the trainer would proceed to work with the trainee on the third behavior. If changes occur in each of the behaviors only when training is introduced, then the trainer can assume that his/her training program was responsible for the change. A multiple baseline design also could be used with two or more subjects who had common behavioral deficits. In this usage, the training is instituted with one subject at a time rather than with one behavior at a time.

ASSESSMENT AFTER TRAINING

Assessment after training is designed to determine whether training resulted in changes in behavior that are being maintained in the absence of training. The ideal method for assessing such changes is through unobtrusive observation of *in vivo* trainee behavior. Some ingenious attempts (e.g. determining whether a trainee would refuse a magazine sales pitch on the telephone) to develop *in vivo* follow-ups have been made by McFall and his associates (McFall & Marston, 1970; McFall & Lillesand, 1971; McFall & Twentyman, 1973). However, such procedures are not without their problems (Galassi, 1973; McFall & Twentyman, 1973) and may be impractical on a large scale basis for the practitioner.

In the absence of direct behavioral observation of trainees in "real life," the trainer is left with several options. The first is to place the trainee, at one or more times in training, in simulated interactions which call for assertive behavior (e.g. with a live or tape recorded confederate) and observe the trainee's behavior. If large numbers of trainees are involved, this approach also may be impractical for the practitioner.

Some more practical approaches would involve asking the trainee to complete the paper-and-pencil inventories which were used for screening and to continue to record his/her behavior, with or without validity checks, and to give these records to the trainer at one or more times after training has concluded. A "buddy system" can be an effective method in group training. Based on these data and an occasional telephone call, the trainer and trainee can decide whether additional or "booster" assertion training sessions are desirable.

In summary, assessment should play an important role in assertion training. The type of assessment procedure which will be most useful to the assertion training practitioner will depend on the purpose of the assessment: for screening, for monitoring changes during training sessions or outside of training, or for determining the maintenance of gains after assertion training has concluded.

REFERENCES

Alberti, R.E., & Emmons, M.L. *Your perfect right: A guide to assertive behavior*. San Luis Obispo, CA: Impact Press, 1970, 1974.

Bates H.D., & Zimmerman, S.F. Toward the development of a screening scale for assertive training. *Psychological Reports*, 1971, *28*, 99-107.

Bodner, G.E. The role of assessment in assertion training. *The Counseling Psychologist*, 1975, *5*(4), 90-96.

Buss, A.H. *The psychology of aggression*. New York: John Wiley, 1961.

Dalali, I.D. The effect of active-assertion and feeling clarification training on factor analyzed measures of assertion. (Doctoral dissertation, University of California, Los Angeles, 1971.) *Dissertation Abstracts International*, *32*, 1B-1291B. (University Microfilms No. 71-21, 322)

Fensterheim, H. *Help without psychoanalysis*. New York: Stein and Day, 1971.

Friedman, P.H. The effects of modeling and role playing on assertive behavior. In R. Rubin, A. Lazarus, H. Fensterheim, & C. Franks (Eds.), *Advances in behavior therapy*. New York: Academic Press, 1971.

Galassi, J.P. *Assertive training in groups using video feedback*. Final progress report in National Institute of Mental Health Small Research Grant MH22392-01, 1973.

Galassi, J.P., DeLo, J.S., Gallasi, M.D., & Bastien, S. The college self-expression scale: A measure of assertiveness. *Behavior Therapy*, 1974, *5*, 165-171.

Galassi, J.P., & Galassi, M.D. Relationship between assertiveness and aggressiveness. *Psychological Reports*, 1975, *36*, 352-354.

Galassi, J.P., & Galassi, M.D. Validity of a measure of assertiveness. *Journal of Counseling Psychology*, 1974, *21*, 248-250.

Galassi, J.P., Galassi, M.D., & Litz, C.M. Assertive training in groups using video feedback. *Journal of Counseling Psychology*, 1974, *21*, 390-394.

Galassi, J.P., Hollandsworth, J.G., Jr., Radecki, J.C., Gay, M.L., Howe, M.R., & Evans, C.L. Behavioral performance in the validation of an assertiveness scale. *Behavior Therapy*, 1976, 7, 447-452.

Galassi, M.D., & Galassi, J.P. A critical review of assertive behavior: Definition and assessment. *Psychotherapy: Theory, Research and Practice*, 1976, in press.

Galassi, M.D., & Galassi, J.P. *Assert yourself! How to be your own person*. New York: Human Sciences Press, 1977.

Gambrill, E.D., & Richey, C.A. An assertion inventory for use in assessment and research. *Behavior Therapy*, 1975, *6*, 550-561.

Gay, M.L., Hollandsworth, J.G., Jr., & Galassi, J.P. An assertiveness inventory for adults. *Journal of Counseling Psychology*, 1975, *22*, 340-344.

Hall, R.V. *Behavior management series: Part I. The measurement of behavior*. Lawrence, KS: H. and H. Enterprises, 1971.

Hersen, M., Eisler, R.M., & Miller, P.M. Development of assertive responses: Clinical, measurement and research considerations. *Behavior Research and Therapy*, 1973, *2*, 505-521.

Hollandsworth, J.G., Jr., Galassi, J.P., & Gay, M.L. The adult self-expression scale: Validation using the multitrait-multimethod procedure. *Journal of Clinical Psychology*, 1976, in press.

Jakubowski, P.A., & Lacks, P.B. Assessment procedures in assertion training. *The Counseling Psychologist*, 1975, *5*(4), 84-90.

Lange, A.J., & Jakubowski, P. *Responsible assertive behavior: Cognitive/behavioral procedures for trainers*. Champaign, IL: Research Press, 1976.

Lawrence, P.S. The assessment and modification of assertive behavior. (Doctoral dissertation, Arizona State University, 1970.) *Dissertation Abstracts International*, 31, 1B-1601B (University Microfilms No. 70-11, 888)

MacDonald, M.L. *A behavioral assessment methodology applied to the measurement of assertion*. Doctoral dissertation. University of Illinois, Urbana, 1974.

McCarthy, D., & Bellucci, J. The adolescent self-expression scale. Personal communication, 1974.

McFall, R.M., & Lillesand, D.B. Behavior rehearsal with modeling and coaching in assertive training. *Journal of Abnormal Psychology*, 1971, 77(3), 313-323.

McFall, R.M., & Marston, A.R. An experimental investigation of behavior rehearsal in assertiveness training. *Journal of Abnormal Psychology*, 1970, 76, 295-303.

McFall, R.M., & Twentyman, C.T. Four experiments on the relative contributions of rehearsal, modeling and coaching to assertion training. *Journal of Abnormal Psychology*, 1973, *81*, 199-218.

Phelps, S., & Austin, N. *The assertive woman*. San Luis Obispo, CA: Impact Press, 1975.

Rathus, S.A. A 30-item schedule for assessing assertive behavior. *Behavior Therapy*, 1973, *4*, 398-406.

Shelton, J.L. Homework in AT: Promoting the transfer of assertive skills to the natural environment. In R.E. Alberti (Ed.), *Assertiveness: Innovations, applications, issues*. San Luis Obispo, CA: Impact Press, 1977.

Vaal, J.J., & McCullagh, J. The Rathus assertiveness schedule: Reliability at the junior high school level. *Behavior Therapy*, 1975, *6*, 566-567.

Wolpe, J., & Lazarus, A.A. *Behavior therapy techniques*. New York: Pergamon Press, 1966.

PART IV

RESOURCES

Resources for Training:
The State of the Art

Almost every major weekly has carried an article on assertion training (AT). It appears that assertion has arisen out of nowhere to be touted as the miracle-brand solvent for those difficult personal problems left unconquered by TA, TM, or est. Actually, the concept of assertion has been around for many years, although not popularized until the past few years.

A Brief Historical Perspective

The concept of assertion was first introduced as part of the emerging behavior modification literature in the late 1940s. In 1949, Salter described what he called the excitatory reflex response and personality in his book *Conditioned Reflex Therapy* (republished, 1961). Nine years later, in 1958, Wolpe devoted most of one chapter of *Psychotherapy by Reciprocal Inhibition* to "assertive responses," a term he preferred to Salter's "excitatory" label. Wolpe's writing included some important additions to and revisions of Salter's basic theory. In *Behavior Therapy Techniques* (1966), Wolpe and Lazarus gave an entire chapter to "assertive training." This chapter was revised by Wolpe in *The Practice of Behavior Therapy* (1969, 1973), while Lazarus discussed assertion further in a chapter of his *Behavior Therapy and Beyond* (1971). With these publications, Salter, Wolpe, and Lazarus had laid the foundations of assertion training,[1] but none had devoted an entire book to the subject.

In 1970, Alberti and Emmons published the classic (and now revised) forerunner of the current outpouring of assertion literature: *Your Perfect Right*.

Revised and expanded from Colleen Kelley, "Assertion: The Literature Since 1970," pp. 264-275 of the *1977 Annual Handbook for Group Facilitators*. John E. Jones and J. William Pfeiffer (Eds.). La Jolla, CA: University Associates, 1977.

[1] For a more complete summary of this line of development, see D. C. Rimm & J. C. Masters, "Assertive Training," in *Behavior Therapy: Techniques and Empirical Findings*. London: Academic Press, 1974.

Since that time, the term "assertion training" has skyrocketed to fame and continues to inspire books on the subject. Of the thirty-nine assertion books and looseleaf publications considered in this review (including *Your Perfect Right*), all but two have been published since 1974.

Some see this sudden popularity of assertion as a transitory fad. Others (Jakubowski-Spector, 1973, reviewed in this article) see it as the result of three important cultural changes of the 1960s: (1) people began to value personal relationships more highly, (2) social acceptance of alternate life styles and social behaviors grew, and (3) the women's movement encouraged women to be effective as well as sensitive. Thus assertion filled the need for increased personal effectiveness. The increasingly humanistic approach of behaviorists in recent years is also cited as an important contributing factor to the current status of assertion training.

As the literature of assertion has grown in volume and has become more available to the general public, people have found it more and more difficult to know which assertion book would best meet their needs. This confusion is complicated by the fact that one assertion book may offer some unique and useful section of information not included in another otherwise similar book. Even the most inclusive book may fail to explore a significant aspect of assertion in the depth desired by the reader.

Recent vs. Pioneering Works

Assertion has distinguished itself, since its inception, by its emphasis on (1) anxiety reduction and on (2) skill training in new and more effective behaviors, involving (3) self-expression and the basic personal rights of people in interpersonal situations. The recent literature, however, differs from the pioneering works in several respects:

1. In contrast with the earlier works, the more popular literature is less oriented toward one-to-one therapy and centers more on group training or self-help.

2. Whereas emphasis had been on patients who were almost never assertive or who had very high anxiety levels, assertion training now focuses on clients with normal anxiety levels who wish to become more assertive in one or two specific areas.

3. Prior to 1970, emphasis was on basic behavior modification techniques as they applied to assertion; today assertion has emerged as a separate entity, and behavior modification techniques are only some of the means used to achieve its goals. Among the more recent techniques are structured exercises and instruments.

4. The behavior modification books addressed men's and women's asser-

tion problems; many of the more recent assertion books direct themselves to women.

5. The earlier literature addressed itself solely to the professional therapist; some of the newer books are geared to the professional trainer, and a large number have been written for the general public.

Within these basic distinctions, the new literature varies in terms of content and of stance on basic issues. For example, the questions of what assertion is; who, with what qualifications, should conduct assertion training; whether assertion training is therapy or not; whether the cognitive, affective, or behavioral (nonverbal or verbal) aspects of assertion are the most important focus of training; and whether certain responses are assertive or aggressive are answered in a variety of ways.

Concerns for This Review

In view of the sudden increase in the volume of assertion literature, the newness and smallness of the field, and the diversity of approach, an attempt has been made to consider all books devoted entirely to assertion and published between 1970 and January 1979. Although the intended audience, organizational flow, and readability have been taken into account in reviewing these books, the major concern has been with the answers to three questions: (1) What is the book's basic approach? (2) Are the techniques presented effective and ethical? (3) Does the book present a good overview and is it inclusive in the following areas: definition of assertion and an introduction to the topic's basic concepts; examples; behavior modification techniques; other techniques and a variety of approaches; structured exercises; scales; special helps in application areas; and special features or unique contributions?

Five areas are covered: popular books, subdivided into introductory works and more specialized works; professional books and looseleaf publications; films; audiotapes and filmstrips; and other aids. An attempt has been made to place books of more general interest before those that meet more specific needs. This principle has been adjusted only for books that could be easily confused, e.g., two books by the same author or two books with similar titles. In this case the two titles have been placed next to each other to make it easier for the reader to compare their differences.

Some of the more common assertion terms used in this review and elsewhere in this book are briefly redefined:

- *Anxiety-Reduction Techniques:* Methods to help reduce anxiety, such as relaxation or graduated exposure to the person or object evoking the anxiety.

- *Behavior Modification (Behavioral, Behavioristic) Techniques:* Techniques that teach one to change one's behavior in order to resolve problems or to relieve anxieties, as opposed to methods that simply help one to understand these problems.

- *Behavior (Behavioral)-Rehearsal Procedures or Techniques:* Role play, usually combined with other techniques, such as covert rehearsal, modeling, role reversal, and positive reinforcement for the purpose of practicing a skill, rather than for insight or catharsis.

- *Cognitive Restructuring, Rational-Emotive Procedures:* Procedures that teach one to become aware of one's present thought patterns and to develop more rational ways of thinking about situations, in order to change one's emotional reactions and behaviors in a particular situation.

- *Covert Rehearsal:* The process of imagining oneself responding successfully, or as one would like to, to a particular problem situation.

- *Covert Reinforcement:* The procedure of bringing to mind a pleasurable, or positively reinforcing, image in order to reward oneself immediately following a desired response and to increase the probability of responding similarly in the future.

- *Modeling:* Demonstrating for an observer a behavior that the observer wishes to learn.

- *Role Play:* The technique of acting out or replicating a situation in which one plays a role.

- *Role Reversal:* The process in which one role player in a role play exchanges roles for a brief time with another role player.

- *Thought Stopping:* The technique of controlling unwanted thoughts through negative self-reinforcement, specifically through using the word "stop," at first shouted aloud and eventually simply said silently to oneself.

To facilitate location of resources in this chapter, the entries are listed here in the order in which they appear:

Popular Books

Your Perfect Right
Stand Up, Speak Out, Talk Back! The Key to Self-Assertive Behavior
The Assertive Option: Your Rights and Responsibilities
Don't Say Yes When You Want to Say No
How to Be an Assertive (Not Aggressive) Woman in Life, in Love and on the Job: A Total Guide to Self-Assertiveness
The New Assertive Woman

The Assertive Woman
Self-Assertion for Women: A Guide to Becoming Androgynous*
    (*fully human)
How to Become an Assertive Woman: The Key to Self-Fulfillment
Confidence in Communication: A Guide to Assertive and Social Skills
Assert Yourself! How to Be Your Own Person
Woman, Assert Your Self! An Instructive Handbook
Asserting Your Self: A Practical Guide for Positive Change
It's Up to You: Developing Assertive Social Skills
How to Listen Assertively
Get Yours! Dynamic Assertiveness Training Techniques for Men & Women
Project: YOU. A Manual of Rational Assertiveness Training
I Can If I Want to: The Direct Assertion Therapy Program to Change Your Life
When I Say No, I Feel Guilty: How to Cope — Using the Skills of Systematic
    Assertive Therapy
Taking Charge on the Job: Techniques for Assertive Management
Assertive Skills for Nurses
Becoming Assertive: A Guide for Nurses
Liking Myself
The Mouse, the Monster and Me: Assertiveness for Young People
You Can Run Away from It!

Professional Books

An Introduction to Assertive Training Procedures for Women
Responsible Assertive Behavior: Cognitive / Behavioral Procedures for Trainers
Assertive Training for Women
Assertion Training: A Humanistic-Behavioral Guide to Self-Dignity
Personal Effectiveness: Guiding People to Assert Themselves and Improve Their
    Social Skills
Introduction to Assertion Skills Training
Assertion Skills Games
Achieving Assertive Behavior: A Guide to Assertive Training
Assertiveness: Innovations, Applications, Issues
Approaches to Assertion Training
Assertive Consumer: Credit and Warranties
Assertion Skill Training: A Group Procedure for High School Women
Assertive Black . . . Puzzled White: A Black Perspective on Assertive Behavior
Leader's Manual for an Assertive Skills Course in Correctional Settings

Films

The Confidence Game
Assertion Skills: Tintypes
Responsible Assertion: A Model for Personal Growth
Actualization Through Assertion: A Behavioral Approach to Personal Effectiveness
Assertive Training: The Teaching of Appropriate Behavior
Coping with Parents
Coping II: Getting What You Want
Assertive Training for Women (Parts I and II)
Improving Personal Relationships: Assertion Issues for High School Women in Relating to Men (Parts I and II)
What Could I Say? An Assertion Training Stimulus Program
Assertive Management

Audiotapes and Filmstrips

Assertiveness Training for Women
Assertion Training Series: A Guide to Self-Dignity
Assertion Training (in The Art of Parenting: A Complete Training Kit)
Assertiveness Training for Career and Personal Success
Assertiveness Training
Assertiveness Training: A Teaching Program for Professionals
The How To's of Assertive Management

Other Aids

Assert
Management Dialogue
Assertive Behavior Training: An Annotated Bibliography

POPULAR BOOKS

Introductions to Assertion

The first nine books in this section have such similar content that it is easier to talk about how they are alike than it is to describe their differences. The books all serve as introductions to assertion for the lay reader. To this end, each is written in a somewhat informal style and contains some or all of the following:

(1) a definition of assertion, (2) an exploration of personal rights, (3) a number of anecdotes demonstrating nonassertive, assertive, and aggressive responses in particular situations, (4) techniques and structured exercises designed to be used in a self-help program or as part of group training, and (5) methods of applying assertion in various application areas, such as personal development, communication, social relations, and work.

Your Perfect Right

Robert E. Alberti and Michael L. Emmons
San Luis Obispo, CA: Impact Press, 1970 (2nd ed., 1974). 118 pp., hardbound; paperbound.

This is the landmark book that put assertion on the map for the popular market. The book has two sections: one for the lay reader and one for the professional. The lay material consists of an introduction to, and discussion of, assertion — what it is, personal rights underlying it, situational vs. general nonassertion and aggression, clear definitions of nonassertion/assertion/aggression — to which most of the later books have deferred, referred, and added. Good case examples are sprinkled throughout the text. There is a short, step-by-step description of how to use behavioral techniques to become more assertive and a section on dealing with the consequences of assertion.

The professional part of the book briefly covers therapist preparation, client diagnosis, and some basic facilitation techniques — chiefly, covert rehearsal, modeling, and behavior rehearsal. Additional features include the Universal Declaration of Human Rights, a 35-item Assertiveness Inventory, and an annotated bibliography.

Stand Up, Speak Out, Talk Back! The Key to Self-Assertive Behavior

Robert E. Alberti and Michael L. Emmons
New York: Pocket Books, 1975. 206 pp., paperbound.

This is an expanded and popularized version of *Your Perfect Right*. Additions include a set of assertive vignettes and responses within each of several application areas: personal development, social relations, work, consumer relations, and school. Alberti and Emmons suggest that the reader use these vignettes to practice their step-by-step program of behavioral techniques. Assertive ways of expressing anger/conflict and caring/joy are discussed in separate sections, and there is a more understanding approach to handling put-downs than most other books advocate, an approach that allows both parties to come out ahead.

The authors have dropped the topics of client diagnosis and facilitator preparation in favor of a chapter on "helping others learn assertion." Whereas the earlier work advocated four key steps for facilitators of assertive behavior (knowledge of basic learning principles, familiarity with the literature, practice with components of the training process, and personal assertiveness in the facilitator's own life), this newer version makes everybody an instant winner. It encourages the reader to pass his or her assertive learnings on to a friend or relative, especially through such techniques as modeling and role play. Some very brief guidelines are offered for doing so.

The Assertive Option: Your Rights and Responsibilities
Patricia Jakubowski and Arthur J. Lange
Champaign, IL: Research Press, 1978. 336 pp., paperbound.

This book is as extensive and informative as the book written for professionals by the same authors. A good definition of assertion is presented, as well as a very good introduction to the basic assertion concepts and theory. Basic human rights, cognitive assertion, and verbal assertion (including effective listening and conflict resolution) are covered in depth. The reader is encouraged to integrate assertion skills by taking them immediately to the real-life situation through successive approximations. To this end, guidelines are presented for practicing assertion in situations that more and more closely approximate the target situation, using SUDS and relaxation techniques. Role play, videotapes, and use of a mirror are suggested, although the role play (behavior rehearsal) technique is only briefly described and should be accompanied by more specific guidelines. Participants are told what to look for and what to expect when they join an assertion group.

Thirty-three structured activities are interspersed throughout the text, and two inventories (Asserting Your Body Language and a 30-item Discrimination Test on Assertive, Aggressive, and Non-Assertive Behavior) are included. Special application areas include communications and social situations: aggression, anger, tender feelings, conversation, and requests.

A relatively small portion of the book is devoted to nonverbal assertion. Some new and useful material on irrational thinking, rational thinking, and rationalizations is presented in the cognitive assertion area.

Don't Say Yes When You Want to Say No
Herbert Fensterheim and Jean Baer
New York: David McKay, 1975. 304 pp., hardbound; paperbound.

This book presents perhaps the most erudite and behavioristic approach of this group of nine, and one of the most inclusive. Strongly oriented to setting behavioral goals and developing action plans, the authors present a series of behavior assignments and over twenty structured exercises within various application areas. Many of the structured exercises are really behavioral techniques (relaxation, covert reinforcement, thought stopping, and behavioral rehearsal), which are discussed in more detail than in most of the other popular books. The application areas include personal development, social relations, close relationships, sex, work, weight reduction, and sexual variants; discussion within these areas goes beyond basic verbal and nonverbal assertive responses to an exploration of the topic and ways of developing skills within each area.

Negative aspects of the book include occasional displays of sex stereotyping ("If you're a wife, don't pick half-time of the Jets game. If you're a husband, don't start talking before dinner when she's busy at the stove" [p. 136]) and a "beginner's guide to put-downs" which admonishes the reader to "observe the principle: don't be afraid to hurt the innocent" (p. 115).

A short theoretical background of assertion, a 23-item Assertiveness Inventory, and a 19-item Uptight Inventory are included.

How to Be an Assertive (Not Aggressive) Woman in Life, in Love and on the Job: A Total Guide to Self-Assertiveness
Jean Baer
New York: Rawson Associates, 1976. 311 pp., hardbound; paperbound.

This is a more personalized and slightly less behaviorally oriented book than the one Baer wrote with her behavior-therapist husband. The book is geared more to a woman's point of view than the previous book, and the author shares much of her own struggle to be assertive — a process for which she gives her husband a great deal of credit. The traditional behavior modification techniques accompany new structured exercises applied in much the same areas as the earlier book: personal development (including dealing with anger), communication (criticisms and compliments), social relations, close relationships, sex, work, courtship for singles, and children.

Baer's interviews with a number of prominent women on the subject of their own assertion problems constitute one of the book's unique features. There is an expanded and somewhat more constructive section on the handling of put-downs.

One area that seems incomplete is a discussion of assertiveness training. According to the author, there are two kinds: (1) educational lecture series in the basic concepts and (2) therapeutic sessions, either individual or group, which only those holding an M.D., Ph.D., or M.S.W. are qualified to run. Skill training by group facilitators is left out in the cold.

The New Assertive Woman
Lynn Z. Bloom, Karen Coburn, and Joan Pearlman
New York: Delacorte Press, 1975. 230 pp., hardbound; paperbound.

Here is an introduction to assertion that is both smoothly paced and well balanced. Over twenty-five structured exercises and useful questionnaires are evenly distributed in this book as it progresses through a discussion of assertion concepts, the identification of assertive problems and blocks to assertion, ways to develop skills in challenging irrational beliefs, reducing anxiety, listening, and nonverbal communication. The authors suggest a role-play/role-reversal/role-play training method and assertive messages that include empathic statements, expressions of feelings, and statements of wants.

No special helps in application areas are included, although there are chapters discussing sex and the woman's transition from home back to school or work.

The Assertive Woman
Stanlee Phelps and Nancy Austin
San Luis Obispo, CA: Impact Press, 1975. 177 pp., hardbound; paperbound.

The consciousness-raising emphasis of this book helps put the reader in touch with his or her role-related assertion problems through more than forty structured exercises and enlightening inventories. Many of the special helps are power oriented and are offered in the following application areas: personal development (anger and humor), confident communication (how not to apologize, how not to answer, how to get an answer, how to say no, how to initiate a conversation, how to handle compliments, criticism, or rejection), sensuality, and children.

The focus is on the assertor's self-understanding and attitude change and on the content of the assertive message; behavior therapy techniques are almost nonexistent. There are short sections on reducing anxiety, developing the nonverbal aspects of assertion, and setting up men's and women's consciousness-raising groups. The authors present two separate types of aggression in their assertion model: direct and indirect.

The more positive assertive skills, such as empathy, listening, and making friends, seem neglected in this book. The broken-record technique is presented without a full explanation of its potentially negative consequences, and the two countermanipulation techniques described seem more defensive than assertive.

Self-Assertion for Women: A Guide to Becoming Androgynous (*fully human)*
Pamela E. Butler
New York: Harper & Row, 1974. 307 pp., hardbound; paperbound.

This is a very readable introduction to assertion for women. The book is well written and well organized and has many entertaining and elucidating anecdotes and illustrations. Stereotypical women's roles and problems resulting from those roles are explored, and approaches for becoming more assertive are described in the areas of awareness and verbal, nonverbal, and cognitive assertion.

The book does not describe the major assertion techniques and no definition of assertion, exploration of human rights, or next steps for practice and acquisition of skills in an assertion group are included. However, extensive chapters are included on two special application areas: learning to say no and dealing with criticism. The professional woman, female/male relationships, and power are also discussed.

How to Become an Assertive Woman: The Key to Self-Fulfillment
Byrna Taubman
New York: Pocket Books, 1976. 214 pp., paperbound.

Taubman has interviewed trainers and therapists and drawn from a variety of written sources to create a "compendium" of quoted ideas and suggestions, plus over twenty structured exercises in assertion. The result reads something like a book of Heloise's Hints. If the reader is looking for a systematic and comprehensive introduction to assertion, this one is not for him or her, but there are some useful tips and pointers for those not afraid of a few contradictions now and then.

No real theory of assertion is included, nor any specific application areas. Much discussion focuses around self-awareness, identifying problem areas, setting goals, and practicing the words and behaviors appropriate to an assertive response. The book tends to ramble and to be diffuse at times.

The reader is encouraged to teach himself or herself assertion or to form a led or leaderless group, with very brief guidelines for doing so. The broken-record technique is presented in a more flexible form than usual, although its potentially negative aspects are not discussed. Special attention is given to recognizing various irrational fears, hidden aggressions, and manipulations.

More Specialized Books

The following sixteen books differ from the first nine in that they are more specialized. They concentrate in depth on one or two of the areas (techniques and/or applications) covered by the first nine books.

Confidence in Communication: A Guide to Assertive and Social Skills
Ronald Adler
New York: Holt, Rinehart and Winston, 1977. 334 pp., paperbound.

This workbook contains a good amount of practical, articulate, and interesting reading matter in a nicely organized format. The book is divided into four parts. The meat of the book is contained in Part II (Assertion Techniques) and Part III (Special Application Areas: Communication).

Although only selected techniques are discussed in Part II, those selected are discussed very well. These include: identification of problems and goal setting, nonverbal elements of assertion, shaping, behavior rehearsal (including modeling, coaching, feedback), covert behavior rehearsal, hierarchy building, SUDS, progressive relaxation, desensitization, recording data, and self-modification. Part III includes conversation skills, feelings, criticism, conflicts, and requests.

Part I is a definition of assertion and identification of some basic theoretical concepts; Part IV contains some charts and fifty-three pages of detachable duplications of all activity forms from other parts of the text. This provides the reader an alternative to writing in the text itself and is useful in a class, where assignments may need to be collected. An Assertiveness Inventory is included.

Assert Yourself! How to Be Your Own Person
Merna Dee Galassi and John P. Galassi
New York: Human Sciences Press, 1977. 237 pp., paperbound.

What most distinguishes this workbook from other assertion books is its emphasis on special application areas. The Galassis have created a systematic workbook in which the reader can (1) choose an application area from among fourteen, (2) study some guidelines particular to that area, (3) read a series of counterproductive or erroneous beliefs generally associated with the area and some challenges to those beliefs, (4) fill in his or her own responses to standard lines associated with a particular situation and compare those responses with some model responses, (5) write his or her own practice situation within the particular area, and (6) set some homework goals.

The application areas fall under the headings of communication, family/children, close relationships, work, and school (college students). Except for a section on standing up for rights, application areas comprise Chapters II, III, IV, and V of this six-chapter book.

The book also provides a good discussion of assertion theory and gives some brief attention to verbal delivery, thought stopping, SUDS, deep muscle relaxation, and homework assignments. There are an Assertion Self-Assessment Table, an Assertion Assessment Table for Children, and a form for learning to discriminate among assertion, nonassertion, and aggression. A sequence of procedures that can be used with the special application area chapters is provided, as well as a short overview for the trainer.

This is a good workbook in special application areas, but one thing lacking is a detailed discussion of techniques (behavior rehearsal or role play, verbal assertion techniques, etc.) used to develop basic assertion skills, as well as guidelines and cautions regarding these techniques. For example, although role play is mentioned, the technique described is to have another person read lines to the assertor in a conversation format, to have the assertor practice responding assertively to each line, and, when the assertor is more comfortable with the situation, to have the other person change and vary the lines (p. 33). More technique guidelines, cautions, and variations would seem appropriate.

Woman, Assert Your Self! An Instructive Handbook
Blanche Adams et al.
New York: Harper & Row, 1976. 89 pp., paperbound.

This work was first published as a pamphlet, under the title *Assert Your Self*, by Seattle-King County NOW (National Organization for Women) in 1974. Revisions in this edition are minor: the self-image techniques have been edited, and there are several illustrations and an expanded bibliography.

The book is a collection of assertive techniques and guidelines, which the authors, members of an assertion group, have found useful for themselves. It includes a 20-item Assertiveness Inventory; five structured exercises dealing with self-image; and helpful techniques, suggestions, and practice situations in the areas of social relations, close relationships, work (interviews and business meetings), and consumer relations. There is also a section focused on the reactive communication skills (speaking up, resisting interruption, saying no, stating what bothers you, giving and receiving criticism). Several behavior modification aspects of assertion are mentioned, and some very brief guidelines for a ten-week leaderless assertion group (assertive rap group) are given, including useful rules for giving feedback. There is a short annotated bibliography.

Asserting Your Self: A Practical Guide for Positive Change
Sharon Anthony Bower and Gordon H. Bower
Reading, MA: Addison-Wesley, 1976. 244 pp., hardbound; paperbound.

This systematic workbook presents a step-by-step assertion program that is quite broad, clear, and useful. The Bowers — a counselor and former actress and director, and a psychologist specializing in the study of human learning and memory — have combined their talents in this volume. The book emphasizes both (1) the development of verbal assertive statements — scripting — and (2) the use of behavior modification principles and techniques in becoming assertive.

The chapter-by-chapter skill-building sequence involves: (1) identifying and understanding personal situations in which assertion is lacking and situations in which assertion is desired, (2) improving self-esteem, (3) reducing anxiety and doing some beginning assertion exercises, (4) developing assertive scripts, or verbal replies, and (5) a nine-phase method for practicing assertion. This nine-phase method strongly emphasizes vocal (projection, clarity, expression) skills accompanying the script and includes attention to other nonverbal assertion cues. The workbook includes over fifty original structured exercises within this sequence.

Five of eleven chapters are devoted to various aspects of scripting, a topic that has received only passing attention in other assertion literature. There are guidelines, samples, and directions for writing one's own script. Special pointers and examples are offered on scripting in response to one-shot or long-term harassment or aggression. The focus is on negotiation, not power or put-downs. While the authors suggest that scripting is not bound to the proposed four-stage formula, exercises tend to focus more on knowing exactly what to say and practicing how, when, and where to say it than on developing spontaneous reactions.

The book has several deficiencies. It contains little discussion of a definition of assertion or its theory. Covert- and behavior-rehearsal techniques are not discussed, nor are assertion groups, and the nine-phase training method presented is written to be used entirely by oneself. A few of the sample scripts seem abrasive and not open enough to negotiation, and some of the "I" statements expressing feelings would be better if they excluded the word "you." Those who object to the use of self-punishment as a technique are free to eliminate its minor role, as the reader is encouraged to tailor the program to his or her needs. A brief description of several defensive techniques does not discuss the potentially destructive results of their repetitive use.

The book uses several acronyms and special terms to aid in remembering assertion concepts developed by the authors. Illustrations are creative, although somewhat male dominated. There is a special section on social skills and a 14-item Assertiveness Questionnaire. A companion 69-page Instructor's Manual (by Sharon Anthony Bower and Beverly A. Potter) is available that presents an organized eight-class format for teaching assertion. Approximately twenty structured exercises are offered, some of which incorporate written exercises from the workbook. The manual includes brief introductions to systematic desensitization, relaxation, and role play.

It's Up to You: Developing Assertive Social Skills
Eileen Gambrill and Cheryl Richey
Millbrae, CA: Les Femmes, 1976. 168 pp., paperbound.

This excellent book specializes in one application area: positive social skills, in particular meeting people and carrying on group conversations. Initiating, maintaining, ending, changing participation in, disagreeing in, and making conversations more enjoyable are all discussed in depth with examples and useful guidelines.

Other assertion techniques are described as means to develop and practice these social skills. Techniques discussed include: positive self-talk (cognitive assertion), relaxation, goal setting, fogging, role playing, record keeping, self-reinforcement, and monitoring of behavior. Ways to use the book in a group situation are discussed. Appendices contain useful written forms and three scales: Identifying Behavior Checklist, Assertion Inventory, and Activity Inventory.

How to Listen Assertively

Baxter Geeting and Corinne Geeting
New York: Simon and Schuster, 1976. 232 pp., paperbound.

Listening is discussed here under three headings: Process, Skills, and Applications. Listening is categorized into several types (TLC, creative listening, listening for information, etc.) that merit study. The description of each of these types of listening is accompanied by corresponding guidelines.

"Listening assertively" is perhaps not the most appropriate title for this book. The basic concepts of assertion are not discussed, although a brief definition of assertion is given in which the importance of standing up for both one's own rights and those of others is emphasized. Although assertive listening is usually associated with active listening, very little space is devoted to discussion of this skill. The reader is told that "as an assertive listener . . . it is your perfect right to stop listening when you are sure this is a waste of time" (p. 65). The reader is cautioned not to make snap judgments, but the option of checking out the judgment is never mentioned in the suggested guidelines, which basically advocate intense listening followed by a decision on whether to leave or stay, (pp. 25, 42). When reading nonverbal cues, the listener is advised to listen carefully, but is never advised to check out with the speaker what the nonverbal language means (pp. 34-36). Instead, the importance of one's "intuitive voice" or sixth sense is mentioned.

Nor is the possibility of interrupting a long-winded speaker considered. Only areas such as starting to talk before others are finished are mentioned. The authors say, "Probably the most unforgivable habit one can acquire is that of interrupting others . . . If you hear yourself interrupting, consider it a danger signal of deeper trouble" (p. 220). The legitimate use of interruption is never discussed.

The book contains many examples and some guidelines, although not many techniques. Application is discussed in the following areas: personal development, communication, social relations, family/children, close relationships, work, and school.

Get Yours! Dynamic Assertiveness Training Techniques for Men & Women

Ruth Halcomb
Canoga Park, CA: Major Books, 1976. 158 pp., paperbound.

This book is a somewhat more organized and more specialized Heloise's Hints. The book is generously interspersed with guidelines, questionnaires, and exercises in selected special application areas: social relations, close relationships, and sex. Topics include, among others, how to assertively form and follow up on new relationships, how to make your sexual needs known, how to deal with conflicts, anger, and anxiety in close relationships, and how to deal with falling in love. The book includes a definition of assertion; a discussion of the three assertion response styles and basic human rights; and a brief summary of the DESC script, thought stopping, and the SUDS technique.

Project: YOU. A Manual of Rational Assertiveness Training
Claudine Paris and Bill Casey
Denver, CO: Institute of Living Skills Education, 1978. 85 pp., paperbound.

This is a short, practical book, written in a concise style. It presents short discussions of predominantly cognitive-behavioral assertion areas and techniques. (The authors have chosen to include only those techniques that have been "well researched.") The book gives basic useful descriptions, examples, and suggested activities in each of the following areas: goal setting and attainment; establishing baseline data; irrational beliefs and rational-emotive philosophy; cognitive, covert, verbal, and nonverbal practice methods; principles of learning; and the special application areas of communication, social relations, and consumer relations.

An Assertiveness Inventory is included.

I Can If I Want to: The Direct Assertion Therapy Program to Change Your Life
Arnold Lazarus and Allen Fay
New York: William Morrow, 1975. 118 pp., hardbound.

Rational-emotive in approach, this book aims at helping people identify and change (1) the mistaken beliefs that cause them emotional disturbance and (2) the resultant behavior. The volume is an organized catalog of twenty "mistakes," or mistaken beliefs, each identified and illustrated with an example. The basic misconceptions underlying each mistake are listed, and a program for change toward more assertive thinking and behavior is described. Each program consists of several activities that can be carried out by the reader.

There is very little discussion of assertion per se in this book, although the definition of assertion offered is clear and functional. A 17-item Therapist Selection Questionnaire and five case studies are included.

When I Say No, I Feel Guilty: How to Cope —
Using the Skills of Systematic Assertive Therapy
Manuel J. Smith
New York: Dial Press, 1975. 324 pp., hardbound; paperbound.

The first three chapters of this controversial book deal with our inherited survival responses, ways in which other people violate our prime assertive human right, and the common means other people use to manipulate us. This sets a good tone for the theme song of the book: survival in a manipulative world.

Within this first section, a number of irrational or "childish" beliefs concerning how one "should" behave are presented, as well as ten basic human rights with which to contradict the beliefs. Some of the childish beliefs are perhaps not so irrational (Example: "You need the cooperation of other people to survive" [p. 61]), and the basic human rights are more asocial than those presented in other assertion books (Example: Right #10. "You have the right to say 'I don't care'" [p. 67]).

Chapter 4 discusses "the first thing to learn in being assertive: persistence." The remaining chapters center around the seven techniques that form the book's core. Three of the seven techniques — volunteering free information, self-disclosure, and seeking a workable compromise — are positive and equitable. However, these techniques have been allotted just over twelve pages of discussion.

The book concerns itself mainly with four techniques known as broken record (repetition), fogging (agreeing partially or in principle), negative assertion (agreeing with criticism), and negative inquiry (requesting criticism). The stated main purpose of these techniques is to respond to manipulative attempts, benign or not, to control behavior; the second purpose is to reduce defensiveness and anxiety in unpleasant situations. Numerous dialogues demonstrate how to use these techniques in response to attempted manipulation. Many of these dialogues make the a priori assumption that the other person is attempting to manipulate. For example, a person asking for an explanation is perceived as trying to induce guilt. This assumption seems to close off avenues of negotiation prematurely and to promote distrust.

Although Smith denigrates manipulation as a technique, suggests workable compromise whenever self-respect is not in question, and proposes verbal problem solving as the alternative to aggression and flight, there is little in the book that demonstrates real dialogue or that speaks to the rights of both parties involved.

Perhaps the greatest objection that has been made to this book is its approach to the ethical questions involved. While empathy is mentioned as important in dealing with persons close to oneself, Smith does not discuss many of the limitations and the potentially destructive effects of the techniques. In response to a student's request for some safeguards in using the techniques, Smith states (p. 83) that these skills are amoral. Another student's question as to how sincere Smith was in agreeing with criticism while using the fogging technique is answered: "Does it really matter?" (p. 113).

In general, this book seems to deal more with power than with assertion.

Areas of application include communication (saying no, responding to criticism), social relations, sex, work, and consumer relations.

Taking Charge on the Job: Techniques for Assertive Management
Lyn Taetzsch and Eileen Benson
New York: Executive Enterprises, 1978. 144 pp., hardbound.

This is the book for managers seeking a general introduction to assertion. Good examples of how to apply assertion in management situations can be found throughout the text, along with very readable discussions of these examples. The book is divided into three parts: Idea, Method, and Practice. Part I contains a 12-item inventory and discusses the nonassertive, assertive, aggressive, and mixed-response "manager types." Part II contains some aspects of self-confidence and of verbal and nonverbal assertion, and some well-spelled-out directions for broken record and workable compromise. Fogging is described, but with an incomplete discussion of its inherent dangers, one of which is the fact that it is an indirect means of handling a situation. Part III deals with applications in the communications area: feedback, giving criticism, taking directions, and making requests.

Behavioral and rational-emotive assertion techniques (behavioral rehearsal, thought stopping, etc.) are not discussed in this book; however the authors recommend books for further reading and suggest that readers supplement the book with an assertion training workshop in which role play is used.

Assertive Skills for Nurses
Carolyn C. Clark
Wakefield, MA: Contemporary Publishing, 1978. 236 pp., paperbound.

Nurses should find this book extremely useful, and others may profit from studying it as well. It is a very practical, "programmed" book designed for use by either trainers or individual nurses. For this reason, the book has two introductions: one for self-study and one for nurse educators and consultants.

The main section of the book is divided into seven modules. Each module focuses on an assertion area and contains a prelearning evaluation, module goals, an information section, a set of learning activities, inventories and structured experiences, problems within the area to solve or study, a post-learning evaluation, and an evaluation of the module itself. The book is programmed to allow the reader to "test out" of modules with which he or she is already familiar. Modules include information on various aspects of theory (a looser definition of assertion than most is presented); verbal, nonverbal, and cognitive assertion; identification of rights; application areas; and special needs. The book is very oriented toward nursing, and all examples and forms are designed with nursing content.

Most assertion techniques are described here; however, areas such as behavioral rehearsal (role play) are described very briefly. Although facilitator instructions are good, they are not comprehensive enough to give an inexperienced trainer the necessary guidelines. Although Clark recommends that the book be used with a partner or a self-help group, a caution is included for those with special needs. Self-instructions are clear, but it would have been helpful to include a few additional cautions concerning potential hazards of using the book. A somewhat broader discussion of limitations of the broken record technique would have been helpful. The term "acquiescent-avoiding" is used in place of nonassertive, and "h/ir" replaces the traditional him or her.

Special application areas include communication (criticism, anger), work (nursing), and culture (women).

Becoming Assertive: A Guide for Nurses
Sonja J. Herman
New York: D. Van Nostrand, 1978. 189 pp., paperbound.

This is a self-help book written especially for nurses. Although it is a nice introduction to assertion itself, the most outstanding thing about this book is the large number of examples related to nurses. According to the author, "all examples are based on real hospital or health care facilities" and could be of interest to anyone who has been involved in health care, including patients. The book also places a great deal of emphasis on reasons nurses need assertion and barriers to nurses being assertive.

Elements of assertion discussed include: a definition of assertion, examples of the three response styles, a short history of assertion, an overview of rights, and some brief coverage of self-confidence, verbal, nonverbal, and cognitive assertion, as well as special applications in the area of communication: making and refusing requests.

A self-help model is provided in order to help the reader develop assertion skills. The model consists of eleven learning modules, most of which contain an "exercise" (reading assignment or activity) and a set of questions regarding the exercise. Role play, SUDS, relaxation, and diary techniques are included in this section. Very few guidelines and cautions are offered for role play and other techniques, which makes the chapter on maintaining skills more important. In this chapter the author suggests that the reader seek further growth from workshops, support groups, self-reinforcement, watching other models, and using a hierarchy of situations when practicing. Although the majority of the situations presented are excellent, several portray what seem to be somewhat curt or unnecessarily confrontive responses.

Liking Myself
Pat Palmer
San Luis Obispo, CA: Impact Press, 1977. 80 pp., paperbound.

One of two existing assertion books for children, *Liking Myself* is written for people five to nine years of age. The word assertion is never used, although the book is advertised as an assertion book and it does focus on assertion concepts. Instead, Palmer employs a simple, easy-to-understand vocabulary and several structured activities to help the reader (or person read to) learn to be his or her own friend; express his or her own thoughts, feelings, and wants to other children and adults; allow himself or herself to be who he or she is; listen to his or her body; and briefly practice relaxation and meditation.

Basically well organized and well presented, the book can give some useful direction to a child developing basic assertion skills. It is illustrated throughout with line drawings and is hand lettered.

Liking Myself does leave out several important cautions: (1) Children should be cautioned about the possible negative outcomes of assertion, especially when considering assertion with adults. Even adults are cautioned about this! (2) Children should be cautioned about situations in which they make legitimate choices and someone else is disappointed or hurt, e.g., the child does not want to play, and his friends feel bad as a result. (3) Children should be cautioned about possible side effects of relaxation exercises (p. 62).

The Mouse, the Monster and Me: Assertiveness for Young People
Pat Palmer
San Luis Obispo, CA: Impact Press, 1977. 78 pp., paperbound.

The Mouse, the Monster and Me is a children's assertion book, written for people eight to twelve years old. It can be used alone or as a sequel to *Liking Myself.* The two books have similar format, organization, and quality of presentation. *The Mouse, the Monster and Me,* however, covers more advanced assertion concepts. Assertion is defined, as are the three response styles (the mouse — nonassertion, the monster — aggression, and me — assertion). Basic human rights and cognitive assertion are presented, as is a short relaxation activity (the same caution concerning relaxation is needed as in *Liking Myself*). The child is given guidelines for identifying his or her strengths, making and refusing requests, receiving and responding to criticism, and giving and receiving compliments.

This book is meant to be read by the child. It contains a number of written exercises to complete. The reader is encouraged to practice the various skills discussed in the book with a friend or family member.

One caution: Children should be warned about the possible negative outcomes of assertion. Children *can* be physically forced to do things against their will, contrary to what this book might lead them to believe.

You Can *Run Away from It!*
Julian Meeker
Santa Monica, CA: Gutenberg 2000, 1977. 91 pp., paperbound.

This is not an assertion book, but an "anti-assertion" book. Anyone who conducts assertion training will probably enjoy this spoof of the field. Here, the broken-record technique becomes "slipped disc," one of *the* concession training techniques. A 40-item Concession Inventory is included to help the reader determine whether he or she is manic-concessive, simple-unassertive, assertive, or aggressive. Sample item (p. 24):

"Someone steals the parking space you were getting ready to back into. What would you do?

a) Jump out of your car, start a fist fight with the driver of the other car, and ask questions later.

b) Open your door, look back and yell, 'Hey, that's MY space, buddy!'

c) Grumble that it's your space and drive on.

d) Jump out of your car, open the hood, pretend like you just stopped to check your battery fluid, smile, jump back in the car and drive on."

If the results of the inventory indicate "manic-concessive," chapters with titles such as "Don't Say Yes When You Want to Say Yes, Sir!" offer such worthwhile aids as concession training exercises and verbal rationalizations ("Who needs it?" "It's more trouble than it's worth" "I wouldn't take it if they gave it away" "Money is not everything" [p. 46]) and so on.

PROFESSIONAL BOOKS

Although many of the books already mentioned describe exercises useful in designing assertion sessions and contain short sections addressed to group leaders or discussions of some aspects of assertion groups, the following books have been written specifically for trainers.

An Introduction to Assertive Training Procedures for Women
Patricia Jakubowski-Spector
Washington, DC: American Personnel and Guidance Association, 1973. 24 pp., paperbound.

This monograph gives a brief introduction to the theory of assertion. Topics include developing a belief system, plus a brief discussion of behavior-rehearsal, rational-emotive, and anxiety-reduction techniques. A preliminary theory of phase changes that people go through as they learn assertion is included. A unique feature is a series of examples of assertion as a continuum:

borderline between aggressive and assertive, borderline between nonassertive and assertive, and high-quality assertion.

Responsible Assertive Behavior: Cognitive/Behavioral Procedures for Trainers
Arthur J. Lange and Patricia Jakubowski
Champaign, IL: Research Press, 1976. 323 pp., paperbound.

This is my nomination for a trainer's good buy. Lange and Jakubowski, who also co-authored a popular book in the field described earlier, have taken a textbook approach to a comprehensive overview of the field. The book opens with a summarization of the current status of assertion training and devotes subsequent chapters to (1) a definition and analysis of assertion, nonassertion, and aggression, (2) the development of an assertive belief system, (3) over twenty structured exercises for use in assertion training, (4) cognitive-restructuring procedures, (5) behavior-rehearsal procedures, (6) methods for planning and conducting various types of assertion groups, (7) general applications of assertion training, (8) assessment procedures, and (9) ethical considerations. The only section dealing specifically with special helps in application areas, in this otherwise comprehensive book, is a special chapter by Thomas V. McGovern on assertion training for job interviewing and management/staff development. Review questions and exercises at the end of each chapter are designed to help the reader integrate and apply the material.

Treatment is extensive and informative. The definition of assertion includes an analysis of six different categories of assertive statements. The chapter on assessment procedures contains an up-to-date summary of paper-and-pencil instruments available for assessing assertion change. The book contains a 60-item Discrimination Test on Assertive, Aggressive, and Nonassertive Behavior and a topical assertion check list.

Negative aspects of the book are minor, including a small type face, a rather dry style, an inordinate number of references to Jakubowski's books, either earlier or "in press," and a pollution of the assertion vocabulary with newly coined words like "nonassertive circle" and "unassertive." The authors also seem to have had difficulty deciding whether modeling is or is not a behavior-rehearsal procedure (pp. 155, 176, 177).

The book's approach is an integrative one, offering resources and a philosophy permitting any trainer or therapist to design a course suited to his or her particular goals and orientation.

Assertive Training for Women
Susan M. Osborn and Gloria G. Harris
Springfield, IL: Charles C Thomas, 1975. 204 pp., hardbound; paperbound.

For most trainers, the appeal of this humorously illustrated book will lie in Chapter 5, "An Innovative Approach to Assertive Training." This single chapter offers over sixty structured exercises that can be used as presented, in a twenty-five hour, ten-session approach, or employed selectively in designing assertion training modules. The course design differs from conventional practice in two respects: (1) there is little attention paid to the theoretical basis for assertion or the idea of personal rights and (2) the course opens with a series of nonverbal activities.

Much of this volume is strongly oriented to the report from research, with few anecdotes or examples. Although it lacks the range that Lange and Jakubowski offer, the book has a number of unique features for those with special interests: (1) a chapter on group dynamics; (2) a chapter devoted to the message from research as regards aggression, assertion, and power; and (3) sections on assertion and the women's movement and applications of assertion to the woman's social, sexual, work, and family life.

An Appendix contains a 60-item scale designed to assess assertiveness levels, a group evaluation form for feedback to the trainer, and several other useful entries. There are also assertion check lists developed by Lazarus and Rathus and a chapter briefly describing basic behavior modification techniques.

Assertion Training: A Humanistic-Behavioral Guide to Self-Dignity
Sherwin B. Cotler and Julio J. Guerra
Champaign, IL: Research Press, 1976. 229 pp., paperbound.

Cotler and Guerra's approach to assertion training lies in anxiety reduction and social-skill training, in that order. The heart of the book consists of (1) a package of behavioristic techniques designed to measure and reduce relatively high anxiety levels in assertive situations and (2) sixteen structured exercises for developing conversational and other social skills.

The basic program relies heavily on an adaptation of Wolpe's "Subjective Units of Discomfort Scale" (SUDS) to measure anxiety and on relaxation and behavioral-rehearsal techniques to reduce anxiety and to develop assertion skills. The Assertive Data Collection Package (ADCP) used to accomplish these goals includes a 43-item Assertiveness Inventory and diaries and scales designed to document changes in anxiety levels, behavioral and emotional responses in assertive situations, and assertion goals.

Although the language is heavily oriented toward a "therapist" in the "treatment" of clients, some of the instruments in the basic package and most of the structured exercises for social-skill development can be used equally well by group trainers in designing their own assertion sessions.

A section on "protective skills" includes eight defensive techniques and discusses most of the pros and cons involved in this controversial area. Additional features include a good review of the literature and an interesting assertion matrix model designed by the authors.

Personal Effectiveness: Guiding People to Assert Themselves and Improve Their Social Skills

Robert Paul Liberman, Larry W. King, William J. DeRisi, and Michael McCann
Champaign, IL: Research Press, 1975. 169 pp., paperbound.

"Personal effectiveness" is the authors' term for their view of assertion training, which focuses on "enlargement and refinement of social and emotional skills." The method was developed in mental health and clinical settings, and the language is geared to "therapy" and "treatment" by "counselors" or "helping professionals." In general, the approach is a behavioristic, highly structured, directive, and somewhat elementary approach to assertion training.

The manual is divided into three sections, each corresponding to one of the three phases of a Personal Effectiveness Session:

1. A Planning Meeting in which each client reports on the completion of homework assignments from the previous meeting and chooses a feeling or action he wishes to practice in the Training Session;

2. A Training Session in which each client role plays, under the direction of the group leader, the chosen feeling or action with co-leaders or other clients and receives a homework assignment for the next meeting; and

3. An Evaluation Meeting in which group leaders receive feedback on the Training Session and discuss clients' progress.

Behavioral rehearsal is the core of the approach, with major emphasis on nonverbal behaviors rather than on verbal or cognitive content. Review questions, suggested answers, and practice exercises for the professional are included at the end of each chapter, and there are flow charts throughout the book.

The book has several rough spots. Many questions in the review sections and in examples for use with clients are either simplistic or leading. Illustrations throughout the book label certain postures as *ipso facto* effective or ineffective and depict such scenes as a therapist patting a client on the shoulder upon successful completion of his homework assignment. Although the emphasis in training sessions is totally on positive feedback ("one cannot give a client too much positive feedback" [p. 79]), therapists are encouraged to discuss positive and negative aspects of a client's performances ("I don't know what Tim's problem is ..." [p. 123]) in the Evaluation Meetings while clients listen.

For the trainer who wishes to use a more flexible, varied, and inclusive assertion program, the book does contain a set of nine structured exercises. Two of these, however, include the broken-record technique, with no attention given to its potentially destructive effects, and an exercise, mistakenly called "fogging," that corresponds more to empathic assertion than to the generally accepted (Cotler & Guerra, 1976; Smith, 1976; Lange & Jakubowski, 1976) definition of the term.

A 30-item Assertiveness Inventory, Rathus' 30-item Assertiveness Schedule, and an annotated bibliography are included. An accompanying 32-page Program Guide, a six-page Client's Introduction, and a demonstration film are available.

Introduction to Assertion Skills Training
Patricia L. Cameron, Joseph J. Ferrandino, and Herbert A. Marlowe, Jr.
Tampa, FL: Florida Mental Health Institute, 1979. 45 pp., looseleaf.

The *Introduction to Assertion Skills Training* and *Assertion Skills Games* (see following entry) share authorship and were developed for the same purpose: to codify and standardize the assertion training program for the mental health system of Florida. Although these materials were developed especially to serve the mental health client who has a short history of residential treatment (less than four months), they contain activities and designs that can be used profitably with any client group.

The *Introduction to Assertion Skills Training* (formerly known as *The Assertion Skills Training Manual*) contains a very short theory and background of assertiveness training and outlines twelve designs for assertion sessions in which the central technique used is role play in a hierarchy of situations accompanied by feedback. The client begins by responding to a video vignette, then progresses to assertion board games involving role play; homework; use of a journal; group role play with feedback; and actual practice in the real-life situation. (Role play is understood here to refer to behavior rehearsal.)

The design sessions outlined are very succinct and straightforward. Various structured activities and other useful aids are included that can be adapted by assertion trainers to any setting.

This publication is probably best considered as a resource for new designs or activities, rather than as a primary resource for the inexperienced assertion trainer, since theory and technique are not discussed in any inclusive way.

Assertion Skills Games
Patricia L. Cameron, Joseph J. Ferrandino, and Herbert A. Marlowe, Jr.
Tampa, FL: Florida Mental Health Institute, 1978. 44 pp., looseleaf.

Assertion Skills Games outlines directions for six assertion board games designed to help participants develop assertion skills. (One of these activities is included in a somewhat modified version in the *Introduction to Assertion Skills Training*.) Trainers are required to construct their own materials and boards based on rough sketches and directions provided. Activities are centered around identification of the three types of assertive response, self-disclosure around assertion issues, and role play of assertive situations. These games are useful training tools; however, training guidelines are sparse and should be supplemented with a good background in assertion for trainers. For example, in the "Role Play Game" participants are told to give feedback about how the practicing participant's behavior could have been more assertive. Here, participants should be encouraged to concentrate on positive feedback in keeping with standard role-play guidelines for assertion practice.

Achieving Assertive Behavior: A Guide to Assertive Training
Harold H. Dawley, Jr., and W. W. Wenrich
Monterey, CA: Brooks/Cole, 1976. 121 pp., paperbound.

Into this thin, no-frills little book has been poured much concise information about assertion. The authors oriented the book especially toward the student in the "helping" professions and related fields, but say it could also serve as a "self-help" guide and be useful to therapists.

In fact, the book seems too formal and condensed to serve as a self-help manual, or even as a trainer's manual. It is behavior-therapy oriented. Although it is readable and contains illustrative anecdotes, it also cites a fair amount of research supporting the assertion areas discussed, and it is written in a rather academic style, unlike a workbook.

The purpose this book would seem to serve best is as a supplementary reference or "pocket mini-encyclopedia" on some behavior-therapy-based assertion techniques. As such, the book contains a brief discussion of aspects of respondent and operant behavior, a history of assertion, the three assertive response styles, situational versus general nonassertion and aggression, behavioral analysis and evaluation, reality testing, cognitive restructuring, verbal skills, nonverbal skills, behavioral rehearsal and role play, and more. Entries are not so much comprehensive as informative. One typically misunderstood area, which also seems to be confused here, is the difference between behavioral rehearsal and role play (p. 69).

Some guidelines in the special application area of communication are included, as well as some relaxation exercises and some tips on trouble shooting. An Assertive Behavior Checklist, Rathus' Assertiveness Schedule, and a recording form are included.

Assertiveness: Innovations, Applications, Issues
Robert E. Alberti (Ed.)
San Luis Obispo, CA: Impact Press, 1977. 386 pp., hardbound.

Another first from Robert Alberti and Impact Press, *Assertiveness* has the distinction of being the first book of edited readings devoted entirely to assertion. The readings were written by thirty-six practitioners in the field who have geared their writings to other practitioners. This leads to an extremely interesting, if uneven, book.

Assertiveness contains diverse articles of varying length and weight. Chapters are organized into five sections: Background, Innovations in Technique, Assertiveness Across Cultures, Applications of Assertive Behavior Training, and Issues and Ethics in the Practice of Assertive Behavior Training. Within each section, topics read like a "what's what on the cutting edge of assertion" or, as Alberti describes it, "unique contribution(s) toward a comprehensive presentation of the state of the art . . . at once a useful handbook and a progress report on an evolving therapeutic/training procedure" (p. 20). Every assertion trainer should be able to find something of interest in this book.

Application areas include: personal development (weight control, phobias, alcoholics), communication (anger), family/children (daughters, adolescents, juvenile delinquents, children), close relationships (marital counseling, divorce), work (job hunt, nurses), and cultural (blacks, Mexican-Americans, Asian-Americans, women).

Approaches to Assertion Training
John M. Whiteley and John V. Flowers (Eds.)
Monterey, CA: Brooks/Cole, 1978. 269 pp., paperbound.

Approaches is the Brooks/Cole edition of the original *Counseling Psychologist* issue on assertion training ("Assertion Training," 1975, 5(4)). Some of the original articles have been edited, and new articles have been added. All are consistently excellent in quality.

These readings explore assertion as a counseling technique and as an adjunct to other counseling approaches. Although assertion is dealt with as a therapeutic process, many of the readings should prove useful to trainers in general. Many of the sixteen articles were written by well-known practitioners (Rathus, Jakubowski, Lange, Rimm) and contain good descriptions of techniques and discussions of problems. Part One includes six articles that introduce approaches to assertion training, giving a definition, history, theory and general practices, techniques and concepts. Research issues and findings are presented, as well as a description of specific assertion designs currently in use by the writers.

In Part Two, application areas and special client populations are discussed, including the elderly, job interviews, sexuality, and other cultural and work areas. Part Three deals with issues in assessment and with the training of trainers. The reader should note that the terms unassertive and nonassertive are employed in a somewhat confusing way.

Assertive Consumer: Credit and Warranties
Barbara Clark, Wanda Veraska, and Michael Emmons
Washington, DC: National Consumer's League, 1978. *Student's Manual*, 60 pp.; *Instructor's Guide*, 60 pp.; *Administrative Model*, 43 pp.; looseleaf.

The *Assertive Consumer* is a series of three publications developed under a grant from the U.S. Office of Education's Department of Health, Education, and Welfare by the National Consumer's League. The goal of the series (available in Spanish or English) is to teach consumers their legal rights concerning credit and warranties and assertive behavior that will secure these rights.

The publications contain extensive credit and warranty information and very little information on assertion training, although this is being rectified. In general, the program is well planned, well suited to its goals, and should be welcomed with open arms by consumers.

The *Student's Manual* includes twenty-one pages of questions and answers on credit and warranty, plus seventeen pages of model letters for consumers. Assertion is accorded eleven pages, focusing essentially on a problem-solving approach.

The *Instructor's Guide* assumes that a reader has enough knowledge about credit and warranty to teach the course. It consists mainly of a thorough, detailed design for conducting an experiential three-day course in being an assertive consumer, focusing on acquiring and sharing credit and warranty knowledge and experiences (consumer) and role playing these same experiences in order to practice assertive ways of responding to them (assertion). The guide lacks thorough guidelines for relaxation activities or role plays. The authors are in the process of publishing a supplement containing guidelines for conducting role plays and information on teaching techniques. (Personal note, June 26, 1978). Until this supplement arrives, the inexperienced assertion trainer should probably couple this manual with a good assertion trainer's guide of his or her choice.

The *Administrative Model* is a guide to setting up assertive consumer training courses similar to those that have been conducted through the National Consumer's League. It includes a number of press releases and course-evaluation questionnaires, as well as instructions for setting up an office promoting the event and other such administrative details.

Assertion Skill Training: A Group Procedure for High School Women
Catherine M. Steel and Janice M. Hochman
Washington, DC: American Personnel and Guidance Association, 1976. 63 pp., looseleaf.

This is a straightforward, "bare bones," "how to" manual for high school counselors or other professionals wishing to teach assertion skills. The publication contains useful guidelines for reaching, informing, interesting, screening, and selecting high school women for a seven-week (two one-and-one-half-hour sessions per week) assertion training program. A training design for six or eight group members and two co-trainers is described; films and eight structured activities are used.

A Process Guide chapter gives some very useful background information and guidelines for the techniques of reinforcement, modeling, role playing, goal setting, and logs.

On the negative side, the "bare bones" of the book could stand to be fattened with some detail on possible problems that may occur and some "how to's" on helping participants cope with them, as well as next steps for participants completing this design. No design rationale is given, and some design activities seem out of sequence (Line-Up, p. 43) or missing (role play).

The manual contains an Assertion Scale for High School Women.

Assertive Black . . . Puzzled White: A Black Perspective on Assertive Behavior
Donald K. Cheek
San Luis Obispo, CA: Impact Press, 1976. 132 pp., hardbound; paperbound.

This book, unique in its subject matter, explores the how and why of adapting assertion training to the black client's needs. The book is easy to read and covers several important aspects of the black view of assertion. For example, the behaviors blacks label as assertive, nonassertive, or aggressive may differ from those recognized by whites, because most blacks have a different history, culture, or lifestyle and run different risks in the same situations. Cheek lists a number of problem assertive situations for blacks (p. 21) that are very different from those a group of white clients would list.

Suggestions are offered of ways in which the trainer can modify his or her approach to make assertion more valuable and effective to blacks. Chapters on black language, mode, and styles; assertion training tools from a black perspective; and design and guidelines for a black assertive training program are included.

One area not addressed, but which might prove a helpful addition, is how to deal with "degrees" of blackness or blacks who have been "brought up white."

Leader's Manual for an Assertive Skills Course in Correctional Settings
Elizabeth P. Kirchner and Robert E. Kennedy
University Park, PA: Institute for Research on Human Resources, Pennsylvania State University, 1978. 123 pp., looseleaf.

Probably the biggest asset of this manual is the relevance of the examples, inventories, role-play situations, and other participant materials to the correctional setting. The materials were developed over a three-year period of offering assertion skills to men held at the State Correctional Institution at Rockview, Pennsylvania; the authors have focused on "assertive behaviors that research and experience indicate are especially needed by and useful to correctional clients."

The manual contains few guidelines for trainers about teaching specific techniques or potential training problems and contains no assertion history or theory. Participants are taught a basic definition of assertion, a version of the DESC script, other verbal assertion techniques, and some nonverbal and cognitive skills. Modeling, role play, coaching, and the use of video equipment and feedback are advocated, although, again, few guidelines are provided for implementing such techniques. Application areas include communication: dealing with criticism, anger, hurt, and disappointment.

The manual is divided into color-coded sections for easy reference. Sections include (1) a general course outline for an eight-session course (two hours each), (2) handouts for participants on each of the areas taught, (3) homework assignments (written forms and check lists) for each of the areas taught, and (4) additional materials for course leaders. Other notable items include a 14-item Assertiveness Quiz, a 35-item Interest Inventory, eleven suggested structured activities, and a list of over one hundred typical assertion situations for use in role play.

A few potential problem areas exist. A sample advertisement for the assertion course assumes that the reader knows what assertion is, and the course evaluation form asks the respondent to "be brutally frank" in answering items. The manual will need to be supplemented by additional readings if the facilitator knows little about assertion techniques or training. Workable compromise, fogging, and broken-record techniques are taught as basic core skills. Cautions are provided for these techniques; but a warning that the other person's rights should be taken into account is not provided.

A Special Application Areas Chart (Table 9) is included here to aid trainers in finding areas of special interest.

Table 9. Special Application Areas

SPECIAL APPLICATION AREA   AUTHOR

Cultural	School	Consumer Relations	Work	Sex/Sensuality	Close Relationships	Family/Children	Social Relations	Communication	Personal Development	AUTHOR
	X		X	X			X	X	X	Adams et al.
								X		Adler
X			X		X	X		X	X	Alberti
										Alberti & Emmons (1974)
	X	X	X				X		X	Alberti & Emmons (1975)
X			X	X	X	X	X	X	X	Baer
X	X			X						Bloom, Coburn, & Pearlman
										Bower & Bower
X			X	X	X			X		Butler
										Cameron, Ferrandino, & Marlowe (Skills Games)

Table 9 (continued).

SPECIAL APPLICATION AREA   AUTHOR

Cultural	School	Consumer Relations	Work	Sex/Sensuality	Close Relationships	Family/Children	Social Relations	Communication	Personal Development	Author
										Cameron, Ferrandino, & Marlowe (Intro. to Training)
X										Cheek
X										Clark, B., Veraska, & Emmons
			X							Clark, C.
								X	X	Cotler & Guerra
									X	Dawley & Wenrich
					X	X		X	X	Fensterheim & Baer
	X		X		X	X		X		Galassi & Galassi
								X	X	Gambrill & Richey
									X	Geeting & Geeting
				X	X			X		Halcomb
			X							Herman
										Jakubowski-Spector
								X		Jakubowski & Lange
X										Kirchner & Kennedy
			X							Lange & Jakubowski
										Lazarus & Fay
										Liberman, King, DeRisi, & McCann
										Meeker
X										Osborn & Harris
							X		X	Palmer (Liking)
							X		X	Palmer (Mouse)
		X						X	X	Paris & Casey
X					X		X	X	X	Phelps & Austin
		X	X	X				X	X	Smith
										Steel & Hochman
			X							Taetsch & Benson
										Taubman
X				X	X					Whiteley & Flowers

FILMS

The assertion film market has begun to grow only recently. Distributors vary as to their willingness to loan their films for review purposes. Six films are described here. A list of other assertion films and their respective distributors follows. These latter films were either not available for review or were not yet available for distribution by January 1979.

The Confidence Game
16mm. or videocassette/color/sound/1 hour
Educational Resources Foundation, P.O. Drawer L, Columbia, South Carolina
    29250

The Confidence Game consists of three films that build on one another, three accompanying audiotapes, a 133-page leader's guide, and a 102-page student workbook. The package includes practicing some skills during the sessions and outside of the training setting.

The films are titled: Part I: The First Step (15 min.), Part II: Keeping Your Balance (18 min.), and Part III: Walking the Wire (18 min.). The setting is an office and plant and the films spotlight employees (executive vice president, administrative assistant, secretaries, receptionist-typist, production manager, plant foreman) as they interact with one another and react to various office-plant problems and events. In Part I, Tracy, the "new girl" in the office, consistently models assertive behavior, while various aggressive, assertive, and nonassertive reactions by other members of the office staff are shown. Gradually, as the series progresses through Parts II and III, a team spirit develops. Individuals learn to interact in more assertive and problem-solving ways.

The office-plant is located at the middle-management level in a manufacturing company. Situations are typical and well chosen, and acting is well done. The film moves along at a good pace and maintains interest as well as continuity.

Areas explored include getting and giving information, making and refusing requests, active listening, giving and receiving criticism, making and responding to complaints, problem solving, dealing with work-related discontent, sources of and responsible use of power, being persistent (broken record), receiving compliments, making mistakes, handling crises, and sharing one's own strengths. Nonverbal assertion and a version of the DESC script are also included.

The films teach through modeling, rather than through any specifically stated guidelines. The term assertion is not mentioned, although being honest and protecting both one's own and others' rights are stressed. The theme of the package is described as becoming cooperative, confident, and competent on the job.

Some of the early situations presented seem more emotional (expression of anger) than most office norms allow, and most company members seem relatively open to change. This office has a norm of sharing feelings, thoughts, and opinions, and a relatively flexible use of "personal spaces" (boss sits on employee's desk to talk to her, secretary sits on same couch as boss while taking dictation) contributes to the portrayal of a somewhat informal office atmosphere.

The three audiotapes are narrated by a professional-sounding, yet easy-to-listen-to male voice. The films are analyzed and discussed by the narrator, who gives cognitive input and guidelines, interspersed with segments of relevant dialogue taken directly from the films.

Transcripts of these tapes are included in both the student workbook and in the leader's guide. In addition, the leader's guide contains brief notes to the facilitator on timing, things to watch for, and a workshop evaluation form.

Assertion Skills: Tintypes
16mm. or videocassette/color/sound/20 min.
Conceived and developed by The Ralston Purina Company. Available from Salenger Educational Media, 1635 Twelfth Street, Santa Monica, California 90404

This film opens with alternating male and female guitar players singing "Assert Yourself," a gentle but persistent song that explores the concepts of assertion, aggression, and nonassertion and sets the film's tone. The guitar players are shown playing the song at regular intervals between groups of tintypes.

The tintypes are brief vignettes focusing on various assertion-related situations in the office or corporate setting: an assistant asks the boss for information and the boss brushes off the request; a woman voices her concern about transferring from a male to a female supervisor; a man in the production or maintenance area wonders why a job he has been hoping would come his way has not been given to him; employees make requests and propose new ideas on the job; a nagging manager gives orders to his secretary; a woman tries to pay for a business lunch her company has initiated and her male companion refuses to give her the check, which was handed to him by the waiter; a manager asks his male subordinate to run errands for him over the lunch hour; a wife listens to her husband complain about the problems he has on his job and suggests some assertive solutions which he rejects. Nine such short, well-acted vignettes are presented, as "tintypes of today and yesterday." They are interesting and believable and involve blacks and whites and men and women.

Up to this point, the film is very well done and it would be a fine opener for an assertion program. It sets a tone and holds attention and provides good stimulus for discussion. It could be used as a stop-action film to identify response styles and to practice developing assertive ones.

The film ends with a "tintype for tomorrow": Mary Wells Lawrence, chairperson of the board of an advertising firm in New York, talks about "presence." Although she presents a good pep talk on presence, it seems to detract from, rather than add to, the film. Assertion, not presence, has been the subject of the film to this point, and the entire scene seems a bit too "cutesy" and out of place.

The film has two sets of participant worksheets and a 14-page manual that discusses possible uses and goals and gives questions (and answers) for discussion of each vignette. Directions (although incomplete) on how to use the worksheets and a brief bibliography are also included. The worksheets essentially set up a structured activity in which each partner alternately makes a request of his or her partner and later refuses a request from the partner. Partners are unaware that the instructions have set the situation up in such a way that all requests are denied. They must rate their feelings each time in response to their partner's behavior. The worksheets are exchanged after the activity is completed and the experience is debriefed.

Several potential problems exist in relation to these worksheets: (1) directions to the trainer do not equip him or her to mediate the strong feelings that may result from the interaction; (2) this activity is labeled role play, which may be confusing in light of the more complex activities involved in behavioral rehearsal; (3) directions for giving feedback *only* include feedback on *offensive* behavior. This is not in keeping with the focus of assertion on reinforcement of behavior that approximates assertion.

Responsible Assertion: A Model for Personal Growth

16mm./color/sound/28 min.
Research Press, Box 31770, Champaign, Illinois 61820

This film blends segments of an actual assertion training workshop conducted by Arthur Lange and short talks on assertion concepts featuring Patricia Jakubowski, with flashbacks to real-life situations. Assertion is defined, and the concepts of basic human rights and cognitive assertion are discussed. Role play and homework techniques are incorporated.

The film is basically an introduction to assertion training, presenting selected glimpses of the kinds of situations, concepts, and techniques that are usually covered. The film is well presented, lively, and entertaining.

Actualization Through Assertion: A Behavioral Approach to Personal Effectiveness

16mm./color/sound/28 min.
Research Press, Box 31770, Champaign, Illinois 61820

Two of the producers of this film are also authors of the book *Personal Effectiveness: Guiding People to Assert Themselves and Improve Their Social Skills*. As is true of the book, the film is group-therapy and behavioral-rehearsal oriented, and the focus is almost totally on nonverbal assertion. The film shows segments from a group session in which four "mental health technicians" conduct behavioral rehearsals with four respective clients. The rehearsals are conducted with much coaching and positive reinforcement. Modeling and homework assignment techniques are also shown.

The film is well put together and would probably be of greatest interest to trainers and therapists for the techniques modeled. One caution: one technician comments to a client, "You got what you wanted" but does not warn that getting what one wants is not always the final result, nor the primary goal, of assertion.

Assertive Training: The Teaching of Appropriate Behavior (Film #782)
16mm./color/sound/29 min.
California State Department of Health Film Library, 744 P Street, Sacramento, California 95814

This film is one-on-one therapy oriented. Basically, the film follows a man named David through several assertion sessions with his therapist. He learns to make eye contact, raise his voice, stand straight, and express himself with his hands and arms. After this, David begins behavioral rehearsal with a role player brought in from outside, and through shaping, videotapes, positive reinforcement, and homework assignments, demonstrates more and more assertive behavior. Several other useful techniques are demonstrated.

The film is designed to show how to deal with "severely lacking" or "malfunctioning" behavior (such evaluative terms occasionally are used) and will probably be of most use to trainers as a model of the type of client who would probably learn best with a therapist in the one-on-one setting.

Coping with Parents
16mm./color/sound/15 min.
Filmfair Communications, 10900 Ventura Boulevard, Studio City, California 91604

This film presents four vignettes in which four different teenagers practice being "straight" or assertive with their parents. The film was made in 1973 and is somewhat dated by miniskirts, but the problems are contemporary. The film is behavior modification oriented; assertion techniques and concepts are not discussed per se. The film would probably be best used in working with teenagers and applying assertion theory and concepts to the sample situations.

Other Films and Distributors

FILMFAIR COMMUNICATIONS
10900 Ventura Boulevard
Studio City, California 91604

Coping II: Getting What You Want
16mm./color/sound/20 min.

AMERICAN PERSONNEL AND GUIDANCE ASSOCIATION
1607 New Hampshire Avenue N.W.
Washington, DC 20009

Assertive Training for Women: Part I
16mm./color/sound/17 min.

Assertive Training for Women: Part II
16mm./color/sound/18 min.

Improving Personal Relationships: Assertion Issues for High School Women in Relating to Men: Part I
16mm./color/sound/15 min.

Improving Personal Relationships: Assertion Issues for High School Women in Relating to Men: Part II
16 mm./color/sound/15 min.

(Booklets can be purchased separately with each of the above pairs of films.)

RESEARCH PRESS
Box 31770
Champaign, Illinois 61820

What Could I Say? An Assertion Training Stimulus Program
16mm./color/sound/18 min.
(Comes with a leader's guide.)

VISUAL EXCHANGE INCORPORATED
2617 Harlesden Court
Hollywood, California 90046

Assertive Management
16mm. or videocassette/color/sound/23 min.

AUDIOTAPES AND FILMSTRIPS

Assertion audiotapes remain a fairly rare commodity. Four tapes are reviewed here, and three others and their distributors are listed.

Assertiveness Training for Women
Janet Wolfe
New York: BMA Audio Cassette Programs (270 Madison Avenue, 10061.)

This forty-minute tape spotlights women's assertion problems from many different angles. Wolfe packs a large amount of information into a small tape. Geared to therapists and counselors, as well as trainers, the tape contains a definition of assertion; a discussion of the three response styles to an assertion situation; the reasons women have problems being assertive; preliminary procedures; role play, modeling, and homework techniques; and some general assertion principles for professionals. Major emphasis is on irrational beliefs and cognitive assertion. Approximately half the tape is devoted to an exploration of these topics.

Wolfe seems to favor an individually tailored assertion program, although it is not clear exactly how this is to be worked into the group setting. Preliminary examples tend to lean toward women with fairly emotional problems.

Although the language is somewhat stilted and the tape is basically a long talk, the tape is clear, concise, and presented in a logical sequence. It will prove especially useful to those seeking an introduction to cognitive assertion concepts.

Assertion Training Series: A Guide to Self-Dignity
Julio J. Guerra, Sherwin B. Cotler, and Susan Morgan Cotler
Champaign, IL: Research Press (2812 North Mattis Avenue, 61820)

Two of the three "authors" of these tapes have also written an assertion book for trainers: *Assertion Training: A Humanistic-Behavioral Guide to Self-Dignity*, reviewed earlier. The tape-training series contains four tapes, each approximately sixty minutes in length. They capture the essence of the Cotler-Guerra assertion approach and thus are a good introduction to this program for trainers. The first three could be used profitably to give clients a "feel" for this particular approach.

Tapes one, two, and three deal with a definition and theory of assertion, a guide to skills for special needs (progressive relaxation and guided fantasy), nonverbal assertion, basic verbal assertion skills (open-ended questions, free information, self-disclosure), and special-application-area skills (protective, anger, apology). Tape four is for trainers; it provides some basic guidelines for setting up a behavior-modification-oriented assertion training program like the one described in their book.

The tapes are lively, as they were recorded at actual assertion training events (hopefully, there is normally less "talking at" in the real situation). Three trainers take turns contributing to the session, and the atmosphere is relaxed. A spontaneity results that makes the presentation only slightly less systematic than it might otherwise be and helps hold the listener's interest.

Assertion Training (in *The Art of Parenting: A Complete Training Kit*)

Bill R. Wagonseller, Mary Burnett, Bernard Salzberg, and Joe Burnett
Champaign, IL: Research Press

This filmstrip, audiotape, and accompanying twenty-four page Parent's Manual are part of a package of five such units *(The Art of Parenting: A Complete Training Kit)* designed to train parents in effective child-rearing techniques. (Topics of the other four units are communication, motivation, methods, and discipline.) The kit also contains a Leader's Guide.

The assertion filmstrip consists of a series of colorful drawings (forty-three frames) depicting men and women — black, white, and native-American — in various situations. (The text is recorded on one side of the audiotape with an audible pulse added and repeated on the other side with inaudible pulse.) The first three-quarters of the filmstrip is narrated by a man who briefly defines assertion and makes some remarks about the importance of assertion and the three response styles (assertive, nonassertive, aggressive). He then mentions eye contact, body language and gestures, voice tone and pitch, body posture, and place and timing and suggests that parents not only need to act as assertive models, but also need to teach their children assertive skills and reinforce their children's assertive acts.

Ten simulated situations portraying typical parent-child problems complete the filmstrip. The situations are described by a woman who suggests that viewers discuss each situation and similar situations that they have trouble dealing with.

The Parent's Manual elaborates on the information presented in the first part of the tape-filmstrip and includes a transcription of each of the ten simulated situations. Twelve pages of the Leader's Guide are devoted to the assertion training module. Included are a script of the tape that accompanies the filmstrip, an analysis of possible reactions to each of the situations presented, and a page of suggested activities.

Probably the most useful part of this unit is the set of situations, which can be used as take-off points for discussion of parent-child problems relevant to assertion. The Leader's Guide provides guidelines for leading participants in a discussion of these situations.

The presentation of assertion that precedes the situations contains some remarks that may be confusing to the listener or to the person conducting this training, since few professional guidelines are provided. For example: one should assert oneself "without hurting someone else"; "when parents are good models, the children will learn assertive behaviors"; and "parents who are assertive become happier." Also, rather than speaking of assertive, nonassertive, or aggressive *responses,* parents are described as nonassertive, assertive, or aggressive *people*, and emphasis is almost exclusively on the nonverbal aspects of assertion. ("Assertive behavior is not so much what you say but how you say it.") Three other minor limitations: responses are called both *levels* of assertiveness and *types* of assertiveness; only a male scientist (white) is shown on the filmstrip; and the unit seems to be geared to children who can be reasoned with and are at least of speaking age.

Although the Parent's Manuals in this kit can be ordered separately, the filmstrip and audiotape must be bought with the complete training kit.

Assertiveness Training for Career and Personal Success
Robert A. Moskowitz
New York: AMACOM (The American Management Association Building, 135 West 50th Street, 10020)

This set of six tapes is divided into twelve learning segments in a program designed to teach assertion in the work setting. The focus is on career and personal success, and tapes are stopped at intervals for directed work in an accompanying 163-page workbook.

This series is an easy-to-listen-to presentation in which male and female narrators alternate; each tape is interspersed with short dramatized vignettes. Each tape is approximately forty-five minutes long, but takes longer to complete because of the workbook exercises (no time indications are given). The pace of the tapes is fairly casual; the speakers give many examples and relevant tie-ins with each new segment of information. The series progresses through a definition and discussion of assertion, its importance on the job, causes of nonassertion, assessment, some focus on rights, verbal, nonverbal, and cognitive assertion, ways people avoid assertion, assertion guidelines, and some cautions. Special application areas include: communication (requests) and work.

The workbook is well put together and contains many useful forms, questionnaires, inventories, activities, and a case study. The program concludes with a final exam that can be mailed in to be scored. One Continuing Education Credit is offered through AMA for successful completion of the program.

The tape series is a good introduction to assertion for people in the work setting who wish to familiarize themselves with some assertion concepts, explore their own assertive behavior, work at improving their assertion in day-to-day situations, and set realistic personal goals. The series could profit from more concrete guidelines for assertive action, a detailed discussion of assertion techniques, and, of course, a competent trainer to facilitate learning. The final exam measures only cognitive knowledge; it cannot measure assertive growth.

Other Audiotapes and Distributors

Assertiveness Training
Robert Alberti and Michael Emmons
Brooklyn, NY: Psychology Today Cassettes (P.O. Box 278, Pratt Station, 11205)

Assertiveness Training: A Teaching Program for Professionals
Arlene Levin
West Los Angeles, CA: Viewpoints (P.O. Box 84315, 90073)

The How To's of Assertive Management
Terry Paulson
North Hollywood, CA: The Assertion Training Institute (P.O. Box 9468, 91609)

OTHER AIDS

Assert, a newsletter published by Impact Press, reviews many assertion materials as well as journal articles and theses as they are made available; it attempts to keep readers informed about the latest developments in the field.

Management Dialogue is a newsletter published by Paulson and Associates (P.O. Box 9468, North Hollywood, California 91609). The stated purpose is to "provide a practical forum for input for managers." Application of assertion issues to management are discussed; useful approaches to or resources for maintaining assertive effectiveness as a manager are shared by readers; and problems sent in by readers regarding people problems in management are answered in light of assertion principles. A large amount of space is also devoted to advertising for Paulson and Associates' seminars.

Impact also publishes *Assertive Behavior Training: An Annotated Bibliography* by Donna M. Moore (1977) that lists 258 research articles and books directly related to assertion. This bibliography is scheduled to be updated.

REFERENCES

Kelley, C. Assertion theory. In J. W. Pfeiffer & J. E. Jones (Eds.), *The 1976 annual handbook for group facilitators*. La Jolla, CA: University Associates, 1976.

Lazarus, A. A. *Behavior therapy and beyond*. New York: McGraw-Hill, 1971.

Salter, A. *Conditioned reflex therapy*. New York: Putnam, 1961.

Wolpe, J. *Psychotherapy by reciprocal inhibition*. Stanford, CA: Stanford University Press, 1958.

Wolpe, J. *The practice of behavior therapy*. New York: Pergamon Press, 1969, 1973.

Wolpe, J., & Lazarus, A. A. *Behavior therapy techniques*. New York: Pergamon Press, 1966.

Bibliographical Sources

References

Addington, D. W. The relationship of selected vocal characteristics to personality perception. *Speech Monographs*, 1968, *35*, 492-503.

Adler, R. B. *Confidence in communication: A guide to assertive and social skills*. New York: Holt, Rinehart and Winston, 1977.

Alberti, R. E. Issues in assertive behavior training. In R. E. Alberti (Ed.), *Assertiveness: Innovations, applications, issues*. San Luis Obispo, CA: Impact Press, 1977.

Alberti, R. E., & Emmons, M. L. *Your perfect right* (2nd ed.). San Luis Obispo, CA: Impact Press, 1974.

Alberti, R. E., & Emmons, M. L. *Stand up, speak out, talk back! The key to self-assertive behavior*. New York: Pocket Books, 1975.

Alberti, R. E., Emmons, M. L., Fodor, I. G., Galassi, J., Galassi, M. D., Garnett, L., Jakubowski, P., & Wolfe, J. L. A statement of "principles for ethical practice of assertive behavior training." In R. E. Alberti (Ed.), *Assertiveness: Innovations, applications, issues*. San Luis Obispo, CA: Impact Press, 1977.

Baer, J. *How to be an assertive (not aggressive) woman in life, in love and on the job: A total guide to self-assertiveness*. New York: Rawson, 1976.

Bain, A. *Thought control in everyday life*. New York: Funk & Wagnalls, 1928.

Bandura, A. Modelling approaches to the modification of phobic disorders. *Ciba Foundation symposium: The role of learning in psychotherapy*. London: Churchill, 1968.

Bandura, A. Psychotherapy based upon modeling principles. In A. C. Bergin & S. L. Garfield (Eds.), *Handbook of psychotherapy and behavior change*. New York: John Wiley, 1971.

Bernstein, D. A., & Borkovec, T. D. *Progressive relaxation training: A manual for the helping professions*. Champaign, IL: Research Press, 1973.

Bloom, L. Z., Coburn, K., & Pearlman, J. *The new assertive woman*. New York: Delacorte Press, 1975.

Bower, S. A., & Bower, G. H. *Asserting yourself: A practical guide for positive change*. Reading, MA: Addison-Wesley, 1976.

Bower, S. A., & Potter, B. A. *Instructor's manual for asserting yourself: A practical guide for positive change*. Reading, MA: Addison-Wesley, 1976.

Cautela, J. Treatment of compulsive behavior by covert sensitization. *The Psychological Record*, 1966, *16*, 33-41.

Cautela, J. Covert reinforcement. *Behavior Therapy*, 1970, *1*, 33-50.

Cautela, J. R., & Kastenbaum, R. A reinforcement survey schedule for use in therapy, training and research. *Psychological Reports*, 1967, *20*, 1115-1130.

Cooley, M. L., & Hollandsworth, J. G., Jr. A strategy for teaching verbal content of assertive responses. In R. E. Alberti (Ed.), *Assertiveness: Innovations, applications, issues*. San Luis Obispo, CA: Impact Press, 1977.

Cotler, S. B., & Guerra, J. J. *Assertion training: A humanistic-behavioral guide to self-dignity*. Champaign, IL: Research Press, 1976.

Dawley, H. H., Jr., & Wenrich, W. W. *Achieving assertive behavior: A guide to assertive training*. Monterey, CA: Brooks/Cole, 1976.

Egan, G. *Interpersonal living: A skills/contract approach to human relations training in groups*. Monterey, CA: Brooks/Cole, 1976.

Ellis, A. *Reason and emotion in psychotherapy*. New York: Lyle Stuart, 1962.

Ellis, A. *Growth through reason: Verbatim cases in rational-emotive therapy*. Palo Alto, CA: Science and Behavior Books, 1971.

Ellis, A. *Humanistic psychotherapy: The rational-emotive approach*. New York: Julian, 1973.

Ellis, A., & Harper, R. A. *A new guide to rational living*. Englewood Cliffs, NJ: Prentice-Hall, 1975.

Fensterheim, H., & Baer, J. *Don't say yes when you want to say no*. New York: David McKay, 1975.

Flowers, J. V. Simulation and role playing methods. In F. H. Kanfer & A. P. Goldstein (Eds.), *Helping people change*. Elmsford, NY: Pergamon Press, 1975.

Flowers, J. V., & Booraem, C. D. Assertion training: The training of trainers. *The Counseling Psychologist*, 1975, *5*(4), 29-36.

Freedman, P. H. The effects of modeling and role-playing on assertive behavior. In R. D. Rubin, H. Fensterheim, A. A. Lazarus, & C. M. Franks (Eds.), *Advances in behavior therapy: Proceedings of the third conference of the Association for Advancement of Behavior Therapy*. New York: Academic Press, 1971.

Galassi, M. D., & Galassi, J. P. *Assert yourself! How to be your own person*. New York: Human Sciences Press, 1977.

Gambrill, E., & Richey, C. *It's up to you: Developing assertive social skills*. Millbrae, CA: Les Femmes, 1976.

Gaw, B. The pendulum swing: A necessary evil in the growth cycle. In J. W. Pfeiffer & J. E. Jones (Eds.), *The 1978 annual handbook for group facilitators*. La Jolla, CA: University Associates, 1978.

Gordon, T. *P.E.T.: Parent effectiveness training: The tested new way to raise responsible children*. New York: Wyden, 1970.

Jacobsen, E. *Progressive relaxation*. Chicago: University of Chicago Press, 1938.

Jakubowski, P. A. Self-assertion training procedures for women. In E. I. Rawlings & D. K. Carter (Eds.), *Psychotherapy for women: Treatment toward equality*. Springfield, IL: Charles C Thomas, 1977.

Jakubowski-Spector, P. Facilitating the growth of women through assertive training. *The Counseling Psychologist*, 1973, *4*, 75-86. (a)

Jakubowski-Spector, P. *An introduction to assertive training procedures for women*. Washington, DC: American Personnel and Guidance Association, 1973. (b)

Johnson, D. W., & Matross, R. P. Attitude modification methods. In F. H. Kanfer & A. P. Goldstein (Eds.), *Helping people change*. Elmsford, NY: Pergamon Press, 1975.

Kahn, M., & Quinlan, P. *Desensitization with varying degrees of therapist contact*. Paper presented at the meeting of the Association for the Advancement of Behavior Therapies. Washington, D.C., September, 1967.

Kanfer, F. H. Self-management methods. In F. H. Kanfer & A. P. Goldstein (Eds.), *Helping people change*. Elmsford, NY: Pergamon Press, 1975.

Kelley, C. Assertion theory. In J. W. Pfeiffer & J. E. Jones (Eds.), *The 1976 annual handbook for group facilitators*. La Jolla, CA: University Associates, 1976.

Kelley, C. Assertion: The literature since 1970. In J. E. Jones & J. W. Pfeiffer (Eds.), *The 1977 annual handbook for group facilitators*. La Jolla, CA: University Associates, 1977.

Knapp, M. L. *Nonverbal communication in human interaction*. New York: Holt, Rinehart and Winston, 1972.

Lange, A. J., & Jakubowski, P. *Responsible assertive behavior: Cognitive-behavioral procedures for trainers*. Champaign, IL: Research Press, 1976.

Lange, A. J., Rimm, D. C., & Loxley, J. Cognitive-behavioral assertion training procedures. *The Counseling Psychologist*, 1975, 5(4), 37-41.

Lazarus, A. A. Behavior rehearsal vs. non-directive therapy vs. advice in effecting behavior change. *Behavior Research and Therapy*, 1966, 4, 209-212.

Lazarus. A. A. (Ed.). *Clinical behavior therapy*. New York: Brunner/Mazel, 1972.

Liberman, R. P., King, L. W., DeRisi, W. J., & McCann, M. *Personal effectiveness: Guiding people to assert themselves and improve their social skills*. Champaign, IL: Research Press, 1975.

McDonald, M. L. Teaching assertion: A paradigm for therapeutic intervention. *Psychotherapy: Theory, Research and Practice*, Spring 1975, 12(1), 60-67.

McFall, R. M., & Marston, A. R. An experimental investigation of behavior rehearsal in assertive training. *Journal of Abnormal Psychology*, 1970, 76, 295-303.

McMullin, R., & Casey, B. *Talk sense to yourself!* Lakewood, CO: Jefferson County Mental Health Center, 1975.

Meichenbaum, D. Self-instructional methods. In F. H. Kanfer & A. P. Goldstein (Eds.), *Helping people change*. Elmsford, NY: Pergamon Press, 1975.

Moreno, J. L. *Who shall survive? A new approach to the problem of human interrelations* (2nd ed.). Washington DC: Nervous and Mental Disease Publishing Company, 1953.

Osborn, S. M., & Harris, G. G. *Assertive training for women*. Springfield, IL: Charles C Thomas, 1975.

Paris, C., & Casey, B. *Project: YOU. A manual of rational assertiveness training*. Denver, CO: Institute of Living Skills Education, 1978.

Paulson, T. Short term group assertion training with token feedback as an adjunct to ongoing group psychotherapy. *The Counseling Psychologist*, 1975, 5(4), 60-64.

Percell, L. P. Assertive behavior training and the enhancement of self-esteem. In R. E. Alberti (Ed.), *Assertiveness: Innovations, applications, issues*. San Luis Obispo, CA: Impact Press, 1977.

Phelps, S., & Austin, N. *The assertive woman*. San Luis Obispo, CA: Impact Press, 1975.

Porat, F., & Quackenbush, M. *Positive selfishness: A practical guide to self-esteem*. Millbrae, CA: Celestial Arts, 1977.

Rathus, S. A., & Nevid, J. S. *Behavior therapy: Strategies for solving problems in living*. New York: Doubleday, 1977.

Rich, A. R., & Schroeder, H. E. Research issues in assertiveness training. *Psychological Bulletin*, 1976, 83(6), 1081-1096.

Rimm, D. C., & Masters, J. C. *Behavior therapy: Techniques and empirical findings.* London: Academic Press, 1974.

Rosen, G. M. *The relaxation book: An illustrated self-help program.* Englewood Cliffs, NJ: Prentice-Hall, 1977.

Satir, V. *Peoplemaking.* Palo Alto, CA: Science and Behavior Books, 1972.

Schmidt, J. A. Cognitive restructuring: The art of talking to yourself. I think _____, therefore I am _____. *Personnel and Guidance Journal*, October 1976, *55*(2), 71-74. (a)

Schmidt, J. A. *Help yourself: A guide to self-change.* Champaign, IL: Research Press, 1976. (b)

Smith, M. J. *When I say no, I feel guilty: How to cope — using the skills of systematic assertive therapy.* New York: Dial Press, 1975.

Steel, C. M., & Hochman, J. M. *Assertion skill training: A group procedure for high school women.* Washington, DC: American Personnel and Guidance Association, 1976.

Suinn, R. Body thinking: Psychology for Olympic champs. *Psychology Today*, 1976, *10*(2), 38-43.

Taylor, J. G. Personal communication to Joseph Wolpe, 1955. Cited in J. Wolpe. *The practice of behavior therapy* (2nd ed.). Elmsford, NY: Pergamon Press, 1973.

Ullman, L. P. Making use of modeling in the therapeutic interview. In R. D. Rubin & C. M. Franks (Eds.), *Advances in behavior therapy.* New York: Academic Press, 1968.

Webster's seventh new collegiate dictionary. Springfield, MA: B. & C. Merriam, 1965.

Wolpe, J. *Psychotherapy by reciprocal inhibition.* Palo Alto, CA: Stanford University Press, 1958.

Wolpe, J. *The practice of behavior therapy* (2nd ed.). Elmsford, NY: Pergamon Press, 1973.

Wolpe, J., & Lazarus, A. A. *Behavior therapy techniques: A guide to the treatment of neuroses.* Elmsford, NY: Pergamon Press, 1966.

Further Readings

Adams, B., et al. *Woman, assert your self! An instructive handbook.* New York: Harper and Row, 1976.

Alberti, R. E. (Ed.). *Assertiveness: Innovations, applications, issues.* San Luis Obispo, CA: Impact Press, 1977.

Alberti, R. E., & Emmons, M. L. Assertive training in marital counseling. *Journal of Marriage and Family Counseling*, 1976, *2*(1), 49-54.

Bakker, C. B., & Bakker-Rabdau, M. K. *No trespassing! Explorations in human territoriality.* San Francisco: Chandler & Sharp, 1977.

Bandura, A. *Principles of behavior modification.* New York: Holt, Rinehart and Winston, 1969.

Birdwhistell, R. L. *Kinesics and context: Essays on body motion communication.* New York: Ballantine, 1970.

Bodner, G. E. The role of assessment in assertion training. *The Counseling Psychologist*, 1975, *5*(4), 90-96.

Bower, S. A. Assertiveness training for women. In J. D. Krumboltz & C. E. Thoresen (Eds.). *Counseling methods.* New York: Holt, Rinehart and Winston, 1976.

Briggs, D. C. *Celebrate your self.* Garden City, NY: Doubleday, 1977.

Butler, P. E. *Self-assertion for women: A guide to becoming androgynous.* New York: Harper and Row, 1974.

Butler, P. E. *Self-assertion for women: A guide to becoming androgynous (fully human).* New York: Harper and Row, 1974.

Cameron, P. L., Ferrandino, J. J., & Marlowe, H. A., Jr. *Assertion skills games.* Tampa, FL: Adult Programs Department, Florida Mental Health Institute, 1978.

Cameron, P. L., Ferrandino, J. J., & Marlowe, H. A., Jr. *Assertion training manual.* Tampa, FL: Adult Programs Department, Florida Mental Health Institute, 1978.

Cameron, P. L., Ferrandino, J. J., & Marlowe, H. A., Jr. *Introduction to assertion skills training* (Rev. ed.). Tampa, FL: Adult Programs Department, Florida Mental Health Institute, 1979.

Cautela, J. Covert sensitization. *Psychological Reports*, 1967, *20*, 459-468.

Cheek, D. K. *Assertive black . . . puzzled white: A black perspective on assertive behavior.* San Luis Obispo, CA: Impact Press, 1976.

Clark, B., Veraska, W., & Emmons, M. *Assertive consumer: Credit and warranties* (student's manual, instructor's guide, administrative model). Washington DC: National Consumer's League, 1978.

Clark, C. C. *Assertive skills for nurses*. Wakefield, MA: Contemporary Publishing, 1978.

Cotler, S. B. Assertion training: A road leading where? *The Counseling Psychologist*, 1975, *5*(4), 20-29.

Davis, F. *Inside intuition: What we know about nonverbal communication*. New York: The New American Library, 1971.

Deibert, A. N., & Harmon, A. J. *New tools for changing behavior* (Rev. ed.). Champaign, IL: Research Press, 1970.

Egan, G. *The skilled helper: A model for systematic helping and interpersonal relating*. Monterey, CA: Brooks/Cole, 1975.

Egan, G. *You and me: The skills of communicating and relating to others*. Monterey, CA: Brooks/Cole, 1977.

Eisler, R. M., Hersen, M., & Miller, P. M. Shaping components of assertive behavior with instructions and feedback. *American Journal of Psychiatry*, 1974, *131*, 1344-1347.

Eisler, R. M., Hersen, M., Miller, P. M., & Blanchard, E. B. Situational determinants of assertive behaviors. *Journal of Consulting and Clinical Psychology*, 1975, *43*, 330-340.

Flowers, J., Booraem, C., Brown, T., & Harris, D. An investigation of a technique for facilitating patient to patient therapeutic interaction in group therapy. *Journal of Community Psychology*, 1974, *2*(1), 39-42.

Flowers, J. V., Cooper, C. G., & Whiteley, J. M. Approaches to assertion training. *The Counseling Psychologist*, 1975, *5*(4), 3-9.

Flowers, J. V., & Guerra, J. The use of client coaching in assertion training with large groups. *Community Mental Health Journal*, 1974, *10*, 414-417.

Galassi, J. P., DeLo, J. S., Galassi, M. D., & Bastien, S. The college self expression scale: A measure of assertiveness. *Behavior Therapy*, 1974, *5*, 165-171.

Galassi, J. P., Galassi, M. D., & Litz, M. C. Assertive training in groups using video feedback. *Journal of Counseling Psychology*, 1974, *21*, 390-394.

Galassi, J. P., Kostka, M. P., & Galassi, M. D. Assertive training: A one year follow-up. *Journal of Counseling Psychology*, 1975, *22*, 451-452.

Gambrill, E. D., & Richey, C. A. An assertiveness inventory for use in assessment and research. *Behavior Therapy*, 1975, *6*, 550-561.

Gay, M. L., Hollandsworth, J. G., Jr., & Galassi, J. P. An assertiveness inventory for adults. *Journal of Counseling Psychology*, 1975, *22*, 340-344.

Geeting, B., & Geeting, C. *How to listen assertively*. New York: Simon and Schuster, 1976.

Goldstein, A. P. *Structured learning therapy: Toward a psychotherapy for the poor*. New York: Academic Press, 1973.

Halcomb, R. *Get yours! Dynamic assertiveness training techniques for men and women*. Canoga Park, CA: Major Books, 1976.

Hall, E. T. *The hidden dimension*. New York: Doubleday, 1966.

Hartsook, J. E., Olch, D. R., & De Wolf, V. A. Personality characteristics of women's assertiveness training group participants. *Journal of Counseling Psychology*, 1976, *23*, 322-326.

Herman, S. J. *Becoming assertive: A guide for nurses*. New York: D. Van Nostrand, 1978.

Holmes, D. P., & Horan, J. J. Anger induction in assertion training. *Journal of Counseling Psychology*, 1976, *23*(2), 108-111.

Jakubowski, P. A. Assertive behavior and clinical problems of women. In E. I. Rawlings & D. K. Carter (Eds.), *Psychotherapy for women: Treatment toward equality*. Springfield, IL: Charles C Thomas, 1977.

Jakubowski, P.A., & Lacks, P.B. Assessment procedures in assertion training. *The Counseling Psychologist*, 1975, *5*(4), 84-90.

Jakubowski, P., & Lange, A. J. *The assertive option: Your rights and responsibilities*. Champaign, IL: Research Press, 1978.

James, M., & Savary, L. *A new self: Self therapy with transactional analysis*. Reading, MA: Addison-Wesley, 1977.

Johnson, D. W. *Reaching out: Interpersonal effectiveness and self-actualization*. Englewood Cliffs, NJ: Prentice-Hall, 1972.

Kanfer, F. H., & Goldstein, A. P. (Eds.), *Helping people change*. Elmsford, NY: Pergamon Press, 1975.

Kazdin, A. E. Effects of covert modeling and model reinforcement on assertive behavior. *Journal of Abnormal Psychology*, 1974, *83*, 240-252.

Kirchner, E. P., & Kennedy, R. E. *Leader's manual for an assertive skills course in correctional settings*. University Park, PA: Institute for Research on Human Resources, Pennsylvania State University, 1978.

Lazarus, A. A. Behavior therapy in groups. In G. M. Gazda (Ed.), *Basic approaches to group psychotherapy and group counseling*. Springfield, IL: Charles C Thomas, 1968.

Lazarus, A. A. *Behavior therapy and beyond*. New York: McGraw-Hill, 1971.

Lazarus, A., & Fay, A. *I can if I want to: The direct assertion therapy program to change your life*. New York: William Morrow, 1975.

Lemaire, J. G. *La relaxation*. Paris: Payot, 1964.

Maier, N. R. F., Solem, A. R., & Maier, A. A. *The role-play technique: A handbook for management and leadership practice*. La Jolla, CA: University Associates, 1975.

McFall, R. M., & Lillesand, D. B. Behavioral rehearsal with modelling and coaching in assertion training. *Journal of Abnormal Psychology*, 1971, 77, 313-323.

Meeker, J. *You can run away from it!* Santa Monica, CA: Gutenberg 2000, 1977.

Mehrabian, A. *Nonverbal communication*. New York: Aldine-Atherton, 1972.

Noursund, J. *Us people: A mini-max approach to human behavior*. Monterey, CA: Brooks/Cole, 1972.

Palmer, P. *Liking myself*. San Luis Obispo, CA: Impact Press, 1977. (a)

Palmer, P. *The mouse, the monster and me: Assertiveness for young people*. San Luis Obispo, CA: Impact Press, 1977. (b)

Percell, L. P., Berwick, P. T., & Beigel, A. The effects of assertive training on self concept and anxiety. *Archives of General Psychiatry*, 1974, *31*, 502-504.

Rathus, S. A. Principles and practices of assertive training: An eclectic overview. *The Counseling Psychologist*, 1975, *5*(4), 9-20.

Salter, A. *Conditioned reflex therapy*. New York: Creative Age Press, 1949.

Sansbury, D. L. Assertive training in groups. *Personnel and Guidance Journal*, 1974, *53*, 117-122.

Scheflen, A. E. *How behavior means*. New York: Gordon and Breach, 1973.

Scheflen, A. E., & Scheflen, A. *Body language and social order: Communication as behavioral control*. Englewood Cliffs, NJ: Prentice-Hall, 1972.

Schutzenberger, A. A. *Introduction au jeu de rôle*. Toulouse, France: Edouard Privat, 1975.

Schwartz, R. M., & Gottman, J. M. Toward a task analysis of assertive behavior. *Journal of Consulting and Clinical Psychology*, 1976, *44*(6), 910-920.

Stone, G. L., & Vance, A. Instructions, modeling, and rehearsal: Implications for training. *Journal of Counseling Psychology*, 1976, *23*(3), 272-279.

Strayhorn, J. M., Jr. *Talking it out: A guide to effective communication and problem solving.* Champaign, IL: Research Press, 1977.

Taetzsch, L., & Benson, E. *Taking charge on the job: Techniques for assertive management.* New York: Executive Enterprises, 1978.

Taubman, B. *How to become an assertive woman: The key to self-fulfillment.* New York: Pocket Books, 1976.

Wenrich, W. W., Dawley, H. H., & General, D. A. *Self-directed systematic desensitization: A guide for the student client and therapist.* Kalamazoo, MI: Behaviordelia, 1976.

White, J., & Fadiman, J. (Eds.). *Relax.* New York: Confucian Press (Dell), 1976.

Whiteley, J. M. (Ed.). Assertion training. *The Counseling Psychologist*, 1975, *5*(4), 3-116.

Whiteley, J. M., & Flowers, J. V. (Eds.). *Approaches to assertion training.* Monterey, CA: Brooks/Cole, 1978.

Wilson, G. T., & Davison, G. C. Behavior therapy: A road to self-control. *Psychology Today*, October 1975, 54-60.

Winship, B. J., & Kelley, J. D. A verbal response model of assertiveness. *Journal of Counseling Psychology*, 1976, *23*(3), 215-220.

Withers, J. Don't talk while I'm interrupting. *Ms.*, March 1975, 106-109.

Wolfe, J. L., & Fodor, I. G. A cognitive-behavioral approach to modifying assertive behavior in women. *The Counseling Psychologist*, 1975, *5*(4), 45-52.

Wolpe, J., Salter, A., & Reyna, L. J. *The conditioning therapies: The challenge in psychotherapy.* New York: Holt, Rinehart and Winston, 1966.